MW00998408

Rock Burst

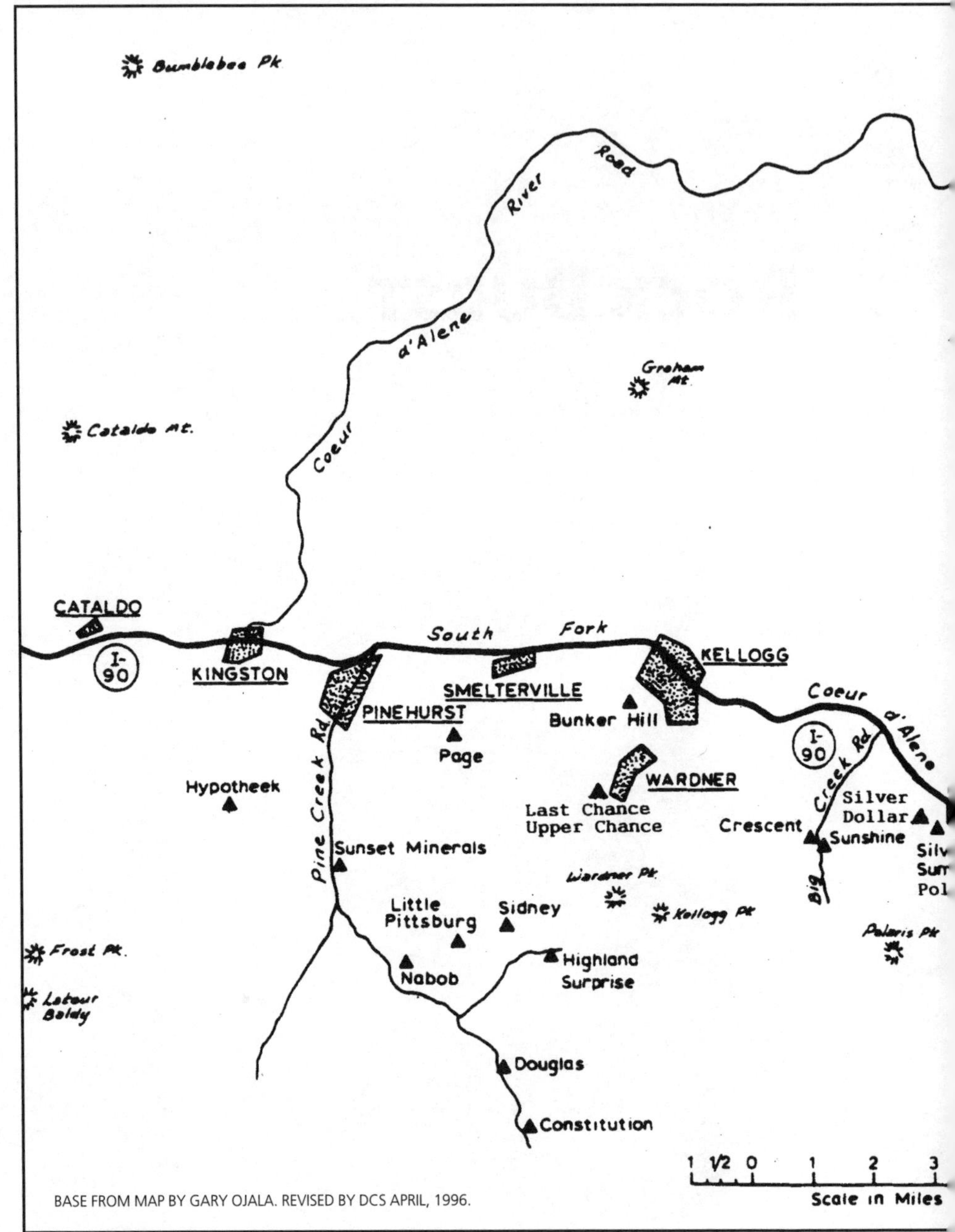

BASE FROM MAP BY GARY OJALA. REVISED BY DCS APRIL, 1996.

Coeur d'Alene Mining District mines mentioned in *Rock Burst*:

Bunker Hill & Sullivan
Bedroom
Caledonia
Canyon Silver
Constitution
Daddy Lode
Formosa
Frisco
Galena
Golden Chest
Hecla
Hercules
Hummingbird
Interstate
Last Chance
Lucky Friday
Mammoth #1, #2, #3
Mayflower
Midnight

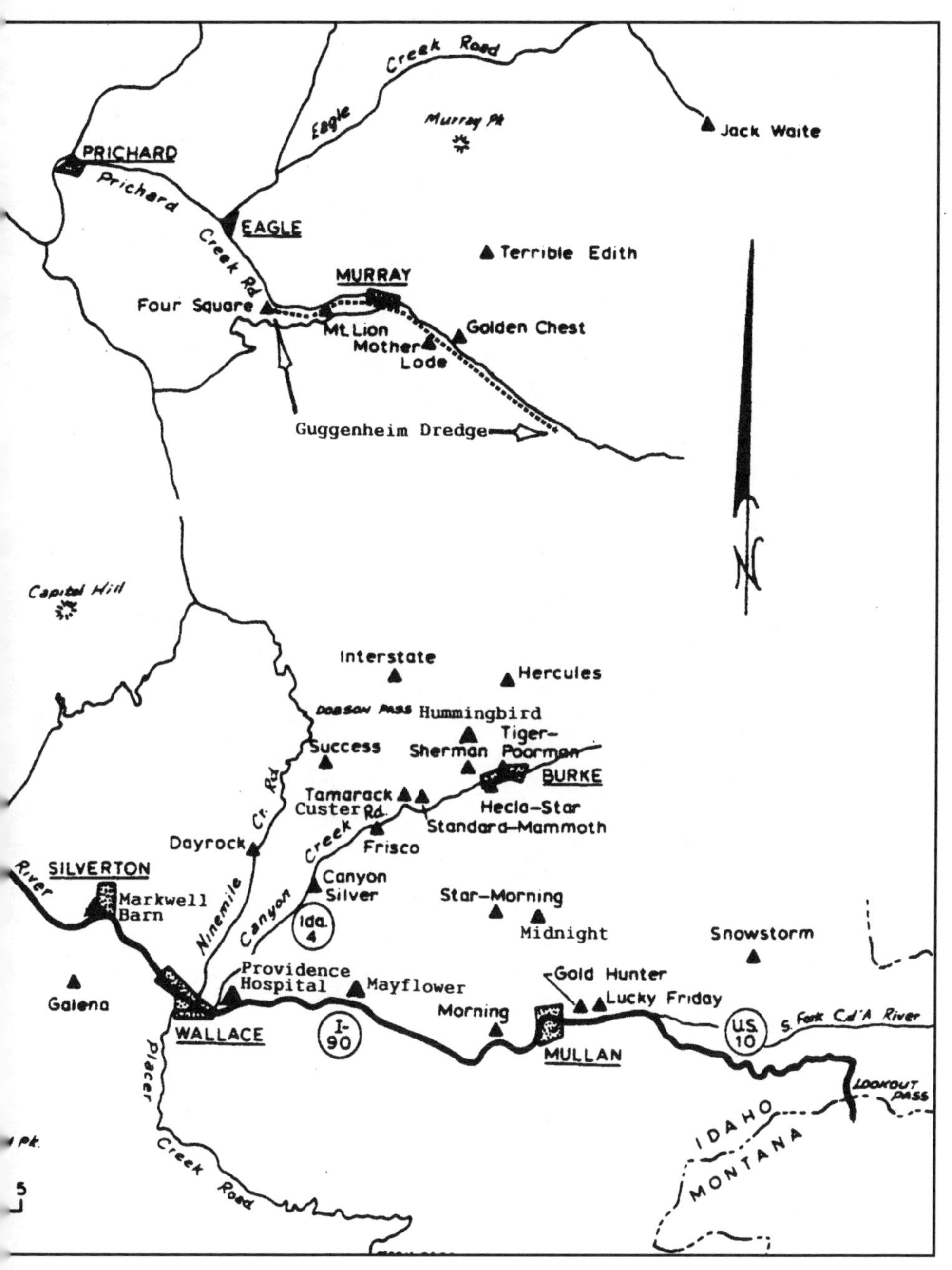

Monarch
Morning
Mother Lode
Page
Palisades
Pittsburgh
Polaris
Sherman

Sierra Nevada
Silver Dollar
Silver Summit
Snowstorm
Spokane-Idaho
Standard
Star
Sunshine Silver

Tamarack Custer
Terrible Edith
Tiger-Poorman
Tyler
Upper Chance

ROCK BURST

Bert and Marie Russell

Living the West

UNIVERSITY OF IDAHO PRESS
Moscow, Idaho
1998

Published by the University of Idaho Press
Moscow, Idaho 83844-1107

Printed in the United States of America

2002 2001 2000 99 98

5 4 3 2 1

Library of Congress Catalog Card Number 94-77720

LIBRARY OF CONGRESS CATALOGING-IN-PUBLICATION DATA

Russell, Bert, 1909–1997
Rock burst / by Bert and Marie Russell.
p. cm. — (Living the West)
Includes bibliographical references and index.
ISBN 0-89301-197-5
I. Russell, Marie, 1921– . II. Title. III. Series.
PS3568.U76554R63 1997
979.6'03'092—dc21

97-9491
CIP

Dedicated to Bert
his intelligence, wit, humor and love of life

and to our children,
Judy Marie and Walter Bert
who share his concerns and compassion.

The homespun yarn that wove together the many patterns of Bert's life as he worked as logger, river driver, shipyard electrician, timber cruiser, rancher, and writer was understanding and writing about the lives of working people wrestling their livelihood from above and below the earth of north Idaho. That weaving was halted by Alzheimer's disease. It is my hope that in 50 years of working together, the patterns of our lives merged so that the fabric of this work blends with his.

CONTENTS

ILLUSTRATIONS

ACKNOWLEDGMENTS

I wish to express my sincere appreciation to all those who have helped me in the preparation of this book. A very special thanks goes to Barbara A. and Peter A. Dahl who read the complete manuscript, encouraged me with their enthusiastic interest, and made many helpful suggestions. Walter B. Russell and Robert D. Hanson read parts of the manuscript and also made helpful suggestions. Barbara Howard Meldrum read the complete manuscript and encouraged me to submit it to the University of Idaho Press for publication. Donald C. Springer prepared the wonderful map of the Coeur d'Alene mining district showing all of the mines mentioned in the stories. Without his help I could never have had confidence in the authenticity of the mining terms in the glossary. Aaron Robinson, Lloyd C. Russell, and Waverly Reeves were helpful with logging terms and A. P. Ross with railroading terms. Peggy Pace is responsible for my adding many more terms to the glossary, which makes the stories more understandable.

Many thanks to Marcella J. Hanson for coming to my rescue when I had problems with the computer.

I appreciate, and future generations will appreciate, all the people who have shared their life stories for this book. The way we earn a living is changing dramatically from their time as we move from an industrial age to one of ever-higher technology. But the need to learn from them about how to engage life with dignity, strength, compassion, and humor will never change.

INTRODUCTION

Grassroots cultural history: this is what Bert and Marie Russell offer us in this engaging collection of interviews with ordinary people who often lived extraordinary lives in the mining district and neighboring areas of north Idaho. Here are the stories of miners who worked in the shadow of Death, an all too frequent visitor, who was summoned by rock burst, fire, other accidents, or the painful, life-shortening disease, silicosis. These are stories of comradeship, families, woodsmen, nurses, shoemakers, dancers, teachers, farmers, and storekeepers. Many regional readers will find contributors whom they know or their parents knew. Their stories will be eagerly read for the insights they give into the past of people and places familiar but imperfectly known.

Other readers will find much of interest in these pages whether the interviewees are personally known to the reader or not. These pages contain a wealth of information about how certain processes were performed: how ice was cut, stored, and sold for refrigeration; how to walk on floating logs and how to roll them (birling) in competitions; how the responsibilities of various jobs in the mines were performed; how candles were used for light in the mines before the introduction of battery-operated cap lamps; and how logging crews were fed and the food prepared. Here too are details about working conditions: how early miners were totally unprotected from particulates that damaged their lungs and shortened their lives; how they emerged from the hot mines with wet clothes that froze in the winter chill; how lack of safety regulations put their lives in unnecessary danger; how men worked constantly under the pernicious threat of an unpredictable rock burst; how loggers plunged waist-deep into icy water on log drives; and how young children performed the work of adults for minimal pay.

The book begins with newspaper accounts and other information as well as poetry about the tragic Sunshine Mine Fire of 1972; the appendices includes newspaper accounts of destructive snowslides and a summary of the labor disputes of the 1890s. These materials give a grim frame to the personal accounts that form the body of the book. They are included because they help to corroborate and amplify references to these events by a number of the contributors. But it would be a mistake to think that this book is primarily about the dangers and disasters that befell those who chose to live and work in this region. What I find most interesting about the references throughout to accidents, loss of life, and perils survived is the spirit expressed by the contributors. Granted, the events are usually recounted after the pain of the immediate experience has been eased by time, but the vividness of remembered detail speaks of the impact of these events.

The spirit these contributors convey is of fortitude, adaptability, courage with humility, a will to survive, and, sometimes, a strain of fatalism. Moreover, a number of these stories are funny, and others are heartwarming tales of accomplishments and satisfaction. There's a delightful account of two girls who won a tree sawing contest and were given a trip to New York, where they were featured in newsreels and demonstrated their skills in Central Park. Another story tells how a double amputee made dollhouses for the 44 surviving daughters of miners killed in the Sunshine Mine Fire "to help put a smile on their faces."

Quite a few contributors shed light on labor relations over a period of several decades. The need for unions becomes apparent from references to working conditions and the low pay received in the early days. Later contributors are often strong supporters of the unions. Some immigrants became embroiled in labor disputes through accidents of time and place as well as difficulties with the English language. Others in the post-World War II period endured the witch hunts of the McCarthy Era. Several women tell of their experiences with gender discrimination both regionally and, especially, while doing men's work for women's wages in the shipyards and aircraft assembly plants of World War II. But not all the labor relations were discriminatory or oppressive: the Canyon Silver story of a weekend in Hawaii seems almost too good to be true, yet it is.

Mobility and versatility characterize the careers of these contributors. Sometimes the changes of location and job resulted from preferential choices. More often than not, the changes were acts of survival or attempts to get ahead and live a better life. Sometimes the changes did result in improved conditions and greater personal happiness, but often they did not. There are many stories here, and more stories beneath the surface for those who wish to use these vignettes as launch pads for their own imaginative reconstructions and extensions.

These contributors demonstrate a variety of place, position, and ethnicity. Of the 27 interviewees included here, ten were born in the Coeur d'Alenes and "down the valley," and two of these were children of European immigrants. Six contributors were born in foreign countries, another four were children of immigrants, and at least four more were grandchildren of immigrants. Nine contributors came to the region from other states. At least three were homesteaders or the children of homesteaders. These accounts include many references to the experiences of immigrants and to the ways various ethnic groups interacted.

Several of the contributors refer to ecological issues, such as the belated recognition of the pollution caused by mining, and a weighing of values in determining how to deal with natural resources. The careful reader can discern from their stories where certain contemporary attitudes originate.

The order of the narratives follows a roughly geographic/occupational pattern. The pattern is not precise primarily because these people moved around considerably. But the miners, and those closely associated with mining in various business enterprises, begin the book, followed by those involved in the timber industry in the forested areas surrounding the mining district. Last are the valley people, some of whom are linked to the timber industry (if not included earlier) and others who are primarily farmers. The chronology is generally mixed. Birth dates of the contributors span 44 years from 1880 to 1924. Consequently, the range of experience within the region is considerable. The most recent interviews were conducted in 1994 and the earliest in 1972, which is fortunate because most of those early contributors have passed away. Many stories would have been lost if these interviews had not taken place.

Bert Russell collected and recorded stories from "old-timers" for 30 years. Many of these accounts were published in three of his books: *Hardships and Happy Times*, *Swiftwater People*, and *North Fork of the Coeur d'Alene River*. Bert knew the region he wrote about and the people he interviewed. He was born in Harrison, Idaho, and worked a variety of jobs; as his wife Marie writes in the dedication of this book, "he worked as logger, river driver, shipyard electrician, timber cruiser, rancher and writer." Bert could relate to the experiences his subjects described. This rapport no doubt helped break down the hesitancy some might have felt in telling their stories—Bert was an insider, not an outsider.

Bert's first published book, *Calked Boots*, was written like fiction. It drew from stories and people he had known while working on his ranch and in timber-related jobs. *The Sawdust Dream*, his most personal book, was also written like fiction. It is his own remembered story of the people and events of the Russell & Pugh Lumber Company. His other books are primarily oral histories in which people tell their stories in their own words. Bert's writing consistently displays his love for the region and its people and his desire to stick close to the known facts. As he said once in a published interview, "I think reality is so much more interesting than fiction. You can't play with the facts—they allow us certain yardage all right—but you can't just dream them up." (Susan M. Stacy, ed. *A Companion Book to Idaho Public Television's "Proceeding On Through a Beautiful Country."* Boise: Idaho Educational Public Broadcasting Foundation, 1990, p. 238.) Yet both Bert and Marie are well aware that facts are slippery and may exist in several versions. Marie has said to me that the stories in this book consist of "people's *perceptions*. There's no way of checking all the details in these accounts. Some are colorful tales. There may be discrepancies in people's perceptions, reflected in these accounts." Nonetheless, these "perceptions" have value as personal versions of events that are not reducible to concrete truths.

These stories are presented in the words of the interview subjects, but they have been edited. The most obvious omission is the voice of the interviewer: we hear a monologue, not a dialogue. Bert intentionally placed himself invisibly in the background, and Marie did likewise when rendering the stories she collected. The accounts are trimmed and shaped for ease of reading (just imagine what a direct transcript would be like with false starts, silence-fillers, and sentence shifts and fragments). More substantive changes relate to style and the impact of written text versus oral conversation. The principle followed has been to preserve the flavor of the original speaker without overloading the written text. Most of the grammar and diction follows the speaker's words unless confusion would result; dialect is suggested without being overdone (for example, the "g" is dropped from "-ing" some of the time, but not as frequently as the interviewees did when speaking). But enough has been preserved to characterize the narrator's speech pattern.

The earliest interviews were conducted by Bert, but Marie often accompanied him, and she gradually became more involved in the process. This project extended over a 24-year period, but Bert's health terminated his participation in its completion. Of the 27 interviews in *Rock Burst*, Bert conducted and wrote up 17 of them; four interviews were conducted jointly by Bert and Marie; Marie wrote up ten of the interviews; and she conducted six interviews in addition to some follow-up consultation. Marie also collected the Sunshine Mine Fire selections, the materials in the appendices, and wrote the glossary and the background essay on labor disputes. Her contributions to this book are substantial, and it is accurately called a coauthored work.

Had Bert and Marie Russell not had confidence in the purpose, significance, and quality of the materials collected over so many years, and had they not taken the initiative and financial risks of privately publishing their earlier oral history collections, we most likely would not have this book. It is a fitting tribute to the labors and the vision of Bert and Marie Russell that this book is now published by the University of Idaho Press. They have preserved for us the living histories of north Idaho people by mining the human resources of our region so that all readers can share the treasures they bestow.

—*Barbara Howard Meldrum*

■ ONE

WE WERE MINERS THEN

■ *The following items are excerpts from news stories.*

Rock Burst

ON DECEMBER 5, 1985 one miner was killed and three hurt from a rock burst at the Lucky Friday Mine near Mullan, Idaho.

BURST KILLS 1, HURTS 3 AT FRIDAY

Shoshone News-Press, Thursday, December 5, 1985
MULLAN—One Lucky Friday miner was killed and three injured after a rock burst on the 5,100-foot level Wednesday afternoon.

John Pilon, 54, Cataldo, was hit in the chest with a 250-pound rock at 3:40 P.M. and killed instantly. The body was recovered at 4:20 P.M. Pilon had 20 years of hardrock mining experience, 15 of them with Hecla Mining Company, owners of the Lucky Friday.

Pilon was . . . in a stope with his partner and three others when the rock broke. . . . The other three suffered minor bumps, bruises and cuts. The three survivors were: Del Marcy, Cataldo; Frank Fausett Jr., Elk Creek; and Herb Travis, Osburn.

Swing crews were just minutes into their shifts before Wednesday's accident. A second rock burst in a different portion of the mine at 7 P.M. prompted Hecla officials to call the swing shift in and send them home. When the graveyard reported, miners were sent underground but kept at their stations for the entire shift. Eyewitnesses reported frequent movement and periodic rumbling in the mine Wednesday, and some Mullan residents reported broken windows.

"Most of the time our experience with rock bursts is there' s not a hell of a lot anybody can do," said [Martin Rosta, District Supervisor for the Mining Safety and Health Administration] in Seattle.

Rock bursts are caused when pressure on the walls of a mine's underground tunnels cause rock to break away with violent force.

ROCK BURST KILLED POPULAR MINER

The Spokane Spokesman-Review, May 17, 1994
Correspondent, Bekka Rauve
KELLOGG—James Finlay, who died Friday in a mine accident, was the best liked employee at the Sunshine Mine, his partner says.

Finlay, 50, and Capparelli, 45, had worked together since 1979. When the explosion took place, they were working to clear out a raise, a vertical shaft connecting one level of the mine to another.

"There's no way to describe what it was like," Capparelli said. "That kind of explosion is very loud—I didn't hear anything. The skin of my back is all torn up from where the rocks were embedded—I didn't feel anything. There was no time. One second we were standing there, the next second we were totally buried and in pain. Totally packed in rock."

Capparelli said that the rescue crew, finding it impossible to work from above, instead removed the timbers below the two miners.

He doubts the rescue took long, but it seemed like a long, long time.

"When the rock comes in around, it compresses you. When you exhale, it sifts around tighter. You can't get air in your lungs. It keeps crushing you. I knew my partner was there. I could feel him struggling to breathe. Then he quit."

Capparelli expected to die himself, he said. But when he was lowered to a stretcher, still conscious, he found the mine foreman and the mine manager waiting in the darkness. "And I saw cap lamps as far as I could see. The whole mine was there."

Capparelli escaped with cuts and bruises. . . . He' s still struggling to cope with the loss of his partner, he said. Capparelli describes Finlay as "an easy-going guy who never complained and did every job to the best of his ability . . ."

"I'm sure the bruises will heal," Capparelli said. "Maybe time will heal the rest. I hope so."

The Sunshine Mine Fire, May 2, 1972

On May 2, 1972, a fire broke out just before noon in the Sunshine Silver Mine, six miles east of Kellogg, Idaho, trapping the 201-

man shift underground. That afternoon, 108 men escaped. Two more were rescued on the eighth day. Hope, alive in the breasts of relatives and friends, faded day by day. As rescuers working feverishly found bodies, hope was extinguished on the tenth day when the last 40 of the 91 miners who perished were discovered.

A full account of the 1972 Sunshine Mine fire appears in *Muscle and Blood* by Rachel Scott. The following is a brief account of the disaster as reported in Spokane, Washington's, *Spokesman-Review*. Note the excerpts are not in chronological order.

FIRE

MAY 8, 1972—At six A.M. Tuesday, May 2, a group of men coming off the graveyard shift at the Sunshine Silver Mine smelled smoke at the 3,700-foot level, three-quarters of a mile below ground.

"Do you smell that?" one miner asked his partner.

"Yeah. Probably somebody lighting a cigarette."

They didn't report it.

Some six hours later the fire that had been smoldering undetected—perhaps for days—in some abandoned corner of the mine burst with a fury that engulfed in minutes the crucial shaft and escape routes with high-density carbon monoxide smoke.

ESCAPED

MAY 7, 1972—William Mitchell, 26, one of the 108 men who escaped . . . said he had learned of the fire by word of mouth, about one-half hour after the time officials said it started.

He and others at the 4,400-foot level rang for a skip [elevator bucket] to take them up the shaft. The skip, which normally descends to the 4,400-foot level in a little more than a minute, took nearly one-half hour to arrive that day.

When it finally came, Mitchell found he could not squeeze aboard because it had been filled by men boarding before him. That was the luckiest thing that would happen to him that day.

Mitchell and others who were unable to board stood at the edge of the shaft and watched the skip, carrying some 30 men, rise through thickening smoke toward the surface and safety. The men aboard it were not seen again.

About 20 minutes later a second skip arrived. Mitchell boarded it and descended to the 4,600-foot level to pick up other miners. The group then rode the skip up to the mine's 3,100-foot level, walked the three-quarters of a mile to the main Jewell shaft, and took a second skip to the surface.

Out under the clear night sky, Mitchell realized the men in the first skip had not made it.

"They never did reach the surface," Mitchell said. "I believe they got off at 3,700 and that's where they perished."

May 4, 1972—Roger Sindley, Smelterville, Idaho, who said he was the last person to escape the mine after the fire, said he believes some of the miners who were trapped in the mine's deepest shaft, several hundred feet below the location of the fire, may have a chance of surviving.

"The story was different at the higher 3,100-foot level where I was when the fire broke out," he said. "I saw all persons who died on that level. I would have been dead there also if a safety man hadn't pulled me out," he said. "I was on the verge of passing out from smoke inhalation."

RESCUE EFFORTS

May 3, 1972—The trapped men were estimated to be on horizontal levels off the main shaft of the mine, but rescue workers had not determined just where they were. Platform stations are in the vertical shaft, where the main elevator stops, but horizontal shafts branch out from near those stations in many directions.

A company spokesman said . . . there are two escape routes from the mine. The first route was described as "a very long walk," but a route through which the miners could safely make it.

May, 4 1972—The main rescue efforts have been moved from the Jewell shaft to the entrance of the Silver Summit Mine shaft, which is on the opposite side of the mountain from where the rescue work began after the fire broke out before noon Tuesday.

Silver Summit is about five highway miles over the mountain from Jewell shaft.

The Silver Summit shaft goes downward on a slope to a distance of 3,100 feet to an area immediately above Tuesday's disastrous fire, which already has claimed 24 lives.

Work at the 3,100-foot level continued through the night in an effort to reach the major No. 10 vertical hoist shaft—with workers within 200 feet of the vertical shaft at last report.

It is through the No. 10 shaft that rescuers hope to descend to the

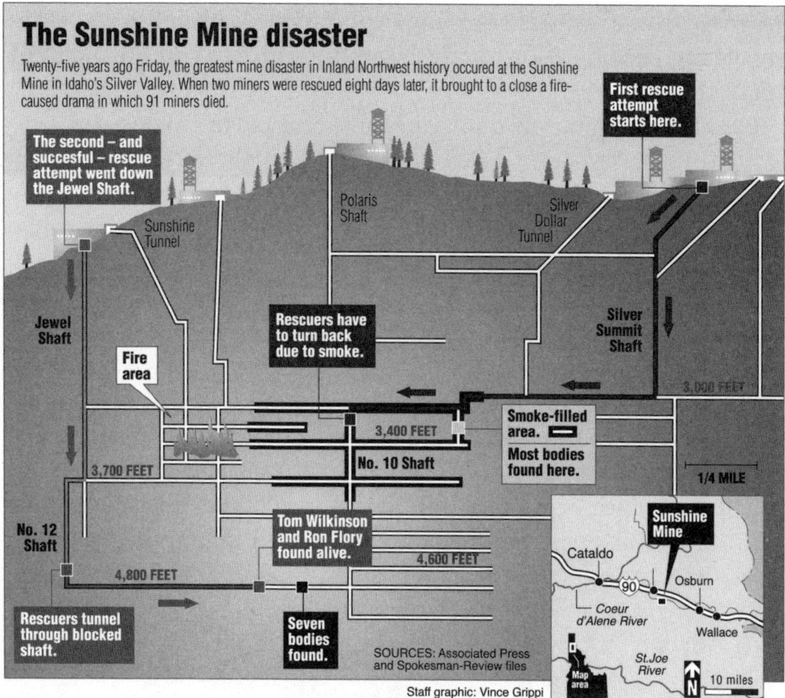
The Sunshine Mine disaster
Twenty-five years ago Friday, the greatest mine disaster in Inland Northwest history occured at the Sunshine Mine in Idaho's Silver Valley. When two miners were rescued eight days later, it brought to a close a fire-caused drama in which 91 miners died.
The second – and succesful – rescue attempt went down the Jewel Shaft.
First rescue attempt starts here.
Sunshine Tunnel
Polaris Shaft
Silver Dollar Tunnel
Jewel Shaft
Silver Summit Shaft
Rescuers have to turn back due to smoke.
Fire area
3,000 FEET
3,400 FEET
Smoke-filled area.
Most bodies found here.
No. 10 Shaft
3,700 FEET
1/4 MILE
No. 12 Shaft
Tom Wilkinson and Ron Flory found alive.
4,600 FEET
4,800 FEET
Rescuers tunnel through blocked shaft.
Seven bodies found.
SOURCES: Associated Press and Spokesman-Review files
Staff graphic: Vince Grippi
Sunshine Mine
Cataldo
90
Osburn
Coeur d'Alene River
Wallace
St.Joe River
Map area
N
10 miles

■ Map shows details of successful rescue attempt deep in the Sunshine Mine. *From the April 27, 1997, edition of the* Spokesman-Review.

one-mile level, where the trapped men are thought to be located. Marvin C. Chase, general manager and vice president of Sunshine, said rescuers "had a good chance of reaching the No. 10 hoist" by dawn today.

That shaft is one of the principal shafts into the depths of the mine. It doesn't open to the surface, but does reach deeper into the mine than does the Jewell shaft, through which many of the 108 miners escaped to safety after the fire first broke out.

About 40 rescue workers boarded a 40-unit enclosed steel tram-like vehicle near midnight to descend into the mine. The train runs backwards down into the shaft on a narrow gauge truck, but is driven forward from an underground station.

The one-way trip to the 3,100-foot level takes about 45 minutes. Ron Strand, one of the 40 men from an earlier rescue party, returned from an eight-hour shift Wednesday night and told of conditions in the mine and of the rescue operation.

"Work is slow at this stage," he said. "The tunnel now is filled with smoke and contains a lot of carbon monoxide gas."

He said workmen were constructing bulkheads in the tunnel leading to the No. 10 shaft. Large fans are located with their "backs" to the bulkheads, he said—blowing the heavy poisoned air past the men and out of the shaft.

Clean air being pumped into the mine replaces the toxic gases, [which] enables rescue workers to move the bulkheads farther into the tunnel and repeat the process.

Air tanks carried by each of the rescue workers contains sufficient oxygen to last an average-sized man about two hours, Strand said, adding that once one tank nears empty, the men leave the shaft.

Chase said that most of the men working in the mine when the fire broke out Tuesday were below the 4,600-foot level. The 24 bodies were found at the 3,100 and 3,700-foot levels, and the 58 missing miners are believed to be well below that—but searchers are not sure of just where.

The fire, which began in an unused portion of the mine at about the 3,700-foot level, is still burning among the older timbers between the 3,400- and 3,700-foot level.

VIGIL AT MINE

MAY 3, 1972—Families and friends of those still trapped in the mine waited in a cordoned-off area throughout Wednesday, May 3. About 40 remained at midnight.

MAY 4, 1972—Mrs. Joanne Reichert, Big Creek, Idaho, sat in a folding chair facing the entrance of the Sunshine Mine Wednesday, waiting for news of her husband. . . . She had been waiting in the same spot for nearly 30 hours. About 100 relatives and friends of other miners trapped underground . . . waited nearby.

"The worst part of this tragedy is the waiting," Mrs. Reichert said. "It's worse than a nightmare."

Mrs. Reichert said she had not slept Tuesday night and would not sleep Wednesday night until she learned what had happened to her husband.

Most other waiting persons voiced similar feelings. Few had slept since Monday night.

Despite the grim environment of the gathering, most of the waiting persons helped and consoled each other.

"All Tuesday night and Wednesday morning other waiting persons were offering me blankets and food," Mrs. Reichert said. "Everyone remained together."

One man, whose brother was trapped below, said he and others kept trying to help because "it's the only way you can keep your head straight."

When temperatures dropped Tuesday night many of the waiting persons entered a nearby mine warehouse to keep warm. There were few chairs and most sat on the floor.

However, volunteer workers, most of whom were recruited by the American Red Cross, converted the warehouse into a dormitory and cafeteria by Wednesday night.

The volunteers brought sandwiches, doughnuts, coffee, and milk by the truckload, set up a snack bar, brought in numerous chairs and set up several rows of beds. They also supplied blankets, cooked hot meals for everyone Wednesday night, and set up a nursery in Kellogg for the children of waiting persons.

Many of the 108 miners who escaped the mine mishap Tuesday were present, hoping their colleagues would be rescued.

May 5, 1972—Mrs. Virgil Bebbs, Kellogg, fell unconscious to the ground at the entrance to the Sunshine Mine Thursday afternoon. She had been waiting since Tuesday for word about her husband. . .

Several . . . who also were waiting to learn the fate of their relatives and friends trapped below quickly came to her aid. A doctor at the scene brought her to consciousness.

Mrs. Bebbs, who hadn't slept since she arrived at the mine more than 50 hours earlier, was only one of many in the crowd who were feeling the inevitable, bad physical effects of being under constant emotional strain for a long period of time.

Another woman, who said she had high blood pressure problems, was given tranquilizers to calm her and allow her to sleep. She nevertheless refused to sleep until she heard news of her husband who also was trapped below.

A young man whose father was still missing said he was deeply worried about his mother's health. He said she had a heart attack only three weeks before.

"I just don't know if she can take it if my father dies," he said. "She had a previous husband who was killed in another mining accident."

Liz Ahartz, a volunteer nurse from Silverton, Idaho, said it was amazing that the health of the persons in the crowd was holding up as well as it was.

"They just refused to sleep," she said. "But, then I guess I wouldn't either, if I were in their position."

Despite the prolonged strain of waiting for news, members of the crowd continued to do what they could to help each other's morale.

After hearing her husband was one of the confirmed dead in the disaster, Mrs. Robert Bush remained at the scene, helping to distribute sandwiches.

Others distributed blankets, set up chairs and helped to console those around them.

Two teenage boys, who said their father didn't like their long hair, went to Kellogg to get haircuts after hearing their father had died in the mine.

RESCUERS

May 5, 1972—One rescuer, who wished to remain unidentified, said he knows more than half the men trapped in the mine.

"It's extremely dangerous down there," he said. "But you just keep going back."

The workers said the smoke was so thick in some parts of the mine Thursday that "you can't see the end of your nose." He said a person without a breathing apparatus would die in a matter of seconds.

"There are a lot of hazards down there," he said. "It would be easy to miss seeing a vertical shaft because of poor visibility and fall 2,000 feet to your death."

". . . There's also the possibility a rescue man could trip and fall causing his breathing apparatus to pop from his mouth," he said. "A breath of smoke and carbon monoxide could make you too weak to get the apparatus back into your mouth."

. . . [He said] it was difficult to breathe even in the mine's lowest depths.

May 6, 1972—It was learned Friday that one of the men found dead Wednesday was actually a rescue worker. Donald Beehner, 38, Wallace, was a rescue worker who died when he removed his oxygen mask in order to share his air supply with a fellow miner, a mine official said.

Both of the miners perished.

By Friday, rescue workers at the nation's deepest and richest mine numbered 155 men.

May 8, 1972—It is believed if trapped miners are alive, they will be between the 4,800- and 5,200-foot levels at the bottom of the No. 10

shaft. Fresh air has circulated throughout that area since the Tuesday fire trapped the men.

[Marvin C. Chase] said there also is a possibility some miners may be trapped and alive somewhere at the 3,400-foot level.

Mine officials said rescue teams are making their way to the No. 10 shaft hoist room from the Jewell shaft entrance at the 3,700-foot level and another No. 10 hoist room at the 3,100-foot level from the Silver level entrance.

"We're still optimistic that people are alive down there," Chase said. "As long as they have water and air they have a chance."

MAY 9, 1972—Several miners expressed a dismal theory of the fate of miners trapped in the mine Monday afternoon.

They said because No. 10 shaft hoist operators apparently had died trying to bring their elevators to the surface, most of the miners could have been trapped while riding up hoists in the No. 10 shaft.

WILKINSON AND FLORY RESCUED

MAY 10, 1972—Two miners, trapped at the bottom of Sunshine Mine for more than a week, walked out of the mine at 8:20 P.M. Tuesday [May 9] amid cheers, applause, and tears.

Located at the 4,800-foot level in the mine by a four-man rescue team, Tom Wilkinson, 29, Kellogg, and Ron Flory, 28, Smelterville, emerged from the eight-day ordeal apparently unharmed.

MAY 11, 1972—The two men snatched from the grave that so far has claimed 47 lives said Wednesday seven mates who tried to flee [deadly] smoke with them "just didn't make it" to safety. . .

While Ron Flory. . . and Tom Wilkinson . . . were swigging beer while resting in a hospital following their eight-day burial within the 4,800-foot deep cavern, workers pressed their rescue efforts with renewed hope of finding more survivors.

Flory and Wilkinson, partners at their job for more than a year, were released from the hospital, each about 14 pounds lighter, still bearded and saying in chorus, "We feel great."

Several days later, as air pumped in by rescuers dissipated the smoke, the two went back in search of the others. They found them dead.

"We know we've got all the men who are alive on the 4,800-foot level," Elburt Osborn, director of the federal Bureau of Mines, had said Tuesday night.

May 15, 1972—Flory and Wilkinson were working near the bottom of the No. 12 shaft when the fire touched off the gas and smoke higher up in the shaft. The men raced for the elevator station.

Flory said: "We got up to the lift station and several buddies were already there. Some were watching for the cage. One was listening on the phone. They tried to get respirators to everybody. The smoke just got so thick we had to keep moving back. Tom Wilkinson was gonna get on the phone and tell supervisors at the upper levels where we were gonna be and everything, and they just didn't make it."

Wilkinson passed out and was taken along the tunnel on top of a motorized ore car. He related later:

"I was kind of delirious, and they put me down on the ground, kept talking to me and telling me I was all right and was in good air. My partner [Flory] went back out and told them there was good air and to get back there. Ron stayed and Dick [unidentified] said he would get the others back to us.

"Dick went out to see and he never came back. Ron said, 'I'm gonna find out what's wrong' and he started walking out. He came back and said, 'They're lying all over'; so I jumped on the motor, and I says, 'Let's go,' and we went out of there.

"First one we seen was Dick. We just grabbed him and drug him back down the track. He was gone. It looked like somebody had fallen off the ore car and they all got off and tried to help and none of them made it."

There were seven bodies. Flory and Wilkinson said they were unable to help them so they took the lunch buckets and retreated with the ore car.

They went back about 1,500 feet into the tunnel to a drill station, a small room where drill bits are kept. They shut the steel doors behind them and remained there most of the time. Once they walked through a dark No. 12 shaft offshoot and found a telephone on a pile of rubble.

"The line was dead," Wilkinson said

The phone had been dropped down the shaft by Bureau of Mines rescue crews, but the wire snagged on a rock outcropping and was cut through.

Their lonely ordeal then began. Flory, a six-foot-two bear of a man who speaks slowly and deliberately, said simply, "I am not a praying man, but I prayed a lot down there.

"We kept up each other's spirits. One man would get down and the other would talk him out of it. We were scared for a whole week, but we never really gave up hope until about a half hour before we were rescued.

"So when I first heard banging on the pipes I didn't believe it."

That came from the two-man team which inched down a narrow ventilator shaft in a bullet-shaped "torpedo" cylinder.

"We banged back, and pretty soon we really did hear voices," he continued. "We hollered back, and pretty soon, we saw flashing lights."

The pair signaled with the headlight on the ore car, the only light they had. The battery held out the whole week.

Weak but not too bad off, they walked with the help of the rescuers about 2,500 feet to the torpedo and the miracle of escape to the open air.

Flory was the first to reach the safety of the main shaft. Asked if he wanted to go straight up, he replied, "No, I want to wait for my buddy."

The men came out together, still wearing their helmets, a week's growth of beard, and supported by other miners. They emerged to cheers from the crowd of anxious people for whom they meant hope for their own men . . .

THE WAITING ENDS

MAY 12, 1972—Ten anguished days of waiting and wondering ended at the Sunshine Mine late Thursday when word came that the last of 91 missing miners had been found dead a mile underground.

Many announcements had been made since fire erupted May 2 in the nation's richest silver mine. But only one meeting with newsmen had been joyous—that coming Tuesday night [May 9] when Thomas Wilkinson and Ronald Flory had been found alive and well at the mine's 4,800-foot level.

Wilkinson and Flory were the only survivors after an initial group of 108 had fled safely from the smoke, gas, and flames May 2.

BATTLING THE BLAZE

MAY 15, 1972—Larry L. Marshall, a United Steelworkers Union official here, said the fire was continuing to burn so intensively that crews were unable to reach the blaze.

"As a result, the workers are trying to isolate the blaze with bulkheads in the mine's tunnels in hopes it will burn itself out," Marshall said. "If this fails, it is hoped the bulkheads will stop enough air from getting to the fire, thereby starving the fire out."

Marshall said the last of the 91 persons who died in the mine were removed Saturday.

CAUSE

MAY 3, 1972—Mine officials said they have not been able to determine the cause of the blaze, but there was speculation that it was attributed to electrical failure.

MAY 4, 1972—While the exact cause of the fire is still unknown, [Marvin C.] Chase said the fire probably started due to spontaneous combustion. He said it apparently burned for some time and finally built up sufficient pressure to burst a bulkhead at that level. At that point, he said, a heavy concentration of smoke poured into the Jewell shaft.

MAY 14, 1972—Stanley Jarrett, assistant director of the U.S. Bureau of Mines said Saturday that . . . investigation into the cause of the fire will not be undertaken until the fire is out and officials can inspect the area firsthand.

Adding to the list of possible causes, mine authorities said Saturday that the disastrous fire could have been caused by a welding torch touching off a gas pocket, sending the blaze spreading through the timbers in a long-unused portion of the mine. Other possible causes include . . . a carelessly-discarded cigarette.

Some of the 108 miners who escaped the underground inferno said smoke had been noticed inside the mine at least two days before the fire and had gathered sufficient momentum to break through a bulkhead and spread carbon monoxide-laden air down the mine's vital No. 10 shaft.

Shoshone County Coroner Albert M. Peterson said Saturday the miners still below were dead within 60 seconds after the poisoned air filtered through the workings.

"It was like getting hit by a train or having a rock fall on you," he said. "Blood tests we ran on the first 11 men to be brought out of the mine indicated the air was between 70 and 80 percent carbon monoxide."

MAY 14, 1972—Meanwhile, a mass memorial service will be scheduled for the 91 men. Selected as a site for the service was the auditorium at Kellogg High School because of its large seating capacity.

[The Sunshine Mine Memorial lists 92 names: the 91 miners and the rescue worker who also lost his life.]

We Were Miners Then

by Senator Phil Batt

Our tongues have not tasted the bitter dust,
The roar of the drills has never reached our ears.
Unfelt to us is the darkness of the shafts,
Yet we are Idahoans
And we were miners then.

We are farmers
We run the water from the melted snows
Onto parched desert soil.
The planted seeds take root and grow;
The harvest fills our granaries.
The pits are strange to us
But we are Idahoans
And we were miners then.

We are loggers
We are your neighbors
We share the high country with you.
But we sing our song
To the buzzing of the chain saw
And do our dance on the spinning logs.
There is no room in the mine
For trees to fall
But we are Idahoans
And we were miners then.

We are cattlemen, innkeepers, merchants,
Men of the law and men of the cloth.
Ours are a thousand trades.

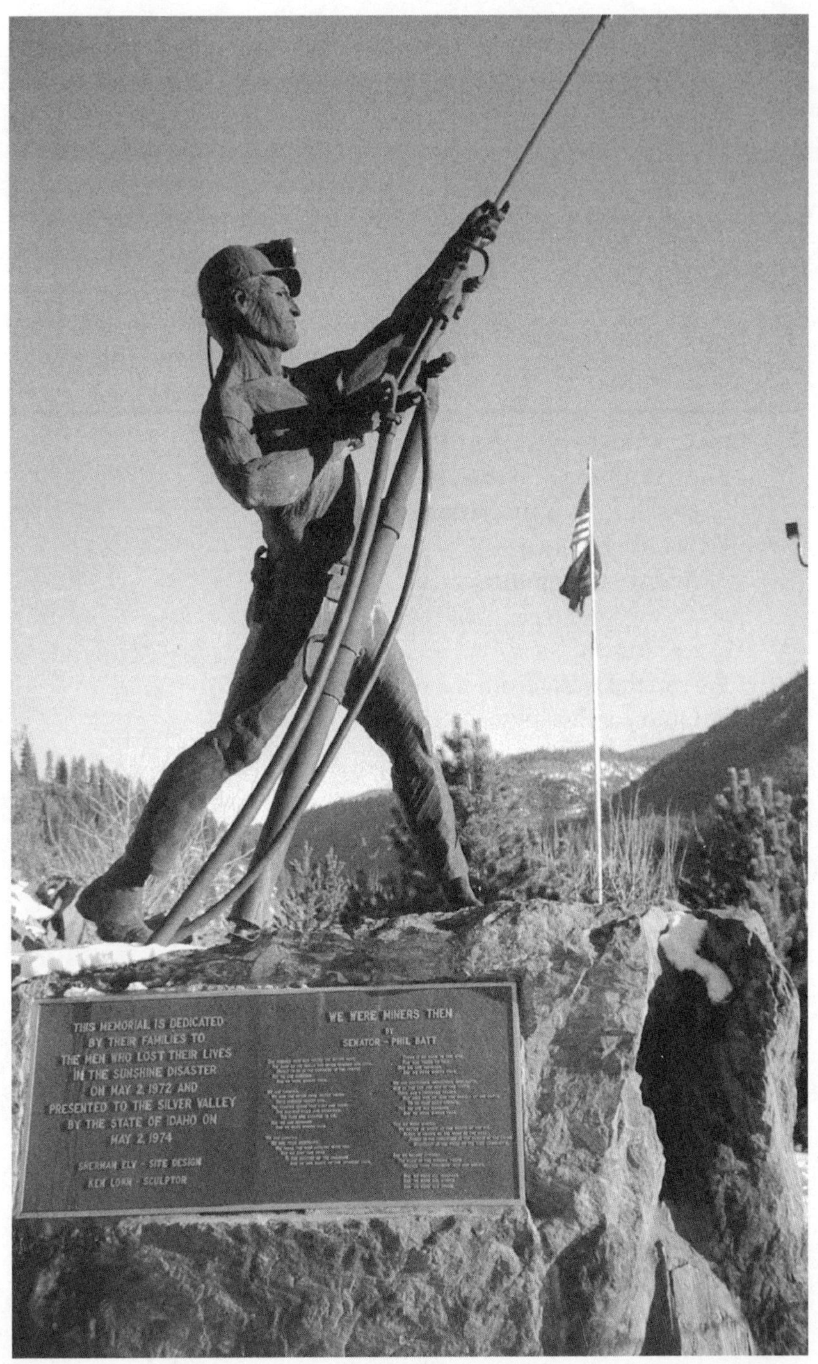

■ Memorial to the 91 miners and 1 rescue worker who lost their lives in the disastrous Sunshine Mine Fire, May 2, 1972

But only you go to the bowels of the earth
To do your daily chores.
Yet we are all Idahoans
And we were miners then.

Yes we were miners:
We waited in spirit at the mouth of the pit
Ached in unison at the news of the dead
Joined in the jubilation at the rescue of the living
Marveled at the poise of the tiny community.

And we became strong;
The flux of the widows' tears
Welded strength into our bodies.

And we were all Idahoans
And we were all miners
And we were all proud.

Sherman Ely, Site Designer
Ken Lonn, Sculptor

Proudly we pay tribute to the men who lost their lives in the Sunshine Mine, May 2, 1972

Alexander, Robert H.
Allen, Billy Wayne
Allen, Wayne L.
Allison, Richard Marlin
Anderson, Arnold E.
Anderson, Robert L.
Armijo, Jose Edumino
Barber, Benjamin
Barker, Robert E.
Bebb, Virgil
Beehner, Donald G.
Bewley, Richard Donald
Birchett, George William
Blalack, Wayne
Bush, Robert W.
Byington, Floyd L.
Cae, Clarence
Carlos, Carter Don
Casteel, Charles
Croker, Kevin
Crow, Duwain D.
Davenport, Roderick B.
Davis, John W.
Delbridge, Richard
Delbridge, William R.
Diaz, Roberto, Sr.
Dionne, Gregory
Don Carlos, Carter
Fee, Norman Seager
Findley, Lyle M.
Firkins, Donald K.
Fleshman, Howard Laurel

Follette, William Robert
Garcia, Richard (Dick)
George, Richard G.
Goff, Robert W.
Goos, William L.
Guertner, John P.
Hanna, William F.
Harrison, Howard
Hobson, Patrick M.
House, Melvin L.
Hudson, Merle E.
Ivers, Jack B.
Johnson, Fred E.
Johnson, Paul E.
Johnson, Wayne L.
Johnston, Michael J.
Keough, Custer L.
Kester, Sherman C.
Kitchen, Dewellyn E. (Kitch)
Kitchen, Elmer
Lavoie, Kenneth C.
Lynch, Richard
McLaughlan, Donald J.
McNutt, Delbert J.
Moore, James C.
Mullin, David J.
Naccarato, Joseph R.
Nelson, Orlin Wayne
Norris, Richard Dale
Orr, Donald R.
Patrick, H. B. (Pat)
Pena, Casey (U. S. Navy)
Peterson, John W.
Phillips, Francis W.
Puckett, Irvin L.
Rais, Floyd A.
Rathbun, Leonard D.
Rawson, John R.
Reichert, Jack L.
Rhoads, Delbert (Dusty)
Rossiter, Glen R.
Russell, Paul M.
Sargent, Allen
Sayler, Gene E.
Sayler, James D.
Scanlan, Robert B.
Serrano, Juan Raul
Sharette, Nick D.
Sisk, Frank R.
Stephens, Darrell Eugene
Thor, Gustav Gayle
Truelock, Grady E.
Waldvogel, Robert E.
Walty, William Roy
Whatcott, Gordon
Wiederrick, Douglas L.
Wilson, Ronald L.
Wilson, William E.
Wolff, John Sam
Wood, Don B.

PART ONE

WORKING IN THE MINE DISTRICT

■ John Appleberg, 1973

TWO

JOHN APPLEBERG WITH ARTHUR NORLEN

Interviewed 1980 at home up Big Creek.

JOHN: My dad, John Jacob Appleberg, was born in Colorado of Swedish parents. When he was seventeen, he went back to the old country to stay with relatives at Vaasa, Finland. Over there, he and a cousin got into trouble fighting, so the relatives told Dad to go back to America and take the cousin with him.

They came into a Canadian port, beat their way across country on freight trains and then slipped across the border into Minnesota. They were caught by U.S. Customs. The cousin was deported. They checked and found Dad was born in the United States and said he could stay.

My mother was Swedish, but lived across the bay from Sweden at Vaasa, Finland. She graduated from high school there and could speak and write a mixture of a border dialect that, when mixed with English in the United States, gained the name of "Swenglish" or "Finnglish" depending on which language was dominant.

In Minnesota, Dad logged and joined the Industrial Workers of the World [I.W.W.], called "Wobblies." And that's where he married my mother. I was born there in 1909. Then Dad moved the family to Everett, Washington.

To the Coeur d'Alenes

In 1915, Dad moved us to Wardner in the Coeur d'Alene mining district, and he became a miner at the Sunshine [Mine]. He never tried to hide his Wobbly beliefs, and that soon got him fired and blacklisted by the big mines. But he was a good miner and the leasers [leaseholders] would still hire him.

Dad worked in the district in 1915 and 1916 and in Butte, Montana, mines in 1917 during the first world war. Then he came back and worked several leases in the No. 5 tunnel of the Morning Mine at Mullan. Dad made good money. You betcha! A thousand dollars a month. Good money in them days.

First Job

In 1925 jobs were hard to get for an inexperienced kid. John George and Mike Savage were leasers in the Upper Chance at Wardner, the upper part of the Bunker Hill Mine. Dad got John George to let me work on a conveyor belt picking out the big chunks of waste rock. The fine stuff would go through, and the big chunks of ore I'd throw in the ore pocket. Dad sent me down the drift to get something. On my way back, I met this trammer who was pulling cars with a mule as the ore came out of a chute. He handed me a miner's pick and told me the muck was hanging up in the chute and to go pick it down. I was just a kid of sixteen. I didn't know any better. I went up to the incline in the back of the chute and picked enough to fill that car and two or three more. I was working in a chute that went 200 feet straight up to the next level, and they were dumping muck up there at the time. Fortunately, nobody dumped any while I was in there.

Just as I was coming out of the chute, here come my dad. He said, "What the hell are you doing up in there?"

I said, "This guy told me to help him load his train."

Dad grabbed a piece of starter steel, that's a steel drill about two and one half feet long, and ran the trammer clear outside the mine and over the dump. He couldn't catch him or he might have brained him. The guy didn't come back that day.

Dad was running one of those dry-drilling machines. Those machines used water and had a five-gallon tank, so he carried his own can of water. When he used up that water, he'd finish the rest of the day dry. The rock dust would hang off everything. It would be an inch thick on Dad's shoulder.

A coupla weeks later payday came. I think miner's pay was three or four dollars a day. John George paid me off at about a third of that, maybe $1.40. The check was given to Dad and he never told me exactly what I got. But Dad told me not to go back to work. He was a strict union man and believed, since I was doing man's work, I should have been paid man scale.

Injured Dad

The Page Mine is down below Smelterville and way up on the hillside from the sand pile. The second and last job I ever had with my dad was in the Page in 1925. The stope inclined up 70 degrees. Dad sent up a load of six-foot-long, green, heavy posts. He climbed up the ladder and was below me, helping me unload them. The posts were standing vertical in the timber cart—called a pickleboat—and I was standing alongside. I'd reach down and sink my pickaroon near the bottom of the post, then heave the post up into the stope where I was, and Dad, at the same time, would give a push with both hands at the bottom end of the post. We worked fast, in rhythm. Well, this time he bent over and grabbed hold a little ahead of me, and when I swung down with the pickaroon, it sunk right into his cap alongside his carbide light. It didn't hurt him any—just drew blood. But if the pickaroon had been a little further down, it would have penetrated his skull.

Mad!? For ten minutes, he really told me off.

I climbed down out of the stope and walked out of the mine. It scared me so bad, I went to Texas.

Dad died of silicosis at age fifty-three. The year before he died, he couldn't even walk across the room.

Sticky Cake Fault

Next time I worked in the Page was 1929. In the Page there's no solid rock anyplace. You drive a rock bolt in to bind rock layers together. To do this, you bore a hole and drive a crooked rock bolt into it.

There was a cake fault, too. It was between one and twenty feet wide. There wasn't much water with it, and it came out crumbly, like cake crumbs. Then between the 1,800- and 2,200-foot level, there was another cake fault, only it was full of water. It was a fright! Sticky. You couldn't drill it. Couldn't do nothin' with it. Pick it up in your shovel, hold the shovel upside down, and it would still stay in it. They tried putting paper in the mine cars to make it let go. It would still hang to the sides of the cars. Tip the car to empty and it would take the car with it into the dump. Once, a whole damn train went over the dump. Took a bulldozer to pull the train back around. Then when we tipped the car to empty, we had to chain the car to the track. The stuff would start oozing out of the car and finally drop off, all in one gob. Miners called that "crapping."

Pickleboat Tipped

I was working on the 3,400-foot level of the Page. I had just brought a load of muck out and dumped it, and the cager was landing a

 40-foot-long pickleboat out of the incline shaft, into the station. The station was maybe 40 feet square and 16 feet high. The timbers were chained in the pickleboat, and the pickleboat was still fastened by a cable to the bottom of the cage.

This guy should have unhooked the cable and left the pickleboat there for someone else to unload, but he wanted to use the timber cart somewhere else. This guy was unchaining the load of timbers when, I don't know where in the world the cager got three bells from, but the cage started going up.

When I saw the cage taking off, I run across the station alongside the pickleboat, grabbed the cord, and gave one bell to stop. At the same instant, the pickleboat tipped at an angle, which caused its long timbers to hit the top of the station. That broke the cable. The guy unchaining it jumped backwards to safety. Me, right there in the middle of it all with timbers raining down. It's a wonder I wasn't killed.

Kindest People

Then came the Depression and no jobs. I set off in 1930 to see sunny California. I was walking along a highway after dark, and a car hit me from behind. I was thrown clear off the highway into a brushy ditch. When I woke up, I could hardly make my legs move. I tried raising up and my back pained awful. I kept trying to work my numb legs and finally crawled up to the edge of the highway. I raised up on my knees with the help of one arm and started waving the other arm for help. Cars just kept on going.

After a long time, a car stopped with some black people. They took me to a hospital in a nearby small town. They carried me in to the front desk. The [hospital] woman said they couldn't take me in without no money. Those blacks argued and argued till I was put on a stretcher and wheeled to a room.

I had no broken bones, but my legs were hurt and my back hurt. I spent weeks convalescing. Those black people were the kindest people I ever met!

1933–34 Flood

As soon as I was able to travel, I headed back home. I went into the business of cutting stove wood with my brothers Harry and Gunnard. Our yard became a woodyard. We delivered wood all over the mine district in an old Model T Ford truck. Then we set up a woodyard down by the Division Street bridge in Kellogg and the flood of 1933–34 washed our wood away along with our woodsaw. But the flood had damaged the railroad, and so we all went to work on the section.

The Morning Beanery

About 1931, I worked at the Morning Mine at Mullan. The Mullan Beanery was twice as big as the Tiger Beanery at Burke—all wood, five or six floors, and an enormous dining room. They had their own bakery. I boarded there two years.

The beanery set out a table loaded with cold cuts and pie, cake and cookies for the guys coming off night shift. But they had to quit it because all the other miners in the community drifted in there to eat free. Even miners from Wallace and Kellogg came in to fill up their lunch buckets for the next day.

Ten-Day Nelson

I worked with a tramp miner called "Ten-Day Nelson." He just stayed ten days on a job and was gone. In the early 1930s it seemed like 99 percent of the miners were ten-day men. Most of them were single. They worked long enough to get a little stake and then moved on to the next mine.

One morning, Nelson had a poisonous hangover. I don't know what happened to set him off, but he had his whole box of dynamite laid out and his primers [blasting caps] all made up with fuses getting ready to load the holes. Those days the blasting caps were filled with fulminate of mercury. All of a sudden he started jumping up and down on those primers with his leather boots and howling, "Go off! You sonofabitch! Go off!"

You should have seen me take off down the ladder and down the drift. I met Dean Fleming down there. He was shifter [boss].

I said, "That Nelson went nuts! He's jumping up and down on those primers." When I went back, Nelson had gone.

Shifting Ground

The Morning [Mine] ground was the worst in this country for shifting, squeezing in all the time. You could cut a timber and just hold the headboard up there between the end of the cap and the wall for ten minutes and it would be tight. On the 4,000-foot level, we put in 20-inch drift caps—20 inches through! A cap is the timber that runs horizontally overhead and is held up by posts.

You can't imagine the force moving in that mine. We had to put five headboards crisscrossed between the end of the cap and the tunnel wall. Headboards were generally made 2 ¾-inches thick, 10 or 12 inches wide, and 18 inches long. If we put in only four headboards and the boss checked them, he made us take them out and put in another, [so] there would be over 13 inches of wood between the ends of the cap and the tunnel walls. They'd soon be so squeezed, they'd weld into one piece about 3 inches thick. The result would be a block so hard you couldn't drive a concrete spike into it. We'd use two caps, one above the other, with a saddle block between, and even those would break within a couple of weeks.

A shaft crew of 70 to 80 men worked there 24 hours a day for I don't know how many years. Replacing timbering constantly was costly! That's why the mine eventually had to shut down.

Horse Play

I worked at the Interstate Mine 1935 and 1936. It closed down in 1937. When Bill Hightower and I would come to work in the morning, there'd be a bunch of guys coming out of the mine, and we'd hang onto the trolley wire with one hand and touch somebody going by. We were in dry boots and they were wet, and wherever our hand touched them, it sent like a shot of lightning through them. Catch them guys unsuspecting and you'd knock 'em down like you hit 'em with a two-by-four.

Hungrier and Longer

Bill and I got off shift at four o'clock one morning and went through the Interstate and come out on the other side of the mountain. Outside it was just daylight and raining like the devil. We started climbing the mountain through the brush and run into an old lean-to. We crawled into it to dry and thaw out.

I said, "The longer I sit here the hungrier I get!"

Bill stretched out with his back against a wood block. He was a long, tall drink of water.

He says, "The hungrier I sit here, the longer I get!" I laughed about that for a long time.

Years later, Bill Hightower retired. He sold dynamite for powder companies, drilled steel, and run a beer hall at Osburn.

Cold Trip

When the Interstate closed down in '37, Ten-Day Nelson and I and Beans Fleming decided to rustle a job in Butte. The day before we left Wallace, Ten-Day had parked his car next to the depot. The snowplow came along and peeled one side, knocked out the windows, and tore the doors off the driver's side. It was 15 below zero. We didn't do anything to close up the gaps and by the time we got over as far as Drummond, Montana, boy, we damn near froze to death!

We got a room in a three-story old wooden hotel. There was a big skylight over the center of our room. There was no glass in it, and the snow came drifting down on our bed. We never did thaw out that night.

Poor Beans! Going from Drummond to Butte the next day, I had to sit on his feet to keep them from freezing.

Visit the King

Butte didn't appeal to me, so I came back and went up to Wallace to see the King. At that time it was [George T.] Edminston. He was the hiring agent for all the mines in the Coeur d'Alene district. If you were blacklisted with him, you couldn't work at any mine. Now they have a different system. The members of the Mine Owners Association trade information and the personnel manager of each mine has a dossier on every miner.

Old-timers tell me that at the time of the 1899 blowup of the Bunker Hill Mill, the miners gave the King a ride out of town on a rail. But when the soldiers filled the streets, he came back [refer to appendix 3].

Morning Mine Cable Broke 1936

This time the King gave me the good word and I went to work again at the Morning Mine. It was six months after the Morning disaster of October 6, 1936.

The cable that broke and dropped the miners to their death was flat, five inches wide, a half-inch thick, of indeterminate length, and woven out of whatever pieces they had in their own shop. It was never tested. It wound up on a narrow drum, one wrap on top of another. I believe the drum was twelve feet in diameter. It only went to Level 3,850.

It wasn't the main hoist, it was the chippy hoist that broke. It was a smaller cage alongside the main one. They loaded some men and lifted to take them out, and the cable broke.

Other miners heard them all the way down the shaft, screaming. Just a streak of fire going down. Set the wooden guides on fire. The guys dropped close to 2,000 feet.

ART: I worked for a time on the shaft maintenance crew at the Morning. At the time of the accident, miners told me the chippy cage set

■ Miners drilling a round of holes to be loaded with explosives. The blast will break out an advance of approximately six feet. They are using a twin boom jumbo, a drill holder for drilling upward or at angles toward the floor and mounted on a car on rails. Ernie Damiano says he built quite a few jumbos in Bunker's shop during the 1960s and 1970s.
Manley photograph

■ Miner using a Lyner Swedish-made Jackleg Drill. The expandable air cylinder gives support at almost any angle. The "timber set," used to prevent cave-ins, is of vertical stull on either side topped by the "cap." A "headboard" is wedged between the rock wall and end of the cap. "Lagging" on either side, which prevents loose rock from sloughing in, is sometimes placed outside the stull.
Manley photograph

down below for half a shift. The shifting earth squeezed the shaft narrower. The shaft crew hadn't fixed the jacket sets, so when the men got into the cage and started up and reached the tight place, the cage stopped and broke the cable. The cage hung there a few seconds or a minute. The cable had broke far above. It came down the shaft, striking the top of the cage with such force that it knocked the cage loose.

JOHN: This John Maxwell that I worked with was there at the time and helped clean up the mess. A thousand feet of this flat cable went down on top of the cage. They found one man on top. They didn't know where he come from. He couldn't have got out of the cage, so he must have been sucked in from some station on the way down.

The cable had worked its way into the cage and through the timber and around. The men in the cage were tore to pieces. When they found a hand or a leg, they didn't know who to put it with. They had to burn out some of that cable with maybe a guy's arm sticking through it.

Union at the Sunshine Mine

I worked in the Sunshine 1939, '40, and '41. I knew one of the miners that rode to work in a bus. Joe was strong union and the others were against. They got to arguing. When they got off the bus, a half-dozen ganged on Joe and beat the stuffin' out of him. My wife, Myrtle, was working at the boardinghouse at the time, and she saw him when he came in to get doctored up. He was beat up pretty bad.

The strike for union recognition and more pay at the Sunshine was lost in 1937. But during World War II, the War Labor Board ruled that the Sunshine had no right to interfere with any of the labor organizers and had to recognize the union and give back pay to the miners it had fired for union activity.

The board told 'em: "Pay up or we'll come over and run the mine and pay up for you." Even after the Board ordered Sunshine to pay up, the Company waited six months.

ART: I was recording secretary to the Mine, Mill & Smelter Workers Union and was in on the talks with the lawyers. We filed a class action suit to force the Sunshine to pay. Finally they did send checks to the men—over a period of about three weeks—in late 1944 or early 1945.

JOHN: Several guys got over $3,000. Sunshine had 300 men working. It was said it cost the Sunshine a half-million dollars.

Sunshine Powder Magazine

About 1942 they unloaded 22,000 pounds of dynamite in the concrete powder magazine over against the hillside at the mouth of Big Creek Canyon below the Sunshine [Mine]. There was some dynamite that could have been too old and unstable already in the building. It blew up that same day. The building vanished—disintegrated. It had two big steel double doors. They never found a trace of them.

There were two boxcars on the railroad siding a hundred or more feet away. It knocked the tops off the boxcars, but they were both loaded with concentrates, so they stayed on the rails. But one of the tops went clear across the river and landed on the highway. The power lines and telephone lines between the powder magazine and the highway blew to hell.

In Mike Kelestros' big house that was less than a quarter of a mile away a baby girl was sleeping upstairs. It didn't even crack a window. Blasts go in waves—it must have arched over.

The Sunshine posted a reward for years. They figured somebody had set it off—but nobody was missing afterward.

ART: Now they use nitrocellulose instead of dynamite. It's safe even when it freezes. Only one stick of dynamite is used in the bottom of each hole and the rest is fertilizer—ammonium nitrate.

The caps aren't sensitive now, either. You can drive a spike right through one of them. In fact, that's how the salesmen demonstrated how safe they were when they first came out. They drilled a hole in a lagging, stuck the cap in the hole, and drove a 40-penny spike right through it.

It takes 120 foot-pounds of energy or an open flame to set them off. You've even got to hit them hard with a sledgehammer to set them off on an anvil.

The Sunshine and the Galena are both bad on account of siderite [iron ore]. Siderite has real hard walls and will kind of slack off in layers, maybe half an inch, or maybe four feet thick, when you're drilling. Siderite is associated there with copper, silver, zinc, and gold.

You're running a buzzy and drilling underneath, and a couple of tons come down. It can break your arm or cut your hand to pieces. There's no limit to what can come down—maybe 50 or 100 tons. That's how a lot of men in the Sunshine and the Galena get hurt.

Danger from rock bursts is a different proposition. You got a drift all mined out, and you get a rock burst caused by a changing point of stress in the rock. The pressure shifts from one point to another, close to this place that you've relieved.

JOHN: It happens just like that! [Snaps finger.] An explosion! Crack! Like a rifle shot. No way to get away from it anymore than you could jump sideways to get away from a rifle bullet. And the whole wall will come in.

In our house on Big Creek below the Sunshine, a half-dozen times a night—the small ones—we hear them. Several times we've had big ones that shook the house like an earthquake. Well! That's what an earthquake is. Just a changing point of stress in the rock. Vibrations will travel through the rock and shake rock down all over the mine.

ART: There is much confusion in people's minds about what causes an air blast. Just as on a much smaller scale a miner sets off a blast with dynamite and blows rock into a stope, a rock burst [travels] with the speed of an explosion [and] blows highly compressed rock into a tunnel. Each yard of compressed rock swells instantly 40 percent. This compresses the air into traveling out the tunnel at high speed and makes an air burst capable of knocking men end over end and tearing out timbers.

JOHN: Like Edson and Muir, those two we dug out of the Sunshine about 1940. They were killed in a rock burst. It took us three days to move 600 cars of ore and rock to get to 'em. We could see the last guy all the time, leaning against the footwall with his hand up, just standing there, crushed to death. No bones broken. The rock had come in around him, crushed him, and he couldn't breathe. Oh, boy! Did he stink!

ART: How about that guy in the Sunshine? A big rock burst caved in the whole doggone tunnel ahead of him and the air blast knocked him down. That got him so scared he spent the night in the hospital. After that he went selling soap—never did come back to the mines.

JOHN: One of my hoistmen became an electrician's helper. He was in this stope on 2,400 at the Y where the drift forked. He was laying down on a lagging, eating lunch, and a rock burst come down and broke his leg. And just past him a little ways, the tunnel closed up tight!

Sand Filling Stops Rock Bursts

One of the best things the mines ever did was run the sand back into the mines, filling the stopes that have been worked out. The sand packs like concrete and prevents rock bursts. The sand is rock that has gone through the crusher, separated from the slimes, that can be pumped underground. They tried pumping sand and slimes in that old drift at the Bunker, but after several years, the sand still hadn't settled. So now, the slimes go outside to the settling ponds. Sooner or later, they run out of room in the mine for the sand. The highway fill, from the smelter slag pile to the Miners Hat, is sand from the Bunker settling pond. And the settling pond at the Sunshine is only good for another five years.

Too Many Bosses

I worked for the Bunker three or four times but I never did like the Bunker. Too many bosses. Terrible. In 1942 I was working there. On account of World War II, you were supposed to stay at the job. I was offered a job gypoing—that's contract work where you're paid for what you produce—at Pine Creek in the Spokane-Idaho.

I quit the Bunker and went to the War Labor Board at the courthouse to see about transferring.

They said, "You have to go back to Bunker Hill."

I said, "No! I'll wait till the war ends and I'll go work where I want to."

They classified me 1-A and took me to Spokane to be inducted in the army. I got into a fight with the colonel down there. Then I got into a fight with some headshrinker they sent me to talk to. The headshrinker said I was too antagonistic and classified me 4-F.

So I come back to Kellogg. I waited a week and the War Labor Board phoned me and ordered me to go to work at Pine Creek.

The Galena Mine

The Galena is up Lake Gulch about a mile on the west side of Wallace. I went there in 1956, and that's where I worked 17 years until I retired. The big hoist at the Galena has a 14-ton flywheel. When it gets going, it's enough to pick up a cage at the bottom of the mine and hoist it clear to the surface after the power is kicked off. It takes four or five hours for it to stop rolling if they don't use the brake.

Chopping Ice

I was on the shaft crew, and every winter we had to chop ice. The main hoisting shaft of the Galena mine is the Callahan shaft. A regular hurricane goes down that shaft all the time. Imagine how cold that is when it's ten below zero outside! Pretty soon the cages are scraping ice as far down as 400 to 600 feet.

We had to stand on top of the deck top of the cage and go down with pickaroons chopping out this ice. Your hands get numb and ice builds up on your shoulders. The pickaroon handle ices up so big you can't hold onto it anymore. Twenty minutes is actually all a man can stand.

As you go down, you have to be sure to free the cord of the shaft bell and keep it free because it's the only way you can signal the hoistman—and the hoistman can't move without a signal. Of course, guys on top were supposed to look down every few minutes to see we're all right.

But we had a bonnet [metal cone] over our heads to protect us from ice or anything falling down from above, so the men above can't see anything unless we get our heads out from under the bonnet far enough so they can see our lights. If you're 400 feet down the shaft, it's almost impossible to let anybody up above know what's going on.

My partner McCulloch and a crew got trapped. They had already reached the maximum time they were supposed to be down there. When they went to signal the hoistman to move, the bell rope had froze. Most places you can't force your way into the manway. Fortunately, they were just two sets above the 200 level. Just above and just below stations there are openings to give you access to the manway. Five feet further up, they wouldn't have had a chance.

They chopped like hell and were wringing wet with sweat before they got through the ice, knocked out the paneling, and got into the manway and down the ladder to the 200 level station. Another ten minutes in that shaft and they'd have been dead. It's like the sailors that are dropped into the North Sea; 20 minutes is the maximum they can stay alive.

The ice work is dangerous but I liked it. The ice you chop loose falls on down the shaft. I've chopped out icicles that were four times the size of a table. You can hear them banging back and forth on the timber and breaking into pieces. The ice melts before it reaches 4,300 feet.

But you remember to keep one hand working for yourself and one for the Company all the time. You never, ever forget it. You have to stand, sometimes with one foot on one wall plate and one foot on the other wall plate, and beneath you stretches a black hole 4,000 feet deep that tapers down to a tiny light. It never bothered me. Yet if I get out on the roof of my house and look down 20 feet, it scares me to death.

Dropped Steel Rails

One time we dropped a load of steel rails and none of 'em went over 600 feet. These were 90 pounds-to-the-foot rail, the size that had been used on the Union Pacific Railroad. A 20-foot rail dropping 100 feet punches through a 12-by-12 timber like it's butter—and maybe through a couple more timbers underneath it. We went down and hooked onto each rail with a hoist and tried to pull it out. No chance! We had to use the torch and burn them off in pieces. It took two days to get that load of rails out.

Motors Can Kill You

A self-contained battery motor to pull ore cars weighs 15 tons. It uses batteries eight or nine feet long. The batteries are heavier than the motors. They run eight hours, and then they are recharged. The drifts down there are a mile or better long, and these motors pull 15 ore cars on these main hauls. I've helped put these motors back on the rails thousands of times with big jacks and lagging. In most of those drifts you can't get alongside the motor to work on it. There are more accidents in transportation underground than from anything else.

If you see a motor coming, you'd better get in between the timbers and flatten out because 99 percent of the time there isn't room between the motor and the rock walls. It makes no difference if the motorman sees you with his light. He can set the brakes and stop the wheels, but he'll go 500 or 600 feet down the drift before he can come to a standstill. A lot of guys get caught on the hip and it rolls them and crushes the pelvis.

If you're in a place where they've got those ditches alongside the track to carry water, you can lay down in the ditch in the water and let the train go over your head. But on these Granby cars, they've got that big roller that sticks down flush with the top of the rail and it'll scrape you up unless the ditch is wide enough and deep enough. Motors are ugly things underground. A lot of guys I've known have been killed.

Fatal Rock Burst

A rock burst caught one guy at the Galena. To get him out, we went down through a raise and then over. We always posted a guard at the head of the raise where we went down. These rock bursts would come about every five minutes. If they continued to get stronger, he'd wait as long as he dared, then he'd call everybody out. We'd go down the drift and wait maybe 20 minutes till the bursts got weaker, then we'd go to work again.

First, the crew set a dragline and sucked off the muck. When it got down to him, they hollered for us on the shaft crew to come. In that drift, the 12-by-12 caps and posts were mashed together and looked like a pile of matches. We chain-sawed all the timber out of the way and put in temporary braces to hold the wall so we could bring a stretcher. It took 24 hours a day for three days and three shifts to get his body out.

Accident Prone

Some guys are dangerous to work around. Like this John Marshall I worked with at the Galena. He hooked a pickaroon in a 12-by-12 timber and turned it over without taking his foot out from under it. So he broke the arch and was laid off six weeks. He came back to work, turned another 12-by-12 over on his foot, broke the same place. He was off nine weeks that time.

Another time, we were putting ten-inch drain pipes of heavy steel under the sill timber and had to wiggle them around to get them in place. Marshall put his hand over the end of the pipe and told me to push the other end. It mashed his hand against the timber and his fingers popped like watermelons. Didn't break them—just mashed. I never figured why he didn't get killed or seriously maimed.

Galena Settling Ponds

The Galena had five settling ponds like steps. A spring flood washed out the whole thing in 1974 and carried all the slimes and chemicals down the Coeur d'Alene River.

Trading Stock

Nowadays, they use carbide bits on their drill steel. At the Page, you could use one for weeks at a time. At the Galena, you could only get one or maybe two holes with a bit because the ground is so full of iron. Carbide bits were expensive. Lots of men stole 'em and traded 'em at the cathouse [house of prostitution]. Then the cathouse sold them to the leasers.

Claustrophobia

I didn't suffer from claustrophobia underground till I got this emphysema. Then, in a close place, I'd run out of breath. Of course, I knew to sit till I calmed down. But if I couldn't get my breath, even in an open station, pretty soon I'd be so scared I'd feel like running over to the shaft and jumping in. I had to talk myself out of it. What caused the emphysema in the first place was too many years underground in too much bad air.

■ Art Norlen, 1973

THREE

ARTHUR NORLEN

Interviewed 1980 and 1991 at his home on Tamarack Ridge.

I WAS BORN NEAR Arvika, Sweden, in 1909. My dad had a farmstead that included a lot of timberland. By law, the cultivated field and the woodland could not be sold one without the other. In summer, we grew barley, oats, rye, and potatoes on our small acreage and took care of milk cows. In the fall, up until Christmas, Dad made boots in a room set aside in our house as a shop. After Christmas, we cut pulpwood and logs in the forest. At age nine, I was given a small hatchet and expected to do my part, just as I was expected, in my youth, to learn bootmaking and to do my part of the farm work.

Depression and Emigration

Sweden sank into a terrible economic depression in 1922. There was no work except on government roads and harbors. My dad handled a road tunnel contract when I was sixteen in 1925. Most jobs were unionized at that time, an outgrowth of a 1910 general strike when [Prime Minister Hjalmar Branting] was elected and labor laws and social programs were established. Capital punishment was abolished. It was, in fact, the beginning of democracy in Sweden. I worked with strong union construction workers who taught me how to drill and blast rock.

As work became more and more scarce and conditions harder, young men were emigrating from Sweden in droves. There was another reason which prompted men to leave: military conscription. At eighteen, a young man had to register. At nineteen, he had to enter the service for two years, attend military camp thirty days each summer for three years, and thereafter, so long as he was within military age, he was subject to call.

After we saw the bloodbath of nearby combatants in World War I and suffered from the German blockade of our harbors, Swedish youth learned the bitter lesson that Sweden, with a population of only five million, was too small to mount an adequate army for its own defense and that military solutions were stupid.

I had two uncles and an aunt in America, but no idea where. Carl Torkelson, a guy who had emigrated to America in 1905, had visited his mother in Arvika the year before, and had promised me a job working on his farm in Bear Springs, Montana. So I sailed to the United States from Gothenburg on the *SS Drottningholm,* November 5, 1926, to work for him.

Bear Springs

I had to get up at 4:30 in the morning, milk 11 cows, feed ten calves, and separate the milk so they could churn butter. Then, after I hauled wheat to town and came home late, I had all those cows to milk again.

Bull pine grew along the edges of his field. I cut, peeled, and hauled enough bull pine to build him another house after he had a sawmill cut it into lumber. At one dollar a day and board for 15 hours work, I was being paid 6¾ cents an hour!

I left the farm after two months to trap coyotes along the Judith River all winter. In the spring of 1927, with my pockets jingling with money from the sale of the furs, I headed for the mines at Butte [Montana].

With the Mad Swede

I was still only seventeen, but I was big for my age and told them I was eighteen. I said I'd had experience in drilling and blasting rock, so they hired me as a helper for the Mad Swede, a crackerjack miner. Whenever something went wrong, they sent for him to fix it. He had just come off a drunk that morning and slept all day in an abandoned spot in the mine, leaving me nothing to do.

The men I rode to work with warned me, "He's a company stool pigeon. So talk about women, liquor, and the old country. But don't let him know there's a big organizing campaign going on. We're talkin' union!"

Sandpoint and Uncle Andy

I'd only worked at the mine seven or eight weeks when a chance conversation with a Swede miner gave me a lead on the whereabouts of my uncle. This miner not only said he knew my Uncle Andy Norlen at Sandpoint, Idaho, but he had worked with my other uncle, Nels, in the woods at Headquarters, Idaho. I wrote Uncle Andy, and he sent me a letter that he'd line up a job for me.

Andy Norlen lived with his wife and son on an 80-acre farm near Sandpoint. An old employee of the Humbird Lumber Company, he had bought lumber from Humbird and built a house, and everything was clear and paid for. But he was finding it difficult to make much off the farm and complained that the farm work left him too little time to work at the sawmill for good wages.

No wonder Uncle Andy ran short of time. He was endlessly enterprising. He had a first-class gun shop in Sandpoint, too. I have been crazy about guns ever since I was a kid in Sweden. He let me help in the shop and taught me how to replace parts in guns, then how to blue them [apply a protective coating], and, finally, how to shape gun stocks. I found it interesting to learn but I'll have to admit, I didn't do Uncle Andy much good financially.

When I collected my pay for lumber piling and loading lumber on railroad cars at the Humbird mill, if I had any spare cash I bought me a bottle and went dancing!

When fall came, I worked in the woods. The snow got so deep I spent most of my time shoveling out the trees so I could use the crosscut saw, and then even more time shoveling out the logs so I could cut them to length. I decided that winter logging in the United States wasn't for me.

Chasing the Greek

The next summer I worked in the logging camp for Humbird at Clagstone. They had a Greek saw filer who hated Finns, so he left the crosscut saw rakers long, making it hard for the Finns to pull the saw. And the Finns told me that during the previous winter, when the timber was frozen, he put too much set in the teeth. This meant a wider saw cut that required more effort to pull the saw. One Saturday night the Finns drank a gallon of moonshine and chased that Greek out of camp, and he never did come back. I had learned saw filing in Sweden. It took me four 16-hour days to work those saws back in shape.

Swenglish and Finnglish

People in Swede settlements in the United States would often speak a broken English mixed with Swedish words that resembled English in pronunciation. As newcomers picked up this dialect, they thought they were speaking English. The Finns would do the same. And so there evolved dialects we called Swenglish and Finnglish.

Then there were Swedes who had grown up along the border of Finland who already used a dialect made up of Finnish and Swedish. When they came to America and mixed their dialect with English, they were impossible to understand by someone who had not been raised on the border.

Mine Trouble at Butte

In the winter of 1929, I headed for Butte, Montana. I had worked at the Leonard Mine, so I stopped there first. It had pickets at the portal and scabs working inside. The Company offered me a job scabbing, but I went on to the Tramway Mine and then to the East Colusa—all copper mines and all on strike. I joined my friends on the picket line.

The second day, a wall of police and deputies came in on both sides of us with clubs. To keep from getting beaten up and arrested, we took off up the 45-degree hillside, in an inch of snow, dodging on all fours through the tall grass and brush. At the top of the ridge, we got to our feet and bunched up. The deputies were still on the road 350 yards below us when someone standing with them fired at us with a .45 automatic, but the bullets fell far short. Some of the pickets said it was probably a Jugoslav [Yugoslavian] bootlegger who had been hanging around. He just wanted to make a good fellow of himself with the powers. No doubt he figured the union would die anyhow and we were just a bunch of hated radicals.

There were two Finlanders in our bunch who couldn't speak much English. I was told about a year later that one caught this Jugoslav bootlegger in an alley and left him with his face and body ripped with shallow knife cuts. By the time the police found the bootlegger, he had bled so bad that he nearly died.

Frank Little

My striker friends showed me around the town. Down toward Meaderville there was an effigy hanging over the sidewalk from the one and only tree. Ninety-nine percent of the guys who worked there had to go by this place, and if you walked straight, its feet would kick you in the face. A placard pinned to its chest read "Frank Little."

Frank Little was an official of the mine union and a Montana Indian. August 1, 1917, Frank Little had been taken from his bed by six men and dragged to death behind a car. His lynched body had been left hanging from a railroad trestle further out of town. My friends showed me the place. They said in the biggest funeral Butte had ever seen, over 50,000 people followed Frank Little's body to his grave. That showing of support marked the end of the vigilantes!

Being Fingered

My miner friends said we had lost this strike, so I went to Missoula and then down river to Noxon. The Anaconda Company had several logging camps cutting mining timber and hauling it back to Butte. I got a job in the first camp.

The woods boss, named Charley Walk, found out I could do a little of everything, so he put me on as a handy extra at day's pay and promised me a job sawing as soon as one was open.

A couple of guys, Hodini and Finch, came into camp. I remembered seeing them hanging around the picket line in Butte. The next morning, this Charley Walk didn't say anything to me when it come time to give out orders for the day. When the office was empty, the timekeeper wiggled his finger through the window at me to come and get my check.

I moved on down to the next camps. I'd eat lunch and supper in one and stay overnight and eat breakfast, then I'd go on to the next one for lunch.

The lumber camps were organized Wobbly while the mines were Western Federation of Miners. I located Wobblies in every camp and told them who the buggers were that were moving through and putting the finger on strikers from Butte.

Quite a few miners that got blacklisted at Butte moved to Sandpoint and bought little stump farms [farmland that has been logged but not had the stumps removed]—my mining partner, Erickson; the Backlunds; the Coolas—almost all Scandinavians.

The White Delph

I found work that winter of 1929 at the White Delph Mine on Big Lightning Creek, a mile and a half from Clarks Fork, Idaho. The White Delph had a crew of 11 men. Compton White was its president and dragged down $500 a month salary for himself.

I said to him, "I only want to work three months. That's all. If you want more, then don't hire me." I only wanted to work in the mine until work in the woods opened up.

Compton White had a funny habit. When he got ready to speak, he'd blow out his breath. He blew and then said, "That's the smartest thing I've heard."

Clarks Fork had about 100 population and at least six bootleggers. Two bootleggers were women. It seemed like the whole town was making homebrew and peddling it and whiskey. The druggist had the best booze with no fusel oil in it. He cut pure grain alcohol with water, colored and flavored it.

Ride with Dynamite

One day Compton White told me to help him haul a load of powder from his main magazine, which was always a safe distance from the mine. I stood in the back of the pickup with the sides stacked high with boxes of dynamite. The road was rocky and rough. He drove like the devil was after him and I was hanging onto the top boxes as they slid back and forth. Pretty soon I lost a box overboard. It broke into splinters on a bunch of rocks and spread pulverized powder all over the road. It was a miracle it didn't blow up. The deer came down and licked that salty powder all spring.

I've often wondered that there weren't more blow-ups from frozen powder. If the dynamite froze, the nitroglycerin separated into little droplets. Nitroglycerin then became so unstable that if you broke a stick of dynamite in two, that little droplet could go off if the droplet happened to be where you broke it.

Accident Prone Partner

My partner in the White Delph was John Tolliver during most of those three winters I worked there. We were using pickaroons, which have a point on only one side. One time in the shaft, I drove a regular double-pointed pick into a timber. I mentioned to John that the pick wasn't in tight enough. He tried to drive it deeper with his open hand as though it was a pickaroon. Bang! He drove the point of the pick right through his hand. It made me sick when I helped him pull it out.

Hugo

My younger brother Hugo, only sixteen, came from Sweden in 1930 on the very day our Uncle Andy Norlen dropped in the field, dead from heart failure. Hugo found six weeks work piling brush for the Forest Service at three dollars a day. Then he hitchhiked everywhere looking for work. At Selle, north of Sandpoint, we built a two-room shack so we'd have a place to come back to. We built it out of lumber taken from an old flume, and made an agreement with the land owner that when we left it would be his.

I rode freights to find odd jobs. I had to keep working to pay our expenses. It didn't take much compared with today's standards, but jobs were few and pay very low—whatever someone wanted to pay. It was worse for Hugo. He got work on a fire one Fourth of July and work on the flood on Christmas day 1933. Nothing more. The folks sent money and Hugo went back home in 1935.

The King

The fall of 1932, I hit the mines in the Coeur d'Alenes looking for work. A guy named Murphy had a shaft job up at the Tamarack. He wanted me for a partner. The job had to go through George T. Edminston, who was hiring agent for all the mines in the district. He was the man who held the blacklist. Everybody in the mines referred to him as the King.

We went up to Wallace. In Edminston's office, Murphy said, "By Jesus! If I was you, I'd hire the lad. He's a good man."

The King said, "Fill out the application and come back tomorrow."

The next morning, the office girl handed me my application. Stamped on the bottom was the one word "NO." I could read the handwriting on the wall. Much as I hated making and repairing shoes and vowed never to do it, I knew I must get a shop and make my living at the skill I had learned as a kid in Sweden.

Dusted

I went back to the White Delph at Clarks Fork and told Compton White I needed more than three months work this time.

I started running a dry buzzy in a stope that was all slate rock on St. Patrick's Day. By Thanksgiving I was sick. I'd lost my appetite and a lot of weight. I went to the doctor.

He fluoroscoped my lungs and says, "You're full of rock dust! What kind of rock dust is this?"

I says, "It's gotta be slate because I've been in it for eight months."

He said, "Get lots of rest. When you feel sleepy, go to sleep. And don't be runnin' around town!"

He prescribed a diet that included raw liver.

I says, "I'll heave at the thought!"

He says, "I'll tell you what to do. Cube the liver into small pieces. Wash them. Put a little salt on them, then swallow them down. Don't chew. They won't taste that bad."

 So I learned to eat raw liver.

Slate dust is not as damaging to the lungs as the silica dust, which comes from rock with a high quartz content. In about the same length of time it took to get that dust into me, I got rid of it. I was fine afterward.

First Shoe Shop

I had hung onto every cent I'd made at the White Delph. I set up a shoe shop in Coeur d'Alene at 819 Fourth Street.

Times were hard, so all my work was shoe repair. Then, as conditions began to get better under President Roosevelt and the Rural Electrification Program shaped up and furnished work for power linemen, I began making climbers to order. Around 1937, as the lumber industry picked up, I began making calked boots to measure for loggers. I ran my shop nine years until I was drafted into the service in 1942 for World War II.

World War II

It was the job of the Second Air Force to keep watch over the Japanese submarines and shipping in the Pacific, but after 1944 the Japanese didn't possess enough navy to threaten the nearby Aleutians and Alaska. At Fort Lewis a notice went up on the bulletin board that anyone experienced in nonferrous mining was needed and would be given a furlough. I signed up and was one of the 4,000 men released by the service to help out mines all over the country. My army pay was to stop but I could expect union wages. I chose the Bunker because it brought me closer to home.

I worked a couple of months and then for no reason I was called back to the air force. Then I was told the Bunker had written a letter requesting I be furloughed to them again.

This time I was put to work with John Appleberg as partner. John had emphysema and puffed hard on heavy jobs, but he was a willing worker. I gathered that for a long time he had worked steady and drank up everything he made. He and Myrtle were married in 1942 and she was trying to convince him to take better care of himself, but he still fell off the wagon sometimes. He went on a one-week drunk. Two days after he came back on the job, he told me he had never stopped drinking till there was nothing left to drink and was in debt $1,100.

Muck Roaring Past

There was a timbered chute running down on about a 50-degree angle. A big rock hung up in there. Bill Collins was the push.

He says to me, "Drill a hole in that big boulder, take a stick of powder, and blast it out."

So we rigged up a jackhammer and lowered me down in there. I had drilled the hole and was loading it. The jackhammer was wheezing and I couldn't hear anything. Suddenly, little pebbles started hitting me on the head and shoulders. I knew I had only a split second to save myself. I drove my pick into a timber above me—deep, almost to the eye of the pick—and grabbed hold with one hand next to the wood. I swung my other hand around to grab, and in my panic, drove my forearm onto the point of the pick. It didn't go clear through my arm and missed the bone. Down the chute came a load of muck—anywhere from six to 12 tons of rock. I hung there, half-crucified, with my feet pulled up while the muck went roaring past.

A guy named Sargent was tramming into this chute. Any trammer should have known not to dump his carload till he checked to see that nobody was in the chute. The air hose running down to my jackhammer was clear evidence that someone was working below.

I charged up there to break every bone in his body. A half-dozen guys were already there screaming at him and so goddamn mad that I felt sorry for the poor devil and made excuses for him.

Nine Bosses to Six Men

We worked night shift and there were nine shifters to run six men on our level.

Going down in the skip, gentle old Big Mike Gnatovich, he'd say, "They don't work nothing like they used to do. Why! Back in 1905, so and so and I drilled a round with a jackhammer and mucked it out, put in a set of timbers and hand mucked that out. Done it every shift, too!"

John said, "Mike! Your drift was only four feet wide and four feet high."

I'd say, "Mike! What ever happened to your partner?"

"Oh," he'd say. "He died in 1912."

And I'd say, "You see, Mike, what happens when you work like that?"

John Blows Up

On the 2,300-foot level, there were only the two of us and we had a shifter over us. John went out to the station for something and here were three shifters standing around giving advice to one another about how to run their crews.

John came back to me and says, "It burns the hell out of me to listen to shifters. Three of 'em out there airing their knowledge about mining and they don't know nothing. They're lazy and they got no principles."

I said, "Over the years, I've watched these guys buckin' for sergeant. Some begin as pretty good guys. They become shifters and most of 'em give up their principles. Anything comes from the Union Hall, they scream. Anything from management, no matter how stupid, they praise. They carry gossip from the union meetings to the management.

"You remember Perry Matthews? Well, I was running around with him and he was about to be crowned shifter. We were drinkin' down at Dan's and I said, 'Perry! I know the situation from A to Z, and if you don't want me around, you're not hurting my feelings a goddamn bit. But you'll never make the shift job if you associate with a union man like me!'

"Perry said, 'I don't want no shift job.'

"I said, 'Don't kid me, Perry! I know what you want.'"

John said, "You've just made up my mind for me. I'm goin' where I can work contract and don't have to listen to dumb shifters beatin' their gums. I'm quittin'!"

Working with Dum Dum

They brought me Dum Dum for a partner. We were on only day's pay, but he was high flying—always working at contract speed. While I worked with John, I never lost a drop of blood. With Dum Dum, I was jangled nerves and covered with bandages.

I walked out and went to the hiring agent. "Either you get me a job on Pine Creek at the Spokane-Idaho or I'll just wait till the army calls me back."

I worked at the Spokane-Idaho three days and was called back to Fort Lewis. I no more than arrived when here came a request from Tubby Garrett, manager of the Spokane-Idaho, wanting me back.

Contracting with John

This time I worked with John Appleberg, contracting. I was also appointed shop steward for the union and took up grievances with the manager. I liked [Tubby] Garrett. So long as I had a grievance worth considering, he listened.

Originally the mine had been the Constitution. It produced 45 percent zinc ore. As we drilled, it looked like blood coming out the hole. Pine Creek zinc was blood red.

You had to make more holes and space 'em properly. If you took six inches too much ground, they'd bootleg big holes. It's called "bootleg-

■ Jack Stout and Jack Welch mining in 1928. They are wearing carbide lamps, and Jack Welch is using a jackleg drill, sometimes called a "buzzy" or "stoper." The stope they are working is on an incline vein at the Cedar Creek mine.
Courtesy Jack Welch

ging a hole" when the hole blows out leaving a big cavern behind it that looks something like the shape of the leg of a boot. So then you have to run a pipe up into the hole and keep shoving more powder up in there. And stuffing dynamite up there, you're getting powdered dynamite dropping down in your face and over your clothes and inside your shirt collar and you get the goddamndest powder headache. Then you take gunnysacks or most anything to stuff the mouth of the hole to prevent it blowing out again.

Colder'n hell there, too. But not quite as cold as the Sunset Lease where John worked one time. He said in wintertime, he could look out and see the moon up the raise from the stope he was working in. There was a breeze coming down another shaft and sweeping up his that would blow his hat off. He'd wear two suits of long underwear, two pairs of pants, two coats, and two pairs of gloves to drill. Walkin' in water. Wet. Drippin'. The machine would freeze up and he had a helluva time!

We'd change off. One week I'd drill and John would timber and the next week he'd drill and I'd timber. It was my week drillin' and my machine went dry. I was drilling up holes with a buzzy stoper machine. I brought the thing down and looked at the end of the drill. It was squirting water like mad. I put it back up the hole—standing there—shaking my head.

John says, "What's wrong?"

I said, "I don't know. I can't get any water."

John came toward me and he saw it. That whole roof, or back as they call it in the mine, had a crack four feet deep and my drill had reached into that crack and the water was running out about 30 feet further down the stope. Normally, water runs into the machine, out the end of the hollow drill and comes back out the hole being drilled, wetting and flushing the rock dust. It was so foggy around the machine from the dry dust, I hadn't seen it. There was a thousand tons of rock hanging over our heads and I had drilled into the whole damn works.

We got all the lagging and planks and timbers for cushioning on top of the timbers so if the whole block fell down and the dynamite in it exploded on the timber, it wouldn't wreck our timber. We blasted at noon and got it down without any trouble. We were lucky.

On that contract we'd go down to work an hour late and quit an hour early and take two hours for lunch. We loafed four days at the end of the period. We knew we could get out still more ore but we didn't do it because if we made too much money, the company would cut the price on us. We made $14 a set on that stope.

The guy that measured us up said, "Well! You each made $21.50 per day *again*!"

Day wage for a miner at that time was $8.75.

The Spokane-Idaho produced 45 percent zinc and so did all the other mines on Pine Creek. When the wartime subsidies on minerals were dropped in 1949, they could no longer produce at a profit and had to close down.

Altogether, I only worked with John Appleberg one year and three months, but I liked every hour he worked with me. Our ideas about unions were alike. He was a staunch rank-and-file union man who earned the respect of everybody for his honesty and hard work. But he had such an aversion for chiselers, scabs, and finks that he was too radical. There was no gray area with him. Once he judged a man to be a fink or scab, he opened up on him and never let up. He suffered from emphysema, not only from breathing foul air underground, but from chain-smoking three packages of cigarettes a day. Drinking rotgut didn't help, either. But he knew mining! Every move counted.

Sunshine Strike 1937

The International Mine, Mill & Smelter Workers Union organized the Sunshine in 1937, and when the management refused to recognize the union and fired every man it could uncover, the union pulled a strike.

At about this same time, the majority of workers in the Bunker voted for Mine-Mill, but the Bunker also refused to recognize the union. In 1942, soon after World War II began, Harry Bridges, leader of the Longshoremen's Union, came up to the Coeur d'Alenes twice to let the Mine-Mill union know that if the mines continued to refuse recognition of the union, our brothers in Longshore would stop handling ore shipments. He also said the Longshore had an agreement with the Teamsters Union that if one union hot-cargoed anything, the other would follow suit. I was away in the air force at the time, but old-timers my age later told me that it was this threat of being hot-cargoed plus pressure from Franklin Roosevelt's War Labor Board that forced Sunshine and the Bunker to recognize the union and stop discriminating against union men.

Why Can't They Work Together?

I quit the Spokane-Idaho October 15, 1945, and next day went to work as organizer for the Mine, Mill & Smelter Workers Union. A little later, I was also appointed recording secretary. The secretary received no pay, but as organizer I was given miner's day pay—$8.75. My wages were paid by three local unions at Kellogg, Wallace, and Mullan. The International only paid a couple of vouchers for gasoline.

The International Mine-Mill leaders raised the idea of delegates going to Washington to lobby for laws that would help labor. A faction in the local union accused them of being communist. I tried to act as intermediary and thought: They're all workers. Why can't I get them working together for the common good?

All the fight they were waging should have been with the companies for better conditions—not with each other. You see, the red issue is one the Company can't raise. If the Company fires a laboring man, charging him with subversive thoughts and actions, everybody is going to rush to his defense, especially his union. But if the Company can get enough of their own stooges into the union, then the union factions can carry out attacks like that.

But I soon found that trying to make peace between those two factions was like ramming your head against a stone wall.

In Seattle, Harry Bridges had called a meeting of the Longshore Union to form a united front with Woodworkers, Boilermakers, Mine-Mill, and other unions. Mine-Mill had no money to pay expenses, so I volunteered to drive. One of the delegates was Lefty Lane. Back in the 1930s we used to tease him at lunch time. Lefty was a rabid socialist. I don't remember if he was called Lefty because of his politics or because he was left handed. Anyway, when he got started talking socialism, he couldn't quit. One of us would eat lunch while the other guy asked questions, and then the other would eat while the first asked questions and kept Lefty talking. Poor Lefty never got a chance to eat.

Jim Ames was a delegate, too. There was a tremendous crowd at the meeting. We stayed three days. But Lefty talked nonstop from Kellogg to Seattle and back.

The night we returned, we stopped at Jim's house for coffee. He had been digging out a basement and Lefty went out in the darkness to use the outhouse. It was black dark, and as he went out the door he was still talking, and he closed the door, still talking, and all of a sudden his voice was coming up through the floor cursing and screaming. I ran out with a flashlight, and there he had fallen down into the basement. He was clawing at the dirt and trying to climb out and I got to laughing so hard, I couldn't even help him.

Scabs at the Star

In late 1945 and early 1946, we were working to organize the Star Mine at Burke. We had about three-fourths of them signed up—that is, they signed cards that they wanted an election. We'd think we had a majority because they had signed up, but then when the Labor Board held an election, they'd vote against the union.

We got the lowdown on them in this way: Enough signed up for the union that Hanley, the manager, had to turn over the whole list of employees to us. The National Labor Relations Board required it. Hanley was Hecla and the Hecla leases the Star. The Star was 75 percent owned by the Bunker and 25 percent by the Hecla. We sent this list of employees to the International office of Mine-Mill and the names came dribbling back as they did research on them. Page after page: where they had scabbed; what they had done; their aliases.

[The mine owners imported nonunion men to infiltrate the union organizing effort and sabotage it.] There were 90 imported scabs hid away in that Star Mine, scabs and gunmen from Longshore, Steel, Auto, Electrical—everything. We had four of the ones who worked under Harry Bennett and used machine guns on the Ford workers in Detroit in the 1934 Bloody Thursday Massacre when 91 were killed. The scabs had settled down as permanent fixtures in Burke Canyon, down to and including Woodland Park.

If the Mine-Mill had gotten in, there would have been a hell of an exodus from the district. That bar that used to be in Burke, the Hoist Room, had a couple of pool tables and cards. I was on the picket line outside and went in there to use the bathroom. It was a silly thing for me to do. A whole bunch of those guys were hanging around. When I started back out, these guys started moving and about six of 'em divided on each side of the only door. Just as I went by the rack of pool balls and cues, I grabbed a cue. I carried it by the small end and walked right through with it at the ready. I'm telling you, I was scared.

Butte was sort of the mother of the unions in the Coeur d'Alenes. But here, the companies held the union out by raising wages. For years the scale at the Hecla and the Star was two-bits higher nonunion than Butte was with a union. When they'd see a raise impending, they'd give their men a raise. It's smart policy for the company. They'd pay the wages but otherwise they run the mine the way they please. If they had a union mine and fired a man, they've got to have cause or the union will take up the grievance. They even evolved pensions to take care of their faithful employees when they get old.

So what it amounts to, the unions struggle for better pay, working conditions, pensions, and medical coverage, and the nonunionists get them for nothing. It's not fair, but there's nothing you can do about it.

We had three elections for Mine-Mill, the Steel Workers had one election, and the Star has never been organized.

Three Dollars for Ten Hours

I have great respect for the Mine, Mill & Smelter Workers Union, the Western Federation of Miners, and before that the Federation of Miners, and the part they played in labor history. All of them struggled for a living wage and decent working conditions back when miners were paid only three dollars a day for ten hours and died like flies from silicosis—only then they called it miners consumption, or miners con for short. It was the Miners Union that set up the Providence Hospital in Wallace and the first adequate medical care for miners injured on the job.

It was the Miners Union that struck in 1892 to maintain a barely living wage of $3.00 when Bunker and its followers cut to $2.50. Help rolled in from all other big mining camps to feed the strikers and their families. The struggle against Bunker's lower scale continued into 1899 when it was finally organized and struck.

Back in 1930, we had begun asking that May first be designated Joe Hill Holiday because he was labor's troubadour and was executed by a firing squad in Salt Lake City, November 19, 1915. Joe Hill came from near Arvika, Sweden, where I came from. They celebrate Joe Hillstrom Day in Sweden yet.

Site of the Old Concentrator

I lived at 202 East Portland in Kellogg. I had to dig a ditch because water was backing into my garage. Down about eight inches in the gravel, I ran into the concrete of the old mill yard. It runs all over this area and is hard enough that you can hardly break it with a pick. This is the mill yard, and the mill itself would have been across the street about where the motel or apartment house office is. Milo Creek ran down through here. I believe this is the location of the old concentrator of Bunker Hill that masked men blew up in the 1899 troubles. [See appendix 2.]

Bull Pen 1899

From the hill road, we took a picture, holding the camera so as to show Italian Gulch as it appears in the original bull pen picture. This puts the center of the bull pen maybe 200 feet east of the Kellogg Lumber Company, but across the tracks from it. As nearly as we can figure out, the railroad track was in front of the bull pen in the picture—in front being closer to the camera or south of the bull pen.

We place the location of the center of the bull pen in the 100 block of Railroad Avenue on the south side of the railroad tracks. About at house number 114. There was an exhaust or tailing flume that ran out to the river over by the site of the bull pen. The flume ran down from Wardner. It dumped all the tailings into the river at that time, although, of course, the river was not where it is now.

I talked with a man named Fitzhugh, dead now, who appeared to know the location of the bull pen. He said the buildings were not new; they were where the Bunker Hill stored their equipment—wagons for hauling ore down from Wardner in summer and sleighs in winter. He said the bull pen was made by partitioning off the old buildings already there.

Back to Sawing Logs

I had done some good for the Mine-Mill by organizing the Silver Dollar and the Zanetti Lease over toward Murray, but I was getting discouraged over the gullibility of the neutral miners to swallow the communist scare. I took a withdrawal card from the Mine-Mill, June 5, 1946, then joined the Woodworkers Union and went over on the North Fork to saw logs for Ohio Match on Stewart Creek. After three months of sawing, I took a withdrawal card from the Woodworkers and on September 10 set out on a six month's trip to Sweden. I visited my mother and brothers, worked in the woods there for three months and became reacquainted with everybody I had known in my youth. Then I came back to the States and headed for Kalispell, Montana, where they were building the Hungry Horse Dam.

Hungry Horse Dam

Money was rolling into town from the Hungry Horse Dam. I bought a little furniture and sporting goods store and set a room aside for a gun shop. I worked on guns all week in my spare time and then my wife, Verna, and I kept the store open late Friday nights and I blued them. After three years, I left Kalispell because from the first of November till late in April the deep snow shut down all dam work and blanked out business for six months out of the year. During that period, people simply survived on unemployment checks.

Old Friends

In 1950, I bought a shoe store in Kellogg on McKinley across from the YMCA. I installed a shoe repair shop in the store to make a complete service. It was like coming home. My old friends and neighbors came in to greet me, like John Appleberg, Preston Dieter, George Blackburn, Fred Blackwell, Hazel Corbeill, Andy Hightower, Grant McGlade, Tony Matovitch, Wayne Jarvey, Fred Derby, and Jack Aho.

Tubby Garrett, who had been superintendent at the Spokane-Idaho when I worked there, came in and shook hands.

He said, "It sure is nice to see you back in the country again."

I said, "By God, Garrett! You say that like you mean it."

He said "I do."

I said, "After all the times I argued with you when I was shop steward for the union up there?"

He said, "Every argument you put up had validity. You came with somebody's grievance. You didn't come in just to pick a fight with me."

I was really surprised and pleased.

Phil Wilkes

I missed seeing my old union friend, Phil Wilkes. He had been killed about 1948 in a motor accident in the Pittsburgh mine.

Along in 1946 or '47, his son, young Phil, borrowed his dad's car one night to go get some smokes at Morbeck's store in Pinehurst. He parked around back where it was dark. Some Bunker thugs knew the car and thought they had his dad, Phil Sr. They were drunk, I suppose.

One of them said, "That you, Phil?"

The kid said, "Yes."

He was just getting out of the car. He hadn't worked in a mine, didn't know anything about the union or danger. He reached back into the car for something. The guy slammed the car door shut on his arm and heaved his weight against the door. Another guy started beating on him and two more came along and helped 'em.

Afterwards, somebody heard him moaning back there and called an ambulance to take him to the hospital.

Expanding Business

We had a chance to buy a building on 308 Main, and after that bought two more buildings adjacent to the first one. Over a period of time I remodeled them to give me a two-man shoe repair shop and a shoe store. I was kept busy but took time off to go fishing with John Appleberg and to hunt with him in the fall.

During the Korean War, the newspapers were screaming about the Red Chinese Menace. Senator Joseph McCarthy was riding high on the wave of publicity created by his hearings and a steady string of accusations against "red plotters" and "fellow travelers" in Hollywood, in political places, and in labor. I believe the man was actually insane. He kept accusing high and higher-up people of being involved in communist plots till he even denounced President Eisenhower as a communist dupe. That finished off McCarthy.

Johnny Appleberg said the FBI came around and questioned him and some others about me. But they didn't give a damn about me. What they were after was evidence against Travis and the other International Union leaders because there was to be a witch hunt, an Internal Security Committee Hearing, in Wallace with lots of media publicity to blast the union. They couldn't find any credible witnesses and the hearing had to be canceled.

1960 Strike at Bunker

The Mine-Mill was locked out in an election at the Bunker Hill in 1960 in competition with the company-fostered Northwest Metal Workers Union. The strike started April 6. With no smelter smoke to kill off the vegetation, it got so green on the hills around Kellogg you hardly knew the place. The Bunker hadn't been able to sell 10 percent of the sulfur dioxide they produced. There was no market. Consider that 2,300 tons of sulfur dioxide had been released from the stacks of the smelter and the zinc plant every three shifts.

The Sunshine was struck at about the same time as the Bunker, but the Sunshine settled soon. We let the union use our store as a collection center for financial help to needy miners and their families.

The business community of Kellogg swung its sympathies to the Bunker except for about five of us small businesses. Of course, some of the bars pretended to be on the side of the union.

When it came time for school, and other stores wouldn't give credit to miners and their children, I made the union a proposition. The union could buy shoes from us and pay up every two weeks and get them for 10 percent mark-up on our cost—and we pay the freight. We about broke even on it, but we sold $5,000 worth of shoes. They weren't expensive shoes, mostly $3.95 and $4.95, so that was a lot of shoes.

We depended on shoe repair income for our living and running expenses. We had a hard time, though, because that's when I had borrowed $8,000 for remodeling the two buildings we had bought. I had intended hiring it done, but now I had to do the remodeling myself, nights and weekends.

Christmas Radio Voices

Beginning around the first of December, the radio commercials were featuring little voices with, "I want a dolly for Christmas, Mommy."

And Mommy's voice would reply, "You can't have a dolly this year, dear. Daddy is on strike."

Then little voices would say how sad it will be with no toy bears or trains or kiddie cars for Christmas.

The seven-month strike was settled suddenly with miners going back to work in time to get one check before Christmas.

I didn't come out too bad. I got back the cost of the shoes, so the following season I was able to buy a whole stock of the latest shoes. The competition were still stuck with last year's stocks while I had the latest styles. That helped our sales, too. In the year following the end of the strike, I was able to pay off the $8,000 I had borrowed.

End of Mine-Mill

In 1946, the Steelworkers had raided the Sunshine and beat out the Mine-Mill by joining management in claiming the upper echelon

Mine-Mill leadership was communist. In 1960, Mine-Mill lost the Bunker, and the Bunker had been their big foothold in the Coeur d'Alene district. It wasn't long after that, they lost Metaline Falls to the Northwest Metals Union. Metaline was a partial Bunker operation. Mine-Mill still held a number of smaller mines.

Then in Butte, Mine-Mill had to merge with Steel to prevent being swallowed by increasing raids. The only local that held on for years afterwards, one that absolutely refused to join any other union, was the local at Sudsberry, Ontario, Canada.

Rubber Boots

One of the items always on the agenda for Mine-Mill negotiations had been boots for the miners. Both Sunshine and Bunker sold boots at reduced prices under union contract. In the zinc plant, the men had to wear rubber boots to protect them from the electric current in the floor due to the electrolytic process. The chemicals would soften boots till they'd begin to leak and make men do a monkey dance. The Bunker sold the boots, through their office, to the men for two dollars. They made the men turn in the old boots to prevent them from selling boots to their friends cut rate.

About 1962, Bunker began buying boots from us in lots of 500. By 1965, I was making trips back East and buying boots in large numbers for many mines.

Sunshine Fire 1972

I was again visiting Sweden in 1972. We were riding past my brother Andrew's place when he flagged us down and said he had just heard by radio of a big fire in a mine at Kellogg, Idaho. I thought it must be at the Bunker and was concerned because of two women working in our store. Ann Cannon had a husband working at the Bunker, and Margaret Ferguson had a boyfriend working there.

I waited till 11:00 that night so I could catch the store at 8:00 opening time at Kellogg. That's when I found it was not the Bunker but the Sunshine that was afire. Next day, Swedish TV gave accounts of how really disastrous it was.

Three weeks later, I flew home. By this time, the newspapers had printed the names of the dead miners. Of the 91 lost, 85 of them were our customers. There had already been many private funerals, but I was in time to attend a general Memorial Service at the high school gym at Kellogg. I went early but was barely able to get a seat. Even the aisles were jammed and the back was filled with people standing. Five or six ministers from different denominations spoke briefly at the service.

Some of the rescue equipment in the Sunshine had been allowed to get old and defective. One of the best things that has come about since the disaster is the organizing of a real search and rescue school in the district, not only attended by people here, but with links to other mining communities in other states.

Busy Retirement

I sold my shoe store and repair business in 1973 and set up a gun repair shop in an old house in Kellogg. Then I built a house for myself and my wife, Ruth Hussa, on Tamarack Ridge, and I carry on gun repair in my gun shop in the basement.

Hunting with John

John Appleberg had retired in 1973, and he and I continued to hunt and fish together. When I quit fishing, he didn't go anymore, but we still hunted together each fall. When John came to a new hunting area, he started walking it and in a couple of days he knew every game trail and ridge. He was a lucky hunter, but it wasn't all luck. He always hunted against the wind. His hearing was bad, but his tremendous eyesight made up for it.

And he was a nice guy around camp. First off, he'd dive in and set up a tent or lean-to. He'd grab the chain saw and cut up a bunch of wood. If I didn't get up early in the morning and beat him to it, he'd have the fire going and breakfast ready. In the evening hours, we'd sit around the fire recounting stories of men we had worked or hunted with.

I learned on trails to let him take the lead. He'd set the pace and I'd follow. A few times I forgot and took the lead. I'd be walking uphill at my ordinary pace and I'd turn around and here he'd be down the hill, bent over with his hands on his knees, puffing hard and gasping for air.

John put in 38 years underground. He died on Election Day, November 1982.

[Arthur Norlen's busy retirement included writing two books: *The Vanishing Immigrants* published in 1976, and *Death Of A Proud Union* published in 1992.]

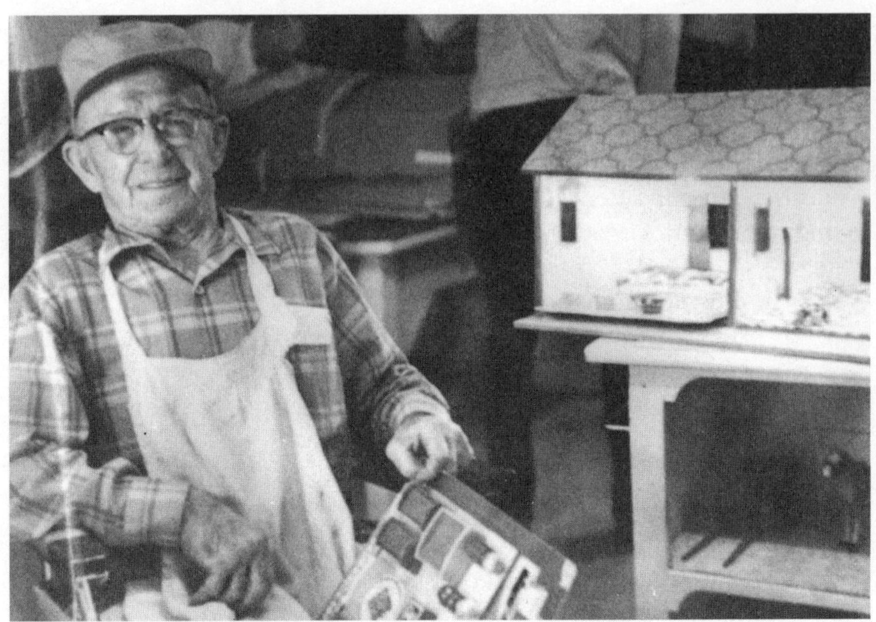

■ Otto Starke built a dollhouse for every girl who lost her father in the 1972 Sunshine Mine Fire

FOUR

OTTO STARKE

Based on a 1974 interview with Otto Starke at Silverton, Idaho, and a 1993 interview with his daughters, Evelyn Prindle and Elaine Drews, at Osburn, Idaho.

Dollhouses

WHEN THE Sunshine Mine Disaster of May 2, 1972 took the lives of 92 miners, Otto Starke, a double amputee, set about making a dollhouse Christmas gift for each of the 44 little girls that were left fatherless "to help put a smile on their face."

Dixie Stevens brought him the names of the girls. His two daughters, Evelyn Prindle and Elaine Drews, bought materials. Larry Loftus, maintenance man at the Shoshone County Nursing Home at Silverton, Idaho, hauled them to the basement where Otto worked. Fred Prindle cut the back walls of the dollhouse pattern to make the size of the plywood manageable for Otto. Shoshone Glass Company in Kellogg furnished all the double-strength glass to make shatter-proof windows for the protection of the little girls. The houses were wired with Christmas tree wiring fitted with night light bulbs "because they don't get too hot." Josie Gunderson, a resident at the home, made the drapes.

[See *Swiftwater People* by Bert Russell for more on Josie Gunderson.]

They were all excited when three weeks before Christmas the Fisher-Price Company in New York telephoned that they were sending a free gift of furniture for 50 dollhouses. A company in Oregon sent stuffed animals, one for each house, but sent them anonymously. A lady in Oregon who makes wedding dresses sent 30 eleven-inch dolls dressed like brides. Another sent three-inch dolls made of various-colored beads. Tiny Christmas wreaths were sent for each house. Someone sent a huge Christmas wreath made of wrapped peppermint candies that could be pulled out individually for Otto's enjoyment.

Hanging on Otto's wall are a commendation from the governor of Idaho, Cecil Andrus, and another from the president of the United States, Richard Nixon.

OTTO: "Roy Loftus, the maintenance man here, was a big help to me. Each week he goes down to Wallace or Kellogg, and if I need screws or paint, glue, a dozen things, he gets it for me. He charges it and they send the bills to my daughters.

"I tried to use a lot of color in my dollhouses because children like bright colors."

As news of Otto's thoughtfulness and generosity spread, cards and letters poured in from every state in the Union, each of which was answered by Evelyn and Elaine. And orders also came for dollhouses, which he filled for only his actual cost. But, of course, all the dollhouses for the miners' daughters were free gifts of love.

"You see, the material for a dollhouse costs $15, and it takes me three days to make one. If I was to charge even a little over three dollars a day for my labor, that would add ten dollars to the price, and half the people couldn't afford it. I've made 130 houses. I make 20 more and I stop. Altogether I will make 150.

"It gives me pleasure to know I'm making little girls happy. When my own girls were three and four years old, and I worked at the Polaris Mine Mill, I build 'em each a dollhouse. Evelyn played with hers till she was too old to play anymore, and I put it in the loft. Then when she had a girl, she takes it down and papers it and fixes it up.

"Then I say to my granddaughter [Gail], 'There's a little girl comes up here and plays with you all the time with your dollhouse. So why don't you give her your dollhouse and I make you a new one.'

"She said, 'My mama played with this one, and if I have a little girl, she's gonna play with it.' She still got it!

"And Elaine, her dollhouse is in the basement. She hasn't got any little girl. But her boy—he's over six feet—sometime I'll have the job to fix up that dollhouse for a great-granddaughter."

Escapes Military Service

Otto Starke was born in Dresden, Germany, in 1890. He was working on ships, stalling off compulsory military service, when the mate of one ship let go of a big block. It swung and smashed him in the right eye and ear, permanently injuring them.

In 1909 at age nineteen, while working as a steward on a German passenger ship, he jumped ship at Hoboken, New Jersey, with an accordion and 75 cents. He rode the subway for five cents to New York City. He knew not a word of English. Walking down the street, he saw a saloon with a German sign. He went in and told his story to the owner.

The owner told him, "An angel must have sent you. I need just such a boy like you," and gave him the job of "swamper" [cleaning up the saloon] and fixing free lunches for the customers.

Otto wanted to learn English, but at this place he heard none. Although he was treated like a son, after nine months he left.

OTTO: "In New York, I worked as busboy helping the waiter. I thought I knew enough to be a waiter, so I went to the New York Club and hired out as a room waiter. But I couldn't manage.

"The boss told me, 'Otto, they like you, but they can't tell you what they want. You learn a little more English and you come back.'

"So I went to Rochester, and then to Chicago."

Chicago

He tried to work as a waiter a number of times, but his lack of English killed the jobs for him.

He had gone to Chicago with the $300 he had saved up. A broker invested his $300 and increased it to $700. Then the broker told him that he had information the German government was looking for a chance to kidnap him, load him into a car, take him to the German consulate, and ship him back to Germany. This was 1912.

OTTO: "In Chicago they were getting pretty close to grab me."

The broker advised him to get out of Chicago and into the hinterlands.

Heads for Arkansas

Otto bought a team of horses. It turned out that one of the horses had distemper and the other was wind-broken and had the heaves. But he headed for Arkansas and was learning a little more English all the time.

 OTTO: "I drove on through into Arkansas and back into the Ozarks. I found I couldn't make myself understood. Every place I stopped, I could stay overnight and never charge you a penny. I got acquainted with some German farmers back in the hills. One had good mules, so I bought a team and traded them other horses off. The gray horse, the one with the distemper, I traded off for a little calf.

"I stayed there in the hills and made white oak barrel staves and ties, but I couldn't make any money.

"On the start it was OK, but oh my! It was lonesome."

Montana

In 1914 Otto homesteaded on 320 acres of dry and windy eastern Montana ground. While there, he applied for citizenship. He also took a claim in the Cat Creek Basin but let it go. He says they struck oil there later.

OTTO: "It was midwinter, and I needed a couple horses. A fellow showed me two French coach horses, a black and a dappled gray. They woulda been worth $200 apiece, but they were skin and bones and had lice.

"I says, 'What you want for 'em?'

"He says, 'Give me $15 each. You'll probably lose them horses. It don't look like they're gonna pull through.'

"Well, I had buffalo hay at home on my place. I had a nice warm barn. I had a neighbor to help me. I went over there and fed them horses plenty of hay and oats. I put shoes on both of 'em that wouldn't slip on the icy ground. We take 'em home one at a time, with me leading and my neighbor hanging on to the tail so the horse won't fall down—they was so weak. We get 'em in the barn and scrub 'em down with coal oil and then soap and water to kill the lice. We put blankets on to keep 'em warm. In the spring the guy that sold the horses to me couldn't believe his eyes. They were beauties!"

To Canada, Then Idaho

After eight years, Otto left his homestead with the fine looking team and a hack, driving first to Canada, then to Idaho, where he worked at mining on the South Fork of the Salmon River.

And there, he heard of mining in north Idaho.

Elizabeth

Through friends, Otto learned of a German girl coming to America. When she arrived, he met her with his shoes all shined up like glass.

■ Elizabeth Raithel sailing from Germany to be Otto Starke's bride

OTTO: "She came over on the *Bremen*. She was thirty-one. I was forty. I couldn't let her slip away. You got to be a fast worker. She came in October and we were married about six weeks later.

"She told me, 'Daddy! If you hadn't had your shoes polished, I'd never have given you a second look.' So that's why I never got over it. I always keep my shoes polished."

Otto and Elizabeth were surprised to learn they had lived within a few blocks of each other in Dresden.

They had two daughters. Evelyn was born in Grangeville, Idaho, in 1934. Elaine was born fourteen months later.

OTTO: "Elizabeth and I were married 38 years. I lost her five years ago. Cancer."

Twenty-One Years in the Mine

Otto worked 21 years in the Polaris Mine mill. He was a flotation operator.

In 1965, when Otto was seventy-five, he had a heart attack.

 OTTO: "I had a heart attack the same week President Eisenhower had his heart attack."

Stays Strong

Four years ago, Otto had two blood clots in his right leg. The doctor took an artery out of his left leg to help the circulation in his right leg. Finally, his left leg was amputated below the knee and the right leg, just above the knee.

To keep his strength to hoist himself around with hand power, Otto constantly exercises his arms and hands, raising himself off the seat and staying strong enough to swing himself into and out of a bathtub without help.

OTTO: "But I'm strong. Each night before I go to bed, I make a dozen hand raises."

FIVE

CANYON SILVER STORY

As told by Robert Leetch, with reminders by Rhonda Starchman and Burnice Leetch, in 1974.

THERE WAS AN old mine two or three miles north of Wallace going out toward Burke. Bill Morrow and his brother, Roland, bought it from Bill Beatty and made a junked car lot out of it. At one time, there were a couple hundred wrecked cars there.

Fritz Anderson lived right close by in a little house. Fritz told Bill he'd worked this mine 40 or 50 years ago when it was the old Formosa Mine and he knew there was ore there that hadn't been uncovered. Fritz took Bill down and pointed where the ore was, maybe 500 feet away through solid rock.

Bill Morrow was a plunger. He had bought 1,200 sheep one time while in a bar. This fellow had these sheep and he was worried about transportation. Bill offered him a couple dollars less than Bill knew he could get on the market, and the guy took it. Bill made money on them.

Then another time, he bought a dog team in Coeur d'Alene—sled, harness, dogs, the whole bit. Right on Sherman Avenue.

Bill Morrow was common, just like me or you. He wasn't a miner. He didn't know one end of a steel from the other, but he and his brother were both super workers.

They organized the old mine under the new name "Canyon Silver" and set out to find the ore. There were about 12 in the crew working for him. His brother, Roland Morrow, worked there as electrician and plumber. It was 1969 when I went to work there. He paid pretty good. We got 50 cents a foot. If you needed something, he'd get it for you—a good guy to work for.

Everybody had nicknames. The "Gallopin' Swede" was Pete Christianson. He was the one that his wife sent him sandwiches in the dinner bucket wrapped in a road map, and when he came home, his stuff was set out on the porch in cardboard boxes.

I was called "Orville Wemple" after a comic-strip character. I worked ten years before I learned the track man's name. Everybody called him Frog because that's a part of the track switch. Another one was called "Popcorn John." He'd get one of these big grocery sacks and pop it full of popcorn and take his kids to the movie.

Miners like to tell stories like the one I told my wife: Clete and me went down in the drift and blasted and the devil come climbin' right over the muck pile. I said, "You ain't scarin' me a bit! I married your sister."

We sunk that shaft down from the 120-foot level already there, to the 400-foot level. Along a vein, we worked out what they call a "kidney of lead," big as a car of pure lead. Then we went down to the 600-foot level and started drifting.

My partner Clete Startchman and Ben Walters and Dick Eickinger—all three of them, wanted to crosscut to the left. The engineers and geologists said the ore had to be to the right. I bet five dollars it was on the right, too.

We crosscut 50 feet to the right and ran out of all indication. It was costing the company a bundle. Drifting cost $15 a foot and the shaft at least $45. The experts gave up.

We started left. We were making six-foot rounds with maybe 25 or 30 holes. That means we were drilling holes six feet in depth in the end of the tunnel or drift and the blast would kick loose six feet of rock or muck and lengthen the tunnel by another six feet.

The Promise

On payday, we was all in the Metals Club in Wallace. We'd been givin' Bill Morrow a bad time. If you get a good boss, razz him.

He got up and said, "All right! If we strike ore, by God! I'll take all you guys to Honolulu for a steak dinner."

Of course, we thought he was talkin' through his hat.

I was working day shift and I dumped that shift. When I didn't show up, my partner, Clete Startchman, drilled one round by himself, blasted, and mucked it out. The night shift that followed him drilled and the first round uncovered a real good showing of ore. February 17, 1970. If I'd worked that day with Clete, we'd have probably put in two rounds and so we'd have been the ones to uncover it.

■ Canyon Silver crew on Hawaii vacation February 17, 1970. All expenses were paid by the Morrow brothers after striking high-grade ore. Names furnished by Mrs. Robert Leetch. Left to right: Richard Anderson, Barbara Anderson, Connie Eickinger, Robert Leetch, Lawrence Leetch, Leslie Anderson, JoAnn Starchman, Rhonda Starchman, Cletus Starchman, Wilma Wallers, Mrs. Bill Morrow and grandson, Joey Anderson; Ben Wallers, Bill Morrow and son, Steve Morrow, Art Udstead, Tom Castille, Lennie Morrows Castille, Steve ?, a friend from college; Jean Udstead, Jerome Bundy, Bradley Wallers, Rickie Eickinger, Anna Bundy, Mrs. Roland Morrow (Roland stayed home to look after the mine), Nancy Eickinger, Andy McKorkel, Burnice Leetch, Carrie Lee Leetch, Doris Eickinger, Dick Eickinger.

When I went to work at a quarter to seven that next morning, I walked in the door of the dry house where miner's change clothes, and it looked like the Metals Club. They had everything to drink. A real party.

Kept His Promise

Morrow says, "You better call home. We're going to Honolulu tomorrow morning at six o'clock. Families and all."

At the airport, the guys started to carry their own luggage and Bill says, "No. You set 'em down. That's all paid for."

When we got to the hotel in Honolulu, they had a mix-up on the luggage and the rooms and everything.

Bill was fit to be tied. He says, "You guys wait right here on the bus."

He goes into the hotel, comes back about five minutes later with this guy who was a-bowin' and "Yes, sir! No, sir!"

He put us up in the Hawaiian Hilton on Waikiki Beach. Forty-one dollars a day for the room we had.

Next day, waitin' for the tour bus, we had already drank four or five of those damn mai tais.

That bartender said, "Nobody can drink four of these mai tais and still walk!"

He wasn't going to serve us another one, but Bill flat out told him, "You either bring them and put 'em right here on the table or I'll buy you out."

So we tipped that one up, and that bartender was still shakin' his head when we left.

Bill Morrow told me it cost him $21,000 for the trip—hotel, mai tais, meals, tours, everything.

When we came back, we reserved all of Albi's Steakhouse in Wallace and gave the Morrows an appreciation dinner, a plaque and a scrapbook of pictures of the trip. Bill sat there with his feet on the table the same way as he had done at the Hilton. He was at home anywhere.

Bill didn't take the geologists and engineers to the islands. It was his crew that found the ore and it was his crew that got royal treatment from then on. That was just the first trip.

He'd call up and say, "Get ready! We're going to Las Vegas."

Or he'd decide the whole crew should go snowcatting at his Waterhole Ranch in Montana. When you were with him, he never let you pay for anything.

Carrie, our daughter, was pretty young at that time. She run a snowcat into a tree and smashed it. When she come in, she was terrified.

Bill put his arm around her and said, "Honey, don't worry about that snowcat. We'll buy you a brand new one."

He took the crew to his place on the Coeur d'Alene Lake. I think it was two o'clock in the morning when he put 21 of us into his $16,000, 22-foot blue boat, powered with a 454 Chevy V8. He touched the throttle and it went 70. Coming across the lake at you, it looked just like Batmobile, that boat in the Batman comic.

He bought that old Providence Hospital in Wallace and donated the use of it every year for the Campfire Girls to have a haunted house to raise money. To really appreciate that, you would've had to gone into that hospital. It was kind of a spooky damn place while it was a-runnin'. In the basement, the ceilings were really low and the rooms were small and dark. Then you go through the scary casket room and before you go down the stairs, all of a sudden, he'd open the door, "Aaaaaagh!" and there'd be a Dracula.

Old Fritz Anderson, who showed Bill where the ore body was, passed away about three months after we went to the islands. He was almost ninety.

About two years after Bill Morrow struck it, the new safety regulations required another exit out of the mine. Bill was standing in a wet place, working on a 440-volt pump to begin making the exit. He was electrocuted. I think Bill was about fifty-eight. After he got killed, they closed the mine.

■ Calvin and Carol Bates, married in Superior, Montana, 1934

SIX

CALVIN BATES

Interviewed 1973 at Harrison, Idaho.

I WAS BORN ON Decoration Day, May 31, 1907, in Woods County, Alva, Oklahoma.

When I hit this Idaho country, July 7, 1934, I could see all the high-water marks from the 1933–34 flood. My mother had wrote me that the bridges and roads was washed out, and they were isolated up there in Burke. The only way they could get eggs and a little stuff like that was by flying it into that little landing strip at Osburn. Wallace was cut off except for that airfield there.

Bear Jones

When I first come here, I was like a stranger coming to a foreign country. I got acquainted with Bear Jones, an old, broke miner who lived in Burke.

He said to me, "Now you stay as long as you want. You'll always have a place to sleep."

Before he got too crippled up, Bear Jones was working the gold 250 yards below the first switchback that you come to on your way to King's Pass. All that area in there was loaded with little shacks of prospectors. That was the way they made their living during the Depression.

They called him Bear Jones because he was a good hunter and liked hunting with a rifle for bear on the hillsides above Burke.

He told me, "Let's go over and put out a salt lick and this fall we'll get us a deer."

 We throwed out some hunks of salt. When September come, it wasn't the season, but it was time to kill deer.

So he said, "Now you can go up and kill some birds and I'll kill a deer, or I'll go up and kill some birds and you get the deer."

I said, "You're probably more used to shooting deer than I am. I never shot a deer in my life, so I'll go after the birds."

So I went up and got six or eight grouse. I went back to camp and there Jones was with half a deer. He'd give out, so I went up and found the other half where he'd left it.

There was a lot of deer poaching going on in that district during the Depression. I was told that if you wanted to put down five dollars, you could have a deer left at your door.

This game warden, name of Sneed, was out there checking on poachers when he disappeared. His car was found locked up between Wallace and Mullan. They dug up places where something had been buried, but it always turned out to be offal of deer. He wasn't very well liked and could have been dropped down a mine shaft. They never found the man.

It was after that Jones made the remark that if a game warden caught him to report him, why he wasn't comin' back. I never took that serious, but you know, that old sonofagun would have killed a game warden—just like that! You see, if he'd got caught and fingerprinted, he was a goner because he'd escaped from the pen. But it couldn't possibly have been Jones that killed the warden because the time didn't mesh.

As time went on, Jones quit and I didn't know what had become of him. I was up at the Tiger boardinghouse one day and coming down the hallway was Bear Jones, more crawlin' than he was a-walkin'. He'd got arthritis in his feet so bad he couldn't hardly walk.

I was shocked by the man's appearance. He had grown old in the few years he'd been gone. I thought the man was ready to drop.

I said, "Come to my room and rest up a little. You look tired."

While he was a-restin' on the bed he told me how he'd always dreamed of gold laying around on the ground like chicken feed. He said a few years back he had sold his car and had around $1,000.

He got acquainted with a guy who said, "You buy in on this fishing boat with me and we'll go to Alaska and make a fortune."

But after they got up there, the guy told him, "Jones. You can't do anything. You'll just have to get out."

Jones told that guy, "I want my money, every dime of it. If you don't give it to me, I'll blow you in two!"

He went down and got his shotgun. Well, the guy was smart enough to count out the money to him, but afterwards Jones counted it and he said, "You know that sonofagoat beat me out of $5?"

He told me that many years before, he'd killed his brother-in-law with a shotgun. While he was in the penitentiary, he got in a scrape and then escaped. He changed his name from Henshaw to Jones and worked the mining district in Tennessee till he come out here.

Then he kinda rolled up on his elbow and wanted to know if I'd help him and I said, "Yeah. What do you want me to do?"

They used to sort the rock out by hand on a conveyor belt, so he said, "Get me a job on a sorting."

I said, "There's no sorting plant anymore."

Well, then he said he had a sister in Tennessee and he wanted to see her again. I think the ticket cost me $60. He had enough money to eat on.

He got back there and the minute the law saw him, they grabbed him and threw him back in the penitentiary again. But they see what shape he was in and they turned him loose and paroled him to his sister. He was drawing $13 a month.

The first month I got $10. The second month I got $10. I knew Christmas was coming on and he must be awful short of money so I bought a carton of cigarettes and sent it to him.

Went on quite a long while, and finally his sister sent the cigarettes back to me and said her brother had died, that they didn't any of them smoke.

But I know, if that old man had lived, he'd have paid me every dime he owed me. His word was just like gold. If he told you he'd kill you, he would do that, too!

Morning Mine Was Hot!

Unless you keep air moving, it'll get hot. There's several things that create heat underground. If there are any electric lights, electric motors, rotting timbers, and whenever you blast, you heat things up good. Unless you keep the air moving, all these things together will make it hot.

I never worked at the Morning, but they said in the Morning, the first thing you did was take off all the clothes you could spare. The first day or two, you worked a little bit and they maybe carried you out. You just caved in till you got used to the heat.

The Morning was a mine you could always get a job in. Even during the Depression there was a big turnover. It was so hot that men would quit. And their regular men was all getting so old and been there so long, they'd just go down there and sit. My God, it was hot! The men

■ A miner drilling in a face of a stope at Morning mine.
Photo courtesy Calvin Bates

couldn't produce enough to pay for the operation. And then, because the ground was always shifting, the shaft maintenance was a huge expense. About 1953, the federal [government] had to shut the Morning down because the ventilation wasn't good enough. Now the Star [Mine] is coming in from the other way with good ventilation and they're working the Morning ground.

Rudy Mackey

In 1935, the Morning Mine had hired mostly Finns and they were clannish. If a guy went to do something, there was a Finn stepped right in there and did it for him, and if he started to do something else, there was another one stepped in and done it. And they talked a different language so he couldn't understand what they said. It resulted in this—the guy would quit, he just wouldn't be able to take it.

Rudy Mackey was a young Finn who later worked with me. He'd

worked in iron mines in Michigan and they mostly spoke Finn there. Neither one of his parents had ever learned English.

So when Rudy Mackey came to the Morning, he could easily get a job. They had a company boardinghouse in Mullan for the Morning, and Rudy went there to sign up for meals.

When he came in, one of the Finns said to another, "There's a young punk. He won't last but a few days."

Rudy was older than I was, but he looked just like a young kid and didn't look like a Finn.

The other Finn said, "Yeah. He won't last long. He'll be gone in a few days."

Rudy looked at him and said in Finn, "I'm not a high school punk and I'll be here as long as I want to stay."

You could have knocked their eyes off with a stick.

1936 Church Hill Snowslide

February 27, 1936, when this Church Hill Snowslide happened, I was working. It happened on Monday. Lucky for me I'd changed from night shift to day shift that very day. It happened at nine o'clock in the morning. When I was on night shift, it was like clockwork—I got up in the morning and ate my breakfast and went to the Burke post office at nine o'clock.

I was living in a house up on the hillside behind some poplar trees. There ain't a building left there now, but there used to be an apartment house and a boardinghouse and—you just can't realize how many houses were up there at one time. Just covered. The trees growing there have come up since the slide.

The Church Hill Slide was named after the Catholic Church that is about four or five blocks below the Burke Hotel, but the church wasn't hit by the slide.

The earlier 1910 slide went pretty much down and then went up. It took the pine trees and laid them over just like a big wind had hit 'em. It took the houses—some it just knocked the chimneys off and others—it was just like a big wind on the inside of 'em that blowed 'em up and left nothing but the floor. The air concussion scattered debris all over.

But the 1936 slide never came all the way down.

There was a kid caught and buried. Just the edge of the slide caught him under about three feet of snow. They missed him right away, and started looking for him. They knew about where he had been. There's enough oxygen in snow to keep you alive for quite a little while. They found him alive and got him out.

■ The 1888 Tiger Hotel at Burke, Idaho. The highway, creek, and railroad went through the building. The canyon was so narrow the railroad locomotive whistled in summer for the merchants to come out and raise their awnings so the train could get past. Old-timers said the narrow canyon made it necessary to teach the dogs to wag their tails up and down.

There was a bachelor lived up on the left side. The slide come over some cribbing and knocked the stovepipe off his house. Didn't do a bit of damage otherwise.

Just back of my house there was a house got knocked off its foundations, but the family wasn't at home.

There was a man, his wife, and baby caught in bed in one house. They couldn't get out for a time, but it didn't hurt 'em. In another house that got buried, three boys crawled out a window and got out.

They tell me that back in the early days, miners from Church Hill went down to Bell Crossing and Lower Mace to help dig them out of a terrible big slide that killed a lot of people. After they'd worked so long and so hard, they went home up on Church Hill and after they got in bed, another slide come down and killed a bunch of them, too.

The Star Mine

At the end of a shift at the Star Mine, we'd drive a mile and a half out of a tunnel in a cold car and then get on a truck for the trip down the hill—and for a long time it was an open truck. Many a time my clothes would be wet when I come out from underground. By the time we rode to the big building at the bottom, they was froze stiff. Then we'd take a shower in what they call the "dry room," put on our clothes, and walk right out into maybe 20 below zero. I don't know how we lived.

We hung the clothes on a chain that was raised up, and if they was spread out, they'd be dry next day. Sometimes it was just a little bit hard to scrape the old muck and stuff off the diggers and get into 'em. Made you wonder if it was worth it.

Most of us tried to change to clean work clothes once or twice a week. We'd take 'em into the shower and give them a rench [rinse] and throw 'em down on the floor and stomp on 'em and then hang 'em up to dry. Mining ain't the most refined work in the world.

Gas at the Star

When Tom McAvoy and I got up about 60 feet into the top of this prime raise, there was a chute to be pulled that would leave us a hole to come back down into the tunnel below. But they hadn't pulled the muck like they was supposed to.

I told Tom, "It's too gassy! We got to get out of here."

We was cheatin' on it. Instead of using a ladder in the manway, we were driving in 60-penny spikes to make steps down this incline. My partner, Cletus Starchman, on the outside, was sending up material with the air-winch as we called for it.

I was following Tom back down and I said, "We'd better get out of here fast! Clete will pull the chute and we'll get caught by the muck."

We heard the muck coming and pulled out on a little platform and lit a cigarette, and the next thing neither one of us knew a damn thing.

They climbed up and got Tom McAvoy out. They come to pull me out, and when my subconscious mind felt that muck slippin' under my feet as they took me down feet first, my mind just knew I was going into that chute. It took three of 'em to get me out. They said I fought so hard they felt like leavin' me in there. But I didn't know anything about that.

When they got me out and the fresh air hit me, the first guy I seen was my shift boss, Len Gillette. He wasn't a bad lookin' guy, yet he was a hell of a long ways from being pretty. I looked up and he had rosy cheeks and I never seen such a good lookin' man.

I said, "You're a good lookin' sonofabitch."

He said it was the first time he ever got accused of being good lookin'.

Another 15 or 20 minutes in that gas was all it would have took.

1948 Bell Canyon Crossing Snowslide

It was on a Friday night in 1948 and I just got off shift for the weekend. It was just about dark. The weather was mist and rain with snow hanging heavy on the sides of the canyon—the kind to make slides. It seemed like everything was after me that year. I decided I'd get the hell out of there and go to Spokane for the weekend. So I collected my guns and personal stuff and stuck it into the car. I reached up to turn off the light, and before I could pull the string, the light went off by itself. I jumped in the car and run down the road. Bell Crossing was maybe 10 or 12 blocks below where I lived. I see people running every way and I thought: What in the hell is happening?

I couldn't see anything wrong and I drove right into the snowslide. I got out and laid on my back under the car and put my chains on so I could back up.

When I got unstuck, I turned around and went back up to the beanery. If there hadn't been room at the beanery, I'd have slept in my car. I didn't have much taste for going back into my house. If I'd have left the house just five minutes earlier, I'd have been in the middle of that slide. It was three blocks wide, maybe 30 feet deep. It took bulldozers three days to clear a way through it. I had to stay there three days before I could get out.

The way I happened to get out as soon as I did: It would freeze at night and they'd let the bread truck, the water, and the milk trucks through. I got between 'em on their way back out. I stayed in Spokane with my cousin till I got word the slide was cleared up and we could go back to work.

Rock on the Head

I didn't want to come back. Something kept tellin' me I didn't want to come back.

I was working in the Star and we was in a raise. I was sent down to hoist up some timber and these guys got to crawlin' around up there and a rock got kicked off. It was about a foot by maybe an inch and a half and weighed enough that you could reach out and just barely pick [it] up with one hand. It was traveling pretty good because it dropped 206 feet. Normally, coming down a timber slide a rock will hit and then you'll hear it bounce. But all I ever heard was "shhh!" right before it hit. It smashed my hard hat and cut a gash in the side of the top of my head.

At first I thought: This is it! Then I thought: I got to get off this track or the train will run over me. The train ran back and forth. I knew they wouldn't see me. There was a little hole back in beside the timber hoist and I fell back in there, and far as I knew, I had died. Finally I come to and saw I was still alive. I had left my feet lay over the rail. If the train had come along, it would have run over my legs.

There was a guy workin' back there repairin' and I managed to get back to him and say, "You got to take me out."

I went down to the doctor's office and walked up the stairs. He took a look at me and said, "You better go to the hospital."

He took me up to the hospital, let me out, and never went inside with me to see I got help. It was so icy I could hardly stand up. The front was under construction and I had to go around to the back door. It wasn't until then that the pain hit me hard. It's a wonder I didn't pass out. I gave the slip to the girl and she'd come running every few minutes to see if I was undressed yet. I wasn't too fast. They took some x-rays.

When the doctor came that evening he said, "Was you ever lucky! Not a thing wrong."

Next morning, he asked me if I felt like getting up for more x-rays and I said, "Sure." I hadn't much more than got back in bed when they rushed in. "Don't move! Lay still!" They were afraid of a blood clot.

The first x-rays didn't show the fracture. That's due to the fact that my brain hadn't had time to swell and show it. It'll show a crushed skull, but not a fracture till the skull is pushed apart. And I had a ruptured eardrum, too.

Well, I'd walked all over the hospital already and if a blood clot was going to happen and kill me . . . so when I had to go to the bathroom, I just got up and went.

I didn't have no robe, just a little old short gown, but I'd wait till no nurse was around.

A nurse come in and says, "They tell me you been up and walkin'."

I said, "Ah! What do you mean? Somebody just tellin' you tales. I wouldn't do that."

She said, "Well, I think you are."

So when Dr. Hunter come in, I said, "They jumped all over me for gettin' up and goin' to the bathroom. Tell that nurse to get me a robe so I can go to the bathroom."

He said, "Do you think you feel all right?"

I said, "I have to, I guess. I been kicked around here so far and I'm still alive."

Dead Air

I had lived up Silverton Canyon with Tiny Pugh and his wife for a time before Carol and I were married.

One day, just above Silverton, Tiny and I went back in a mine to an old shaft to gather up some bolts. There was water in there and it was damp. The air was just as cool as anything. Tiny started to light a cigarette, but his lighter wouldn't work. We didn't think anything about that although generally it worked fine.

We come back out into the air and my heart pounded and pounded and beat just like it was just going to jump out. I never had it pound so hard in my life, and Tiny's did, too.

You see, the fresh air goes only so far and then the air is dead. It just cuts off. When you run out of fresh air, you run out of oxygen. It can hit you—just like that! We had just about stayed too long. We could have blacked out. But the air had been so cool! I mean if it had got warm and stuffy, I'd have been suspicious. Then it dawned on us why the lighter hadn't worked. It worked all right outside.

Silver Summit

At the Silver Summit a fellow fell down the shaft.

We had complained that morning we should have screens on the cage so you couldn't fall off. To get on or off the cage you had to step over an eight-inch gap, enough room for a man's body to fall between cage and shaft.

He'd cut his hand and his shifter was sending him up to First Aid. As the hoistman brought him up, he seen his head, his light, and about that time he disappeared. Must be the sight of the blood made the fellow faint, and he fell right straight down 400 feet.

They wanted me to go get this fellow at the bottom of the shaft. I went down and the only mark I found on him, except his cut hand, was from when he fell between the cage and the shaft. He had mashed a kind of indent on the right side of his forehead.

There should have been another man with him going to First Aid. And the guy that should have been with him was his shifter.

From 1965 to 1967, I was lead man at the Silver Summit. I took the place of the shifter on his day off. But I didn't want to be shifter. Now this has been my observation: Most of the time the companies would rather have a shifter that is just a little bit of a heel and not too sympathetic to the men under him. Some way, they don't think a nice guy's quite as good a shifter as the man that's the heel.

The Silver Summit was the last place I worked. My legs were bothering me so I couldn't do the climbing. I came to the mines in 1934 at age twenty-seven and I retired January 1, 1969, when I was going to be sixty-two in May.

Speaking about the cage that fell at the Morning Mine in 1936: The man laying on top of the Morning cage after it fell would have been the man who had been ringing the hoister and spotting the cage to load or unload, and would have been standing right at the edge of the shaft and could have been sucked in.

They generally operate two cages, back to back, using one as counter weight against the other.

Speaking about the 1972 Sunshine Mine Fire: I'll always think that fire at the Sunshine Mine was caused not by internal combustion but by a cigarette. They had a smoking ban up there, but that don't stop cigarette fiends from smoking. The only way they could stop them would be to search every man that went in—his lunch bucket, his hard hat, his pockets—for cigarettes and matches.

SEVEN

VINA GROSBECK

Interviewed 1972 at Osburn, Idaho.

MY FATHER, Edward Burton, was Irish and English. He was born in California and moved to Eagle in 1884. He built ovens of rock and clay outside, set up a bakery, and peddled bread packed on a horse to miners at the diggings. He said the first supplies and whisky were brought in on a good wagon road that ran on parts of the old Mullan Trail from Montana.

Maybe no more than a year later, Murray boomed with a gold strike, so he moved to Murray and built a bakery and later a general store.

Mother met Dad when she came from Nebraska to visit her married sister who was living in Murray.

I was born in Murray in 1890. It had six saloons open day and night. In its heyday, nighttime didn't mean anything. People would get drunk once in awhile, but I was born to it and accepted it. Murray wasn't any wilder than anywhere else.

I used to stand around the edge of a saloon and listen to miners talking about their claims and panning gold and sluice building. People didn't get so awful rich, but they worked hard and made money.

We had a school, of course, and an Episcopal church and a Methodist church. Good and evil seemed to get along without any chewing matches between them.

Dad said that at an earlier time there were troubles over who filed first on mining claims. You only had so many days to record your claim at the county seat, and that was several days away at Pierce. Later, when

Shoshone County was divided in the late 1880s or early 1890s, Murray became the county seat.

Dad grubstaked someone occasionally, but he never wound up with a share in any worthwhile claim.

He said, "The more you grubstake people, the more you find out you shouldn't have."

Smart Lucy

We had a white mare named Lucy. Gosh! She was smart. We took her around town daytimes to deliver goods from the store. At night, we put her in the barn, but sometimes she'd get out and come to the house and knock on our door and shake the handle. If you didn't open up and give her a lump of sugar, she'd tear the door knob off. Dad had to build a steel frame around it so she couldn't get at it.

Dreams of Gold

When I was just a little kid, one old fellow dreamed he had gold on his claim, which was only a hundred yards up the hillside from the saloons. He worked up there all the daylight hours and that gave the old chair warmers at the saloons a good laugh. They made up pet names for him. Later he showed up with some gold, and he wouldn't tell anybody where he found it. After awhile they quit asking him questions about it. He was kinda spooky, and you never can tell what a spooky man will do.

Pretended to Not Know English

Another old sonofagun, he didn't talk to anybody much. Quiet. But when he did talk, it was in broken English. I think he did that to throw people off the track. One time he got mad and rattled off English as good as anybody. He worked a placer claim. Most people worked one place as long as they got colors [flecks of gold] and then they'd move somewhere else. Not him! It worried the old chair warmers.

His name was Howell. Behind his back, we called him "Hoggin" because his face and clothes was so darn dirty.

People would ask where he come from, and he'd mutter, "Philadelphy."

When I was about sixteen, two strangers stopped me in the street and wanted to know if I knew Howell.

I said, "Yes! I do."

They said, "Do you know where we could locate him?"

I said, "No! I don't." I wasn't going to tell them. How did I know what they wanted with him? Maybe they wanted to murder him and take his gold.

They said, "He gets his mail at this post office, don't he?"

I said, "I'm not in the post office. I wouldn't know." But I knew he never got any mail ever. He never sent any mail either.

I told the postmaster, "Those two must be up to some devilment."

So the word spread, and everybody played dumb, and those men never found Howell. Five or six years passed. Howell hadn't shown up in town for a couple of months. People went out to his little cabin and found him laying out there in the timber dead, maybe from heart failure. If he'd found any gold, he'd hidden it. Nobody found any in or around his cabin.

Afterwards, the news got around that Howell had been wanted for some crime back in "Philadelphy."

Wallace Stagecoach

Dream Gulch is the one that goes up from Eagle. There was a couple of places they called Dream Gulch. When the first kinda wore out, the miners went to the other Dream Gulch around Beaver Flats, which was where the Wallace stage changed horses at the foot of the hill.

Five passengers fit inside the stagecoach comfortably—three on the rear seat and two on the front seat, which was narrower. The driver and helper sat outside. Generally the stage used four horses. The old road was steep. It would flatten out and then go steep again. Not graded up fancy like now. Every so far the horses would stop and stand resting. Some steep places, they'd gain only 20 feet then "Oh! Got to stop and take a five." Take a couple hours to climb to the summit. You'd dang near freeze to death in the six hours it took to get to Wallace.

Two Beautiful Girls

There was a young married woman, Gloria Reed, from a nice family of English descent, came with her engineer husband to Murray. She gave birth to two girls and a boy. Gloria was on the drinking order, and it don't do a family any good to have a drunken mother. The two girls grew up beautiful. Hollywood wasn't in it with them. They were elegant.

Meantime, the mother was still drinking. The older girl, Beatrice, equipped herself with nurse's training, and came back to Murray to help the sick. She was fine and dandy till somebody gave her a bottle, and then it was all off.

■ Murray, Idaho, 1890

The younger one, Latisha, was kind of on the roughneck order. Not really bad, but I wouldn't want to introduce her as my chum.

The boy, Henry, went to an eastern university and came back with a degree in engineering. He was a nice kid, and he was awfully ashamed of the way his older sisters were turning out. He couldn't stand their way of doing. He wasn't sick. He just died from being brokenhearted.

The father, Lindrath Reed, died soon after the boy. Then Gloria, the mother, died when Latisha was seventeen. Just the right age to not know what in hell was happening to her. It was a shame. It was terrible. She became a prostitute right at the time when she needed a guide. Instead of that, the only ones that took an interest in her just kicked her a little more till she dropped down to nothin'.

And to show you how sometimes you make a statement, never thinking there's anything to it at all, Latisha was kinda indifferent and she says, "Oh! I don't give a damn what they do with me after I'm dead. I won't know anything about it anyhow."

Oh, Golly! I never will forget her. She was so beautiful.

"Only one thing I hope," she says. "I want to be buried in the Murray Cemetery. But I don't think I'll be in there long."

A fellow says to her, "What in hell you talking about, you ain't gonna be in there long?"

She says, "Because I ain't! I'm gonna fly out of the casket." And she says, "Somebody'll have to get down in the grave and put me back."

That's what happened. Absolutely! I didn't see it myself because I didn't go to the funeral . . . well, I just didn't. But other people saw it.

 She fell out of her casket. Somebody had to get down in the grave and put her back. And she's still there in the Murray Cemetery. And she told all this before she ever died! Isn't that strange?

The older girl, Beatrice, stayed on in Murray nursing people when she was sober, which wasn't often.

She said a number of times, "I really don't have anything to live for. I don't care what I do or where I go or what happens to me. One of these days, if I don't die soon enough, I'll make myself die."

Then she got so darn drunk, she couldn't pull out of it—just the same as suffocated.

I knew of terrible things like that in Murray, but it never phased me. It was just part of life.

Hijacking Gold

I used to help the gosh-darned old miners pan out gold. The gold is heavy and always lays next to bedrock. I panned a little gold on my own, too—not anything regular, just hijacking, you know, borrowing a little here and there from somebody's claim. But it's real thrilling when you find a nice five or ten dollar nugget. It darn near sets you crazy!

Sniping at Daddyville

Daddyville was a half-mile from Murray toward Littlefield. Daddyville had a schoolhouse and a bunch of kids. This woman that Mother knew who was living there and another woman announced they were going sniping [hijacking].

Her son said, "You better stay home, Ma. You won't know whose ground you're on."

She said, "That don't make any difference. There's lots of abandoned ground now."

He said, "Yes, but somebody might shoot you!"

She laughed and said, "They won't be shooting much."

They put on overalls and took a shovel apiece and away they went.

Do you know they hit the mother lode? Nobody else knew it either till one time at the supper table she got to telling about the formation.

A man eating with them said, "Are you sure you're telling the truth?"

And she said, "I never lied in my life, and you ain't worth lying to."

Those two women must have gotten into what had been the end of an old sluice and all they had to do was keep what looked good and throw away what wasn't. Darned if they didn't walk off with around $2,000. Think what that 100 ounces of gold would be worth today!

■ Vina Grosbeck's 80th birthday, May 1964

Mother told me about it because one of the women trusted her and told her. I've always wondered if they had more but didn't tell.

Guggenheim Dredge

The Guggenheims didn't come into Murray country till 1917. They brought two dredges. One was to go upstream and the other was supposed to go down. But the one that went downstream didn't work out—something about the current.

When the Idaho Northern Railroad came up from Prichard, they set the Murray Station. Where the building set wasn't dredged, so after all the excitement about gold faded away, the "beehivers" got in there and cleaned out the gold by hand. And when the railroad got washed out in 1917, the water hadn't any more than receded till people were scratching in the right-of-way for gold.

So word spread everywhere that we were having gold strikes. People rushed in from Wallace, from Burke, from Spokane and further away.

"Do you know of any place I can dig some gold?" [they would ask].

I said, "Why man alive! If I knew where I could dig gold, do you think I'd put it on a poster out there on the fence? Are you crazy?"

Even some people from New York knocked on my door. "We understand you know where we could dig and get some nuggets."

I said, "Who told you all that rot?" It was aggravating and sometimes laughable.

My father died in 1915. He and Mother are both buried in the Murray Cemetery. And here I'm eighty-two already and living in Osburn. I'd like to go over the hill again and visit Ray Simmons at Murray, but it's over two summits and seems so far.

EIGHT

JOHN DENNIS

Interviewed 1972 at St. Maries, Idaho.

Gold Thief

I WAS WORKING on the Guggenheim dredge at Murray in 1917 when the Company got word that someone was shipping gold out of Murray to the San Francisco Mint, and undoubtedly it was coming from this dredge. Murray gold was the purest in the country. The companies commonly got tips from the men at the mint—it was one way of learning of new and valuable properties as well as for uncovering thieves.

So they waited until a chunk of gold got stuck in the drum to catch the thief. The drum had graduated holes from the tiniest to ones you could shove your thumb into. Everybody could see the slug of gold as the tumbler went slowly around. Came time for the cleanup. The cleanup men had been warned not to take that slug of gold out. But when the machine started up again, it was gone.

So the sheriff and a deputy hid out along the railroad track where the men leaving work would have to pass by them. There were only a few men working on the dredge. At quittin' time, Jim Nesbitt and another fellow walked into the sheriff and the deputy.

They looked through Jim's lunchpail and saw he had a couple of baking powder biscuits and said, "Well, go on fellows."

Then the sheriff says, "Oh! Hold on! Let me see that dinner pail again." He broke one of the biscuits open and here was a slug of gold inside.

They took Jim Nesbitt to his cabin and began searching it. Pawing through a shelf of canned beans and fruit and other stuff, the sheriff

■ Guggenheim "purest gold" dredge was operating near Murray in 1917

went to move this baking powder can to one side and Holy Christ man! It was hard to move. No baking powder in the world could be that heavy. The can had been filled with gold and baking powder put on top.

The law gave Nesbitt a couple weeks in the county jail. Then they told him they knew he had learned his lesson and gave him back his job on the dredge. There was a reason for that. They wanted to watch him and find where he might have some more gold hidden.

But Jim Nesbitt didn't give 'em a chance. He waited a few days till he caught 'em off guard. Then he took off cross-country and was gone.

The Emperor Visits

One day, the dredge boss went rushing around looking at his watch. He lined the whole crew up at attention on the deck. He left the machinery running. Here come a long, black limousine. A tall, tough-looking guy jumps out and opens the door and out gets a short little man with a derby hat on. Then another rough looking customer falls in behind him and here they come—one in front and one behind the little guy, marching over the gangplank and onto the dredge.

We stood there like plastered saints while they marched by with never a look to right or the left.

They went to the end of the dredge, turned around, came back again across the gangplank, got into the limousine and was gone.

I said, "Looks like the emperor just passed through!"

The dredge boss overheard me. "My boy!" he says. "You have just seen old Guggenheim, himself, making an inspection."

Howard Drake says: "When I went to Murray in 1909, there were 800 people living there. I knew the bookkeeper for that dredge in 1917 and he said they averaged around $125,000 a month. The dredge was still operating in 1923."

Log Chutes for McGoldrick

In the fall of 1918, I worked at the McGoldrick [logging] camp on the White Pine Flats on Big Creek of the Coeur d'Alene River. I was building chute with Dan Morrison, an expert who had built chute on Marble Creek in the St. Joe River drainage and all over. He was a nice guy to work for. First, he had the mud crossers [cross ties] put down, and then had the long chute logs skidded in and spiked down. After they had built a lot of chute, I scored it with a double-bit axe to the depth the hewers would follow [made a series of cuts to a uniform depth, then the log is cut to that depth]. Then Morrison snapped a chalk line to guide the hewers. Morrison used a left-hand man and a right-hand man for hewing.

Big White Pine

Two Greek saw gangs cut the big white pine. The trees were five and six feet in diameter—breast high—so the butt logs were too big for the chute. They blasted them in quarters and sent them down the chute too.

Hen and Chicks

A foot log ran from the camp to a little island with a few trees on it, and from there to the other shore. An old grouse had her nest and chicks on the island. Every day when we went to work or came home, we'd stop to watch the chicks folly [follow] the mother through the weeds, picking at grass seeds.

One of the sawyers killed the hen, so we held court in the bunkhouse and passed judgment that the man was to be fired. The foreman wouldn't go for us taking the law—his law—into our own hands.

So we said, "O.K. We'll pull camp in the morning—strike!"

The boss, John Clark, argued that we should have the man arrested, but we said, "No! We want to teach him a lesson. The hen had 11 chicks and he, in fact, killed 12 birds when he killed the mother."

The foreman saw we meant business and canned him.

■ John Dennis (91), 1975

The Flu of 1918

Dave Dollar's camp was just a short distance down the creek from us. When I went to work for him, the flu epidemic was on. Everybody had those gauze muzzles on him and a lot of 'em was chewin' snoose [snuff]. Your nose stuck out, but the gauze covered the mouth. It was compulsory to wear them when you were outside.

Dave was holding nine sick men in the bunkhouse that hadn't worked for a month. As Dave said, they would have to pay board, no matter where they were, and the 17-mile trip out to the railroad track would kill them off.

But one man, Bill Leroy, got the idea that if he got into town and took on a couple of real good snorts of whiskey, he would be a brand-new man. Dave tried to stop him, but he went anyway. He hiked through 17 miles of snow to Prichard to catch the train. After that hike and a cold train, we got word four days later that he had died, and they wanted us to take up a collection to bury him. The collection got started but never finished when the timekeeper mentioned that Leroy had over $400 on him when he left camp.

So the foreman said, "To hell with them. Let those who robbed him bury him." And everyone in camp was well pleased with the foreman's suggestion.

But there were no flu deaths in that camp.

Flu from Water Dipper

On construction jobs, a boy went around with a water bucket and gave everybody a snort out of the same dipper. If there was any contagion going around, a fellow was bound to get it.

Three of us went down to Spokane to the Wobbly Hall to raise money to cremate the Wobblies that died. It cost $60 at Smith's funeral outfit in Spokane. We buried a lot of good Wobblies during the epidemic.

One good fellow, Bill Avons, I wouldn't have known he was the same person. Just looked like he'd been pounded with a big hammer. Funny thing, we asked Bill how he was feelin' and he said he wasn't feelin' well at all, but he was standin' in the I.W.W. Hall, so we advised him to go to bed.

I had an extra $10 on me and I said, "Here! Get you some good hot coffee and go to sleep."

He said, "I can't sleep!"

I said, "You got to try anyway."

Next morning, down at the Wobbly Hall, they posted names of fellows that had died and Bill was one of 'em. He didn't even last 24 hours! But it got mostly the young—in their twenties.

Some guys advised, "The more you smoke, the less chance there is of you gettin' the flu. Also, eat lots of garlic!"

[John Dennis appears in two other Bert Russell books, *Hardships and Happy Times* and, as Jack Lynch, in *Calked Boots*. Howard Drake appears in *North Fork of the Coeur d'Alene River* by Bert Russell.]

NINE

FELIX LEGAULT

Interviewed 1975 and 1981 at Silverton, Idaho.

BERT RUSSELL: The human tongue, which can quickly adapt to any language in childhood, finds the complex sounds and word order of another language increasingly difficult by age sixteen. When Felix, with his background of French, confronted English at about age nineteen, he found it difficult to say words like "Idaho" or "eat" without placing an "h" in front of them.

The English-speaking people of north Idaho found it equally impossible to pronounce French names like Fortier and Legault. The words came out Forchey and Legalt instead of Fortyeh and Leego.

There was a welter of foreign immigrants on the Idaho frontier of the early 1900s, including Swedes, Bohemians, Chinese, Germans, Italians, Greeks, and French-Canadian. But the French way of speaking and arranging English was regarded as the most entertaining. Felix Legault's French-accented English is interspersed with more easily-read English throughout his story to preserve its charm.

FELIX: I'm born January 9, 1886, in Quebec, Canada, but I'm raise in St. Emile, Ontario, just across the line. I used to cross the line all the time to play.

My mother died when I am twelve. The bigger kids in the house got bossy, so I left home and worked for farmers for ten cents a day. Dad used to drive out with horse and buggy to find me, but I never lived at home again.

Cheese Maker

That same year, my dad bought a cheese factory. He ask me work for him. By the time I am sixteen, I am running the cheese factory, making sometimes seven or eight hundred pounds of cheese a day.

I was earn $65 a month—a lot of money them days. Two-bits [25 cents] buys a pair of suspenders or a shave and haircut. Overalls cost 35 cents. A great, big loaf of bread cost 7 cents.

I'm starting going to dances. In them days, dances in the big, front room of somebody's home. Roll up the rugs and dance on hardwood floor. They pass the hat to pay for the music and you put in ten cents. One night I ask my dad for a dollar for going to the dance.

My dad tell me my neighbor is workin' for 50 cents a day and he got wife and four or five kids.

Dad say, "You don't need a dollar. Here's two-bits. You're gonna save your money and get rich."

I don't like him tell me how I spend my money.

Later on, our cousin, Joe LaRocque, write from Granite, Idaho, that he has a sawmill and a lot of logging horses. My brother coax me, "Let's go work for our cousin in Idaho long enough to get back money for fare."

"No!" I say. "I got my trade of butter and cheesemaker here."

But after I saved a few hundred dollars, I said, "Let's go."

Ontario to Idaho

In Spokane, they had some employment office, you know. They was writed they want many men. So we go to Granite, Idaho, to see our cousin, Joe LaRocque. He don't have a sawmill. He don't have a big logging camp. He have a couple teams of horses, but he got no job.

I heard of French people living near Lane, so I looked there for work. Across from Lane, behind Killarney Lake, were several French homesteaders: Archie Fortier, old man Soucy, Fred LaVergne, and Louie LaVergne. My brother went back home to Quebec, but I bought half interest in Louie LaVergne's horses and started to work for Archie Fortier. Fortier and his brother had homesteads and they were logging and clearing the land to make farms.

Fresno and Go-Devil

Another homesteader was Carl Graff, a German neighbor to Strobel. Carl Graff built the channel from the river into Killarney Lake with horses and fresno. [A fresno, pulled by horses, was a scraper used for moving and leveling dirt. There were iron hooks on each side and two handles behind, used for tipping up and emptying a full load.] I think it was 1905 because I couldn't speak English yet. Used to be you came from the town of Rose Lake and followed around the hill to go into Killarney Lake. Where there are some old pilings still sticking up over toward the river and parallel to the Killarney channel is where Graff built a wagon road on pilings for the county that connected with the bridge that came across the river from Lane.

Archie Fortier, Arthur Jordan, and old man Soucy built the road going around the end of the lake behind Killarney. I drove team two weeks pulling a go-devil and helping build this road. [A go-devil was a rough V of heavy planks reinforced by iron that was weighted down with rocks or iron. Pulled by horses, it scraped dirt out from the bank to make a narrow road.]

Another man working for Archie ran into the skeleton bones of an Indian. Archie made the man take the bones up the hill and bury them again.

Along the lakeshore we used to pick up lots of arrowheads, made almost heart shape, you know, and very pointed on the hend [end] of him. Kind of a pink rock. Maybe a dozen in a day pick 'em up.

Later, Carl Graff bought land across from Enaville and logged there. He logged behind the schoolhouse at Carter, too.

Dr. Busby

When I first reach Lane, I was sick and go to Dr. Busby in Harrison. He invite me to his home. He talk good French and his wife is talkin' French, too.

Busby told me, "I learn my trade in Montreal."

Dr. Busby was come up lots of weekends to visit Archie Fortier. He was like to be in the timber.

Horse Logging

Louie LaVergne behind Killarney Lake took a contract to log on Two Penny Smith's place on the North Fork of the Coeur d'Alene River. He offered me a job of logging there. I bought two teams. It was a big job for two or three million feet of timber, and the logs was sold to the Idaho White Pine Company at Lane. At that time, they were building railroad grade up the North Fork of the Coeur d'Alene River. It must have been 1907 because the railroad reached Murray in 1908.

At that time, old man Lapp, he live at Lane. He was a kind of fire chaser and he went up and down the railroad track pumping a little handcar and looking for fires that might be set by the coal-burning trains. I know Goodson there, too. He was a nice looking man with a little ranch.

When I got to logging at Two Penny Smith's place, the Idaho White Pine Company went broke. The log scaler for us was a brother to Charley Downey, one of the owners, and he told us about it. Later, the sawmill burned down.

I was out a job. I couldn't find one. When Louie LaVergne came to settle up with me, he didn't have any money.

I said, "I have four head of horses, peavey, and crosscut saw. I sell it to you."

He says, "I'm as broke as you are."

I says, "I'm stuck to sell. I can't hardly talk any English."

He says, "I'm gonna walk up to Murray to see my relation, Oscar LaVergne. He is county road overseer. Maybe he put you on."

So I walk with him up to Murray. That was a long ways from Two Penny Smith's.

Oscar LaVergne say, "I had some good team but they quit me to make more money freighting. So come up!"

Making Road with Team

I walk back and then I bring a team up to Murray. I boarded with Oscar LaVergne for a dollar a day. I was working for $7.00 a day—$3.50 for me and $3.50 for my team. I have to buy all the hay and grain for my horses. It cost $12 to $13 dollars a ton, and rolled oats [cost] $14 to $16 a ton, and I haul it over from Wallace. Oscar has big barn to store the hay. I figure I make clear, maybe $3.00 to $3.50. That was better than $2.00 to $2.50 sawing in the woods and as good as miners cleared working underground.

I work on roads everywhere. Some road is awfully crooked and they make it straight. The road from Murray to Wallace has too sharp curves. You meet a team on a curve and one have to shove over against the bank.

Marie Ann LaVergne

Oscar LaVergne has a little girl, Marie Ann. Only ten or eleven years old, going to school in Murray. She didn't speak French but she understand because her dad and mother speak it at home. Her father was here in America a long time, and then he went back home and got a French girl and come back married.

Marie Ann run around the school yard. Just a little kid. I was twenty. If somebody had told me this was going to be my future wife . . .

Four-Horse Freighter

The next year, about 1908, I bought another horse. I quit the county and started freighting with my four horses. I hauled ore from the Black Horse and Monarch Mines to the mills and came back with a big load of groceries or dynamite.

There was a powder magazine across the road above Silverton and another on the other side of Wallace when you go up to Black Cloud.

They sorted ore by hand and I hauled it over to the Hecla mill. They had 75 men at the Monarch. Sometimes I went empty one way, but with a load both ways, you make good money.

Then I worked for the Monarch in wintertime, too, cutting timber for their own frames and sheds.

Beautiful! I Fall for Her

I was stuck on a girl and going to dances in Murray. I had always thought Marie Ann LaVergne was a pretty nice looking *little* girl. By God! Marie Ann start come to dances. She was fifteen, not quite sixteen. She wear long dresses and cover her hair up. She was beautiful girl! I fall for her.

I was pretty shy with the women, and Marie Ann didn't speak French. I didn't know how to talk about love. I could only say something about horses.

MARIE ANN LEGAULT: I thought he was a pretty fine looking man.

FELIX: We was marry in 1910 at courthouse in Wallace. We went down to Harrison on the train and get on boat running with a great big wheel behind [the *Georgie Oakes*]. We have honeymoon a couple days in Coeur d'Alene and come back to Harrison on the boat running with a propeller [the *Flyer*]. Ross Hall was the captain.

Murray

I bought a house and built a nice barn in Murray. It was an old house from the 1800's. Today [1975], the barn is torn down but the house is still there. It is the second house on the right-hand side from the schoolhouse.

Mines, Stamp Mills, Jig Tables

Back in those days, Murray was a wild place. The Monarch had 75 men working. The Black Horse had a bunch of men. On the right-hand side as you go through Murray was the Mother Lode, then the Daddy Lode close together. On the left was the Golden Chest, then the Terrible Edith—gold mines with hard, white quartz. The Mother Lode and the Golden Chest had big stamp mills that broke the rock to powder.

Then the ore went over the jig tables with water running as the table shakes. You could see the row of gold, then the row of lead, separated by the water. Zinc, they had a hard time to save because zinc is nearly as light as the rock.

Ray Simmons was about seven years old when I went to Murray. His dad had a big store there. The Burton store was there, too. That's still running where the Bedroom Mine is, and the tavern and grocery store. When Burton quit, his daughter took over. She married a man named Keister.

If you go to the tavern that used to be the courthouse, you ask to see the big safe that you walk in. They got a great big key to open the door to the safe. The courthouse is so old she started to lean, so they put big poles against the side.

Homestead in Alberta

In 1912, my wife and I homesteaded in Alberta, Canada, about 125 miles northeast of Edmonton. To get a patent, I had to put up a cabin, stay there three months each year, clear ten acres of land and plow it, and in three years it would be mine.

Sod Roof

So I set up a log cabin. Then I took a team of hoxen [oxen] and was plow the sod in strips and put it on the roof like shingle. Then when I dig my well, I struck clay, so I mixed it thick and smear that over the roof. That is making a sod roof. If it rain all day outside, then at night we have to put umbrella over our head and take oilcloth from the table to cover our blankets because the sod roof is leaking all night. If it rain all night outside, then the sod roof don't leak a drop. But next day when the sun is shining outside, it rains in the house to beat hell.

Big Rooshian [Russian] settlement on one side. Big Hindian [Indian] settlement on the other. All mixed up French, German, English homesteaders. The wheat grow high up over my head. Going through the field, I have to make a jump up to see where I am going. Sometime in the fall, the wheat is too soft. It wrinkle. One year it rain so much the grain go down flat.

Ella and Pauline

One fall when I was ready to come back to Murray, I had to wait for Marie Ann to get her baby. My wife had pains, of course, but an Hindian [Indian] woman, Mrs. Badgeron, was a neighbor there, and she help her. Ella was born November 1913. She is Mrs. Robert Pledger and lives at Osburn.

Lots of Indians around there. The Indians didn't have to homestead. He could get a patent without living on the land. This husband of Mrs. Badgeron, lots of times when he was plowing or seeding, he'd take a notion to go hunting. He'd unhitch the horses, leave the plow and harness piled right there in the field, and go. He live in a log house with a sod roof like mine. He was neglect the roof, so it mostly wash away. You could sit inside and count the stars.

December 21, 1915, Pauline was born at Murray. Sometimes when we went to Alberta to farm our land, we left our two daughters with my wife's parents, the LaVergnes. That's how the girls grow up talking French.

Prichard to Wallace Stage

In 1917, I bought a Chevy for over $400 and moved to Prichard to run stage from there to Wallace. The Chevy had a leather clutch and an old-time brake that you pull up on the outside. Going over the divide, I had a man ride with me to push the clutch and I jumped out and blocked the hind wheel so it wouldn't go backwards.

Sometimes I had too much load for the Chevy, so I bought a seven-passenger Buick that cost me between $700 and $800. The Buick had three seats. In the middle was two folding seats and I could put a board with cushion on it so four could sit.

The back of the Buick was square. I had a blacksmith put a rack on the back to carry packsacks, suitcases, and blankets. All them lumberjack carry blanket in them days. Not many suitcases, but lots of packsacks.

Hundreds of lumberjacks walked 15 or 20 miles up the river packtrail above Prichard to work in the camps. When they came back out, I could go to Wallace by going downriver on a sidehill road on the same side as Prichard to Beaver Creek. [There was not yet a bridge across the river to Beaver Creek.] Then go up Beaver Creek where the road splits, one way to Murray and the other to Wallace.

Other times, I was leaving Prichard in the morning and pick up passengers at Eagle and Murray to take to Wallace. I had nearly all the trade because when them lumberjacks walk in them trails with paychecks they want to spend in Wallace, they wake me up two o'clock, three o'clock in the morning. Sometimes I can't take them all at once. I make two and three trips. Sometimes I had so much load, I had to tie blankets and pack-sacks across the hood with a rope. Then I had to stretch my neck to see where I am driving. People was friendly and honest. Sometimes lumberjack, he was in a poker game and lost maybe $100. I trust him and he pay me later. I never lost a cent.

Those Little Girl

When we live in Murray, my wife tell Ella and Pauline, "You go to the beer parlor, I'm gonna give you a good switch!" And she go get a switch and put it beside her. "Don't go in the beer parlor!"

But first thing you know, they go there. And sometimes they are talking together, those little girl are saying, "You sonofabitch!"

Lumberjack was drunk, you know, and throw them little kid up in the air. And them little kid come with their hand full of nickels, dimes, two-bits, "Look Mama! They give me this!"

She say, "No more of that!"

Ella, she was the oldest one. She meet a lumberjack on the street and say, "Hello, Wobbly!"

Her mother say, "My God! Don't talk like that to that one."

He say, "I'm Wobbly all right. For sure."

Sing on Poker Table

PAULINE LEGAULT BOOTH: I was born in 1915 and I remember living up on the hillside in Murray and looking down to see the gold dredge and all the lights as it worked night and day.

When we were little kids, my older sister, Ella, and I used to walk down the hill to the boardwalk to see Grandma LaVergne who operated a business with her husband in Murray.

We had strict orders from Mother not to stop along the way, and especially not to stop around a saloon. The miners used to capture us on the street and stand us on a poker table in the saloon and plead with us to sing songs in French. They enjoyed teaching us English, too, like "sonofabitch." Then they'd fill a paper sack for each of us with candy and money and turn us loose.

I remember dragging this sack along the boardwalk till the bottom wore out and left a money and candy trail behind us. Money didn't mean anything to us. I can't imagine how many coins fell down the cracks and ended up under the sidewalks.

■ Legault daughters, Ella (4) and Pauline (2) at Prichard, 1917

Go Broke

FELIX: In 1918, at the time of World War I, I set out to become a rich wheat farmer. I leased an 800-acre farm down in the Big Bend country and with the lease, I got all the machinery and 22 head of horses. Fourteen were grown horses, and the rest were young.

I was living in Wallace then and I had to wait for Harvey [my son] to be born, December 16. He was seven days old when I quit running stage, loaded our belongings in a Model T Ford, and headed for Elmira, Washington.

As farms went, mine was small. One of my neighbors had 2,000 acres. I had two dry years with no crop, and it broke me, along with all the other farmers there. At the end, I went over to my neighbor's house to say goodbye. The door was wide open. Nobody home. The breakfast dishes still set on the table just like they left them when they got up, loaded up their old car with everything it would carry, and pulled out. They were nice people. I felt bad about that.

There was nothing left to do but pay what I owed the store and settle up with the bank. I lost the money I paid for the lease and for the machinery and horses, but at least I went back to Idaho with $800 or $900 to buy a team and start logging again.

Back to Team and Logs

[In] 1919, I skidded logs all winter for my cousin, Joe LaRocque, in the draw above the Canyon Garage.

In the spring when I asked for my money, Joe said, "You know I got a truck with solid tires. I can't haul logs out because the mud is too deep. But I got a good job. Next year, I'll pay you."

So I let it go.

Next year, still he didn't pay me. So I come along one day when he was unloading logs into the river between Lane and Rose Lake.

I say, "I'm gonna go to town today. I'm gonna attach them log."

Joe say, "Don't do that! I'm gonna pay you."

I say, "I hear that too long."

So I drove to Springston, and I tell the man at the office of Russell & Pugh Lumber Company, "I come here before with an order from Joe LaRocque and you say he got no money coming. Now I'm gonna attach them log."

He say, "How much Joe LaRocque owes you?"

I say, "Here is the order."

He write me a check.

When I go to the bank at Harrison to cash the check, Joe LaRocque follow me. He was want to borrow $15.

[In] 1920, I log for Joe LaRocque another place.

Drowned Orchard

I take my wife and three kids on a steamboat that stops along the Coeur d'Alene River to unload groceries and hay and oats. We get off across from Medimont and move into the empty Brown homestead house on the flat at the upper end of Swan Lake. It was a big house with bedrooms upstairs and a barn for my horses. The big apple orchard that Brown had planted around the house was dead. When the Washington Water Power raised the dam at Post Falls, the water drowned half the orchard and then the 1917 high water flooded the ground with chemicals from the mine district and wiped out the rest and left the bottom land no good to raise any oats or hay.

Homesteaders had to sell their cattle and get out. They fought the Washington Water Power and the mines in court but lost.

Too old to work and flat broke, Brown and his wife left with only their clothes in a suitcase and went to stay with his son in Spokane.

■ Felix Legault (88), 1974

Somebody tell old man Brown that a family had moved into his house. He came up to put us out. But when he talked with us, he was nice and said, "You can stay as long as you want."

I think the old house is still there (1981) but is caved in. [Remains of the house burned in 1992 in a fire started by careless campers.]

Widow Yarber

That winter, I walked across the ice to visit old Widow Yarber on her homestead in the bay behind Swan Lake. It was so cold she had moved into the cellar. She finally lose her mind. They take her away.

Bachelor Love Kid and Chicken

Every summer, Rufe Dunlop and Archie Smith take kids from Murray or anywhere to their placer claim for weeks at a time. Them old bachelor love kids. Rufe Dunlop, he was raising chicken in a coop across the road on the sidehill from where they live. And that chicken you can pick him up and put him on your lap.

HARVEY LEGAULT: Somebody had failed on payment on a '33 Chevrolet and in 1936, Archie and Rufe took the car over. Here they were, eighty years old and have never driven before. They had a car wreck over on Lookout Pass and put one of 'em in the hospital where he died. Soon after that, the other one followed. They had been partners for over 50 years and were buried side by side in the Wallace Cemetery.

FELIX: I am ninety-five years old now. My wife is gone, but we celebrated our golden wedding anniversary in 1960.

TEN

RALEIGH HUGHES

Interviewed 1983 at St. Maries, Idaho.

MY PARENTS, Henry and Margaret Hughes, started in Illinois, moved to Tombstone, Arizona, and then, about 1888, moved to a homestead near Brookings, Oregon. The place was so isolated, their supplies—like beans, sacks of dried prunes, and barrels of flour—arrived only once a year by schooner from San Francisco. My father went out to the ship with a barge to pick up the groceries.

I was born March 21, 1891, on their 160-acre homestead. A man who rode 40 miles to Crescent City, California, after the doctor, was named Raleigh Scott, so my parents named me Raleigh after him.

My dad was unable to make ends meet on his marvelous stand of Douglas fir and Port Orford cedar. He finally gave up and moved to Crescent City to work in a redwood sawmill for a dollar a ten-hour day. He gave the homestead to a great uncle who traded it for a saddle horse.

To Burke in a Snowstorm

Reading about the Coeur d'Alenes and the thousands of people living there, Dad went up in 1901 to see if there was need for a laundry and found there was.

In Burke he met the grocer, Dan Cardoner, and Cardoner offered to sell him his share in the Hercules Mine for $200. At that time, people called the Hercules prospect "Day's Hole in the Ground." Dad didn't have $200 and if he had, he wouldn't have bought the stock.

Dad came back to Crescent City and continued to work at the sawmill till he saved money enough to move the family.

The second day of May 1903, we took off by team and wagon from Crescent City to Grants Pass, boarded a train for Portland and on to Harrison, Idaho, where my brother Harry lived. From there we took the O. R. & N. [Oregon Railroad and Navigation] again, through Wallace, and arrived at Burke in a snowstorm May 7. I was twelve.

I came down with rheumatic fever so bad I couldn't walk and my folks sent me back down to Harrison to stay with my brother's family and be treated by Dr. Busby. A year passed before I was well enough to return to Burke.

Burke Raised Awnings for Train

The O. R. & N. depot was just below the cribbing of the Hecla Mine. Both the Northern Pacific and the O.R. & N. ran tracks up to Burke from Wallace. But the canyon narrowed down so much at Burke, they had to share the only track going up the town's one street.

The street was so crowded with rooming houses, restaurants, and eight saloons, that the engineer had to whistle so awnings on the fronts of the buildings could be raised to let the train through. Going up the street with team and wagon, you had to keep two of your wheels between the rails.

The Tiger Beanery and Boardinghouse was built over the creek. The railroad ran right through the building and up another 200 yards to Gorge Gulch, which is right in town. The road squeezed past the beanery on the left side.

Delivered Laundry by Horse

Dad and my older brother, Charlie, who was Lillian Blackwell's father, set up the Burke Steam Laundry beside the beanery on the upcreek side. I rode a horse with canvas bag on each side to deliver washed clothes to the men that stayed at the beanery. Most of them worked in the Tiger Poorman Mine. The generous cooks at the beanery wouldn't let me get away unless I ate pie or cookies or cake.

I attended grade and high school in the concrete schoolhouse just past Gorge Gulch but on the right-hand side.

Dancehall Girls

The town's honky-tonk was called the Owl Saloon. They had 15 or 20 girls there who danced with the miners. It cost the miners two-bits [25 cents] a dance. After each dance, they'd go to the bar and the guys would get a drink and the girls would get a ticket. When the evening was over, she cashed those tickets at 10 cents apiece.

Of course, I was too young to go in saloons. The druggist, E. R. Alward, took care of all the girls' medical needs. He was the town doctor, you might say. Anybody get sick, they'd call Old Man Alward. He was also our town photographer—took school pictures, weddings, and happenings like the locomotive blow-up. [The locomotive blow-up is described in appendix 1].

Echoes of the 1899 Strike

[The 1899 strike is described in appendix 3.]

When we arrived, it was only four years after the big 1899 strike in which the Bunker Hill Mill got blown up. People were still talking about it. Al Hutton that put money into the Hercules Mine was the engineer of the train that hauled the dynamite down there, but masked men held a rifle at his back. The miners' union got blamed for it, but I don't think they had a dang thing to do with it.

The Bunker Mill got blown up April 29, 1899, and May 3, Governor Steunenberg declared martial law in the Coeur d'Alenes. Soldiers rounded up union miners and threw them into the bull pen and that caused a lot of hard feeling.

Then in 1905, ex-Governor Steunenberg was killed by a bomb set in his gate in Caldwell. Harry Orchard confessed to setting the bomb and claimed the leaders of the Western Federation of Miners—Haywood, Moyer, and Pettibone—had paid him to do it. I knew Orchard when he peddled milk door-to-door in Burke in a five-gallon can and dipped it out into your bucket or jar. He worked for the Markwell Dairy down the canyon. That Orchard was a rat as far as that's concerned!

Then in the summer of 1907, Haywood, Moyer, and Pettibone were charged with murder. Just before their first trial, May 9, 1907, they came to the union hall in Burke with their lawyer, Clarence Darrow. I saw each one of them get up and make a speech and say how ridiculous it was for anyone to murder an ex-governor.

Injured Hauled by Push Car

Anyway, there was still enmity between the miners and the Mine Owners Association because lots of men were injured in accidents. On their own, the miners paid a dollar a month to the Providence Hospital in Wallace out of their wages. That didn't entitle them to any hospital treatment, but it did entitle them to go to the hospital in case they got sick or hurt.

The quickest way to get an injured man to the hospital was to load him on a push car and coast down the eight-mile, five percent grade to

Wallace. So the car didn't run away, you hauled on a lever attached to a rod running across underneath the car that jammed wood blocks against the rear wheels. You could make it in 20 minutes.

The terrible working conditions made bad feeling, too. In the early days, everything in the mines was run by steam. The fellows in the engine room on the surface had to keep the compressors working to send air underground to run the pumps and keep the buzzys going. The buzzy was a dry drilling machine that filled the air with rock dust that cut the miners' lungs to pieces. That's how they got what was then called miner's con—silicosis.

Washed Dishes for Auntie Fox

Shortly before I came to Burke, May Arkwright Hutton had a boardinghouse there. It was later taken over by Auntie Fox. Auntie Fox served mostly two-bit meals for miners and stayed open 24 hours a day. She was a short, heavy-set woman, way up in her sixties at the time. The miners would do most anything for Auntie Fox. I washed dishes in her place after school.

Violent Burke

Burke was full of violence. One day the superintendent of the Tiger Poorman Mine came down the street and got into an argument with a Cousin Jack—that's what they called a Cornishman [Englishman]. All of a sudden the superintendent knocked the Cousin Jack over those beer kegs in front of the Club Saloon. He must have cracked his skull on a rail. They took him to the hospital on a push car, but he died.

Next saloon down was Swan's. One day a Missourian stabbed a guy in the belly and they loaded him on a push car and took him to Wallace. He died from infection.

Judge Marr

What justice there was, was handed out by Justice of the Peace, Judge M. J. Marr.

He often said, "If you want law, go to Wallace. If you want justice, bring your cases to me."

Ed Murphy was a big, husky blacksmith for the Day boys up at the barn where they kept all the horses for the Hercules Mine. Ed Murphy came home drunk one night, and his wife, who was as strong as a horse, beat him up. The cops heard them yelling and arrested them.

When they came before the judge, he says, "I think yez are both to

■ Burke, Idaho, May 25, 1907

blame. I fine you $20 apiece. If this happens again, I'll give you 30 days and send you down to Wallace."

Judge Marr's office was also his candy store. One day a bunch of kids were milling around in his store trying to steal candy. He chased 'em all out in the street. I never had tried to steal from him, so I was still sitting in the store when he came back in.

He rapped me alongside the head with his cane and said, "Goddamn you! Get out of here, and don't you come back!"

The Hercules Mine

The Day brothers were the main promoters of the Hercules Mine after Harry Day and Fred Harper discovered mineral at the head of Gorge Gulch above Burke. Others, like Edward Boyce, head of the mine union, and Hutton, the engineer, and Paulsen and the Markwells, got an interest in it by working or furnishing money. Dan Cardoner, the Burke grocer, furnished supplies to the tune of $200 and was paid off with a 1/32nd share in the mine.

The Number 1 Hercules Tunnel was too close to the top of the mountain, so they drove another tunnel lower down—called Hercules Number 2—and went in 800 feet.

When they didn't strike the ore body, they sent for a mining engineer and he said, "Turn left!"

They crosscut 12 feet and in June of 1901, they had run into a vein 16 or 18 feet wide—crystallized lead carbonate, all interwound with wire silver. The ore was so pure they could mine it by hand.

Hauled Ore by Six-Horse Team

They built a road down the mountain to the mouth of Gorge Gulch. They took big, heavy mountain wagons and made sleds out of some of them using iron wagon tires, double thickness, on four-inch-wide runners, so they were half-an-inch thick. They'd load a sled on a wagon and the six-horse team would pull it up the mountain. Then at the mouth of the tunnel, they'd unload the sled and pile five or six tons of ore in jute sacks—jute sacks are smaller than gunnysacks. They loaded another two or three tons on the sled and hooked it behind to hold the wagon back. Then they'd run the six-horse team down the mountain.

When they hit level ground at the mouth of Gorge Gulch, they'd unhook the sled and haul wagon and sled, one at a time, over to the O. R. & N. boxcar. The ore sacks weighed 250 pounds. It took two men to load them by hand into the car. They shipped the ore to the Guggenheim smelter in Denver.

Gene Day looked after the barn and horses. He'd had infantile paralysis [polio] and drug one leg when he walked. He had a real nice saddle horse that he rode everywhere. Harry Day was mine superintendent. Jerome Day lived in Moscow.

Big Andy Anderson, a Shoshone County commissioner in later years, was one of the teamsters there. Harry Welton—he married my sister—drove one team. Sid Fernan and his brother that Fernan Lake was named after was drivin' there, too.

Ed Boyce was an official of the Western Federation of Miners and a brother-in-law to the Days. I believe he made arrangements for them to borrow money from the union till they could get returns from the smelter. The Hercules was favored by the union because it signed a closed shop union contract.

Aerial Tramway

Later, after driving Tunnel Number 3, the Hercules set up a mill to concentrate ore at Tunnel Number 4, still lower down, and built a mile-and-a-half aerial tram on cables to carry the ore the rest of the way to dump into railroad cars at the mouth of Gorge Gulch. The loaded bucket coming down furnished the power to move the empty bucket back up.

Then they bought the old Hummingbird Mine property and drove Tunnel Number 5 into the mountain, right across from the Tiger Beanery, to intersect the ore at that level. They mined down another 2,400 feet, and the ore got so poor they couldn't afford to mine any further. So they shut down. The only activity after that was leasers that mined out pockets of ore.

The Rich

The share in the Hercules that my dad had turned down for $200 made old Dan Cardoner $3 million. Edward Boyce ended up owning the Portland Hotel in Oregon. August Paulsen, the Dane who had been milking cows at Markwell's Dairy and earned his stock mostly through labor, got rich enough to set up his medical building in Spokane.

May Arkwright Hutton and her husband, Al, built the Hutton Building in Spokane. Mrs. Hutton had been a waitress in the mine district and ran a cafe in Burke and had sympathy for the poor and unfortunate. She set up the Hutton Settlement at Spokane. She also tried to rehabilitate a bunch of Spokane prostitutes. She paid Art Swisher of St. Maries to locate them on timber claims above Clarkia. I think it was Art who named the creek there Flewsie [or "floozy"] Creek.

Tamarack Beanery

When I was about fifteen, I worked weekends and vacations in the Tamarack Beanery over in Nine Mile Canyon. My shortcut getting there from Burke was to climb two and one half miles up the mountain to the Number 2 Hercules Tunnel. I carried a gallon tomato can with the top cut out and a candle shoved into the side through a hole, for what we used to call a "palouser." With the light tipped down to see the rails and ties, I walked the three-quarters of a mile through the mountain.

At that time, the Hercules had set up a little sawmill over there to cut mine lagging and timbers. The timbers were lifted by tram up to the tunnel entrance and railed on mine cars over to the Hercules. Funny thing! As many times as I walked through there, I never met anybody or any of the rail cars. When I came out of the mountain, I walked downhill past the sawmill and a mile and a half further downcanyon to the Tamarack Beanery.

Last thing at night, I'd set the table for the 40 men that worked in the Tamarack-Custer Mine. The beanery furnished me a bunk. I'd get up in the morning and set out stuff so the miners could make up their lunches. Then they'd come in for breakfast and I'd cart a bunch of hotcakes, bacon, and eggs, and deal 'em out on the table.

"Brown Gravy" Sam was cook. He was a black man. He ordered quarters of beef from Wallace. Back of the beanery was a tall tamarack tree with a pulley set at the top. So the beef wouldn't spoil, we heisted them quarters to the top of the tree clear above the insects. It would keep for weeks up there.

Other stuff sometimes didn't keep so good. Some of the miners sneaked down into the beanery basement one night to swipe a feed of pickled pigs' feet from the barrel. The light was dim down there and it wasn't till Sam had me bring some up to the kitchen next day that we saw the miners had eaten a lot—and they were full of maggots!

Sorting Ore

Then in 1907 when I was sixteen, starting at 4:00 P.M. after school, I worked sorting ore off the conveyor at the Hecla Ore Bin in Burke. They paid me man's wages. Those days, surface workers got three dollars for ten hours.

Five Candles Underground

The underground miners worked for $3.50 for a ten-hour day, seven days a week, and they changed shifts every two weeks.

When miners went on shift, the guy in a little office right off the shaft gave them sharpened steel drills and five candles. Then they rode the hoist down to their working level. The miner stuck one of the candles into the little iron holder and hooked it to his cap so he could see to walk back in the drift. When he got there, he took the little iron off his cap and stabbed it into a timber so he could have light for working.

Usually, the tunnels were built on a slight grade, so when the mucker filled the mine car he could coast it out to the station. He had a foot brake so he could stop it. The load of muck [was] set on a pivot in the center so he could pull a pin and dump it. The grade back up into the drift was so slight, he could push the car back by man power.

You were supposed to have all your rounds drilled and loaded with dynamite and ready to set off by the end of the shift. The fuses were long enough that you could get to the station before the shots went off. You counted every one of those shots to make sure they all fired. A lot of miners have been killed by drilling into missed holes. After the blast, it would probably be an hour before the next crew would be back in the drift, and that would give time for the fumes to dissipate. Of course they pumped compressed air down into the drifts to blow out the bad air, too.

But the morning when the guy at the entrance said, "No candles!" that meant you were fired and might as well head for the outside office and get your pay.

The Washington Water Power put in an electric transmission line to the mines in 1907, and that pretty much marked the end of the candles.

Fell Seventy Feet

Mine work was always dangerous. My brother Charlie, the one that later had the laundry in Kellogg, fell 70 feet in the Standard Mine at Mace. He went down a slanting chute and landed on his feet. As luck would have it, he had enough spring in his legs to break the fall. He was only off two days.

The Fun Special

Every Saturday night the O. R. & N. ran a special train from Burke down to Wallace with two coaches jammed with three people to the seat, aisles full of people standing, and all the guys and kids that could hang to the handles outside with only their feet on the steps. There was always something doing in Wallace, like basketball games, prize fights, drinking, and girls hanging out the windows in the alley [yelling], "Come on in, big boy!"

Train Blowup

One day I was delivering laundry by team down the canyon to Black Bear and Gem. I was less than a quarter of a mile above Mace when a terrific explosion rocked the canyon and a big black cloud of smoke rolled up down there. I tied the team to a tree and ran down. People were boiling out of the houses. The air was full of falling soot.

■ Face of steam gage from the blown-up locomotive

A Northern Pacific locomotive had blown up. The boiler had been lifted by the blast right over against the O. R. & N. track, and the truck of the engine had been thrown a third of the way over. The fireman and engineer were both killed. Bodies of the two brakemen on the cow-catcher were blown over 200 feet up the mountainside—one into his own yard. [See news story in appendix 1.]

It turned out later that the engine was old and had been condemned, but they were short of engines, so they used it anyhow. I've still got the [steam gauge dial] off that locomotive.

First Train to Murray

About 1907, when they ran the railroad up the North Fork all the way to Murray, I was sixteen. I rode up on the first train with Katie O'Rourke, my teacher at Burke. She was daughter of Phil O'Rourke, one of the locators of the Bunker Hill & Sullivan Mine. People danced and celebrated with lots of whiskey at the Murray courthouse that night. Today the road runs on what was the old railroad grade.

Seeing the World

The summer of 1908, I worked at the Tamarack-Custer Mine intending to save my money and enroll at the University of Kentucky to study dentistry. In high school I'd studied two years of German and one year of Latin, but I hadn't quite graduated. But in those days, the universities would let you enroll if you had finished the tenth grade. Then in the winter of 1909, I became discouraged and decided to see the world instead. I drew my savings out of the bank and went over to the Alaska-Yukon-Pacific World's Fair at Seattle.

Afterward, I worked for Western Union laying a single wire telegraph line from Seattle through Chehalis to Portland. When that job ended, I hit a sawmill job in Tacoma where I worked with Ignace Peone, a Coeur d'Alene Indian who later came back to Plummer and became a barber. I liked Ignace. We went salmon fishing together. Then the sawmill closed for the winter.

Fell on Spike

I drifted down to Portland and found a job with a contractor laying out block signals for the Spokane, Portland & Seattle Railroad. One day I was riding on the front of the gasoline-driven work car crossing the bridge over the Columbia from Portland to Vancouver, Washington. As we left the bridge, a work train on a siding ahead of us was unloading rock from flatcars with a big scoop. We were moving fast past the work train. Just as we got opposite the scoop, a rock, maybe 12 by 14 inches and 6 inches thick, slid off the flatcar and derailed our gas car.

I was thrown 50 feet through the air. I landed on my back on a tie with a spike sticking out of the top of it about three inches. It went into my back. Lucky for me it went between my ribs and missed my backbone by about half an inch. Luckier still, it didn't puncture any organs.

They took me to St. Joseph's Hospital in Vancouver. The railroad refused to pay the bill.

I told the Sister, "I haven't got any money. You should collect it from the railroad company." I don't know what they ever did about it. Then I went to work on a dairy ranch milking cows on an overflow land at the mouth of the Willamette River.

Mace Snowslide

In February 1910 I read about the snowslide at Mace. I wired my folks in Burke and got a wire back saying they were all right but that 17 people had been killed in that snowslide. There had also been a snowslide in lower Burke, right across from the Catholic Church. E. H. Pasco, superintendent of the old Standard Mine there, had been killed.

Moved Laundry to St. Maries

In 1911 my dad wrote me that the Hercules Mine had been trying to condemn his laundry property in Burke. The Hercules was just opening the Hummingbird tunnel and had great hopes of getting a lot more ore and wanted more room. Dad got a pretty good price out of it. Then he had the laundry machinery loaded in a boxcar and moved it to the town of St. Maries. He wanted me to come to St. Maries and be a partner in the laundry there.

Homesteaded in Hells Gulch

I washed in the laundry quite awhile. When I became twenty-one in 1912, the Diehls told me about 80 acres of vacant land in Hells Gulch, and I homesteaded it. Later years, I bought another 2,200 acres out there—some of it on tax title from the county.

Met Ida Alver

Around 1915, Ida Alver came up from Kendrick and worked in the laundry. Her dad had immigrated from Bavaria, joined the United States Army, worked up to master sergeant, and retired in Missouri. There he married a woman of Swiss descent and they had a daughter, Ida. Then they moved to Kendrick, Idaho, and bought a farm on Big Bear Ridge.

IDA ALVER HUGHES: I grew up in Kendrick. I was pencil straight and my eyes were snappy. I got a lot of whistles. Down at Kendrick they had lots of men picked out for me—even one guy that stammered.

I said, "I'll pick my own."

When I went to work at the St. Maries Laundry, I said to Raleigh's father, "Who is that man?"

He said, "That's my boy, but don't you get acquainted with him."

RALEIGH: That did it! I was a dead duck!

IDA: No! He asked me to go to the show with him one night, and I said, "I'm busy!" He asked me a second time, and I turned him down again. Third time, I got him!

RALEIGH: It wasn't quite that fast. She went down to Fresno, California, to work in a cannery—stayed there a year or so and came back to work in the St. Maries Laundry again. We seemed to get along all right together, so finally in 1917, we got married. After that, I logged and ranched.

Cutting River Ice

Then I ran the ice business in St. Maries. Usually we got a freeze in December. We cut ice in the St. Maries River right above the Milltown bridge where the St. Maries River runs into the Joe [St. Joe

■ Ida Alver Hughes and Raleigh Hughes with their cargo donkey at their homestead, 1917

River]. The big icehouse for storage was built on the bank almost underneath the bridge.

We had an ice scraper pulled with a horse to keep snow off the ice so it could freeze deeper. When the ice was eight or ten inches thick, we'd mark it both ways with a marker. The marker was like an ice plow with teeth that cut a groove about three-fourths of an inch deep. We'd groove one furrow, then turn around and set the gauge that stuck out the side of the marker into the first furrow and then start marking another. After making 25 or 30 furrows like that, we'd start marking it crossways to make blocks 22-by-30 inches.

Then we'd hook the ice plow to the horse and cut deep furrows down within two inches of the bottom of the ice. Even though my horse, Prince, was shod with sharp caulks three-fourths of an inch long, and the heel of his shoe turned down and sharpened crossways, he'd slip into the drink quite often. We kept a long rope coiled up on the hames [two curved projections attached to the collar of a draft horse] and the end of the line made a choker around his neck. When the horse hit the

■ Raleigh Hughes holding the ice plow for cutting ice on the St. Joe River the winter of 1924–25. The crew of 22 men commonly put up 1,000 tons of ice in the icehouse beside the mouth of the St. Maries River. Ice cutting stopped in 1930 when electric refrigerators killed the demand. Notice the group of sidewalk superintendents watching from the bridge beyond the crew.

water, the rope floated off his hames. We'd hook the rope with a pike pole and grab it and brace our feet. As quick as the horse comes to the surface, he takes in a big breath and you jerk the line tight and choke him off so he don't lose it. He goes under a few more times and each time he come up, you let him take in more air and you choke him off. Pretty soon he floats so high that two men can skid him out on the ice. Soon as you got the horse safe, you haul in the plow that is still attached to him. Old Prince seemed to get used to the dunking and knew what to expect.

Next step, some guys with ice saws cut off single rows of blocks, and two men with pike poles push them into a narrow channel to the icehouse.

The conveyor was powered with a ten-horse electric motor. The man at the bottom used a spud [a heavy bar with a chisel point used for removing bark from trees] to break the rows into individual blocks. Then he shoved the blocks, one at a time, onto the conveyor and they moved up into the icehouse.

The winter of 1929 stayed so warm that the only place ice froze thick enough was down at Hidden Lake near the mouth of the St. Joe River. Through old man Campbell, I hired the Boom Company barge and tug. We hauled old Prince to Hidden Lake on the stern of the tug. Charlie ran the hoist to pull ice into the barge and stack it. Then the tug brought barges two at a time to the mouth of the Maries River, and men let the ice blocks slide into the water where other men could push them to the icehouse conveyor with pike poles.

In a year's time we'd sell 1,000 tons. Generally it took a crew of 22 men a week to put up ice. At the end of a season, we returned the sawdust to the bin at the west end, except for enough to cover the floor about a foot, and left the icehouse empty. Each new season we laid a board floor over the sawdust and as ice cakes came up the conveyor, men set them on edge and packed them in a layer till they filled the floor out to within 18 inches of the walls. We had a special tool to plane the ice into a smooth floor. Then the next layer of ice was turned the other way. We kept adding layer after layer of ice till we had a complete pack of ice reaching almost to the roof.

Then, using old Prince with rope and pulley, we'd pull barrels full of sawdust from the bin and fill in around the walls and finally cover the top with all the sawdust we could find. Ice packed in this fashion becomes like one solid block and melts very little, even in a hot summer.

The ice was delivered door to door; the horses that pulled the wagon knew the route and stopped in front of the right house or business. The driver got out and cut off a chunk of ice, threw it on his shoulder with the ice tongs and took it to the icebox. Grocery stores, restaurants, and saloons took 200 pounds a delivery at 50 cents a hundred pounds. Residences took only 50 or 60 pounds once or twice a week at 75 cents a hundred.

Later, when an old gasoline truck replaced the wagon and horses, most every kid in town learned to drive by running it.

We didn't furnish ice for the Milwaukee Railroad refrigerator cars. They shipped their ice in from Montana to their own icehouse in the railroad yard in St. Maries.

I ran the ice business till 1930 when electric refrigerators came in and killed the demand.

When beer came back with Roosevelt's election in 1932, I distributed coal and beer. During World War II we made a lot of money off beer. We could sell all we could get and they'd come after it.

Looking Back

We've been lucky. My wife and I never lost any of our kids. If it hadn't been for her, these kids might not have turned out so good. She was 100 percent!

Howard got sucked into the army in World War II and sent to Anchorage, Alaska. He was promoted to master sergeant and put in charge of the printing office. Mary went to St. Luke's Hospital in Spokane and became a nurse. Ralph graduated from the University of Idaho in business administration. Paul graduated from the same school in electrical engineering. And they're all here today in Idaho.

My wife was always afraid of losing her mind. She got arterial sclerosis and it cut off the circulation to her brain, and I had to put her in the nursing home.

Because of poor circulation, I've had both legs cut off, but I'm still getting around and enjoying living. If I live till March 21, 1984, I'll be ninety-three.

ELEVEN

MAIDELL CLEMETS

Interviewed 1977 at Smelterville, Idaho.

My DAD WAS born in 1871 in Norway. He was of a family of deep-sea divers. They had bell diving over there clear back to the time of the Spanish Armada. At the time Dad worked underwater, they had diving suits. He did a lot of work underwater.

I lost three cousins during World War II over there. They were divers, and when the German government took over Norway, they conscripted them to raise and work on submarines repairing them. The British come over while they were working on one and bombed it to the bottom, and they went to the bottom with it.

I was born in Bergen, Norway, April 7, 1908. In those days, all inheritances were left to the eldest son and the rest had to do with whatever they could get, so the United States had this heavy migration of foreigners from all over Europe. We came because this was represented as the land of opportunity.

Settled in Wardner

I was two years old when my folks settled in Wardner. My mother being from a fairly large city, Bergen, Norway, thought this mining town was the end of the earth.

Most of those immigrants who came here to work in that period of time were fairly well-educated people. Their background and knowledge was far better than the natives. Even today the average homes in Scandinavia, England, France, and Germany have around 200 books. In the United States it's less than 20.

I think the stories of the mining camps, red lights, and brass chips [used in place of money while playing poker], and things of that nature have been overdone. But wherever there was a boom, gamblers came in to exploit. Like one time when I laid a $50 bill on the counter at a tavern, the bartender noticed it right away. A very friendly person. Another guy and I was sittin' there talkin' to him. And I noticed in the back room, those old fellows sittin' around the card tables, lookin' our way.

The bartender said to me, "I'll go you 20 on that."

I said, "I haven't got any time. I got to get goin'."

"Aw heck!" he says. "You got time for a hand or two."

I told my friend. "Same old story. Inducement. Just a little water in the pump to prime it."

Other people came in to build hotels and stores and furnish services. The funny part of it was that the people who did gain wealth in the area were these merchants. It wasn't the man who came here to work.

Father Was a Miner

My father never worked as a deep-sea diver over here. Instead, he worked as a miner in the Bunker Hill Mine and others like the Last Chance, the Tyler, Caledonia, and Sierra Nevada.

In Wardner the immigrants of Scandinavian descent, like us, lived in one section of town. Those who were Slavic lived in another section. The Welch, they lived at one part and the English at another. The Germans—and like that. Each one of 'em had their own spokesman, and he would represent them on the city council. It was quite a conglomerate city council they had from 1900 to 1915.

Boardinghouses

The Welch boardinghouse was called the Thorton House. The Shannon House was where the Irish stayed. American House for the English. O. E. Johnson's boardinghouse was for Scandinavians. The Slavonian House was set up a little bit different, it was. The kingpin of the Slavonians was John Bogovich. He traveled extensively. He lived on the hillside, and all around him, he had houses he rented to his Slavonian friends. And a lot of them boarded at John's restaurant.

Parents Learning English

I enjoyed playing with children that couldn't talk to me, and I couldn't talk to them. I could go to their home and sit down and eat at their dinner table.

My parents wanted to speak English, they did, and talked English at home as much as they could. My mother had studied in school and was very fluent in German as well as Norsk.

The grocery stores at Wardner would send a man out around town to solicit grocery orders, which they would deliver. Mother traded at C. B. Seelig grocery. He later had a wholesale grocery in Wallace.

When my father, whose name was Clemetson, took out citizenship papers, he had dropped the "on." A man named Bill Voitlander came to take my mother's grocery order and she'd speak to him in German and he'd answer in German. Mr. Voitlander thought this "Clemets" sounded like a German name and would talk to me in German. I couldn't understand a word.

He used to say, "You can't spoof me. I know that you're German!"

Most everything was bought on credit because the area only paid once every 30 days. When miners came in to town, they were given credit right off, they were. No questions asked. But if you didn't pay your bills, though, you soon became known and your trade not welcome.

Mother and Kids Worked

I went to school in Wardner. My father died when I was seven years old in 1915. My Norwegian mother still could hardly speak English. She had four boys and three girls to raise. The youngest was three months and the oldest thirteen years. Mother worked night and day doing janitor work and washings. Us kids picked up and delivered the washing and helped run the old hand washing machine. It was one with a lever that went back and forth and turned a rig like a little milk stool inside.

Us kids did baby-sitting. We'd go to the boardinghouses and chop kindling and pack in wood and coal. I don't think any kid got worked more than I did. I remember doing janitor work at the First State Bank of Kellogg. We'd get up at 6:00 in the morning, I'd go work two hours before school, and then work again in the evening.

Foss's Tea Room

The woman who had Foss's Tea Room in Kellogg hired me to wash her windows. It was located right back of the drive-in area of the Idaho First National Bank. I started washing windows for her one Saturday at 7:00 in the morning. Started right down at the basement, had a ladder there and washed the next floor and the next. Dinnertime, she asked me if I wanted some dinner and I told her, "Sure do!" I was hungry.

First time I saw a plate with partitions. One part for the potatoes and another part for the salad, meat another part. About 4:00 in the afternoon, I got through with the windows. She gave me a quarter.

I guess I had a funny look on my face.

She said, "You want to remember that dinner you had was worth a dollar and a quarter!"

At that time, people didn't think child labor was worth anything, anyway.

Dr. Mason's Dairy

I got a job working for a dairy. It belonged to Dr. Mason, it did. It was not too far from where Safeway store is now along the creek. The old barn on Idaho Street has been made into an apartment building.

Doc Mason bought up some of the local dairies like those of Matt Cooper and Jess Hayes. But he didn't have any place for his stock to run, so he bought a farm down on Pine Creek, and another down on Evans Creek.

They had a milking machine, but it wasn't too successful. It would lose its vacuum. You had to strip by hand. And I don't think the machine was too easy on the cows. Seemed like the milk quality would start dropping off, it would. I'd take the milk from the barn and run it through the cooler and clarifier. I'd go to work at 3:00 in the morning, peddle milk until 7:30, and then I'd go to school. I worked for him quite a few years. I got $15 a month regardless of how many days were in the month or how long the day was.

Wardner Worked Out

About 1916 Wardner became a ghost town almost overnight. The upper workings were getting worked out. Then the tunnel ran from under the upper workings all the way down to Kellogg. Most of the population was moving to Kellogg. Tramways could haul there.

Snowslides

We had a hard winter in 1916. There were snowslides and floods. Many of the buildings caved in. Snowslides had been common in Wardner once the hills were burned off. In 1891, the tramways from the Last Chance Mine had been taken out by snowslides.

Then it went on till about 1931, when a snowslide took out the water system at the upper end of Wardner. Much later, 1956–57, there were record snows in Shoshone County. Mr. Weaver got killed there in Wardner. A snowslide took out his house completely. And then, down about where the Episcopal church used to be, a fellow by the name of Sawyer had his home wrecked.

From *Coeur d'Alene Diary*, by Richard G. Magnuson: February, 1890
"Deep snows and slides near Wardner seriously hindered mining operations; the Last Chance tramway was destroyed in part by slides and would not be repaired until spring.
". . . On March 9th [1891] a snowslide took place at the Last Chance Mine in Wardner causing several thousand dollars damage. No one was killed, but the night shift had a narrow escape. The slide started several hundred feet above the mine, ore bins were swept away and the tramway damaged."

Assessment Work

Then I worked for Gamble, doing his assessment work on mining claims up in Wardner, and the Wardner Fraction and the Bigbee Grand. Most of the drifts were about as small as you could work. Just room enough for your ears on top and the handles of the wheelbarrow on the bottom. I'd help double-jack holes [see single jacking in the glossary]. I didn't know much about it, but I could turn a steel pretty good and keep a hole round and straight. Those old boys could swing a double jack and never miss. I'd muck with the wheelbarrow. Fourteen years old. I only got $1.50 a day.

A Miner at Sixteen

At sixteen years of age, I was allowed to work in the mines. I was a junior in high school 1924. By that time, my older sister was married. My older brother and another brother was working, and my mother was still working, so things were pretty prosperous in our home. 'Course, we worked Saturdays, Sundays, and vacation periods, but I graduated from Kellogg High School.

Hair a Mat of Ice

Later I worked in the Bunker. You had to be underground at 7:30 in the morning, had a 30-minute lunch break, and you'd blast about 4:00 in the evening. Then you had to walk outside. There was no dry houses in Wardner. Some places underground were very warm and you'd be wet with sweat. You hurried as fast as you could. Time you'd get home, your clothes would be froze on you. I've got home, sometimes, I couldn't take my miner's cap off my head. My hair would be a solid mat of ice. When I got my clothes off, they'd just stand up—they were froze.

When I started working in the Bunker, everything was all dry machines. Great deal of dust in the air. Tuberculosis was very common, miner's con—industrial diseases.

You were underground breathing that bad air and hotter temperatures. There were many cases of pneumonia. The average life span of a miner in those days was pretty short!

It wasn't till around 1937 or '38 that we had state compensation laws that recognized industrial diseases. But even if you were a single man, the compensation wasn't enough to pay your bills.

Rock Caves In

About the closest I ever came to being killed was when I was working on a raise in the mine with two Slavonians. I helped 'em get set up. Had two [rock drilling] machines in this raise, they did. I had to carry steel up the raise for them. They were nearing an old stope they didn't know about that was filled with rock.

One of 'em's name was "Papa" John Tolaga. The other was Eli Lokel. When they set up that morning to drill, the face fell out at 'em. Waste rock came in on 'em. Well, Eli, he was crushed. Papa John was laid flat. His leg was pretty badly mangled. He was wearing a Bone Dry boot with a high counter on the outside made of very heavy leather. One big rock pinned John's foot. We got mine steel and pried this rock up as much as we could, but we couldn't get his foot out on account of that shoe holding it. And we couldn't dig underneath his foot any more because we were afraid of more rock caving on him.

He couldn't talk very good, y'know. One fellow there, name of Jenkins. He had a knife. He started cuttin' this boot off. John thought he was cuttin' his foot off.

He began to holler, "No cut 'em off, Jenks! No cut 'em off, Jenks!" But we did get him out.

I went down to the hospital to see Papa John a few days later. "How you makin' it, Papa?"

"Tough!" he says. "Tough! Lay here. Suffer. That's all you do. Lay here in hospital and suffer. Back in the old country, they cut 'em off. In six weeks, be fine."

He got well, and back to work again. At that time, he was about in his fifties, but he seemed old to me.

Charmed Life

Another time in the Bunker Hill, Les Battershell, Benny Benfield, John Mattson, and myself—the youngest—were replacing

■ Maidell Clemets (69), 1977

about 800 feet of water trough that had rotted out up this here shaft—at an angle of about 55 degrees.

There was a skipway there. I was standing in the skip and I'd take a hacksaw blade and short across the open bell wires to give signals to the hoistman. This raise wasn't open very good with the skipway. There was stuff thrown in the manway—rock and stuff like old rollers, debris of every type. These water troughs broke loose and were coming down through there, tearing the lights down. I stood up in the skip and the last thing I could see was Les Battershell going end over end down the incline—rocks hitting him in the hips. Benny got behind a timber. He was pretty well protected.

Well, when things quieted down, I had a carbide lamp that had a draft protector on it. I got that lit. By George, I looked down and here come Les. He was coming back up that shaft just like a squirrel. John Mattson had the end of his tongue cut off. Rock hit that. Benny didn't have many marks on him, just a few bruises. I had stood right up in the middle of all that, and right in the bottom of this skip there was rocks bigger'n my head, rollers, timbers, everything. I was standing in debris almost up to my knees.

Les Battershell had his pelvis bone broken and he was tore up pretty bad. He died as a result of that accident. I still can't understand, today, how I stood upright in the middle of that and never got a mark on me.

Everybody has a certain amount of charm about 'em. They always say the good Lord took care of the fools same as he did the wise people. I guess I was just one of those fools.

TWELVE

SYLVAN AGARLA

Interviewed 1985 at Silverton, Idaho.

FIRST I'LL TELL YOU my father's story—Angelo Agarla from northern Italy. He was twenty-one when he walked to Switzerland to escape military conscription. Then he walked to Bordeaux, France, got a job on a ship, and worked his way to New York City. He said the reason most people came to the United States was because they had heard it was heaven. But they didn't always know what they would be getting into!

He had enough money to ride day coach on the train to Butte, Montana, but he didn't know a word of English. When the fruit hawker came through the car, Dad heard people across the aisle ask for bananas. He practiced the word over and over to himself till he got the nerve to say it. He had never tasted that fruit before, but he ate bananas and nothing but bananas for four days and nights from New York to Butte, Montana.

Honeycombed Mines

In Butte, there were lots of his own countrymen, so he had no trouble getting a job in the mines and picking up some English words.

He joined the Western Federation of Miners union. He said if you lost one job, you had only to walk through the tunnels into another mine and get hired. They had dug till the ground was honeycombed with tunnels. You could even feel the blasting going on beneath your feet as you walked on the sidewalks uptown. Many years later, we visited Butte and only three blocks from the Arizona Hotel the street was cordoned off where a three-story brick building was sinking.

Dad Was a Walker

Dad didn't like Butte, so he climbed a passenger train to Wallace, Idaho. Got a job hand-drilling at the Mayflower Mine up the Nine Mile [Creek]. During the winter, the crew had to pack groceries and other supplies from where the Northern Pacific depot sets up to the mine. They'd load up their packsacks and Dad would be the last to leave. He was a little man. He said it made him feel good to see where the others had set their packsacks on the snowbanks and rested. He kept going with his load, never stopping, and usually was the first man to arrive at camp.

When I grew up and walked with him, I found Dad had a gait that could kill me off. It wasn't the length of his stride; he was powerful and kept setting his feet down in speedy, short steps that never stopped.

1899 Bull Pen

After working at the mine four months, he and the rest of the crew went into town to cash their checks and buy some groceries. They had heard there was trouble brewing in Kellogg, but they didn't know what it was all about. Dad was picked up on the street by the military and thrown into the bull pen in Kellogg. Dad didn't talk English except for a few words so he couldn't convince them he wasn't a striker!

During his seven months in the bull pen Dad's name had been in the papers along with other miners. We had some pictures of him outside of the bull pen drilling with wooden rifles.

This reporter from Spokane said, "They gave 'em guns?"

I said, "They were wooden guns. If they'd been real guns there'd have been a war goin' on."

Dad is in one of the pictures and I can identify him. He is also the man in the picture taken inside the building. He is the one pouring coffee out of a pot.

He hadn't had anything to do with blowing up the Bunker mill, but no sooner than he found a mining job, they'd learn he had been in the bull pen and fire him. He tried changing his name to Murphy, but that wasn't convincing because he had an Italian accent.

In between times, Dad did hand drilling at different prospects. Then he worked on a prospect in Pine Creek with Anderson. In the spring they ran out of groceries. The creek was on a rampage and the only way he could get across was to swim. He took his clothes off and put 'em in a tight bundle and swam across.

I said, "But wasn't the water cold?"

He said, "Sure it was cold, but I was hungry! We had to get some grub."

■ Some prisoners being held in a bull pen in 1899. Sylvan Agarla says, "[Dad] is the one pouring coffee out of a pot." Unable to speak English, the senior Agarla was picked up as he innocently came into Kellogg to buy groceries. *#8-X27, Barnard-Stockbridge Collection, University of Idaho Library, Moscow, Idaho*

Beatrice Marino Agarla

My mother's maiden name was Beatrice Marino. She was raised by a wealthy aunt in southern Italy where they talked a different dialect from Dad. Her uncle and cousins were dealers in horses. If a family wanted a certain class of horse, they'd find it for them. They bought horses for the army. Armies used a lot of horses in those days. They even came to the United States to buy horses. She had a great aunt living in Mullan who sent her money to come to America.

After she had been here a few days, the aunt invited Mother to go downtown with her.

Mother said, "There's snow and ice out there! I come from warm country. I'm so cold, if I could, I'd sit on the stove!"

My folks married in Wardner in 1904. They had three kids. My older sister, Catherine, later, Catherine Eichwal, was born in 1904. She became secretary for Henry Day in Wallace. I was born at Wallace, December 21, 1906. My younger sister, Alice, never married. She became a nurse and worked last as Dr. Fitzgerald's office nurse. She died in 1982.

Mother would say to Dad, "When you're talking to the kids, don't talk dialect. Talk correct Italian."

She learned to read and write English after she was over here. Later, when I went to school, I'd come home with dirty words in English that I didn't know the meaning. She'd wash out my mouth with soap! I can still speak Italian.

Gardener

The way I understood it, all the guys that were in the bull pen in 1899 were still blacklisted years later and couldn't get work no place hardly. But Dad had a leaning toward gardening, so he went to work for Harry Day and those people taking care of their yards—pruning trees, taking care of lawns and flower beds.

As soon as I was old enough, and when I wasn't in school, I worked with my dad mowing lawns and trimming shrubs for people in Wallace.

Kids Hang Out

When I was in high school, in the evenings I'd hang around with other kids at Tabors listening to the latest records in the little rooms they had there. Then maybe we'd go up to Saxton's Ice Cream Parlor next to Morrow's store, or walk up King Street and back. Or we'd loaf till midnight at Walter Frank's garage, which was next door to Sutherland's Livery Stable.

From the Northern Pacific Depot [before it was moved] you cross the bridge toward town and the first saloon was called the Northern Pacific, run by Joe Perla. Next was the Miners Home, last run by Tony Macetta. His daughter, Josephine Macetta Wambold, Dr. Wambold's mother, lives in Kellogg. Next was the El Rey, run by Rizzonelli.

Rocked the *Bonnie Doone*

When our high school team played basketball in Coeur d'Alene, we rode the train to Harrison and then took the *Flyer*, one of the passenger boats, to Coeur d'Alene.

One time we went to Harrison and then walked up the boardwalk to the main street and looked the town over. Then we took the *Bonnie Doone* up the St. Joe River to see the sights at St. Maries and St. Joe City.

On the way back the bunch of us got to moving from one side of the boat to the other and rocking it. The purser came down and warned us that the boat was a sawdust burner and if we got water into the boiler, the whole thing would blow up.

He said, "You smart alecks sit down the rest of the trip or we'll put you out on shore."

I quit school when I was in the eleventh grade.

Learned Lessons

When I was a kid, a big store bought wine grapes by the carload for the Italians to make wine. We had wine with meals. One time Dad gave me a drink of hard liquor and it made me sick. I learned my lesson right then. I never drank. Same way with smoking. Dad had some cigarettes and asked me if I wanted one. Told me to inhale it deep. It made me sick and that's the last time I smoked.

Delivered Coal

I worked with Dad till I went to work for the Garretts. I had a Model T one-ton truck with a dump bed on it, so the Garretts hired me to deliver coal all over town during the wintertime. But I continued to work with Dad in the summer.

Elmer Talvia and County Work

The Shoshone County garage used to be on the big curve coming into Wallace where the Super Stop is now. Once when I hauled coal down to the county garage, I asked Elmer Talvia, a Finlander, if they had any jobs. [His name was pronounced Talvee.]

He says, "One of my men is off on a drunk. If he don't show up tomorrow, you can have the job."

Elmer Talvia was a swell guy. He showed me how to weld and then showed me how to keep records. We had to write down everything we did.

I ran the snowplow and drove truck. I had been driving a pickup, so the first time I got behind the wheel of an FWD, I wondered how you can drive a thing like this. FWD was the name of the make of the truck—a four-wheel drive with a five- to seven-yard box on 'em—made by the FWD Company. You had to throw the FWD into four-wheel drive, but the two Walters were always in four-wheel drive. I think they were manufactured in Long Island, New York. We had a '32 Walters we used to call "Grandma"—powerful as a 'dozer and dependable.

One time I took a Walters with a blade on the front to clear the snow from the road to the Midnight Mine so the crew could go to work. You go past the Morning Club in Mullan and turn left on a narrow, one-way road and go four or five miles up Finn Gulch to the mine. Mike Kinsella ran it at that time. If you ran off a turn on that narrow road, you'd roll all the way till you hit Finn Gulch at the bottom. I said prayers all the way up and all the way down.

We also had to clear the road to the upper workings of the Polaris! When you came to a switchback, you had to back your big truck a coupla times to make the turns.

I worked ten and a half years as maintenance man keeping the equipment in shape which was used on all the county roads.

Sunshine Powder Magazine

I went by the Sunshine powder magazine ten o'clock the night before it happened. I had been down at Kellogg visiting a girlfriend.

Every time I went by that powder magazine, I'd look at that steel door and say a prayer. I knew they had unloaded a carload of powder that day. That night I come from Kellogg and went up to work graveyard shift at the Sherman Mine at Burke. The Hercules went straight into the mountain. The Sherman went in about halfway and made a left turn to go to the hoist room. I was watchman and running compressors. I was goin' through the upper part of the mill above the flotation, where I had to punch a clock, when I heard a funny "Bloooo loooo!" and a big gust of wind came up the canyon.

I went down and asked the flotation operator, "Did you hear that noise?"

He says, "Yes. I wonder what the hell it was?"

When the fellas came in for day shift we told 'em about the sound and the big gust of wind and they said, "The Sunshine powder magazine blew up."

When I went down the hill to go home, I could see that across from where the brick powder magazine had been, the whole hillside was the color of pulverized brick. And they never did find the steel door!

Married

I got married to Donna Stevenson I think in 1943. I'm not sure. My wife worked for the Green Grocery in Kellogg. We lived in Wallace for awhile but that didn't work out, so we moved down to Osburn.

My wife was born in 1910 and died a year ago last October.

Social Security Got It Wrong

I worked for 16 years as welder and maintenance mechanic at the Bunker Hill zinc plant. They were pretty good to me and I got a good retirement pension.

When I first got Social Security, I was makin' over $400 a month. Then I got a letter from Social Security sayin' I owed them $40 for each of several months they had overpaid me, and they held it out of my check.

I went to Coeur d'Alene and said, "What's goin' on here?"

So they called 'Frisco. They had took the first five letters of my name and had figured out I was a woman, "Silva."

I said to that guy in Coeur d'Alene, "What kind of a bunch have you got down there? My Social Security card gives my full name, Sylvan Nival Agarla." They made the mistake and I had to pay for it.

■ Sylvan Agarla (79), 1985

Cemeteries

I know they got a cemetery up the Nine Mile that has all the old-timers, union men, buried there. But Dad is in the new part, in the south end way up on the hillside alongside the road.

THIRTEEN

PALMER "POLLY" ANDERSON

Interviewed 1973 at Silverton, Idaho.

I WAS BORN March 11, 1890, in Wisconsin and came to Wardner with my folks when I was eight years old.

The Girls

When I was maybe twelve, I washed dishes all hours in Big John's place for 50 cents.

In the big hall with pool tables, the girls danced in little bitty, short dresses, shorter than miniskirts. The men paid so much a dance to dance with 'em. They'd buy the girls drinks and bargain with 'em, then go out in the alley to the girls' rooms next door. Part of my job was to carry trays of food and drinks over there. They'd soon kick me out because I was a kid, but it was an eyeopener for me.

John Ponzetti run a confectionery store across from the Connell Hotel. He had a bunch of girls in his place, too. His dive was on that flat back in the hole where Gotty's store used to be. He had a big place, but it burned down. Then he had a beer parlor up at Enaville when the railroad was up there.

Keg on Third Base

Us kids used to head for wherever there was any excitement, like when the brewery burned down on Railroad Avenue. They stored their beer in an icehouse alongside. No one was watching, and during the fire we ran in and saved enough beer to get us all drunk. Even when

■ Palmer "Polly" Anderson at Smelterville, Idaho, in May 1973

we played ball, we had our beer. We kept a keg on third base. If you made it to third, you got a drink.

Stole Handcar

When I was a young guy, two of us stole a railroad handcar one night—the kind you stand up on each side and pump. We pumped it down to Enaville to a dance. I must have been about twenty-one because we pretty near went to the pen for that. We could have met a train. Only way we got out of it was the other guy's dad was section boss at Kellogg.

Nipper Underground

When I was still a kid going to school, I started working underground for Bunker Saturdays and Sundays for $2.50 an eight-hour day. Handled a muck stick [shoveled ore].

Then when I grew up and could work steady, I worked as a nipper. A nipper is a guy that brings the powder.

There was a guy running a machine in there. I run around with his friend, so I knew him well. He was loading the lifters—the bottom holes. He pushed the powder in with the rod handle of a steel scraper and hit the cap. I wasn't over 25 feet away and when it went off it pretty near knocked me over.

It blew his face to hamburger. The poor devil crawled around on the floor and I had to catch him to keep him from falling down the chute. I should have let him fall—he'd have been better off. He lived five or six months, but during that time, he didn't know much of anything.

During the eight years I worked at Bunker, I saw some other bad accidents. That's the reason after I got married, I got out. Since then, I worked for the Auto Freight, 39 years.

CCC Kids

When those CCC kids [Civilian Conservation Corps] came out to Prichard in 1933, they sounded like people from a foreign country. I asked some of the forestry people how they were getting along with the kids.

They said, "Oh! We've got 'em scared to death. We told them if they didn't behave, the hillside lancers would come down and check on 'em." They'd be sitting on the bunks with their chins on their knees, expecting the lancers to show up. They told the kids the lancers were some kind of animal.

One night, the truck driver that was taking a load of CCC's down the other side of Dodson Pass was drunk. On that second curve he ran over the bank and three of the kids got killed. I got pictures of the wreck.

I thought back East was civilized country till I seen those poor CCC kids.

I said to one kid, "What do they teach you in school? Why! We know more about the East than you know about the West."

He said, "They don't teach you anything about the West!"

But some of those boys were pretty talented. They put on shows and stuff and they were good.

FOURTEEN

BETTY AND ERNIE DAMIANO

ERNIE DAMIANO

Interviewed 1987 and 1995 at Osburn, Idaho.

MY DAD, Frank Damiano and his brothers, Tony and Pat, came from Italy to Chicago and worked in the copper mines in Michigan. Then all three of them worked at the Bunker [Bunker, Hill & Sullivan Mine]. My oldest sister was born in Wardner. Tony and Pat homesteaded ground overlooking Anderson Lake. Uncle Pat's place was across the canyon adjoining Waters'. He didn't have any children. His wife died about the time I was born.

I was born November 7, 1916, in a farmhouse up Bell Canyon out of Harrison, just past Bill Lamb's place. Near where Shorty Dudley used to live, we turned left and went three-fourths of a mile up a side canyon. Our place joined that of Tom Lamb, who lived back of where the old gravel pit is. My dad thought real highly of Tom Lamb. All the Lambs were wonderful neighbors. There's no house there anymore.

There were six girls and three boys in our family. Mary was youngest, then me, then Josephine, Edith, Angeline, Lewis, Rose, Carmen, and Ann, the oldest.

Dad hadn't homesteaded our ground. He bought it from Boutillier who had logged the big timber off. Dad had left Kellogg at the time of the 1899 strike. He found work at Grant's Mill in Harrison and sometimes worked his team for others who were logging in our neighborhood.

Our log house was on the left side of the draw going up where a few apple and prune trees still stand. It was about 30-by-20 feet with bedrooms upstairs in the attic and had a shingled roof. For a kitchen, there was a lean-to maybe 16 feet wide attached to the side of the house.

A log barn was built later, for the cattle and horses and for storing hay, across the little creek from the house. We needed cedar shakes for the barn roof. My dad was good friends with Walt Russell. He went to the sawmill office [of Russell & Pugh Lumber Company], and Walt said, "You go downriver to that boom of cedar logs. Take what you need and let the bookkeeper know the length and size of the ones you take."

So we sawed the logs into blocks, loaded 'em in a wagon, and hauled them back home to split into shakes.

Italian Farm

Dad generally milked three cows and kept 30 or 35 head of beef stock. We raised pigs and Rhode Island Red chickens.

Before the timber was burned and cut a second time, the creek carried enough water year around to supply the house, the stock, and the garden, and we could always see little trout in it.

Our garden lay along the edge of the little creek across from the house, close enough to dip water for the tomato and cabbage plants. We grew lots of potatoes. We stored rutabagas, turnips, and apples in our root cellar, and Mother canned a lot of tomatoes and fruit. There was no such thing as lettuce, but early in the spring as soon as the dandelions came up, my mother would clean 'em and cook 'em with a little pork. They tasted good. I still pick dandelion greens.

The Italians could farm steeper land than other people because they were willing to do most everything by hand, like in Italy, instead of with machinery. Dad leveled off a round place, 25 or 30 feet in diameter, and packed it hard. This was before my time. They grew hay and wheat on the bench land back of the house. Come harvest time, they cut the wheat by hand, tied it with straw, and laid these bundles of wheat in this circle and walked the horses 'round and 'round to thrash out the grain as they turned the straw over and over. When the wind was blowing, they picked up the wheat with homemade wooden shovels and tossed it in the air so the wind carried away the chaff and left the grain pretty clean.

From the pigs, we made sausage, pepperoni, and a ham we called "capocolo." They would take the bone out of the loin, which left a chunk of meat, and they'd season it and put it into a cleaned pig's bladder. The bladder would shrink around it in a tight sack. The seasoning would work into it after several months.

Then there was a ham called "brazuto" that used to come from the old country. It's dry. You can slice it paper thin.

Then we'd make sausage and curl it up in a crock and pour lard over it, almost boiling hot, till it covered the sausage. It not only preserved the sausage when kept in a cool place, but they could dig out the sausage and, at the same time, take out lard for cooking.

We had a shed at one end of the house where we hung all these meats to cure.

Logs for Taxes

The folks could usually sell a few logs to get cash to pay property taxes. During the Depression, about 1934, a fire ran through our timber. What logs were left were small. Walt Russell didn't want them for the sawmill because he couldn't sell narrow lumber and the sawmill was in just as tough shape as we were. My folks, being from the old country, were so afraid of losing their land. Finally, Walt Russell did buy the logs. We paid our taxes and took part pay in groceries from the company store at Springston. They only carried staples like dried beans, peas, bacon, flour, yeast, coffee, tea, and stuff like that.

Dad Sang

Most Italian men that came from the old country sang the opera, classical kind of music. Dad sang mostly when he worked. I thought he had a good voice. Of course, he sang in Italian. Dad knew English, but not too good.

Mary Pisani

Mother's maiden name was Mary Pisani. Her father's name was Frank, same as my dad's name. I think Dad sent to Italy for her and she came over with some other women.

When I was small, my mother became very sick so they sold the cattle and everything and moved into Harrison.

Caught Under Snag

Dad worked at the Export Mill, but when he had time, he'd take our little dog and go up to the farm and clear land. One real cold Christmas Eve day, early in the morning, he had set fire around a snag way up on the hill. Then as he was going under a fence, that snag fell on him, broke his leg, and pinned him down. He kept hollering for help and by late afternoon he had just about given up.

In the clear air of winter, the voice carries a long way. Levi Lehman and his brother, Willard, thought they heard someone hollering for help, so they drove down from the Flats and went up toward our place. That little dog started barking when he heard people talking, and they followed the bark of the dog and found my dad. They made some kind of a litter and carried him down to the car and brought him home in Harrison.

The doctor came to the house. My dad asked for a big chew of snuff, put that in, and the doctor set Dad's leg. But it was set crooked and never healed right.

Runaway Team

One day when I was about ten years old, my brother Lewis drove Uncle Pat's team that wasn't too well broke. They went down the narrow road around the steep hillside behind Anderson Lake to the sawmill at Springston to get a load of lumber. It was noon when he came into the mill yard, just bare wagon with four wheels and Lewis sitting on the front bunk. The whistle blew. The team whirled around and bolted. Lewis either jumped or fell off. The runaway team ran down past the office and store, and when some people tried to stop 'em, they swung into the river.

Well, I was walking and driving Dad's team around the Anderson Lake road because where the road went down by the lake, I was to meet my brother and hook my team ahead of his team to pull the load of lumber back up the steep hill. I was coming 'round, high up, and I could see these two horses running down there, and I thought there must be somebody riding them. Pretty soon, they turned up the hill, and suddenly here come Lewis's team around the curve, running. I dropped the reins and ran ahead of my team and stopped 'em. I held onto what was left of a rein hanging from the bit of one horse and talked and calmed them down. Then, because I thought something awful must have happened to my brother, I started bawling.

The runaway team was wore out, so I had no trouble turning them around. I took my team's lines and tied each one on their bit. Then I drove Lewis's team back down the road and led my team. Pretty soon, here come my brother all out of breath. Boy, he was glad to see me, too. He told me how his team had run into the river, the wagon turned over and got stuck in the mud. The horses had broke loose and headed for home. So we went back down and rescued the wagon, loaded the lumber on it, and came back home.

Schooling

I started school at age six in Harrison and began to learn English. I'd come home and sometimes I would talk English to my mother and she'd answer in Italian until I'd realize what I was doing, then I'd speak Italian. But Mother wanted to learn English, and I could help her.

I remember being taught in Harrison by Mrs. Lavigne and Mrs. Howe and liking arithmetic real well. Maria Luchini, Bob Damiano, and Tom Collier, a nephew to "Brown Sugar" Smith, were in my grade.

Boys used to fight a lot. Mostly it was the older kids that would put a chip on your shoulder and dare another kid to knock it off. Some of the older kids were sixteen or seventeen years old. The school was combination grade and high school. I remember some kid would call me a name, but he had to be older or bigger than me to get away with it.

About 1926, when I was ten, we moved back to the farm. There was no bus to ride to school in those days. Jack Lake logged for George Smith and lived up the canyon from us while he logged our place and the Sexton and Lamb places. Jack had kids of his own and let me and some other kids ride to school in his Ford for four dollars a month, apiece. When the snow got too deep, we had to walk the four miles down Bell Canyon and into Harrison.

I was fourteen when I graduated from the eighth grade. I was the only one left at home except for Mary. The others had gone and found jobs or got married. Rose was married to Domenic Nuzzi. Angeline was in Seattle. Carmen had gone to the mine district.

My folks knew I wanted to go further in school, so Dad said, "You're going to stay with your sister Ann in Spokane and go to high school."

Ann had married Michael Pascarello and had a boy of her own. She lived in Hillyard, so I went to that high school. But in November when the snow came, I got to thinking of my folks up there. Dad couldn't get around very good on that leg he had broken. I couldn't take it. I quit school and went home to help him get in the wood and keep the stove going. I never went to school no more after that.

That summer, I helped Dad make the garden, plant hay, and milk cows.

Lied About Age

Some years before this, my brother Lewis had worked at the Export Mill at Harrison. The summer of 1932, I walked five miles to Springston to work, picking edgings for Russell & Pugh. It was in the time of President Franklin Roosevelt and under the National Recovery Act. They had to pay me a minimum of three dollars a day.

One day Walt Russell came up to me and shouted over the screech of the saws, "We're gonna have to lay you off. You're under age."

I said, "Oh, no! I'm eighteen years old all right."

Walt said, "No! You're a year or two younger than my youngest son. You can't be over sixteen."

What could I say? Walt just shook his head and walked away. He had to know I was the only breadwinner. Most of what I earned was going into groceries charged at the Company store and taken home to my family. After that, Walt avoided me and never said no more, and I kept on working.

It was the custom of the farmers to stock up before winter with five or six 50-pound sacks of flour and a sack of sugar and a bunch of coffee. I charged up plenty of supplies before the sawmill shut down for the winter.

Mother Saves Horse

If Dad just brushed his bum leg up against a bush, the skin would break. You know how thin skin gets when you are old. He wore one of those army leggings, but still, he couldn't get around good. Leo Chounard, the sawyer at Springston had an outfit on a frame that he pulled around and sawed wood. So he thought he'd come up and help cut the winter's wood. Leo and I were up on the hill cuttin' wood when down below Dad let one of the horses out of the barn and tied it to the fence nearby. I heard that horse scream.

I said to Leo, "I've got to go down and see what the heck's wrong!" I ran down. The horse had throwed his foot over the barbed wire and was fighting it, sawing that wire into his hoof trying to get loose. I run to the barn and got a pair of wire cutters and cut the wire on both sides. The wire was still in his hoof and I was afraid to pull it out. I didn't know what to do. So I run down and told my mother. I said, "She's bleeding. She's not gonna last."

My mother filled a big pan full of flour. We run up there and then she told me to take the wire out. I took it out. She set the horse's hoof in that pan and kept packing the flour around the wound. As it bled through, she'd just keep packing more on until it made a dough around it. Eventually it quit bleeding. We waited quite awhile and then started washing it out. We saved the horse.

The Fire

We were home. It was on a Sunday right after dinner in July 1936. My folks were Catholic and every Sunday, Dad would read the Bible. Over the sound of his reading, we heard a crackling. My younger sister was there, too. We all ran outside. Our house was a story and a half high with some bedrooms in the top half. Fire was crawling along the roof. The chimney was old and I suppose it caught fire in the attic. Then it seemed to explode and all we could do was back away from the awful heat while everything burned. All that was saved was on a table covered by oilcloth. My mother had grabbed the oilcloth with the dishes in it and ran outside. We looked through the ashes for my father's big gold watch with a bear engraved on the back of it, but we couldn't find nothing.

That night we stayed at my Uncle Tony's place.

After that forest fire on our place in 1934, George Smith and his son, Floyd, had logged it for Russell & Pugh. They had thrown together a bunkhouse shack on our ground. After our house burned, they told us we could move into it. We stayed there and then in Harrison the rest of the summer. That fall, we moved to Spokane.

Ornery Edgerman

I had heard they were going to start a night shift at Long Lake Lumber Company [in Spokane, Washington]. So I went down there—kinda dumb, you know, hadn't looked for many jobs. I stood around a bit and then I went up and asked [Edward E.] Goodwin if he had a job.

He said, "Oh, no. Got all kinds of men."

I hung around awhile watching this poor guy having trouble catching edgings on the double edger. I really felt bad for him. Pretty soon there was edgings all over. The edgerman had to shut 'er down.

Goodwin come over to me and he says, "Did you ever catch edgings?"

I said, "Yeah, at Russell & Pugh at Springston."

He said, "Well, that's just a single edger there."

I said, "Yeah, but I *know* I can do it."

He said, "What's your name?"

I says, "Ernie Damiano."

He says, "You by any chance Frank Damiano's boy?" My dad had worked for him. "Why in hell didn't you tell me! I'd have give you a job."

I had a little trouble, but in 15 minutes I was going good. I think the other guy coulda made it if that one edgerman hadn't butted 'em up against him. He tried that on me a couple of times. The other edgerman knew what that guy was doing. He always gave me a break.

There was always the chance of a guy getting hurt. If the edgings butt up against something, they break. A sharp stick could come right at you.

The trimmerman, one of the Wards from Harrison, come over to me one day, and he says, "You know Ernie, when he butts them up against you, pick up a good heavy edging and walk over there and hit him right between the eyes."

When he started doing that again, I picked up a good heavy edging and I walked over there and I told him, "The next time you butt them for me, I'm gonna let you have it with *this* right between the eyes!"

After that, I didn't have much trouble.

A lot of guys from Harrison ended up at Long Lake. There were the Browns, the Lavignes, the De Andreas—Anton De Andrea.

Lost Parents

Losing the house had been an awful shock to my folks and even more because their citizenship papers burned up. Being immigrants, that meant they had lost their guarantee that they were Americans. Dad was quite sick, but he started in right away getting people's sworn statements so he could get another citizenship paper.

About two weeks before Dad died, the Immigration Service sent some people to the house and gave him the citizenship papers.

After my father died, I took my mother to Kellogg with me and worked at Bunker Hill in the mine for six or eight months until I got laid off. My mother was sick so I took her to Seattle to stay with my sister, Angeline, and her husband, Lewis Alfano. I stayed with my brother Carmen and his wife, Mildred, at Bremerton and looked for work. After Mother passed away in 1938, I came back to Kellogg.

Down to the Last

Meantime, my youngest sister, Mary, had married John Pickolick and was living in Kellogg. I stayed at their home. Every day I would go up to the Bunker Hill Mine and try to get a job and then to the smelter and then to the zinc plant. And that was every day. Every day.

School was out, it was June, and I was watching all those kids go to work. I don't know what the heck made me do it.

I walked into the Bunker Hill office and a guy says, "Can I do something for you?"

I says, "Yeah! I need a job. I need a job damn bad."

He started talking to me and I says, "I don't know why they give these kids work. Their folks feed them. But I haven't got nobody to feed me. I'm down to my last."

That guy sat down and wrote out a letter, put it in an envelope, and told me to take it to a certain guy.

The guy opened the envelope, read the letter and says, "You're to come to work tomorrow morning." I couldn't believe it!

Harrison Men

A lot of guys from Harrison came up here and worked—mostly in the zinc plant. There were the Laffertys—Bob Lafferty was head of the cell room at the zinc plant for a time—Ward Williams, Bill Lamb, Jimmy Miola, Tony Romane, the Benjamins, Bud Turnbow, the Nearings, the Salas.

I worked part of a year at the zinc plant when they were doing some construction there. Emmett Waltman was maintenance superintendent and Glen Waltman was boss of the bull gang on heavy construction.

They finished the construction. Emmett done everything he could to keep me at the zinc plant.

One day he said, "They're just on me. I can't hide you out any longer." So they laid me off.

Then somebody found out I had worked in sawmills, so they sent me over to the Bunker sawmill. That paid 50 cents more a day. I ended up dogging on the carriage. It was a cable-feed carriage, so it wasn't all that fast. Ed Morin was sawyer. Benny Lavigne worked there, too.

Drafted Early

A friend, Pete Rinaldi, and I stayed over night on the St. Joe River and went fishing. While I fried some trout, Rinaldi went to the Trading Post at Avery and bought a copy of the *Spokesman-Review*.

He come back, waving it. "I can't believe it. You're drafted!"

When we returned to Kellogg, the letter from the draft board was waiting. I went into the army in July 1941.

In the Army and Sick

I was stationed at the East Garrison of Camp Roberts. We didn't have howitzers then. We trained with a mock-up made from small logs with an axle and wheels. We weren't issued rifles until the day the Japanese bombed Pearl Harbor. They rushed us to Los Gatos, California, because they thought the Japanese were going to attack there. From then on we didn't have a permanent base. We trained in the desert and even camped in the center of the Santa Anita Race Track.

We thought we'd be sent to South Africa, but they gave us all our shots, loaded our equipment on flatcars, and shipped us by rail to Fort Lewis, Washington, and from there by boat to Anchorage, Alaska.

On the way, I got sick and had a temperature, so I went to the medics and they laughed at me. At Anchorage, they put me on guard duty and I passed out. When I came to, I was sitting by the fire drinking a cup of coffee.

Dan Foley, my buddy from Butte, Montana, told one of the doctors he knew in our outfit how sick I was. The doctor took my temperature and put me in the hospital. The hospital was just some barracks. I got teased a lot about it, but the captain came up and gave me my corporal stripes right there. Some of the guys came up to sit with me at night. They told me I was delirious and never ate. I got down to 90 pounds.

I barely knew the doctor they had flown up from Walter Reed Hospital in Washington, D.C., was talking to me. He started intravenous feedings and made me keep hard candy in my mouth all the time. They fed me everything sweet and no fats. The doctor said this treatment was an experiment. It worked and I started getting better.

The doctor told me, "This whole Alaska Command is full of this. If the Japs only knew it, they could take everything over easy. We're tracing the batch of yellow fever shots you guys got. I think there was some live virus." When they make the yellow fever serum, they inject a horse with something, and he explained there is a certain process that has to take place before they withdraw the serum. They had shortcut one phase because they needed the serum fast, and that phase took place in our bodies. He told me this personally, but nobody else would admit it.

He said, "I'm going to give you this card to keep in your pay book, that they should never give you a yellow fever shot again."

I was in the hospital three months before they released me.

Later, I was breaking some boxes over my knee for kindling, a nail went into my leg and my knee got kinda stiff. I got a tetanus shot. The very next day they were giving tetanus shots.

I was joking with everybody and said, "I don't have to take one. I got one yesterday."

The medic said, "I don't give a damn. I'm givin' you another one today!" So I got another shot. That's the army for you.

I used to bitch about the army, but considering the problems they had, it's no wonder there were snafus—situation normal all fouled up.

Amchitka Island

After I recovered, we were sent to Amchitka in the Aleutian Islands. The island isn't a mile wide and the highest point not over 100 feet. The ground is tundra—black, mucky soil with a permanently frozen subsoil covered with short, coarse grass. No trees, no bushes. Strange, but kinda pretty in a way. There were perfectly formed little ponds about 40 feet across, with some four or five times that big. There were storms, rain, and always wind.

Soon after we arrived, the navy reported a storm warning for winds up to 110 miles an hour. We were living in tents set on top of the ground on a frame. The wind blew 'em all down. Tore 'em all up. Blew some of 'em away. They had a sizable lumber yard there for setting up buildings. The wind blew a lot of that lumber clear across and into the ocean on the other side of the island. Until we got settled, all our food and stuff like that was stacked outside with tarps over it. That blew away, too.

They used to say, you can always tell a man that's come off the Aleutian Islands because he walks bent forward to counter the wind.

Then they made us dig down so the pyramid tents were below the slight slope so when the wind hit, it would shear off. We had a little tin stove that burned coal in each tent. But then the tents filled up with water. So we had to dig ditches about 100 feet to drain it off. Every tent had to have two trenches, enough to take care of all eight men that stayed in it. Four men could hide in each trench. But they filled up with water, too.

At first we had a cook tent and no tables—nothin'. You just went in there and they gave you some chow and you squatted around and ate it. As soon as they got organized, they brought in a prefabricated mess hall and that was nice.

We were only about 700 miles from Japan. We expected the Japanese to attack us.

We were one battery, that's four guns and about 120 men. There were four batteries in a battalion. We were the First Battalion 30th Field Artillery. The battalions were scattered over the island.

We had practiced with these guns in California, but we didn't know how they'd react being fired at these temperatures, like 35 below. That was the first time I ever slept out at 35 below zero! The officers knew how to figure the amount of powder and elevation to reach a target. They learned this from trial and error when the guns were first made. They weighed about 90 pounds and used 155-millimeter shells. The guns were on wheels and had on the back what we called a "spade" which dug into the ground when fired. But the spade wouldn't dig into this frozen ground. They were afraid the gun would kick back and run over you.

When the gun fires, the recoil mechanism on the barrel comes back like a shock absorber, so you have to be out of the way. We were using whale oil, which won't freeze at very low temperatures, in the recoil mechanism, but it had to be tested. We fired the gun with a long lanyard [a long rope] which lets you stand away from it. The book says you dig a ditch and get in the trench, but you couldn't dig no trench up there in that frozen ground!

I got pretty good at firing the guns. I used to go up on the observation post with the officers, and they'd let me fire the guns because, as they said, if anything happened to them, somebody other than the officers would have to take over.

They figured the range of the guns by math. I told Captain Roberts I had only eighth grade education, but I like math and liked to figure complicated problems. Captain Roberts had been a school teacher in Portland, Oregon.

He said, "If you'll take time to study, I'll send for some math books."

I studied all winter with him. Not on a regular basis, but he'd let me know when he had time and we'd meet at the mess hall.

Later the officers came to me and urged me to go to Fort Benning for officers training. But being an officer didn't appeal to me. An officer has to be calm and I had a temper. And I didn't want to separate from the guys of my outfit. It was bad enough being a noncommissioned officer.

They planned to build a big airfield there for the new bombers, and ships came loaded with barrels of asphalt. I've stacked hundreds and hundreds of barrels. But then we got word we were going to leave and all the guys would do was take binoculars and watch for ships! We had been nine months in Alaska and 14 months at Amchitka.

Reunion Later

When we were at a reunion in Colorado about 1980 or '81, the battery commander spoke at a dinner and said, "I want to tell you women and men something that I could never tell before. When we went on Amchitka Island, they told us that they were putting us there so the Japs couldn't take it over and for us to be self-sufficient. If there was an attack, there was no way they could help us. The words they used was that we were 'sacrificial troops.' "

Wrong Charge

From Alaska, we went to Camp Pickett, West Virginia. I think it was there I became a sergeant. We moved around a lot. Went to Fort Bragg, North Carolina. We were school troops, training infantry officers on artillery.

As artillery, we were firing ahead of the infantry to knock out what could be danger spots, such as a machine gun. We were firing on the coordinates given us by the infantry officers. The shells were one size, but the charges put behind the shells—the amount of powder—varied.

We were in the field, firing just ahead of the infantry officers. The danger is that the artillery may drop some shells into them. That's what happened in our battery. Someone misunderstood the charge to put behind the shells and killed two officers. It was daylight, but when the flares went up, we knew something had gone wrong because these flares meant "Cease firing!"

Pack Up and Go

They gave us this big spiel about how we had done our duty overseas—in Alaska—and we were going to stay at Fort Bragg and continue schooling on artillery. And here we got orders to pack up and go to Camp Filmer, New Jersey! One morning, we get up, load into trucks, get on a ferry stacked in there like—you can't believe how many troops they can load standing up. We went across the North River, got on a train, and then into trucks again, and wound up at Pier 10 in New York City. The big ship *USS Brazil* was waiting there. We got on. Then we were pretty sure we were going to Europe.

Guns

In California, we had trained on 90-pound 155-millimeter howitzers, mounted on wheels, pulled with a truck. In Alaska, we had a Long Tom—a 155-millimeter gun with a barrel 27 feet long that would shoot 15 miles. It was so heavy you couldn't pull it off a road unless it was real solid ground. We pulled it with a track-layer Caterpillar. In Europe, we had 155-millimeter howitzers again and what they called "prime movers," which were like a Cat with a rubber track. Not worth a damn.

France

We landed at La Havre, France, February 1945. The big luxury liner, the *Ile de France*, had been bombed and was tipped over on its side, right by the dock.

By this time, the Allied Troops had opened the front to Germany. They sent our outfit to one of the huge camps they had set up, with names like Camp Lucky Strike, Camp Chesterfield.

Our equipment might not be on our ship, so I stayed at the landing with a group to draw out our equipment. When everything was assembled, they brought our outfit back.

We started across France not knowing where we were going, riding in trucks without hoods, four men on each side facing inward, with the ammunition in the center—powder on one side and shells on the other. This was a gun crew of eight, with the noncom [noncommissioned officers] riding in the cab and changing off with the driver. Drove day and night stopping only for gas and to eat. Our cooks were on the trucks and cooked on gasoline stoves with ovens while we were moving. Fixed pretty good meals, too. Surprising.

My section wasn't in a truck. We were pulling a gun and riding in this rubber-tracked outfit that could do about 35 miles per hour, but it wasn't recommended because they had rubber bogey wheels that the tracks run on. Later we found them damn things got so hot they just blowed up and burned if they were driven too long.

Lost in Dark

We were going along in the pitch dark and I fell asleep. Our driver got lost from the rest of the column. At daylight we came to a place where they were selling wine, so we stopped and went in. I met a soldier there that I'd been in training center with and told him we were lost.

He said, "Yeah! I seen that artillery outfit broke down alongside the road by the Moselle River."

What had happened, we were going along in the dark parallel to a railroad track, and somewhere, the rest turned right and we kept going straight on. We found our outfit and moved along with it.

From then on we could see bombers in the air 24 hours a day, pulling gliders, bombing Germany. The Germans were on the run. We moved to different places, but they didn't need artillery. So then General Patton was making a big rush, and they took all our trucks to haul gas.

Occupation Troops

By the time we occupied Germany, I had moved up to sergeant and had seven men under me.

The U.S. military had checkpoints along all the roads so German soldiers couldn't get together and get some guns.

We stayed in a small town in Germany run by the U.S. military. There were hundreds of German soldiers wandering around—going home. Our troops couldn't keep them all prisoners, so we disarmed them and turned them loose. Anybody that wanted to celebrate, hold a big meeting, or a religious celebration, had to get permission.

Special Troops

It was a worrisome thing. We were warned to be on the lookout for German soldiers that had been special troops—the mean ones. Our officers would give us a list of names and we'd try to find evidence linking them to the special troops. I didn't like that kind of work. We went into one place by Jeep and searched the house. Upstairs they had a place hooked onto a chimney where they smoked and cut meat. And in there, we searched and found pictures of this man in the dress uniform of that special troops outfit. We uncovered and arrested him and took him to the American army. He had three daughters and all were nurses working in the hospitals there. But we had to take him. What always bothered me, I never knew what happened to him.

Shipped Home

Near the end of the war in Europe our unit was broken into small groups for reassignment. It was on the point system—how long you'd been in, where you had been, and if you were married and if you had kids. I had been in longer, but I didn't have the points a married man had with kids. All the older guys and married men in our outfit were sent to occupy Austria.

A real good friend from Chehalis, Washington, and I were sent back to the States and our orders read, "Report to Fort Benning for Overseas Duty." We figured it would be the South Pacific for us.

When we reached Fort Benning, we talked it over. I don't know if we'd have done it or not, but we decided we'd been in the war long enough, and we wouldn't rejoin our outfit. Meantime, we were given a furlough and told to report back to Fort Lewis.

We got into Spokane the day the atom bomb was dropped on Japan. The bomb had been a hush secret before that. Everybody was grabbing newspapers, trying to figure it all out.

Soon as our furlough was over, we went to Fort Lewis and were assigned barracks. Next morning, they started reading names of men to be discharged and called our names. A week went by. Two weeks. We were getting apprehensive. The other 20 guys in our barracks thought they were to be discharged, too.

They chose me to be spokesman and I went up to headquarters.

The guy there says, "Go get the right number of the barracks. You got the wrong number. There ain't nobody in that barracks!"

I said, "To heck there isn't! There's 20-some men."

So he sent somebody down there with me, and it seemed we had been lost in the turmoil. They started processing our discharges about midnight, and by morning we were paid off and gone.

And here we got out before the old men with kids they had sent to Austria. I had been in the army over four years.

I was working in the Bunker sawmill when I was drafted. When I came back I worked in the sawmill a couple of years. From then on I worked at the machine shop till I retired.

■ Soldiers traveling by boxcar from Germany en route to being shipped back to the United States in 1945. Back: unknown, Ernie Damiano, Elred Atwood, Reno and Dan Foley. Front: John Cole and two unknowns.

Accident

One day in the Bunker welding room, I stepped on a round welding rod. My feet went out from under me and I fell on my back against a steel sawhorse. They took me up to the Wardner hospital and this doctor kept me in the hospital three or four days.

Then my doctor, Dr. Staley, came in and said, "How's your back doing, Ernie?"

I says, "Not worth a darn, Doc. They're not doin' anything for me."

Then I went home and stayed awhile. Finally my back got so bad I couldn't take it no more. Betty phoned Dr. Staley. He told me to come to the hospital and he put weights to pull on my feet and in a few days this fixed me up. Then Dr. Staley said I could go back to work.

But my release classed my accident as nonindustrial. I took the slip back to the Bunker office and I says, "This is wrong! It happened on the job." I knew that if it wasn't industrial I'd be stuck for the expense if I had problems with my back later on.

The office man says, "You have a history of a bad back."

I said, "Where did you hear that?"

Well, one word led to another and I lost my temper. I threw him down in a chair and held him by the tie and the throat till they dragged me off.

Later on, the public relations man brought the company insurance check up to our shop and says, "You gotta take this, Ernie, and quit foolin' around."

I says, "I'll show you how I take it." I threw the check on the floor and tore it up with my boots.

Some time passed, and the office sent another man to the shop who said, "Can you prove that you got hurt here on the job?"

I said, "You want proof? Come on!" I went to the nearest guy that worked in the shop. "Did you see me fall on my back against that steel sawhorse in the welding room?"

Everybody in the shop knew I was having trouble over the insurance. He says, "Yeah! I saw you fall."

I took him from one man to another through the shop. Each one said the same.

Then I wrote to the State Industrial Board and told them the story. They met with me in Wallace, asked some questions, and said, "We'll have a hearing, here, tomorrow with the Bunker people present. You don't have to be here."

I said, "That sounds like I don't have much of a chance."

The Industrial Board man said, "Son! Take my word for it. You sign any papers they give you. We'll take care of everything."

When I was called to the office to sign the papers, this guy says in front of all those secretaries. "Well! Now we've got you where we want you. We can fire you or do whatever we want."

I says, "Listen! You've got a big mouth. You haven't got the guts to fire me. You know why? My union would shut this place down by morning. You know where you'd be? Out! Those guys from the Industrial Board told me to sign anything and not worry about it."

But in the days after that I stayed mad and worried, so after work I went down to see Charlie Schwab, president of the company. He had met me at Betty's dance recitals and was always friendly. At an affair soon after our oldest daughter, Rita, had graduated, he had asked me, "Now that Rita has graduated from high school, what's she going to do?"

I said, "She'd like to go to the University of Idaho." Then I said, "You know, Charlie, there's sure gonna be one mad Wop if she doesn't get a scholarship."

She had got one, too. I think it was $350 a semester.

In the office Schwab said, "What's the problem, Ernie?"

I told him the State Industrial Accident Board had already ruled in my favor, and these guys in his office were still riding me.

He said, "What the heck's the matter with them guys? You been working for us for years." He wrote out a slip and gave it to the secretary. "I'll put a stop to that!"

Good Old Bunker

You can say what you want, but the old Bunker used to do things for the schools and the city and everybody. Like buying uniforms for the high school band. And I don't know how many days I put in at the YMCA fixing pumps that had broke down—all on paid Bunker time. And there was practically a standing order at the machine shop for us to drop everything and fix kids' bikes. But when Gulf Resources took over, they didn't do any of that.

And the Bunker had always blocked out ore ahead for a reserve. Soon as Gulf took over they used up all those reserves and didn't spend any money to find more. They cashed in on the mine and then shut everything down.

More Math

At the shop, guys with a college education couldn't always figure something out that I could, although I might not do it the proper way. Like the pumps. Once I seen Bob Miller, the mechanical engineer, working on a curve for a pump to pump. It fascinated me.

I said, "Bob! You got to show me how to do that."

He said, "Why do you want to learn that?"

I says, "I'd just like to learn how it's done."

One day he called me at work and says, "Come on down. I've got time to show you."

The boss okayed it so I went down. From then on, when they wanted to pump so many gallons of water and lift it so high at a certain pressure, I'd work out the curve for that pump. I enjoyed doing it.

One morning Bob Miller phoned me, "They say you figured the curve on that pump at the Crescent and it's not working. Explain to me how you did it."

I told him and he said, "You are correct. I'll have to go up and check it."

It made me feel good that he thought I was right.

When he come back he says, "My God, Ernie! Curves are figured without obstructions. They went from a two-inch line into a four-inch line with 20 different elbows on it."

Women on the Job

You know, the pioneer women did a lot of work, but there's something about a mine—I don't think women have any business in a mine.

I never worked as a miner, but sometimes I would go underground to repair or assemble equipment—mostly hoists. But you know, it's so damn hot and dirty in them places. I can't see how in hell women . . .

The management told us, "You've got to get used to working with women. The government says if women apply, we have to hire them."

So first they hired women in the shop. Then one was repairing drill machines and one was running a small hoist. And then they began running trains underground, mostly pulling chutes and hauling muck out of the drifts. Women have worked in the Bunker, the Sunshine, and the Galena.

Air to Breathe

It takes lots of power to push air down into a mine for men to breathe and for cooling. It's generally true that rock gets hotter as you go deeper with some places hotter than others. Some places they use ice machines and convert them into air conditioners. Some mines make a lot of water. Others are dry. They cooled one part of the Crescent with water piped into it from Big Creek.

I went down to the 3,200-foot level at the Crescent to work on a little hoist with another guy. Thirty-two hundred foot means the distance of the drift below the point of entrance—not below the discovery point. Mostly the drifts take off from the shaft every 200 feet.

The hoist man come over, "Say! You're not gonna last very long at the rate you're working."

I says, "What do you mean?"

He says, "It's hot in here and the air ain't good. I've seen guys used to workin' above come down here and pass out. Go look at the thermometer at the station." It read 120.

He said, "Come into the cab a bit. It's only 80 inside. I've got an air conditioner."

Pumping the Crescent

During World War II the Crescent couldn't operate because silver wasn't needed and the government couldn't afford to waste manpower. So they took all the machinery out of the bottom and let it fill up with water. Water will preserve the timbers.

About 1955 they decided to pump all that water out. Johnny Austin and I were sent into the Crescent with a big Pomona pump. We set the pump in the shaft on a double-drum hoist and screwed a ten-foot length of pipe sticking down from the pump's bottom into the water. The other drum held the skip we rode on. Then we screwed ten-foot lengths of pipe on top of the pump to deliver the water outside. As soon as the pump pulled the water depth down ten feet and began to suck air, we lowered the pump ten feet and screwed another ten-foot length on top of the pump. As we went down, we strung out a bell cord so we could give signals to the hoistman above. The bell cord is a stainless steel wire braided like a cable and is strong so it won't break from its own weight.

We moved down pretty fast as long as we were pumping out only the shaft, but when we reached a drift where the water ran back horizontally a long ways, it slowed our progress. And pumping out a drift can be worrisome because back there somewhere there may have been a cave-in that has damned up the water. If your pump has moved down below the floor of the drift, this dam could break and bring tons of rock and water roaring down on you.

We finished the job in three months.

Air Doors and Fans

One winter day, I and Stanley Bencich, who was called "Stanko," went back in the drift that draws air down a shaft to furnish breathing air for the Bunker Mine at Wardner. They use air doors and fans to route the air flow. When the motorman comes out pulling loaded cars of muck, he pulls a rope and air cylinders open the doors for him. On the other end, he pulls another rope that closes them again. Gee! It was cold walking into that moving air. We damn near froze. At night they reverse the fans and draw the hot air up the shaft to melt the icicles.

Our project was to service the fans and set the blades like the engineer had told us. We loosened the set screws and set the blades.

The electrician had told me, "Now, Ernie! When you shut that motor off, it's hot. By the time it's ready to go again, it's gonna be soaking wet. Don't kick the switch on with your fingers. Get a dry board or stick, 'cause it might blow."

So my partner and I put our tools back in the bags and I says, "O.K. Stanko. Are you ready?"

He says, "Ready as I'll ever be."

I took the stick and jabbed that switch and the motor started. The wind from the fan wasn't strong enough to knock us end over end, but we had to keep moving and hugging the wall and didn't have no control.

Stanko has worked in mines since he was a kid. He kept hollering, "Follow me!"

There was a Y there, and following him, I got around into it and out of the wind. At the directions of the electrician we had set the blades too much. Because of the pressure, we couldn't even get them air doors open.

3,000 Volts

Another time, an electrician in the mine scared me. He said, "When you get back in the drift, you'll see a 3,000-volt line laying across the track. The line is armored but it's old and might have some leaks in it. Lift it up with this dry plank and let your motor pass under it."

I remember a guy outside running a jackhammer. His bit hit a 3,000-volt cable, and it blew up the concrete.

Stanko

Stanko knew the underground and its dangers so he was a good guy to work with. His dad had left his mother with Stanko and three sisters. His mother had to take in boarders and washing to support them. So Stanko had known rough times as a kid and it gave him a grudge against life. One time, here came a Red Cross lady into the shop asking for Stanko. They had found his dad dead someplace back East, and the Red Cross wanted to know what to do with the body.

Stanko said, "What do I care? The sonofabitch never worried about me!"

After he got dusted [silicosis], I met him downtown one day wearing an oxygen tank. Medicare paid for the oxygen—and that was expensive—but they would never pay him disability, so he didn't get the extra pay he needed to live.

Him and I had hunted grouse together. He said, "I'd like to hunt one more time. Will you take me?"

I said, "How in hell can you hunt with that oxygen tank?"

He said, "It's portable. I can carry it anywhere."

I said, "But the oxygen won't last long enough."

He said, "Yes, it will!"

When I'd spot a bird, he'd get out and walk, but he tired fast. He finally give it up and climbed back into the car. And the dang oxygen did last clear over to Calder and back.

Him and I were about the same age. That was ten years ago that he died. He would have been about sixty.

Retired

You know, a lot of people don't know what it's like not to be working. There's no hope. You're just nothing. My heart bleeds for the young fellows down at the Bunker that are out of work now and got a family. They're not the same anymore.

Even retiring is rough. For 39 years I climbed that slope to the Bunker Hill. And then they cut you off all at once. It's quite a shock. The first two weeks or month are just wonderful, but then it starts bearing down.

■ BETTY DAMIANO

Interviewed 1987 and 1995 at Osburn, Idaho.

My maternal grandmother was iron-willed, independent, and wanted her girls to have the better things in life. But she also believed you were born to work, and you had your place. My mother accepted those views, but when she exhibited a strong will, independence, and gave up the family religion to develop her own, my grandmother thought her daughter a devil.

In the winter of 1895, my mother talked her parents into letting her ride a horse five miles from their home in Bridger Canyon into Bozeman, Montana, for voice and piano lessons. It was on one of these trips that she met my dad. My father was working just outside Bozeman in a stone quarry where the military was breaking huge stones into chunks and hauling them on wagons to build the foundation for Montana State College.

My mother, Margaret Elizabeth Papke, and father, Ernest Frederick Menzel, married in 1905. They lived on my father's acreage further up the canyon in Bridger bowl, in the cabin that is still there. Later, they moved into Bozeman where I was born April 27, 1924. There were seven children in our family, six boys and me. Our whole family was musical. Dad played piano, violin, saxophone, and trumpet. Music would benefit us all our lives.

There was such freedom and camaraderie in our family! I wanted to do all the things boys do, and hated to have to wear a dress. When Dad left jobs for the boys to do, I made sure they were done before Dad got home so they wouldn't get in trouble. I was a real tomboy and enjoyed all my brothers.

Named Funny

My mother and dad named all of us funny. I was named after all of my mother's sisters, Marie Elizabeth Matilda Menzel, but I ended up just Betty Marie. The second boy, Eugene H. "Gene" Menzel was adopted. And then my brother Herman William, next was William

 Herman, then me, then Fred Floyd "Fritz," and then Robert Donald "Bobby" was the baby. Funny names: Herman William and William Herman, Fred Floyd.

My oldest brother was Carl Ernest, but when my maternal grandmother visited Germany, she discovered an Uncle Adolph who was a famous violinist, so my parents renamed him Adolph. He was three years old then. But when he went to school the kids never called him Adolph, they called him "A." Dad was disgusted and changed his name to Boise.

Boise

Boise was a genius. He could fix anything with his hands. He taught himself piano at an early age and graduated from high school at age twelve. By the time he was thirty, he was playing all kinds of instruments and ended up with a nice band.

When he brought his band into our house for a practice session that lasted till three o'clock in the morning, my folks never complained. We all just loved music.

It was Depression. We had no money, and sometimes we hardly had enough to eat. We learned to laugh at all our troubles. Since we had such hard times, we ended up with lots and lots of laughter.

One night in 1939, Boise was playing piano in a dance hall and a guy came in and started a fight with him.

Boise said, "Not on this job! Let's wait and settle it afterwards."

The guy stood around waiting, and when Boise got out there in the alley, the guy pulled a knife on him and cut his jugular vein. He bled for five hours. They could not stop it. He had inherited thin blood that wouldn't clot from the Hapsburgs in Germany on my father's side of the family.

And the man got away with it because Mother wouldn't testify against him. She said, "We cannot do that. Killing two people does not make it right."

Boise was such a beautiful person. Losing him saddened our family for years.

Bobby

During the 1932 Depression, when Dad had difficulty finding work, Mom sold things door to door to augment our income and she left my little brother, Bobby, in my care. He was two and I adored him.

Bobby was walking around my legs as I was frying bacon. He pulled on my dress. I tripped. The hot grease went down on his head and burned his scalp. He screamed. I don't know what told me to hold him in the sink with cold water running over his head till he stopped crying.

Afterwards, my family, aunts and uncles, railed at me, saying I should have put butter or grease on the burn. It made me feel terrible that I had scarred the little boy I loved so much.

Later years, I've often wanted to take those same relatives aside and say, "See? I did the right thing. You were wrong and you saddled me, a child of eight, with years of miserable guilt."

Lightning

I was ten years old, standing in my room just under the peak of the roof with thunder booming outside, when there was a long crrrrrash! A ball of fire came down right in front of my eyes. My dress flared out and I ran down the stairs yelling, "There's a big ball of fire!"

The rest of the family raced back upstairs with me. There was a two-foot-wide hole burned in the roof right over where I had stood.

Then when I was seventeen, I was on a hiking trip outside of Bozeman with a Girl Scout troop. I was wearing jeans I had borrowed from my brother without his consent. We were on a high mountain peak when it started to rain. The rain came harder and harder. We were soaked to the skin.

I said to the others, "You look so funny! Your hair is standing straight up in the air!"

Our Scout leader said, "We're in an electrical storm. We better get out of here!" Right then, these two unlike charges connected with my hair and crackled like meat frying. I heard CHOOOO! as they went down through my body and slammed me to the ground. I jumped to my feet and started running back down the trail and my hair went up again. It threw me and two other girls down several times.

When I got home, my wet legs were blue, and I was scared it was from the lightning, but then I realized the blue came from dye in the jeans and the rain. My brother said it served me right for taking his new blue jeans.

I was watching Aunt Marie bathing her two-year-old daughter in the middle of the kitchen floor at the ranch during an electric storm. She had just lifted the little girl out of the washtub when this crazy lightning came through the window, went through the radio, then followed the ring around the tub, and went back out the window like it was traveling on a fuse. Other times, I've seen lightning make glimmering lights on the fur of the cattle and on the tips of their horns.

Piano and Dance Lessons

When I was about six, my wonderful mother said to me, "You *must* have piano lessons!"

So she washed clothes to pay for these lessons and took me to every concert that hit the college. I had six years of classical music, but I didn't like to play it. I wanted to dance. My grandmother disapproved and referred to me as the "daughter of a devil!" When I was ten, Mom saw to it that I took dancing, and I worked to pay for my lessons. I loved it! At that time American dancing was undeveloped—many, many years behind the Russians, but I think we're up with them now.

I had graduated from Bozeman High School at seventeen when I heard about this Harry Fletcher. He had been a pianist in the Benny Goodman Band, but had contracted polio and was now teaching piano from a wheelchair.

Why I ever went to see him I'll never know because I never intended to perform on piano. Evidently he saw talent in me because I started one-hour lessons at 7:00 at night, and he stretched those lessons out until 9:00 for nine months. And he made me love it so much. He opened up a whole new world. He taught me the theory and roots of classical music so everything about modern and classical music seemed to fit right in. And I could play! Gosh, I didn't know I could.

And he kept saying, "I know you're going to need this as a dance teacher."

I said, "No, no, no! I'll never play for anyone else!" But his words were prophetic.

Crawled inside the Wings

I was eighteen in the spring of 1942. World War II had opened jobs for women in [the] defense industry. I stayed with my brother and sister-in-law, Gene and Marjorie, in Issaquah and hired out at Boeing as an airplane mechanic.

My job was installing the main gas tank and the smaller gas tank in the wings, and the oil tank in the inboard wing. We also installed the gas caps and de-icers along the wings.

Since I was small, I could crawl inside the wings and tighten or replace bolts that someone else had left loose or stripped. We women did light work but were very conscientious about making sure it was done right. Although we did "A" work we were paid "B" wages. The men got $1.40 for the same work for which we got 96 cents an hour. I was a member of the International Machinist Union. Even the union men didn't realize that women should have equal pay.

■ Betty Menzel (Damiano) age 16, 1940

At the same time I attended Seattle University, a Jesuit school. I moved to an apartment within walking distance in Seattle on Ninth and Seneca. I went to school from 8:00 till 12:00, ran home and got my lunch, changed clothes and went to work from 3:00 to 11:00 at Boeing. Then I'd come home and do my schoolwork.

I also took dance lessons on weekends with the intention of becoming a teacher. There were five dance schools there, so I studied under many instructors: classical ballet with Ivan Novokoff and Mary Ann Wells, and tap with George Barclay among others. And then on vacations I went to San Francisco and Los Angeles for lessons. Once I took a summer off and went to Hollywood and worked a lot of circuits. I worked with Louis DeProne, the tap dance teacher who taught Donald O'Connor. I took lessons from a former Rockette, Linda Gache, Cyd Charisse, Marie Kay and ballerina Jo Rowen.

I was burning the candle at both ends. Gene would often come to check on me. This one time he found me awfully sick. He carried me out to the car and took me home. And then this nose bleed started. This is the only account I've had of that same royal blood that my brother, Boise, had. It stopped after Dr. Hillyard came and packed my nose with yards and yards of gauze, but I had lost a lot of blood. I had to quit college, but I continued to work and I never stopped dancing.

War work was winding down, I was lonely for my family, and in the spring of 1945 I returned to Bozeman. I found a waitress job at 50 cents an hour. Then I learned that Barbara Day, an exceptional dance teacher who came from a family of talented stage people, had opened dance studios in Livingston and Bozeman. I visited her studio, watched her teach and was greatly impressed.

I went up to her, told her about my dancing experience, and said, "I want to take lessons from you, but I don't have any money. I've got willing hands and I'll work for my lessons."

She looked uncomfortable and said, "No, I really don't care to do that. Anyway, my husband and I live in Livingston."

I said, "My name is Betty Menzel. I'm working at the Bobcat Inn if you change your mind."

A few days later I went to serve a table and here she was. She had checked my qualifications.

She said, "We've talked it over. I could use some help around the home, and I need help in my dance classes. But I can't pay much."

I said, "I'm not asking much pay. I'm asking to work for my lessons." It ended up that I did *all* her housework.

After about a year she said, "I need a piano player."

I said, "I don't want to play. The playing I reserve for myself. I'm here to learn dancing."

She was a beautiful lady but she had the heart of a witch. She pushed "Romany Life" into my hands and I played for her as she marked the beat, faster! faster! clapping her hands.

I didn't think I could ever play that classical piece up to her tempo but I speeded up, hating every minute of it. I learned to sit straight on the piano bench for hours and rip through those darned old pieces for her dance classes. But every session added to my slow burn.

One day I was playing "Fire Dance." She kept beating faster and faster till I reached my limit. I jumped up and walked out on her and the whole class. She followed me out and apologized.

I almost screamed at her, "Never, never, never push me like that in front of people. I'll give you 100 percent. Don't ask for 110!"

I ended up playing piano an awful lot and became resigned to it. But I will say this: She gave me all the instruction she promised. It was in the works that I would become a dance teacher and would play for my pupils as Harry Fletcher had forecast for me.

After two years, she called me into her office and said, "I've saved enough money to put my husband through chiropractic school in Davenport, Iowa. You have a choice. You can take over my two schools or you can go to my mother, Mrs. O'Neill, in Wallace, Idaho, as an assistant dance teacher. She has a tremendous background in stage experience from working the Orpheum Circuit out of Seattle. You could learn a lot from her."

I wanted to learn more, so I chose Wallace.

First Show

I arrived in Wallace, Idaho, August 3, 1946. Mrs. O'Neill met me at the bus station.

First thing she said, "Now, Betty! I'm going to be gone two weeks, so it's up to you to do the choreography for the Miners Picnic Show."

I thought: You don't say! Here I'm only twenty-two years old and dropped off into this strange mining town. I don't even know a soul!

Next morning, a Mrs. Clements picked me up at my room on Pines in Wallace and drove me down to the Liberty Theater at Kellogg. On the stage was a cast of three men and three women and a sheet of music, "Tell Me Pretty Maiden," an oldie from the 1890s that I had never seen before, with Mrs. O'Neill's note: "Choreograph this." There were five song-and-dance vaudeville acts to be taught in 11 days and presented August fifteenth. All Mrs. O'Neill had done was lay out the first one and assemble their old-fashioned costumes.

I sat down at the piano and, thanks to Harry Fletcher, I could play. So I put the three men and three women into the old-fashioned dance I dreamed up. Then three girls showed up who could harmonize like everything: Flora and Jean Edwards and Alwyn Kilimann. I placed the girls on stage.

I said, "Now let's project those voices so people will hear you." They sang "Buttons and Bows" and "Gal in Calico" for the second act. I put a few movements with it and they were just wonderful.

I asked Mrs. Clements, "Do you have gingham dresses for these girls?" She says, "We'll make 'em!"

When Mrs. O'Neill came back she asked, "How was the show?"

I laughed. "Oh! We got along."

Then I began taking lessons from her and she was good! On Saturdays I taught her pupils. With Mrs. Clara Taggart playing the piano, we started at 8:00 in the morning and, with never a stop, finished at 5:00.

Locked Eyes with a Man

Mrs. Taggart had a house in Kellogg and took in roomers. Because I didn't know anybody, sometimes I'd stop at her place for supper, and she'd drive me home to Wallace afterward. This November night, just before Thanksgiving, Mrs. Taggart was in the kitchen. I was in the living room playing the piano with her cute little granddaughters, one on each side of me. We were having a heck of a good time singing, laughing, and giggling when this man walked in the door and, boy! I'm telling you, his eyes locked on mine!

I was embarrassed at the length of time this stranger and I looked at one another. Neither of us said anything. He turned away, crossed the room, and disappeared up the stairs.

Then I went home for Thanksgiving and Christmas and came back to start classes in January. Mrs. Taggart had broken her wrist and I came in after class on Saturday to cheer her up and stay overnight with her. She was sitting there and I was stretched out on the davenport in one of her old housecoats and needing a haircut, when this same man came down the stairs into the living room. He was s-o-o-o-o-o handsome! Black hair. Mustache. I liked the assured way he walked. There was an air about him.

Mrs. Taggart said, "Come and meet Betty, our new dance assistant. Betty, this is Ernie Damiano. He rooms upstairs."

He smiled and said, "I'm pleased to know you, Betty." I saw that tremendous gentleness in his eyes and it really threw me.

And then he said, "It's still early. Would you like to go out with me?"

I was painfully conscious of how awful I looked. I pulled the old housecoat tighter around me and I said, "Oh, no! I don't think so," even though it was only about six or seven.

He said, "How about next Saturday?"

So I said, "Oh! I guess that would be all right."

He said, "Then it's next Saturday?"

I said, "O.K." And he left.

The funny part of it was that all week long Ernie tried to find where I lived so he'd know where to pick me up, but nobody knew my last name. Mrs. Taggart thought it might be something like Wertsall. She didn't know my address except it was in Wallace somewhere because when she drove me home in her car, I had always directed her where to go. He really put in a week of worry.

But I was completely at ease because I knew I was going to stay with Mrs. Taggart Saturday night, although I hadn't told her.

When I came through Mrs. Taggart's door Saturday evening, Ernie jumped up from his chair and said, "Gosh! You don't know how glad I am to see you. I didn't know how I was going to find you!"

We went to dinner and then dancing at the Sunshine Inn. And he asked me to marry him. I was shocked. Marriage hadn't appealed to me before. But here was this wonderful man. I could tell I liked him. I could tell!

To show you how fast he was, our first date was January 19. On Valentine's Day he presented me with a beautiful gold compact with my initials engraved on it. But you know what he had done? He had added a "D" for Damiano to my initials.

It was fun to be with him and we did get along well. And he was very considerate. I never ate anything all day long, so when I met him for a date, I was really hungry. Ernie always ate a big meal right after work so all he'd have with me would be a glass of juice or milk, but he'd buy me a steak.

So then he wanted to get married and, boy! I'm telling you, he moved! He lined up an apartment and had me look it over. I really wanted time to think, but I reminded myself I was almost twenty-three years old and my gosh! I should have my own sense about me by then.

Wedding with Some Hitches

The wedding was set at the Federated Church in Kellogg at 2:00 in the afternoon of Easter Sunday, April 6, 1947. Ernie arranged it because I was teaching, and it was his town. Mother, Dad, my baby brother, Bobby, who was seventeen years old, then; my brothers Bill and Gene and his wife, Marjorie, arrived two days early. The only others of my people coming were my Aunt Marie and Aunt Ella, who were to arrive on Saturday but hadn't shown up. Only an hour before the wedding, they came tapping on my apartment door. They were all tattered and torn and looked like they had been through something backwards.

They hugged me and I said, "Marie! Ella! Where have you been?"

They told me the bus had turned over in a ditch. A wrecker had pulled the bus out and it had gone on to Spokane with their suitcases and dress-up clothes. They were all bruised and scratched and Aunt Ella had some glass in her eye.

Both of my aunts are well-educated and Aunt Ella is a poet with a farm woman's sense of humor, so she struck a pose and recited: "Here we are all tattered and torn. Without our clothes on Easter morn."

None of my dresses fit either aunt. Aunt Marie tried to jam her size seven foot into my size five open-toed high heels. We got to laughing and decided they'd have to wear the shoes and dresses they came in.

We arrived at the church twenty minutes before two. I was wearing a pretty, white beaded wedding dress. From the back of the church, I peeked out as all the well-dressed Damiano relatives went past. Ernie's

■ After the long wait at the church, Ernest and Betty Menzel Damiano are all smiles as they stand ready to cut their wedding cake, April 6, 1947

sister, Rose, was there with her two daughters and they were stunningly beautiful. Edie looked like Hedy Lamar. So here they went, just gorgeous, and there went my aunts looking like they'd just come in from traveling around the world on foot. I was not going to impress anybody. And the other relatives that came from Spokane must have thought, "Oh! Poor Ernie. He's gotten into what kind of a fix here."

The bridesmaid was Lois Rinaldi and the matron of honor was Ernie's youngest sister, Mary Pickolick. Her little girl, Mary Frances, was flower girl. Aside from my folks, I hardly knew anybody except Mrs. O'Neill, who was going to sing for my wedding, and some people from around town who only knew me as Betty the dance teacher.

Ernie hadn't come. We waited and waited and we waited. Mrs. O'Neill sang her song at 2:00. She sang another song. And another. The preacher came in looking all worried and rubbed my hands. And where was Ernie? He was always so prompt!

He was waiting at Mrs. Taggart's with his brother, Lewis, who had come by bus from Seattle to be his best man. His brother-in-law, John Pickolick, had taken Ernie's new car to drive Mary and Mary Frances to the church and was supposed to go back and pick up Ernie and Lewis and bring them to the church. But John thought Ernie was at our apartment.

Before she left, Mrs. Taggart had said to Ernie, "Sure you don't want to ride with me? It's ten minutes till two right now!"

Ernie said, "No, because if we do, then John will come and wonder where we are."

It got to be 2:00 and John still hadn't come, so they started walking. A taxi came along. Ernie, all dressed up, little boutonniere and everything, waved it down.

Cab driver says, "Where you going?"

Ernie says, "To a wedding, and I'm late. Do you mind taking us?"

There was a fare in the cab. The guy says, "Well, take them!" And he says, "Whose wedding is it?"

Ernie says, "It's mine! This is my best man and we're 20 minutes late already!"

And there *we* were, Mrs. O'Neill singing four times, the preacher looking at his watch and rubbing my hands, a whole church full of people turning around and looking. I was afraid they were going to leave.

Then the wedding march started and there was Ernie and his best man at the front of the church, and suddenly everything was all right. I went down the aisle on my father's arm and pretty soon we were saying "I do," and the "D" on my Valentine compact was for real.

Meantime, my brothers crossed some of the spark plug wires on Ernie's brand new Chevrolet. Big joke! Ernie finally got the car going but it coughed its way to Coeur d'Alene and I suspected he wanted to kill my brothers. But I knew they were back in Wallace laughing, and I laughed, too. That was like our family. When things go wrong, that's the time to laugh. We were headed for a honeymoon in a nice motel.

Mrs. O'Neill let me have only two days off and I was back teaching dance. Ernie always resented that. We thought we'd take a second honeymoon, but we never did. We started having children right away.

Caged

After I found I was going to have a baby, I kept on teaching till September. Then the change to being caged in the house drove me crazy because I had been taken out of a tremendous life and absolute freedom and I had been going places and all of a sudden I wasn't. I just *never* had been held down before.

I told Ernie, "I need a piano. I know we don't have a lot of money, but I *need* a piano!"

Ernie mentioned it at work to Ed Morin. He and Beulah happened to have one.

Ed says, "It's in storage. You can have it for $100 and pay for it as you want."

Soon I was playing every kind of music on that piano, from morning when Ernie left for work till he came home at night. It was the best therapy in the world.

Children

But after Rita, I never again stopped teaching. Rita was born February 12, 1948; Anita Jo, December 19, 1949; Vicki, March 2, 1952; and Joni, April 20, 1956. Our children were exciting and each one so different.

Ernie as Teacher

Ernie doesn't sing but had heard his dad sing a lot. As the girls grew old enough, it was Ernie that trained them to sing from the heart. He taught them stage presence. For 15 years he delivered them by car to private lessons in piano, organ, or accordion. When I was gone teaching 3 P.M. to 8 P.M. four days a week, Ernie was always there when the kids got home. And when I taught on Saturdays, Ernie would comb their long hair into pony tails and even tie them with a ribbon as I always did.

Teaching Special Children

I had never been able to teach Rita to sew, and she had trouble reading in the first and second grades. Early in her training in my dance class when I was teaching mirror image, I realized she was seeing in reverse. At that time they didn't know about dyslexia.

I taught many children that were considered "slow." I told the mother of one such girl, "Please realize that she is seeing in reverse. Give her time and patience and let her know what she's seeing is not wrong. It's just the way the rest of the world interprets it."

Another mother worried why her third grader was performing for my dance classes but not doing well in school. She had been told her daughter could never make it through the eighth grade and was crying as she told me.

I said, "Sit down. Let me tell you about my Rita and these other kids. Your daughter is not backward. She's sharp as a tack. Imagine yourself with backward vision and having to turn it around and give it back to the teacher within a second. Just love her through these difficulties and tell her she *can* do it." And she could! She became an honor student.

A couple of parents asked me to give exercise classes for handicapped children at the little school at Black Bear up Nine Mile Canyon. I drove up there once a week. Then the Opportunity School at Wallace moved down to Silverton in the old Memorial Hall, so I continued there teaching about 20 retarded or handicapped children whose physical condition made them appear unable to do gymnastics. But I never allowed myself to say they couldn't do it. The kids did soft-shoe, basic ballet, head stands, tap dancing, bridges, and somersaults. They completed the basic skills required for first-year work.

At the end of each year we put on a program, as I did in all my other classes, so parents could see them demonstrate their skills. They performed beautifully. It's wonderful what children can do when you let them think they can!

Montana Vacation

During the miner's strike in the summer of 1961, we loaded the dog, two parakeets, and the four kids into the station wagon and went to Bozeman, Montana, where Ernie had found a job as a machinist repairing and making parts for farm equipment. We rented an apartment from Aunt Ella. The kids were five, nine, twelve, and thirteen. We lived near a cousin who paid Rita to keep her house clean. Rita saved $20 and spent it on a bathing suit even though she couldn't swim.

I said, "You do look beautiful in it, but you're going to find out its utilization. I'm signing us up for swimming lessons at the municipal pool."

Joni was only five years old and had to watch through the fence. It was cold some days, even had snow, and Ernie was concerned about it. I had always been afraid of water so I learned with the little kids. The second day, I was blowing bubbles and here came 'Nita off the high dive. I just panicked. But she hit the water and swam over to the side.

In the six weeks of lessons all three of the older girls and I learned to swim. It's been a wonderful thing!

Meantime, we visited the four ranches of my uncles. The kids rode on loads of hay, watched threshing machines work, and got in on those great big threshing crew meals with 30 at a table. Vicki named herself "Buck" and wore a cowboy hat and boots. She spent a lot of time riding horses and singing in a cowboy voice. It was a wonderful summer. We came back home in time for school.

Ski School and Schedule Change

I had been teaching dance on Saturdays only, which gave me the whole week to be home with my children. I'd start at 8:00 in the morning and quit at 6:00 at night. Made a long day. But then the kids wanted to go to that wonderful ski school that opened at Lookout Pass. That brought about a tremendous change in Ernie's work schedule so he could be home afternoons because I started teaching Mondays through Thursdays. Then we had weekends for skiing.

Spokane Frowned on Me

I taught ballet, acrobatic, and tap dancing because I thought the students needed rounding in all three. Dance teachers in Spokane frowned on me because they thought tap was out of date. But when actress Ruby Keeler came tapping back into popularity at age sixty, tap schools sprang up all over the country.

All My Girls Took Music

When our three oldest girls attended the University of Idaho, degrees in dance were not offered, so all of them took music in addition to a major. They all sing beautifully. Rita took sociology. Anita Jo took voice. She now has a dance school in Nampa, Idaho. Vicki had a liking for math, which she inherited from Ernie, and turned out to be a paralegal secretary. Joni attended Boise State University and earned a degree in voice. She then worked for me a year. But she longed to go further in dancing and won a scholarship to study at Oklahoma University.

When Joni took lessons there from Bill Graham, one of the nation's best tap dance teachers, he was impressed and asked, "Where did you learn to tap?"

Instead of saying, "From my mom," Joni said, "In northern Idaho."

Bill Graham said, "I didn't know there's an Idaho in the United States. And you learned tap in Idaho? I just can't believe it!"

Joan and Don Springer

Joan and Don Springer moved here from New Jersey about 1954, and Joan brought her girl, Diane, to me for dance lessons. I went down to her place, played piano, and coaxed Joan to sing. And my gosh! her voice raised the hair on my arms.

I said, "Joan! You've got a marvelous voice. We've got to have you on stage."

"Oh, no! Not me! I'm big and awkward."

It's true, she was a big, heavy woman, but I felt that strange thing about her voice and couldn't let her alone. It took me three months to talk her into it. When she walked out on stage, she was scared to death. But when she sang, it brought the house down.

Next morning she phoned, "I'm tellin' you, this fat old broad feels ten feet tall and twice as skinny."

From then on, Joan and Don Springer were an integral part of all our productions along with Ernie and me. We couldn't have done it without them.

Community Benefits

Over a period of more than 20 years, our dance studio spent all the proceeds from recitals, programs, minstrel shows, and benefits for community needs. Those who benefited were organizations like the Lions, Kiwanis, and Parent-Teacher Organizations. We bought a resuscitator for the fire department, a wheelchair for a guy that broke his back, fencing for the cemetery, microfilm reader for the library, and the Opportunity bus. For the school we provided many, many lights, matching funds for stage curtains, and the tripod for the grand piano. I could go on and on. Ernie insisted that I donate all those earnings. That way we could always walk away feeling good.

On Stage

I have never felt the need of performing. The last time I had performed was when Ernie saw me do "Fire Dance" on the stage of the Liberty Theater in 1946. In May 1985, Jerrod Krulitz, an eight-year-old, didn't want to go on stage alone. I told Ernie I was going to perform with the boy so he wouldn't get shocked out of his boots. No one else expected to see me on stage because my name wasn't on the program. I donned my costume with leotards and fringe. And man! When I walked out on the stage with that boy, I forgot I was sixty-one years old and hadn't performed in 39 years.

When you go on stage, there's a feeling comes over you like you're another person. Absolutely alone, completely at ease, you feel like you're handing the audience a gift. It's an "at-home" feeling. A wonderful feeling! And that's what makes performers starve to get back on stage. It isn't for fame, it's to be "at home."

People went wild. I couldn't believe how great I felt. I performed two nights in a row.

Last Performance

There was no way I could know this really was my last performance. In the dead of winter, December 14, 1985, I was teaching a small class in gymnastics. I had told the little girl, "Now when you put your hands down, you're going to kick over."

Before I was prepared, she kicked over, and I must have turned my face at the same time. The soft heel of her ballet shoe caught me on the left cheek like a karate chop. It threw me against the wall. I felt the crack as my cheek snapped. My first thought was, "I didn't want to scare any of the kids."

Then I wondered: How does a boxer go 13 more rounds after this happens to him?

I got up shielding my face and went in to the restroom mirror. It was scary looking! My cheekbone was sunk in a hole about the size of a golf ball. It immediately began to swell so then it didn't look so bad.

I came out. A few parents were sitting around. I could not talk to them.

I said to my assistant in a low voice, "Carla, I've been hurt. Here's the keys. Please either lock up or finish the class. They've got an hour left."

She said, "What in the world . . . ?"

I said, "Don't ask questions. I'm hurt bad."

As I walked past some ladies in the doorway, one said, "Can we take you home?" I knew I shouldn't get into anybody's car because I was in shock and couldn't tell them which way to go.

I answered, "No, no. I'm fine."

I knew enough to walk home to Ernie, two and a half blocks over the berms of snow.

I said, "Ernie! I broke my nose."

By this time it was even more swollen and didn't look that bad. He got dressed and took me down to Dr. Scott.

His nurse, Ann Wilson says, "You've been hurt, baby, haven't you?"

I said, "I think so."

Dr. Scott x-rayed me. The cheekbone was completely smashed under and the flange in my nose was smashed up against the other cheekbone.

This was on Monday night. Thursday morning I was back for surgery. Dr. Scott entered from the inside and pushed the bone and tissue back into place, leaving not one mark on my face. A beautiful job!

I didn't tell him I might have a problem with inherited bleeding. He packed my nose.

"Betty!" he says. "If this comes out dry and you're not bleeding, you're O.K." When it came out with no bleeding, I thought: Amen!

This was Christmas holiday time. I ordered $7,000 worth of costumes and put a whole show together. And I don't remember doing it.

Summertime came. I had a real sharp pain in my right eye like a red flash. That must have been my retina tearing away.

In August the eye doctor said, "The retina may grow back if it isn't completely torn off. Why don't we give it a chance? Meantime, don't snap your head or do any hard leaps or jumps."

I signed up a class, but September ninth the eye doctor said I might become blind in one eye. I felt real bad about that. I closed the school. It was traumatic.

I then went to Dr. Lloyd, a behavioral psychologist, who put me, strapped down, through a tunnel while they took pictures [MRI, or Magnetic Resonant Imaging]. It was like being buried alive. I could hear Ernie encouraging me from the other end of the tunnel.

The pictures, clearer than x-rays, showed five glitzes in my head where something had happened to my nerves. Real sharp little lights: one on each side of my forehead and two at the base of my skull caused by the snap of that heel karate chop.

I'm due for another eye examination. The nerves are healing but the retina hasn't changed. Wondering if I'll get sight back in my right eye, I get a clutch in my stomach.

I'm changing my career. I've signed up for a correspondence course in English Composition at the university because I have this urge to write up some of these things I've learned about teaching children.

Postscript June 21, 1994

BETTY: I finished that course with a four point. I have been writing off and on. I was back teaching dance half time until Joni came back to take over for me.

■ BETTY AND ERNIE DAMIANO

Interviewed 1987 at Osburn, Idaho.

BETTY: I thought this mining district was a terrible place when I first came, but learned it did have advantages. When I lived in Bozeman, a college town, it had class distinctions. Over here there were no class distinctions. In school and everywhere else, the millionaires' kids sat next to miners' kids. Another thing that was so neat about this place, the Bunker Hill being a local mine, they cared about kids getting an education. Our first two girls had Bunker Hill scholarships.

ERNIE: The Hecla and Bunker Hill gave out 20 to 25 scholarships a year to students with the right grades. At first the scholarships went only to kids of people who worked at Hecla and Bunker, but then the Internal Revenue ruled that scholarships had to be open to everybody.

Each department in Bunker gave a summer job to four or five college kids so they could earn money for school. I heard one boss from Bunker who was considered a tough sonofagun speak at a meeting: "When they work for me, they work! I put the desire into more kids to go to college more than anyone in the county."

Later, other mines and the Kingsbury brokerage house gave scholarships, too.

BETTY: Those scholarships gave the boost some needed. And the student could go to any college in Idaho.

Ernie wanted to go to college when we were first married, and I wanted him to because he had the ability, even though he had to quit school after the eighth grade. But we had a car and a home to pay for and pretty soon the first two children. Ernie was afraid he'd put us in jeopardy if he quit his job, give up the good Bunker health plan that covered all of us, and went to school. Ernie always felt badly he didn't go. I felt badly, too. I guess I should have pushed harder.

ERNIE: It was my passion to go to school, but G.I. education didn't pay enough to support a family. And I was almost 30 then.

Later, when I worked in the Bunker machine shop, I took a few machinist courses by correspondence, and the Company paid for them.

A Career Woman

BETTY: I knew women *must* have something more than housework, and I had a career. When I first met Ernie I said, "I don't want to give up my dancing." He said, "You won't have to give up your dancing." 'Course I think he has swallowed hard over those words since then. He learned to deal with not only my dancing, singing, and playing musical instruments, but with four girls besides.

We had only one bathroom for five women and Ernie. We had a rule that if anybody wanted to use the bathroom, she must check with Ernie first and tell him how long she'd be there. Remember the "pompy" hairdos? The three teenagers got 20 minutes. And they could do it!

They practiced singing, accordion, organ, and piano in shifts in the morning.

ERNIE: I don't think there was ever another household like this. When I left for work about a quarter after six in the morning, I'd go out the door laughing because there'd be four little girls around the piano singing to beat heck and Betty playing. Other times she'd be in there playing and the kids washing and drying dishes, singing away.

As if Betty didn't have enough to do, other boys and girls joined and pretty soon she had two or three groups coming. The boys came at 6:30 in the morning because she didn't have time later in the day.

BETTY: I always picked the ones who could harmonize naturally. We practiced two times a week and we worked hard at it. We sang all kinds of songs including madrigals. The Peter, Paul and Mary group was popular then and we did a lot of their songs, and folk songs, and a gavotte by Bach that Terry Stevenson still sings. Even wore matching outfits. Soon our groups were singing all over and at different schools and made a big hit.

Early morning practice is not easy. This one boy was a darned good musician, but he liked to party.

I said, "I don't care, Terry! You be here at 6:30 or you're out!"

Know what he'd do? He'd stay up the rest of the night and fall asleep out front in his car so he wouldn't miss the practice.

McCarthy

This was during the time of McCarthy. We were singing songs like "I've Been Working On The Railroad" and Malvina Reynolds' "Ticky Tacky, All The Little Houses" and this lady high school teacher—really, it was kind of breathtaking—she waited till all the boys left and there was just my girls and me there and she came in and pointed her finger at me and said, "You're singing communist songs and you're a communist!"

Later, we had phone calls accusing us. I phoned the head of the Republican Party—two of her boys were singing in our group—and told her our problem. After that they no longer pointed their fingers at me!

But at that time, Ernie was on the city council of Osburn and they started pointing the finger at him.

ERNIE: You remember the McCarthy era? When we negotiated with the Company they brought in a guy who claimed he was one time a communist. He spoke at the school and different places saying our union, the Mine, Mill & Smelter Workers Union, was communist. I don't know if there were communists in it. None of the guys I knew were communists. But it gave the union a bad name and eventually the union was kicked out of the AFL-CIO, which made it worse. Anyhow, the whole object was to bust the union, and pretty soon no decent person would run for any office in the union because you were branded. I couldn't do it. It was too much of a load to carry. Anyway, it finally broke up the Mine-Mill, and the United Steelworkers became our union.

Loyalty Oath

The loyalty oath only involved people who worked for the city, the schools, and the county—people whose salaries were paid by tax money. They had to sign the loyalty oath or they could lose their job. Us members of the Osburn City Council weren't paid.

So I said, "We don't have to sign any loyalty oath. It isn't right! My God, what's happening to this country?"

The others agreed that we wouldn't sign. We'd make a stand.

About two days later, they came over to my house and said, "You might as well give up, Ernie. We've decided to sign it."

I said, "Oh no! I just can't do it." They tried to talk me into it.

BETTY: It was a Sunday afternoon. They came about two o'clock and stayed two hours. "Ernie! You're a good guy. Why can't you just do this?" They said, "Why not? Look what you're doing to your family. What prevents you from signing?"

ERNIE: I told them, "My pride prevents me."

Then they came to the house again and I said, "I spent four years in the army, nine months of it in Alaska, 13 months in the Aleutian Islands, and the rest of the time in Europe. Isn't that enough to prove I'm faithful to this country? Why hell!" I said. "Signing that isn't going to mean nothing. I suspect you guys of being communists. If I was a communist, I would break a leg getting there to sign it so I wouldn't look bad. And here I am, a patriotic citizen, and I'm still not going to sign it."

I got books on the Constitution from the library and made notes to justify my position. There were five men on that council including a lawyer and the city attorney arguing against me. I don't think the attorney had read the Constitution because I caught him up on a lot of things.

The first thing he told me, "Well, you'll have to resign if you won't sign this loyalty oath."

I said, "Alden, you've had a lot of schooling, and you're an attorney, but don't you know the only way you can get an elected city official out is to have a recall election? Even school kids know this."

The councilmen kinda smirked. In a sense these guys were for me, but they didn't have guts enough.

The attorney general of Idaho called me and said if I wouldn't resign, they would hold back any funds going to the city of Osburn. I looked up the law. I don't remember if I wrote him or told him over the phone, but I was laughing. "Yeah! The legislature can legislate a law, but it can't enforce it."

Then he told me any ordinance I voted on wouldn't be legal.

I told him, "I don't care if it isn't legal. I'm still going to vote."

BETTY: Others had heard about Ernie fighting it and people like the police and teachers came and said, "Gee, Ernie! I don't want to sign that loyalty oath. Do I have to sign that?"

ERNIE: I said, "Well, if it means your wages, go ahead. The state can't stop my pay. They can't fire me, but they can fire you. What are you going to gain by being fired? If the whole school refused, it would mean something, but one or two isn't going to mean nothing. Now the Supreme Court is going to decide it because some professors at the University of Idaho instituted a lawsuit." I had seen their names in the paper and wrote them to ask if I could be included in their suit, but they said it was too late.

BETTY: That suit was a light at the end of the tunnel for Ernie. When he found others were fighting against it, too, it made a lot of difference.

Campaigning

ERNIE: During this time, my term on the Osburn City Council ran out. I had told Betty I wasn't going to run anymore. But then I wondered if they would try to prevent me from running and it made me mad.

I said, "Damn it! I'm going to find out if people are for me or against me." I had a little trouble getting the 25 signatures on the nominating petition. Just for dang meanness, I went to one of the councilmen that had signed the loyalty oath and made him sign my petition.

BETTY: They liked him, but they were scared.

ERNIE: I ran again and got more votes than any other one that was running. It made me feel good.

President Kennedy

One of the craziest things happened when President Kennedy got killed. That night when I got home, our kids were laying on the floor bawling to beat heck. I got them quieted down and went over to the city hall to put the flag at half-mast. And this same man that I'd made sign my petition was there, and he wasn't going to put the flag at half-mast. We damn near got in a fight. Some of those people that were always making trouble and calling others communist, that day at school, their kids had said they were glad Kennedy got killed. I went out to the flag pole and put the flag at half-mast like you're supposed to do.

BETTY: Such people don't realize there's the president's office to be respected whether they like him or not. My point is that you've got to protect those who don't think like you do. You might not agree with them, but you'd better support their rights, otherwise there's no freedom for anybody and you're a hypocrite.

ERNIE: At the Bunker, the loyalty oath never came up. I don't think they cared. But I suppose I could have got 100 percent union support over not signing it.

FIFTEEN

CHARLES AND TEG ADDINGTON

CHARLES ADDINGTON

Interviewed 1991 at Harrison, Idaho.

WHEN I WAS TWELVE, I had a cayuse named Pet, half Indian pony and half jack. She would throw you if you got a little bit sassy. About all we ever rode her was just to town—and that was on the level. You didn't want to get her on a hillside, 'cause she'd stop, get her head down or back end down, and you couldn't hang on, you'd slide off. You could never keep a saddle on her, either. [My brother] Glenn and I was the only two of us kids that rode her.

I'll never forget one time when I tied her up in the barn with the other horses to feed 'em. Went back to the barn later, turned all the horses loose and moseyed on out to the barnyard. She quit her feed and come runnin' out. I never paid any attention to her. When she got even with me, she hauled off and kicked me in the stomach and turned right around, walked back in the barn and started eatin'.

Later on, the guy that bought her for packing had to quit usin' her. She'd find two trees that she couldn't get through and go in between 'em till she squeezed the pack off. She was smart.

Ernest, Ermon, and Ethel were still living at home. My sister Lela and her husband, Jack Wagner, lived where Angelo and Joyce Bissell now live. I was the youngest, born April 11, 1909.

Shingle Bay Homestead

We lived at Shingle Bay where my folks, Mary and Winfield Addington, had homesteaded in 1910. There were some mounds up on top of the hill above the house that we figured were Indian mounds. If you stomped on them, they'd sound hollow. We never did dig any of them out. My Uncle Charles lived there and he wouldn't let us. They are still there. But when we plowed the field where Bissells live, there were eight shallow graves and we couldn't help but plow up the skeletons. There was one grave in the bank where the road that goes around the lakeshore had cut through. Glenn dug in the bank and got some Indian beads.

Log Gets Cow

Our spring was up on top of the hill in that draw to the left, if you was facin' uphill, and the overflow ran down to the Miekle place. The Miekle place is now owned by Bissells. They bought it from Billy [Mildred] Ryan, the lady who had the dog kennels. We didn't own the ground the spring was on. I don't know whose place it was on, but Dad built a cement box to hold water and piped it down to the house. We had gravity flow with pretty fair pressure.

When Russell & Pugh [Lumber Company] put in that new log chute, we had two or three milk cows. One of 'em headed for a drink over in the draw. She stepped across the chute, and the very first log that came down the chute got her.

Dad was real easy going. He used his strongest swear word, "Oh, shaw!"

[Russell & Pugh had a logging camp on the Harrison Flats where Jim and Bernice Boe live now. From there, the logs were hauled by team and wagon a half mile down a sloping ravine. Then a donkey engine cable was attached to the tongue of the wagon, which pulled the horses and load up a steep grade to the level of the Flats again. The team then pulled the load of logs another half mile to the Archie Porter place at the edge of the Flats, where a new log chute had been built down the steep mountainside. The chute crossed under the county road and the Union Pacific Railroad track. By the time the logs reached the end of the chute, they had built up terrific velocity. They jumped through the air and hit Lake Coeur d'Alene with a big splash.]

Posts, Wood, and Apples

Shortly after the folks homesteaded, Dad made cedar posts to sell. He loaded them into a railroad car at the siding at Lacon and shipped them into the Palouse country.

He had a woodyard on the beach for selling cord wood to the St. Joe Boom Company. The Boom Company had a sorting gap at the mouth of the St. Joe River. Any log that wasn't branded went into the wood boom. Then they'd take that boom over to Dad's yard. He'd saw the logs into four-foot lengths. He hired men to split and pile eight cords a day for a dollar a cord. They made eight dollars a day. Doggone right! That was big money. A cord is a pile of wood that is four-by-four-by-eight feet.

When the Boom Company had a tow of branded logs ready to be pulled to Coeur d'Alene, they'd send a barge over and Dad would load it up with wood to burn to run the steamboat.

Along about 1932, I was hauling logs out of O'Gara when I run into Jim Keating and he says, "I'd like to get some wood cut. I'll pay you a dollar a cord for four-foot wood."

Norman Woods, my brother-in-law, my brother Ermon, and I took him on for that. Startin' the last of November, we felled the trees, limbed 'em up, sawed 'em into four-foot wood with a cross-cut saw, split and piled 128 cords.

The Depression was on and we had our money comin' when President Roosevelt closed the banks [March 9, 1933].

Jim said, "I've got some money in a safety deposit box in Spokane. I'll go over tonight, and tomorrow I'll get the money and be back tomorrow night."

He come back with the money, paid us off and said, "Now if you want more work, I've got land I want dug up and cleared of redroot." Redroot is a common brush with white blossoms. When rubbed, it makes kind of a soap.

So we took that on and made a little more money. After Ermon and I bought gasoline and the little we just had to have, we turned the rest of our money over to the folks. But that's all the money the ten of us had to live on that winter and spring until May.

Dad grew apples in our old orchard and then started a new one with 400 apple trees of every variety. It was over across on the point toward the old Master's place. The Master's place was right back of Shingle Bay where those tall poplar's were.

Tracking Deer Two Days

Dad didn't eat much meat. He hated to get fat in his mouth, and if he did, he'd spit it out. There weren't many deer in this country then, but he'd hunt around Shingle Bay and get one every year. This one year, there was a little snow on the ground and he started out about daylight, taking his time, tracking this deer. He followed it clear to Grass Mountain, and then it came back to that field, just to the right of the old

 Baron place. Johnny Baron's place was just to the right of the road that turns off the O'Gara road, going up to Bill Lavigne's. It was gettin' dark so he stopped tracking the deer in that field. Next morning he followed it again and got it over toward Keating's place.

Best Schoolteacher

I had to walk three and a half miles to school in Harrison. Seven miles a day. Bert Russell and I were in the first grade together and Miss Carns was our teacher. We had Mrs. Howe in the eighth grade—best teacher there ever was. She made you work but didn't yell at you. We had to pass a state examination to get out of the eighth grade, so we put in the last month studying for it. There was very few kids in her class that didn't pass, but if they didn't, they stayed in the eighth grade.

Crummy High School

I thought Harrison had a crummy high school, so my mother took Glenn and me to Portland where we lived there with my brother Ermon. He was working down on the docks, doing office work for Kerr-Gifford. Dad stayed home, tryin' to keep us in money. My mother just stayed with us one winter. Then we boarded out. I graduated in three and a half years.

Tallyman

After I came back from Portland, I hunted quite a lot. Then I got a job tallying for Jack Glenn. Jack Glenn and Jim Moore were scaling all the logs that came through the St. Joe Sorting Gap. There were a lot of logs come down that river. I liked to tally those big Marble Creek logs. They'd have brail lines on them, and would have a big butt to sit on while you wrote down the scale. Then I went to Kinman Business College for three or four months, but I didn't like it. I'd rather be outside.

Three C's

There wasn't anything to do. That was Depression times. Then Norman and I got in the three C's [Civilian Conservation Corp]. The pay was $30 a month. We got to keep $5 a month, and $25 was sent direct to your parents. That was the purpose of the three C's—to help families.

The camp was run by army men from Fort Wright in Spokane. A sergeant was loaning money between paydays to these guys from New Jersey. One payday when the sergeant came around to collect his money, Norman was whittling fans out of white pine. One of the kids said, "I'll give you a dollar for that fan."

That five dollars we got to keep out of our wages just wasn't enough for Norman, so he was always looking for a way to make more money.

Norman says to me, "We got it made! Let's start making fans."

So we'd make fans for a month, get a box of them down there right behind the lieutenant, and what payday money the sergeant didn't collect for his loans, we took for our fans.

Fed Misinformation

On the Elk River road job, most guys was easterners but there was a few locals to herd 'em around. Norman Woods and Gaylord Donahoe were truck drivers—taking 'em out to work or getting 'em back to camp. I was a truck driver, too, but I was more or less a handyman, taking supplies and tools out to the job.

You could tell those guys from New Jersey almost anything and they'd believe it. We fed them a lot of misinformation, and scared 'em into thinkin' a bear might get 'em.

One of the guys from St. Maries had an old water sack. A New Jersey kid was looking at it and asked what it was for.

The St. Maries guy said, "Well, that's what you carry water in when out in the woods."

The kid said, "You've told me lots of stories but that's one I'm not going to believe!" And that's the only honest thing he'd been told!

Steal Your Women

There were some pretty good guys in the bunch, but some people in town weren't very nice to them. But then, some of them weren't very nice to the people out here, either. They'd try to date some women!

TEG: That's what hurt you local guys. They'd try to steal your women. My brothers used to get so mad. They'd go to dances and say, "All you girls want to do is dance with those old CC's." Some of them were good dancers! But they were from the inner cities and you couldn't understand 'em when they'd talk to you.

CHARLES: By fall we had worked that road up over Elk Butte and down to about eight miles from Boehl's cabin when the weather changed. The easterners were only here for summertime work, so they were sent back home and the locals were moved down to Pocano for the winter.

Building St. Joe River Road

Pocano is on the railroad eight miles below Marble Creek. We stayed in army barracks and slept in bunks—one lower and one upper.

Every morning we crossed the river in a swiftwater boat to get to work. We were drilling and blasting those rock bluffs out, building the St. Joe River road. I only ran jackhammer once in awhile. Most of the time I was packing steel. You didn't have diamond head on your steel drill like they have now. The bits were blacksmith hardened. When your bit got dull, it had to be taken to the blacksmith and sharp steel brought back. That was my job.

In the spring we worked up above Bovill to Collins Creek.

Fighting Fire

I was cutting trails when I left the three C's in '35 to work one summer in blister rust for the Forest Service because they paid more. When we got called out to fight fire, we got really good pay. That was hard work—daylight to dark. You were cutting logs out of the trail, or digging down to mineral soil and throwing the duff back into the fire, making a trail of bare ground that the fire couldn't burn across.

The next year, I went to work for Bob Woods. I worked the next 12 years on brush disposal for Bob all over the country, wherever there was a logging camp.

Bear First Aid

I visited a camp out of Clarkia on Merry Creek. They had a screened-in box for meat above the creek. The cook shot and wounded a bear that was trying to get into it, and I took off after it, thinking to finish it off. How foolish I was! I followed the bear's bloody trail until all of a sudden it stopped. After the bear had got out away from camp, he had packed his wound with needles. I saw needles with blood on 'em, but from there on, there wasn't any blood trail. And I never caught up with that bear.

Many Jobs

After Teg and I were married, she cooked for the camp on Meadow Creek the summer of the last year I worked for Bob.

That fall, we moved back to Harrison and I worked at the Russell & Pugh sawmill at Springston.

During World War II, Teg's sister and her husband had two farms and wanted us to move onto one at Sanders. We stayed one year, but it just didn't work out, so we moved back to Harrison again. I worked for Russell & Pugh, doing just about everything—on the greenchain, the planer, in the yard, and run the stacker for the dry kiln for a couple of years.

In '49 we moved to Kellogg and I went to work in the Bunker Hill zinc plant because the pay was better. You worked year-round and could work as much overtime as you could stand.

Stripper

I started out as a stripper in the zinc plant. There's a solution that runs over cells full of aluminum plates, and the electrolytic process causes the zinc to adhere to those plates and makes sheets of zinc. The plates were about two-foot-eight by three and a half, with seven plates to a cell. You had an electric truck with a handle on it loaded with empty plates. You pulled a plate loaded with zinc out of the cell and put an empty back in. You'd move ahead to the next cell and do the same thing until you got a load. Then you took this load of full plates out to the stripping room, used a chisel to loosen the zinc, stripped and stacked it. You had to make eight loads a day.

Utility Man, Pickler, Shift Foreman

I went from there to utility man. That work was seeing things were taken care of, like checking batteries, checking cells, putting in guides, just doing anything that had to be done.

Then I went to pickler. That was changing solutions. I worked in the basement. The solution was pumped up overhead, then down into the cells, and back down to the basement into tanks. That wasn't as physically hard as being a stripper.

After some years, I was moved up to shift foreman.

When I first went to work at the zinc plant, we stayed two weeks on each shift. Then the rotation changed to seven days of graveyard, then you had two off, and seven days on swing shift, off two, and then seven days of day shift, off two, and back to graveyard.

Stress

The old Bunker—your boss never gave you any trouble there. Gulf Resources—they was always lookin' down your neck. There wasn't a foreman that wasn't prayin' for the day he could retire.

You couldn't stand up for the men and still be a company man; you had to be one or the other. And if you did fire a man, then the union stepped in. Those two things riding you, and at the same time there was bickering between men working overtime about who got the loads. So they started a gypo system and the foreman had to keep track of that.

 Then the superintendent would decide you ought to do things a little different. There was too much stress.

I had a heart attack in 1967. I just couldn't stand the pain. It was more or less in my back. Keller, my boss, took me to first aid and Dr. Whitsel took me to the hospital.

I wasn't in any hurry to get back to work; I got paid while I was off.

TEG: The old Bunker Hill couldn't be beat. That town would still be alive if it were still there. If the school, the town, or anybody needed *anything—anywhere*, all you had to do was go to Bunker Hill.

CHARLES: There was still ore there and the old Bunker Hill would have mined it to keep going. Instead of that, Gulf Resources came in, took the high grade, and got out.

Lost Medical Insurance

I wasn't working there when the mine closed. In 1971, they let out 70 or 80 foremen—salaried men—and that's when I got it. I'd worked there 22½ years. I was retirement age and went on Social Security and the Bunker pension plan. You can draw on both. Teg and I were covered by Medical Service Bureau (MSB) insurance, which had been carried by Bunker, then Gulf, as part of my wages. Teg wasn't considered a member of MSB, but it paid her bills on my membership.

When Gulf closed down, they kept up the pension but dropped our medical insurance. Since I was a member, I could stay on MSB, but had to pay my own premiums. But they wouldn't let Teg become a member because she'd had a little heart problem.

TEG: I had carried MSB with the hospital group plan where I worked and with Bunker Hill/Gulf Resources for 20 years before Gulf closed down.

When I retired, April 28, 1981, I had gone up to the office and asked the MSB man, "Which plan should I carry, the one from the hospital or the one from Gulf Resources?" The hospital group plan had better coverage but I would have to pay the premium. Covered under Charles's plan, we'd pay nothing because Gulf had to continue paying that.

The MSB guy says, "You can't beat that Gulf Resource MSB plan. You better carry it." So I dropped my MSB group plan from the hospital. Two weeks later, Gulf Resources closed down and they canceled Charles's policy. And I couldn't get back on the MSB hospital group plan I had dropped only two weeks earlier. MSB said they couldn't take me because they'd have to consider me a new member. And because of my medical record, I wouldn't be accepted and do that to their old members. And I'd been *paying* for 20 years to both MSB plans!

No company would take me. Being without any insurance was scary. It was making me sick. I'd lay awake at night, wondering what in the world we would do. Finally, after two years, Banker's Life let me buy insurance, but it was very expensive. It was like a policy insuring foreigners coming into the country and it had to be renewed every six months.

Steel Workers Sue

CHARLES: The Steelworkers Union sued Gulf Resources for our medical insurance. Salaried people weren't union members. We didn't pay dues to the Steelworkers, but we were figured as employees of Gulf Resources. So when they won that suit, we were covered by it.

We were reimbursed for all our medical expenses and insurance premiums for five years back. I was paying $65 and Teg was paying $90 a month at the time.

And the beauty of it is, it's the best medical insurance you can find. It pays anything Medicare doesn't pay, including medicine.

I've had a pacemaker about five years. Last summer the specialist put me on some medication because my heart wasn't acting quite right. I had cardiac infarction, but there wasn't much damage. I haven't had any heart irregularity since, so I kicked about taking the medicine and this doctor in St. Maries told me to try cutting down. I cut down all right—I cut it out.

■ TEG ADDINGTON

Interviewed 1991 at Harrison, Idaho.

I was born April 29, 1919, on a little place between Santa and Fernwood, Idaho. Many years later the Seventh-Day Adventists put in a mill there, and it was called Peanutville.

My dad, Richard Marion Seaman, worked in the woods, farmed, and just did everything he could to make a living for his family of six boys and four girls.

Before my father was married, he worked for Jim Angus in Pine City, Washington. When Jim Angus got TB [tuberculosis], he had Dad write to his brother, who was a doctor in Chicago, to come out and take care of him. Then, Dr. Angus stayed and practiced medicine in Rosalia, Washington.

My mother's maiden name was Mabel McClure George. The Mc-

 Clure in her name has been traced back nearly to the year the *Mayflower* came. When she and my dad married they lived in the country outside Pine City. Marion, Lester, Mary, Howard, and Edna were born there.

After they moved to the place between Santa and Fernwood, Wayne, Angus, Elaine, and me, Ethelda (Teg), and Ned were born. The first and last babies were delivered by a doctor, but all the others were delivered by midwives.

Doctored by Mail

My mother would write to Dr. Angus and tell him how one of the family felt and he'd send medicine. Doctors made their own in those days. That was the way we were doctored, and she never lost one of us. That was pretty good nursing.

She had no electricity. In fact, there was no electricity up there until after Charles and I were married. She worked hard and never had any conveniences like we have now. There were no powdered soaps those days. On washdays, she cut up a bar of Fels Naptha soap and boiled the clothes on the kitchen range in the copper wash boiler. Then she scrubbed them on a plain old washboard and got them really clean. In the summertime she canned thousands of jars of food. And it wasn't quarts—she always canned in two-quart jars. No use going out and bringing in a quart for 12 hungry people!

Move to Malden

About the time my youngest brother, Ned, was born, Mother got TB and lost one lung. I was five years old. Dr. Angus said she couldn't stand the cold winters, so we moved to Malden, Washington, where we did have electricity. We were there eight years before we came back. Later on, she had a gasoline-motor washing machine. It worked pretty good, but was so noisy, we had to run it outside on the back porch. During the winter, the house would get cold going in and out, carrying water.

Fun Year

After seven years of school in Malden, I went to Santa with all eight grades in one room. And that was the fun year. Edna Woods was one of the best teachers that ever taught—and I was teacher's pet. I could wave hair and roll it up on curlers, so sometimes she'd keep me in at recess and I'd set her hair. Once in awhile she'd have me come stay with her where she boarded with Mrs. Leonard and the Bunells.

Her father, Bob Woods, was the one that taught me to dance. We danced in the hall that later became the Grange Hall. Bob was good to all the school kids. He'd try to get them to dance and would teach them how. He danced with Trish Yonkin, a seventh grader, and me, an eighth grader. We thought that was wonderful!

Charles Addington was working for Bob. When I was a sophomore, Bob introduced us. In those days, you'd dance with all the guys, so Charles and I danced together, but he never asked me for a date.

Bob Woods had once lived in Harrison. When his son Norman came back from World War I, he married Charles' sister, Ethel.

Huckleberries and Fish

My brother Howard used to take a bunch of us kids fishing on Mica Creek because we didn't need fishing licenses and he did. But then he'd take our fish!

There used to be a big flume going up Renfro Creek. We'd park the car and walk three miles to go huckleberrying, walking up the flume with one foot on each side.

Hard Senior Year

My senior year was a hard year. Shortly before school started, several of us girls were going swimming—my sister Elaine, Maxine Tangat, Leona Peterson and the oldest Kellom girl. My youngest brother, Ned, had a new bicycle and wanted to see how close he could come to us before he'd slam on the brakes. Well, he hit me and broke my left arm about halfway between the elbow and shoulder. When my dad said he was glad Ned hit me rather than one of the other girls because the others would have sued him, I said, "Well—thanks!"

Sideswiped

Until my senior year, Bill Puckett had driven us to high school in St. Maries in the old stage, which served as a school bus. It was 21 miles each way over roads so narrow that sometimes Bill had to back up to pass a truck, especially on the old Thorn Creek road. The stage had five rows of seats running horizontally, and there were four doors on each side of the bus for access to each row, except for the forward jump seats. There were door handles on each door at the beginning of the school year, but all of the handles on the driver's side would be gone by the end of the year from being sideswiped by logging trucks.

One morning when we were about a mile past the Emida turnoff, we came around a curve and there was a mud slide Bill couldn't get around.

 He stopped. We thought, oh boy, we'll get the day off. But he backed up about a quarter-mile and then drove down the pole road that went to the railroad track at the Mashburn Siding, making a loop around the slide, back up to the main road, and took us to school after all.

If Bill Puckett couldn't drive his wife drove—both excellent drivers. They were always on time and never missed a day.

My senior year we had a new driver, who came out from Minnesota where it was flat, to take the job. He was a relative of Keaton, a St. Maries lawyer and school board member. He'd never driven on a mountain road, didn't feel competent, and said so.

He'd growl, "Aw! This job!" He wanted to quit, but the school board demanded he fulfill his contract.

Cattle Truck School Bus

We were to get a new bus, but it didn't come before school started, so they boarded up about three feet of the sides of an old cattle truck, put canvas over the top and down the sides to the boards, and built some steps in the back. They put benches in and then they'd just keep shoving you until they got 60 kids in there. If you were lucky enough to get a place on a bench, you always had to hold somebody on your lap because there wasn't space for enough benches.

My arm was still hurting and I got jostled around because I couldn't hang on. I'd come home at night exhausted and was going to quit school, but my folks talked this bus driver into letting me ride at least one way in the front. We rode that old cattle truck until late October.

The new bus was built to carry 45 passengers, the largest bus made in those days, but this one always carried 60 kids.

Coming home from school, some of us would have a few pennies to spend, and one kid would get off the bus, run into the Santa store real fast, and buy candy. This one icy night in early March, I was sitting clear in the back of the bus, and this boy up front was leaning over the back of his seat collecting money from all of us.

And that's when it happened. We were within three miles of Santa when our bus and a logging truck with piggyback trailer headed for St. Maries sideswiped. The kids said when the bus driver knew we were going to hit, he ducked under the dashboard, and the boy collecting the money got his arm broke from the jolt. They said the trailer chain broke through the back window and hit me. No one else was hurt. The rest of the kids piled out of the bus, looked back, and saw me spread across the aisle with the blood pouring out. I never knew when it hit me.

I had a four-inch scalp wound, skull fracture and was in the hospital ten days and out of school for two more weeks. The bus was smashed and had to have a lot of repair.

Charles Had a Car

Charles came to Santa all the time to the dances, but I wasn't really lookin' at him. Young kids in those days weren't ready to settle down. It was hard times! Charles said none of the guys had transportation but him. He said *he* had a car and that made a little difference.

So just before I graduated, he asked me to go out with him. He still laughs about that because when he came after me, I was gone. I hadn't known where to get in touch with him, so my mother had to tell him I was in Portland.

My sister Edna had come up from Portland and her husband, Dick Chessman, came to my mother and said, "If Teg doesn't go back with us, I just don't think Edna will want to go because she's so homesick." So Mom talked me into going with her.

I didn't know anybody and was bored with nothing to do, so I'd hang around the lunch counter in the Sears Roebuck store until finally, they put me to work as a fill-in soda jerk. And I liked it! I did!

But when I'd been there six weeks, and my sister Mary came down for the Fourth of July, I was homesick and ready to go home.

When I came back from Portland, Charles asked me out again and we went together for over a year and a half.

Meantime, all my brothers were working in logging camps and they said if I'd stay home and help Mother, they would pay me a little money. It wasn't any big amount—but she wasn't well and would have been there by herself.

Mother Was a Writer

Years before, Mother had visited cousins in the St. John's [Washington] area who owned property called Hole in the Ground, so named because it was a hole surrounded by bluffs. She was fascinated with the country and in 1927, wrote a novel about it, but it wasn't published. Although it was short and written in the language of the time, my brother Angus and I published it in 1981.

About 1933, she had spent a summer in Pine City, Washington, where she stayed with several couples she had known when she lived there, and wrote their histories. One was the Kimm family. Her expenses were paid and the histories collected by Whitman County of Washington State. I'd like to read the stories, but I don't know how to locate them.

Just before I got married, she went to Spokane to stay with my brother Marion, who was down with rheumatic fever. His wife gave birth to twins while she was there. About a month after I was married, Mother had a hysterectomy. The doctor said if she'd had two healthy lungs, she'd probably have come out of it, but she didn't because of the TB. She died four days later. She was only fifty-seven. My father lived about eight years more.

Married

While we lived in Malden we had gone to church, but after that I never went much because we had to go two or three miles to Fernwood, and during the summer they never had church. Charles knew a minister living in Spokane who had been in Harrison earlier. We went out to Reverend Moore's home and got married December 2, 1938, and came to Harrison to live.

Dr. Platt came from St. Maries and had a clinic once in awhile in the old Harrison Hospital building. Some of the rooms had been converted into an apartment, and whoever lived there took care of the building. Helen Hull moved out of the Fick house, which was next door, and into the hospital apartment, and we moved into the Fick house.

That summer we lived in Orofino while Charles was working on Deer Creek. We came back to Harrison and lived that winter. The next summer, Charles had a brush piling job, still working for Bob Woods, at Meadow Creek. They were clearing right-of-way for the road between Emida and Harvard. Camp was several miles off to the right going down the Harvard Hill.

Camp and Cold Pancakes

Bob had me come out and cook for 18 to 23 men. I don't know how I had nerve enough to do it. I really don't. They had this one big shack with a big dining table and a little partition, and that was my kitchen. We had to have our bed there because there was no other space. Boy! You had to roll out early and get your bed made.

Charles cut the wood and was my flunky—waited on tables and helped with supper dishes. But all day he worked with the crew.

Ray Porter worked there. He'd come down after supper if we'd give him something to eat. He was young and we didn't think we'd ever get him filled up!

The men fixed their own lunches. I put everything out on a table: bread, meat, and cheese. They thought it wasn't a meal without maple bars and doughnuts, so I made them every other day.

■ Charles and Ethelda "Teg" Addington wedding photo, 1938

■ Charles and Teg Addington 50th wedding anniversary, 1988

I was watching the men fix their lunches and this one little old guy, Shorty Maynard, made his sandwich out of cold pancakes.

I said to Charles, "What's the matter? Isn't there any bread on the table?"

Charles said, "Yeah, I put some out there." So we took the pancakes away.

Next day, Shorty said, "I *like* the cold pancakes!"

We bought chickens from a ranch over on Highway 95. We asked for four-pound chickens and that woman would wade into the flock, grab a squawking rooster, and say, "Well, this one's four pounds!" She'd wring their necks, but we had to clean 'em. It was a lot of work.

There wasn't time to rest in the afternoon because I had to carry my own water quite a distance and heat it on the stove. I used a washboard for our clothes—I still have it. I had to carry meat from down by the creek. They had dug a deep hole to keep it cool and stored it in a shelved box that could be pulled back up. I baked pies, cakes, biscuits, rolls—everything except bread. So when I finally got time to go to bed at night, I was ready!

We never got to leave camp the three months we were in there except to buy groceries—and that was when one or two of the men stayed in Saturday evening. That was hard. We didn't dare leave. We had to guard the logging equipment from people who drove in there for no reason and would steal you blind. And anyway, I had to cook for whoever stayed the weekend in camp.

One night we planned on going to the party for little Shorty Maynard who just got married. Bob's brother, Frank Woods, was going to watch camp. Bob came down and insisted Frank had to go to that party, so we had to stay in camp after all.

Each man paid me $1.50 a day for meals. I had to buy all the supplies and so if I made money it was because I was a good cook and economical, but if I didn't make anything, it was because I wasn't.

The first month I didn't make anything because I had to buy all the staples and cooking equipment. Frank Anderson had run many logging camps, but wasn't running any now, so we went to Emida and bought kettles, pans, and dishes from him—old white bowls, plates and cups, thick pottery that neither I nor the men could break.

Twice I drove out to the Santa store by myself to buy supplies, but usually Charles and I would go. You know, when you used to pay your bill the storekeeper would give you a sack of candy? Big day! Well, we went in there and paid the bill—*I* paid the bill, it was *my* bill—and the storekeeper gave *him* cigarettes!

I was so mad, I said, "I'm not going back there anymore!"

It wasn't right not to go back because the storekeeper had been really good to us, but I was so mad at him.

So then Saturday nights, we went over to Palouse, Washington, which was just as close and over better road, and got our meat and all our supplies. That man gave us such good deals it was cheaper to buy a big chunk of beef than it was to buy all hamburger or roasts, or even boil [meat only suitable for boiling]. And so we had a lot of steaks.

Bob Woods came down one night and bawled me out good. "You're not going to make any money feeding like you are. Always giving these men steaks!"

His brother, Frank, was doing the meat cutting for us. We tried to tell Bob it wasn't any more expensive to feed them steaks than it was something else.

I had to charge the food to begin with. I got that all paid up and my last check was all mine. It was over $300. And that was like a million dollars!

Goofing Off in Seattle

With the job finished, we closed the cook shack and came back to Harrison. After Christmas, my brother Angus—who had been doing seasonal woods work, too—went with us to Seattle and we just goofed off, living on unemployment compensation. Charles and Angus each got $15 a week. We got a motel for $40 a month on 105th Street. Eighty-fifth Street was the city limits then. We'd walk to 85th Street and take a bus downtown. Or we'd drive out to the beach and dig clams. It was a fun time.

We came back to Harrison in April and bought a house from Allen, who was railroad section foreman. It was toward town from what was Joe and Helene Kroetch's house. Later, Vivian Hedlund's father, Chris Jorgensen, owned it and Al and Judy Bruner lived there for awhile.

Dr. Finney

During the eight and a half years we lived in that house, both of our kids were born—Charlene in 1942 and Carol Ann in 1946—and both delivered by Dr. John Finney in the Deaconess Hospital in Spokane. It would be surprising if we knew how many children besides ours were brought into the world by Dr. John Finney after he left Harrison. The same years I had mine, Kate Pettet, Jeanette Bridgeman, Leone Addington, and Louise Peterson had babies and they all went to Dr. Finney.

We moved to Kellogg in 1949, but because Charles' parents were in Harrison, we came down whenever he had a day off and once in awhile I'd come for Rebekahs [Auxiliary of the International Order of Oddfellows].

Radiation

I don't know when it started, but Dr. Loehr in Moscow called it a nodule on my thyroid.

He said, "Now, we'll have to watch that, because if it starts growing, we'll have to do something about it."

By the time I went to see him again—this time about a hysterectomy—it was sticking out so no jewelry would stay straight on my neck.

He said, "Oh! That's grown too much! We've got to get a biopsy of that."

It was malignant. The young doctor who was to do the surgery had been in a cancer center in the Midwest but had done only one surgery in the Gritman Memorial Hospital in Moscow. But after he took two hours to explain the surgery to Charles and me, and even told us everything that could go wrong, we had confidence in Dr. Valder. It was an eight-hour surgery during which they removed the lymph glands, muscle, and jugular vein on my right side and all of the thyroid on both sides. In those days, they usually just took half.

When I complained to the doctor about how awful it looked, swelled straight up and down from the shoulder to my chin, he says, "Well, that's not going to be as bad as you think because it will sink in." It did and that bothered me.

They got it all, but I was to have 24 radiation treatments. I went back and forth from Kellogg to the Fernwell building in Spokane every day except Sunday. If Charles couldn't take me, I'd take the bus. And then I had Nellie Williams, Ward Williams's wife, go with me and I'd drive. My neck was so stiff I could *not* move it. Nellie couldn't drive a car, but she would watch the traffic for me.

The radiation made me sick. I lost my voice, so the doctor doing the radiation put a lead shield over the larynx. When Dr. Valder found out about it, he was afraid the cancer would spread there, too.

He said, "That's where I *want* the radiation." So they eliminated the lead shield and extended my treatments to 30.

I was sick and had an awful skin reaction. It was mattery, and the doctor said, "You are having the same reaction inside. That's why you are so sick."

After that, I got well and have been fine ever since. But it was hard to get the use of my right arm again. I couldn't have the hysterectomy for two years after radiation, and meantime the fibroid tumors disappeared, so I've never had it.

From Pink Lady to Aide

I worked one year for my brother, Angus, in his grocery store in Pinehurst, Idaho, but didn't work again for pay until 1960. When they opened West Shoshone General Hospital in 1958, I had worked as a volunteer—pink lady—and really liked it. When Charlene was ready for college, we did *not* have the money to send her. So I applied for a job as an aide and got it.

Our director of nurses took three or four in a class and showed us how to make beds, give baths, and that. But when you started working, they put an LPN [licensed practical nurse] to work with you for a few days. They put me with Doris Lunde, a good nurse, but so brusque, I was scared to death of her.

After I worked with her for several days, she said, "Now this is your patient. You are on your own. When you've made this bed, I'm coming back, and you'd better have every wrinkle out of it!"

Did I *slave* over that bed? I'll never forget it. And she never came back to look at it.

Hated Pleating Towels

Then I worked in Central Supply. In those days you didn't have packaged stuff. You had to wash, wrap, and sterilize everything. *You* packaged it. It was a nightmare. The towels weren't square in the first place; they had to be pleated with the top and bottom folds exactly the same width, so when the doctor or nurse grabbed it by one corner, it would just come apart. I'd *slave* over those towels; I never could get them right, and I hated them with a passion.

Other towels were called "wraps." You had to wrap those in such a way that when the nurse or doctor picked up a fold, it would open without ever being touched. Everything was *sterile*.

I had to wash surgical instruments at a high sink and developed a painful cyst where I'd had the thyroid surgery. I complained to my superior, so she finally took me out of there. But during the three months it took to heal, the doctor made me wear a strapless bra. Just try to work wearing one of those!

I didn't mind running the autoclave, which was a big sterilizer. Each load had to be timed. Millie Savage wrapped all the surgical instruments, and they had to be timed longer than the rest. Sometimes they wouldn't bring things to be sterilized until just about time for me to go home and then I'd have to stay. Of course, I got paid for it. We had to punch a time clock. We worked by the hour, and they paid time-and-a-half for overtime.

And then I got to work in the nursery. I just loved the babies. And I liked the mothers. *Everybody* was happy with their babies. It was a happy place to be.

Ward Clerk Named Addie

When I was moved up to ward clerk, I worked at the nurse's station on the medical floor keeping the medical charts in order and making up new ones. It was a *good* job and a responsible one. I took the doctor's orders off the charts and made out requisitions for the medicine nurse.

It made me feel good when a nurse would say, "Addie! You can read those orders better than I can."

When I started work, I was asked, "What's your name?"

I said, "Ethelda."

"Well! We can't call you Ethelda."

I said, "Other people call me Teg." But they wouldn't call me Teg and started calling me Addington but soon shortened it to Addie.

When the kids answered the phone at home, they'd say, "It's someone from lodge" or "It's someone from the hospital," depending on how they asked for me. At lodge, I was Ethelda. Family, it was Teg. Hospital, I was Addie.

A woman in x-ray had been doing EKGs [electrocardiograms] but she got too busy, so instead of hiring someone new, they trained me to do them along with my ward clerk job. I was on day shift, so I had to train RNs [registered nurses] and others working swing and nights, so we had somebody at the hospital all the time that knew how to do EKGs. It was a responsible job and I *liked* it.

When they got me to teaching, and then made me head of EKG, and still doing my ward clerk work, the director of nurses, Holly Target, went to the administrator and said that I should have more pay than the other ward clerks.

He said, "Well, you think of a new title for her, and we'll see what we can do about it."

So they made me nursing secretary. Each time I had changed jobs, they upped my pay, and now I got another raise.

Holly Target

Holly Target started work in Kellogg during World War II when doctors were so overworked the nurses hated to call them out another time at night.

She said she called one doctor and told him she had another case that needed stitches and he said, "Holly, you can sew it up." And so she said she did!

None of the other nurses ever tried it, but Holly said she did a lot of that to save those doctors. A nurse wouldn't dare do that anymore.

CHARLES: I was headed home and saw this guy had had a wreck and was layin' there alongside the road with a long gash across his forehead.

Holly was just coming from work, jumped out of her car, went over to him, and ran her finger through the gash and said, "That isn't bad!"

I think she was feeling to see if there was any concussion there.

We didn't have medical insurance in those days, but the old Bunker took care of the men. If you went to the hospital, it didn't cost you anything.

One night I went to the Wardner hospital with a cold and the doctor put me to bed. Doctors from the Day Hospital took care of you at that time.

Holly come in the third day, and I said, "When am I going to get out of here? I haven't seen a doctor since I've been here."

She said, "Well, I'll find out."

She called the doctor and said, "I've got a man here that wants to go home."

He said, "Who is it?"

She told him and he said, "Aw, send him home!" And that's the way they did it. Different than it is now!

TEG: Holly Target said, "If we have something here that we don't want to do, we just give it to Addie!" And they did. But you know, I loved 'em for it.

For every retirement party, Holly would say, "Addie, go down and decorate those tables."

Eighty Cakes

On their yearly anniversary date, every person that worked at the hospital took home a one-layer decorated cake with their name on it.

Holly was disgusted with the store cakes and knew I made wedding cakes, so she came to me and said, "There's no reason why you can't do those."

So I took on that job at home, made whatever kind they wanted and got so much a cake and made 80 cakes a year. Some months I'd make only three, but one month I made 18.

One guy said, "Aw! I'd rather have a pie." So I'd remember and that guy'd get a pie. It was sort of fun.

One vegetarian fellow whose religion prevented him from eating meat or sugar, said, "I don't know what I'm going to do with this cake."

I said, "I made it for you. You can throw it in the garbage if you want to."

But as he left for home, someone watched out the window and saw him eating that cake. He was just starved for sugar! And once, we even caught him eating meat at a potluck dinner when his wife wasn't around.

I taught myself cake decorating. Then I took a few lessons but I couldn't form the roses or do anything else the way the teacher did. I had already created my own style and could not change. I started decorating cakes just for family and friends, but although I didn't make a lot—I never knew what I should charge—I did want to make a little more money. When you start charging, it's not the same as when you are doing it just for fun.

What started me making wedding cakes was when we priced a cake for Mom and Dad's [Mary and Winfield Addington's] sixtieth wedding anniversary reception that was to be held in the Harrison Grange Hall, and I said, "I can make one cheaper than that!"

When our neighbor girl, Shawn Reynolds, saw me mixing up that first one, she said, "You're going to make my wedding cake."

"Oh, yeah, I'll do that."

It wasn't long before she said, "You know what you promised me?"

It was to be a four-tiered cake based on her mother's large mirror. But as I was putting the fourth layer on, the cake started slipping out. Boy, I grabbed it off and so it was a three-tiered cake. Then I learned about dividers and putting pegs in so each layer has something to rest on.

There were three Reynolds girls, two Carter girls and our two, all raised together, and I made wedding cakes for every one—one of 'em twice because she got divorced and remarried.

The middle Reynolds girl, Marjeane, ran off and got married and her mother was so mad, she wouldn't let her have a reception. I always felt bad about it until Marjeane's daughter asked me if I'd make her mother's twenty-fifth wedding anniversary cake.

I said, "I sure will!"

Break a Leg, Dr. Scott

Dr. Scott loved to ski. As he left the hospital after an emergency surgery one Saturday morning, Mary Pierce said to him, "Well, Dr. Scott! This is a good day to break your leg."

He came in that afternoon with a broken leg! That poor girl was so embarrassed. She said, "Me and my big mouth!"

I made a cake in the form of a mountain. Holly and I found tiny trees to put on it and a skier spilled on the snow-frosting with one ski here and one there.

Dr. Cordwell was just going to see a patient when he saw us in the hall and said, "Don't take that cake to his room till I can go with you."

Dr. Scott said that was the cutest thing he ever saw. He wouldn't let anybody cut it, and made his wife freeze it until he got home.

Picnics

There was comradeship. It was a hospital family. I had four or five picnics for them down at the lake in front of our house here in Harrison. This is the house Charles's parents had owned. After Charles retired, we had been living here part-time. Summers, I'd commute to work.

My friends brought liquor. I said, "You can bring it, but I'm not buying it for you because I don't drink it!" They joked about that.

Some who came had never been here before, so they stopped uptown to ask where I lived. Someone must have reported all these people coming down here. I'd never seen a cop down here before nor since. He'd drive down real slow and look, turn around at the city water pumphouse, then he'd come back. He did that a couple times. And the last time, he took off. He could see we were just having a good time.

CNA at Last!

The last year I worked there, they offered a certified nurse's aide [CNA] course. I didn't have to take it, but I did and passed. That made me feel good!

Those were nice years at the hospital, but things were changing. I didn't dislike that job until the very last when they got all these young doctors who believed if you were over fifty, you were over the hill. But their best nurses were over fifty!

The hospital was county supported, so we had the same pension plan as the teachers—only we got less because our pay was lower. And I had Social Security. I worked ten years after Charles retired. April 28, 1981 ended 21 years on the job for me.

Since then we've lived in Harrison full-time.

SIXTEEN

ELEANOR AND BILL LAMB

From a 1994 interview with Eleanor Lamb at Bell Canyon.

BILL LAMB'S STORY starts in Scotland, where his great-grandfather, James Lamb, served many years in the Duke of Wellington's army.

His grandfather, also named James, born in Dundee, Scotland, in 1829, was a blacksmith who served his apprenticeship in the Glasgow shipyards. He married Margaret Galloway Strang of Perth, in 1865. Their first son died. When their second son, Peter, born in 1867, was small, they migrated to the United States to Cleveland, Ohio, where James worked for a railroad company as a blacksmith. Three more children were born there: Thomas, in 1872; Jonathan Leslie, in 1875; and Margaret, in 1877.

Grandfather James moved his family near Cortland, Nebraska, onto land he purchased from the railroad. The youngest son, George, was born there in 1880. While their father continued working for the railroad, the older children helped with the farm work and attended school at Cortland.

In 1887, Grandfather James and several neighbors rented a boxcar from the railroad for their stock and a passenger car for their families, and moved to Perris, California, near the present city of Riverside.

Canadian-born Harry (Shorty) Dudley ran away from an unhappy childhood with a stepmother and ended up in California in the late 1890s with the Lambs. He was always considered part of the family.

In 1898, Jonathan (Joe) and a friend packed their supplies on mules and rode horseback to Harrison, Idaho, where Joe filed on a homestead in Bell Canyon. With the exception of Margaret (Maggie), who had married Tom Dodd, the rest of the family, including Shorty, followed and filed on homesteads near Joe.

Bill's Parents

Thomas left the one-room log cabin on his homestead to live in Harrison, where he opened the Cash Meat Market in partnership with Mox Kuehl. While there, he met and fell in love with Clara Cluphf.

Clara's parents, Frederick and Alpha Cluphf, raised a large family at the upper end of Black Lake. They grew a big garden and stored their fruit, vegetables, eggs, milk, cream, and butter in an earth-cooled cellar built into the side of the hill. When Clara was in her early teens, she and her father rowed their boat down the Coeur d'Alene River to sell the produce and dairy products in Harrison.

In her late teens, Clara met Thomas Lamb when she stayed in Harrison with her older sister and her husband, Grace and Dan Boutillier, and worked in a shop. A 1909 Harrison *Searchlight* newspaper reported on the front page that Clara and Thomas married and took the train to Spokane for a weekend honeymoon. When they returned, they moved into a little house at the upper end of Harrison's main street.

William Thomas Leslie (Bill) Lamb was born in that house, July 6, 1910. Then Daniel McDonald (Mac) was born July 14, 1913 and three years later, Margaret was born January 24, 1916.

Thomas and Joe opened a shop between the Opera House and the Export Lumber Company store. Joe had his blacksmith shop in front and Thomas had a machine shop in the rear.

Bill went to the first grade in Harrison. That summer Thomas moved his family back to the homestead into a three-room frame house he had built. When the town burned, July 17, 1917, the brothers lost their building and all their tools and goods valued at more than $2,500, according to the Harrison *Searchlight*.

Typhoid

Clara's brother George and her sister Grace had moved with their families to Worley. So Thomas moved his family to Worley, where his machine shop and garage business prospered. He was a big, husky man who had never been sick, but he got typhoid fever and died the summer of 1921. Bill was just past eleven.

Without formal training, Clara had worked as a home nurse in Harrison, so she left the children with the relatives and went out on jobs taking care of people in their homes. Bill's uncles helped out by bring-

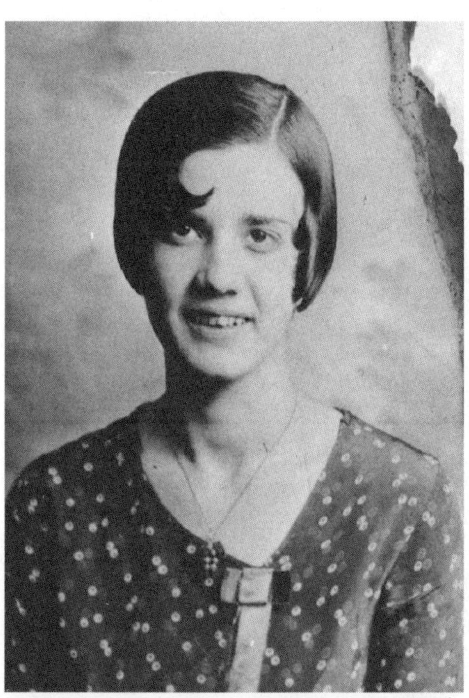

■ Eleanor Courtney (Lamb) in 1931, at the age of 18

■ Ellie Lamb in July 1991, at the age of 78

ing meat to the family. Some time later, Clara's parents left Black Lake and moved to Worley to help.

During one of those years, Aunt Maggie's youngest daughter, Jean, came up from California. She and Mac stayed with Grandma Lamb and the uncles in Bell Canyon and went part of the year to the little Van Dusen schoolhouse on the Harrison flats.

Bill Becomes Breadwinner

Then Clara moved her family to Plummer. Bill quit high school during his junior year to go to work to support the family. Uncle Joe had gone to work at the electrolytic zinc plant owned by the Bunker, Hill & Sullivan Mining Company at Kellogg, and got a job there for Bill. They both stayed at Mrs. Peterson's boardinghouse on Idaho Avenue.

After Bill saved up a little money, he rented a little house where Main Street turns to go up to Wardner, and moved his mother, Mac, and Margaret to Kellogg, too.

Grandmother Margaret Lamb remained on the ranch in Bell Canyon until she died in 1930. Uncle Pete died in 1935.

■ ELEANOR LAMB

Interviewed 1991 at home in Bell Canyon.

I don't know if I was born at home, but I know my sister Helen was. I remember coming downstairs one morning and finding the buggy with a new baby in it that had arrived during the night. I was the oldest of four, then [came] Richard, Arthur, and Helen, all born in five years, so Mother was a busy woman! I was born June 30, 1913, on a ranch ten miles from Pomeroy, Washington, out toward the Blue Mountains on the Pataha Flats.

Mother

My mother, Laura Guernsey Courtney, was born in South Dakota. She taught music there after she had gone to the Ziegfeld Conservatory of Music near Chicago, Illinois. Later she taught music in Dillon, Montana, then moved to Pomeroy, Washington, where she was giving music lessons when she met and married my father in 1911.

Father

My great-grandfather came from Nebraska and homesteaded on the Pataha Flats in 1873. My grandfather built the house there that we lived in later.

My father, Chester Courtney, graduated from Whitman in Walla Walla, Washington, when it was still a three-year academy. He had taken a classical course in German and History, but he didn't know what he wanted to do, so he went back to the ranch. His brother Doane, who was 14 years younger, wasn't interested in farming, so when their father died, it was up to my father to take care of the ranch.

He was a good blacksmith and combine repairman, the highest paid man on a threshing crew. We had an old threshing machine with 32 horses to pull it. And we had two saddle horses, Father's and mine—miserable old Maude—and one outlaw, Pinkie, with those real shiny, skim-milk lookin' eyeballs that would glitter when he looked at you. Father saved him just for the newly-hired men to try to ride. He was not a nice horse at all.

Scarce Water

With 35 horses to water all year long, we had a big cement trough that held the most water I ever saw in that dry country. The closest water was Pataha Creek that ran through Pomeroy, but it dried down to nothing in the spring and left bridges over dry land. After a thaw, water would come down out of the hills, tear all through the fields and pig pasture, but then would leave nothing but a small creek not large enough to do any good except to water the rose bushes my great-grandmother had planted.

Father dug a well and pumped water with a gasoline motor up the hill into a cement-sided cistern covered with a big lid. My brother, Dick, and I were expressly forbidden to go near the cistern because on that sidling hill you could easily slip, overturn, and fall in while peeking down in there. By the time anybody could get a rope, you'd be drowned. But one day when Father was away working and Mother was occupied in the house with the younger children, we took the lid off and had a great time throwing rocks to see how long it took them to plunk to the bottom. Thank heaven Mother never knew what we were doing!

We didn't have water in the house, but there was a sink with a cold water tap on the screened-in back porch where Mother did the washing. She had to heat the water on our big cookstove, lug it out, and pour bucketfuls into the machine.

Two Longs and Two Shorts

I can remember exactly how the old farmhouse looked and where the telephone hung on the kitchen wall. You cranked out a different ring to make calls to each telephone—ours was two longs and two shorts.

In the fall of the last year we were on the ranch, Father went up the hill to repair the phone line. Mother was baking pancakes and was irked because Father hadn't come for breakfast, so she sent us to see what was the matter.

We ran back down the hill, all out of breath and wheezed, "Papa's dead!"

She said, "How do you know?"

I said, "He won't talk to us. He's just layin' up there on the hill!" The ground was frozen. It was November.

My mother grabbed blankets and tore up the hill to stay with Father and yelled back at us to ride the horse down to the neighbors to tell them to send for the doctor and to come up. They couldn't telephone the doctor because they were on the same line, so they had to send someone to town.

Father was a big, heavy man. He weighed 200 pounds and was five feet-eight. He had fallen off the ladder when the old telephone pole broke, giving him a double concussion, one on his left forehead and another behind his right ear. He couldn't work and we had to have a hired man all that winter, but he did get over it.

"Rather Common"

We attended a nondenominational neighborhood Sunday school during the winter months with classes followed by a potluck lunch and visiting. But Dick and I didn't have anybody to play with because Mother really didn't care for many of the neighbors. The most awful thing she could say about anybody was that they were "rather common."

Home School

I can't remember when I didn't know how to read, write, and read music since Mother started teaching me before I was five. As my brothers came along, I had to help them using materials Mother bought from John W. Graham Company in Spokane. We had readers, spellers, phonics charts, and charts with prefixes and suffixes so we could make up words. Boxes and boxes of them. Because I was tiny, my parents wouldn't send me to school until Dick was old enough to go with me. I started in the fourth grade in a one-room schoolhouse on the Scoggins place. They hadn't been able to get a teacher until March and school was to run until August.

When we visited Grandmother Courtney in Pullman for Easter, we all went to church and I caught the chicken pox. I didn't realize it because I felt all right and had only three or four bumps, which I scratched. I still have a little hole on my forehead but the little one on my stomach got stretched years later.

But then the rest of the kids in my family broke out with chicken pox and they really had it! Mr. Scoggins had a lot of kids and insisted we all stay home until everybody was over it, so I didn't get much good out of that year.

The next year the Scoggins kids got the measles and continued going to school because he was on the school board and the board didn't make them stay home. Well, Father had never had the measles and was afraid of them, being an adult, so Dick and I stayed home until all the miserable Scoggins kids got over the measles. We didn't catch measles until years later.

Hershey Bars—"A Whole Carton!"

Mother baked bread every day of her life on the ranch. She canned meat and all kinds of vegetables and fruit. But still there'd be coffee, tea, sugar, salt, spices, and other staples as well as clothing, yard goods, shoes, and hardware that we had to buy from the Emerson Hull Mercantile Company in Pomeroy. Going to town was quite an event in our old Dodge touring car with isinglass side curtains! And you didn't drive *that* in cold weather—then you had to ride the horse or take the sled. The car was just for good weather.

We paid the bill for everything once a year when Father sold the grain. One time Mr. Hull gave us a carton of almond Hershey bars. A carton! A whole carton! We didn't get much candy, so my brothers and I were in seventh heaven.

Bank Takes Farm

The ranch belonged to Grandmother Courtney, and when Father had married, she had taken a second mortgage on it to build a new house in Pullman. Post-World-War-I "prosperity" really wasn't that good. We lived from year to year with no money saved, so when we had three crop failures in a row, that did it. The bank took the farm.

My folks rented storage space in Pomeroy and it was amazing the things that Mother managed to pack and squeeze in. But what a terrible problem having to leave things like our big old coffee grinder on the wall, and the lamp with the bracket by the back door. Being nine and a half years old, I wasn't very happy having to leave my doll bed, doll trunk, my little iron, and my little spurs and quirt—my treasures. But what do you do when you have to leave and don't know where you are going?

There were two families living together close to the school we had been attending: Mr. and Mrs. White, Mr. and Mrs. Ernest Jones, their two little boys, and a grandmother. They were kind enough to let us stay with them that fall and part of the winter.

There wasn't any work for Father, so he went to western Washington and got work in the woods. Mother taught music, sometimes bartering lessons for meat or vegetables. But living was "thin soup."

Santa Claus

Mother never told us about Santa Claus because she felt that would be lying. We knew where our presents came from but were under oath not to tell because she didn't want us to spoil Christmas for other children. We were content and felt sorry for all those stupid kids that believed in Santa Claus.

Dick and I walked from this neighbor's place where we were living to our mailbox to see if there were Christmas packages from our aunt and grandmother. And there were! But it was a long, cold, snowy, three-mile trek lugging them back home.

Pullman

In February, we rented a crummy two-room apartment on Kamiaken Street in Pullman from a man who had a photograph studio. It was on a steep hill fairly close to the business district and above the railroad tracks. Mornings, the boys and I studied at home. Afternoons, I worked for our landlady baby-sitting their little girl or ironing for 50 cents. Not much, but it was a way to make do.

Pomeroy

Early summer after I finished seventh grade, we moved to Pomeroy and rented a little house up against the hill at the edge of town on Baldwin Avenue. With a population of 2,500, Pomeroy was the only town of any size in Garfield County.

Right away Mother started giving music lessons, and I had to take seventh grade exams at the county courthouse. Coming from out in the sticks, my knees shook as I walked up the steps, searched for the county superintendent's office, got the form, and filled it out. And then I had to pass exams in history, physiology, and arithmetic to be eligible to enter the eighth grade that fall.

There were remains of cement sides to the nearly dry Pataha Creek and a bridge crossed over it. The grade school was on one side and the high school on the other. I entered the eighth grade knowing I wouldn't have to endure the anxiety of an exam the next spring because only kids coming in from the country had to take seventh and eighth grade exams.

Water Up to the Floorboards

To go to Pullman from Pomeroy, we drove through the little town of Dodge and then turned north 11 miles to Central Ferry where we crossed the Snake River on a ferry. The ferry was pulled across by cables powered by horses.

One time when we were driving back from Pullman, we could see the ferry coming from the other side but the loading ramp on our side was not up yet. Father got out and was tinkering with the motor when the brakes slipped and the car started down off the bank into the water.

We were screaming, and Father yelled, "Put on the brakes! Put on the brakes!"

Mother had no idea where the brakes were. Father tore around there, lifted the window flap, and set the emergency brake.

We had to stay overnight at the house of the fellow who took care of the ferry while the motor dried out. I had nightmares that night about the river pouring over the top of the car door, but it hadn't been that way; the water had only come up to the floorboards.

Crawdads and Fishing

Once a year when we were little, Father would go fishing in a shallow stretch of the Tucannon River, which was down toward Starbuck and Dayton, but off in the "boonies." Dick and I would be wading and digging for crawdads while Father was fishing. But I don't remember that he ever caught any fish, and we didn't eat the crawdads!

Mother would always buy a big load of loganberries, apricots, peaches, and other fruit to bring home and can.

One of the highlights of summer was getting swimming instructions in the municipal pool. I learned to swim, but not very well.

Chautauqua

The park had a bandstand and was big enough that the Chautauqua people could put up their tents. Orchestras, brass bands, and vocalists traveled with them. Mother took us to see *Daddy Longlegs*, and *The Mikado*, a Gilbert and Sullivan operetta. When I was in the eighth grade, Mother let me go to a lecture on "The Yellow Peril," which at that time was China, not Japan. But the Chautauqua, too, has gone the way of all flesh a long time ago.

Old-School Music Lessons

Theoretically I was still taking piano lessons from Mother, but she was always giving lessons before school, at noon, after school, evenings, Saturdays, or even on Sunday mornings, so I had to practice at odd times. Mother was of the old school: I didn't appreciate having to know all the scales—majors, minors, sharps, flats, and arpeggios—and write them all in a notebook. I didn't like five sharps major, but the minors were worse. And all the chords that went with each scale—well, really! Mother was English and I can't remember her ever giving us a licking, but she'd give you that steely look and say, "You *will* learn this." And you did!

All Mother's pupils had to play by memory for recitals, and I did memorize fairly well then, but that wasn't my bag to play without music. Helen and I played duets and eight-hand pieces with another piano and two more people, and that wasn't all that jolly, but at least you were able to have music for that.

Mother and all her family back to her grandfather, who was a minister, were Congregationalists, but in Pomeroy we went to the Methodist Church. This man, whose boys Mother taught, would sing sometimes, and she'd make me play his accompaniments. That didn't make me very happy, but that was one of the penalties of being able to read music!

Too Young and Too Small in High School

Pomeroy had the only high school in the county, but there were no buses, so country kids would board and room in town during the school year. I got friendly with a girl who lived out toward Starbuck and had fun riding the train to her house. Starbuck was a terminal, and you changed trains there when you wanted to go to Spokane.

I was at a bit of a disadvantage with the other kids three ways: I was younger, only twelve years old; small for my age; and I made quite good grades without spending much time studying. If you had an "A" average, the teacher would post your name outside the room and you didn't have to take semester exams.

At the end of the first semester when I was a sophomore, I hadn't bothered to study because I knew I was going to get out of exams. The teacher was little, red-haired, and just full of hell. She hadn't posted any names! I went in and sat down and began to feel sick. We were about half done and here she came in the door and said, "What are you doing here? You know you are not supposed to be taking this exam."

I could have got down and kissed her shoes. That taught me not to feel quite so smart and take so much for granted.

Little Beasts and Miserable Hound

All this time Mother was giving lessons, and the kids and I were helping what we could. Richard and Arthur had paper routes and Helen helped them. I would baby-sit for the usual 50 cents a night. But there was one place I got 75 cents. The little beasts were such horrors that nobody else would stay with them. They had a dog, a miserable hound, named Kazan from a story about a wolfhound, and after the parents would leave for their dinner and bridge party, the kids would chase each other around the house with a long butcher knife, screaming, with the dog nipping at their heels.

Their father was a druggist, one of those miserable fellows that would never bring you home, so a little before midnight, I had to walk the full length of Arlington Avenue right down the middle because I had this theory that nobody could jump out at you there. I always felt I really earned my 75 cents.

Dime Movies

I regret to say I didn't give Mother every dime I made. I bought movie magazines, cut out the pictures, traded some with my girlfriends, and pasted them in a notebook for drama class. I still have it. We had a nice theater, and shows were ten cents. I was so small the ticket lady never asked me how old I was, so I kept going for a dime until I was fifteen, and then I felt guilty. I had rationalized it this way—the theater got all my money whether I paid a dime or whether I paid adult price. This way I got to see a few more "flicks" for the money.

Purple Knees

All of us kids went to the Methodist Church and belonged to the Epworth League, where we put on some little plays and had roller-skating parties. Thc only paved streets in town—Arlington Avenue, Main Street, and two cross streets—made a large rectangle, so we'd go skating 'round and 'round. About dark, we'd head back to church for hot cocoa and lunch, and every time I'd catch my skates on the railroad tracks and fall and break my knees open. I had scabs on my knees for two or three years. Even years later when I went swimming, I felt embarrassed because when my knees got wet and cold they'd turn purple.

Kellogg a Boomtown

The fall of '28, the year I was a senior, Father went up to Kellogg and got on at the Bunker Hill Mine as a mucker. Kellogg was a boomtown and housing was hard to find, but he rented a little old log cabin. It was on Main Street as you turn, headed toward Wardner, just a stone's throw from the Kellogg High School with the Washington grade school on the end of it.

John Herrett, Sr., was working in the Kellogg post office. He and his wife, Zella, lived up the hill from my parents and were among the first people Mother got acquainted with because they all went to the Congregational Church. Helen was ten and soon old enough to baby-sit the Herrett children as they came along. Later, we would both help Zella with her housework.

The boys and Helen changed schools but I wanted to stay in Pomeroy for my senior year. I was paranoid about having to get acquainted in a much larger Kellogg school and afraid my grades would go to pot with strange teachers.

Senior

My friend, Mary Beale, asked her mother if I could stay with them, and Mrs. Beale said, "If you'll help on Saturdays with the housework, and help Mary with her schoolwork, why that will be fine."

I had been friends with Mary Lou Ledgerwood (now McFadden) ever since I was in the eighth grade because that summer she came to the house for music lessons from Mother. Mrs. Ledgerwood was caretaker of the city library during the school year, and said that I could stay with her and Mary Lou the second semester if I would help in the library and do a little housework—which I don't remember doing that much.

All the summers before, I had worked on farms doing kitchen and housework for board and room and a dollar for a long, long day. I put most of it in the bank. So by the time I was ready to graduate I had $100 saved to buy clothes, graduation pictures, and get a marcel [hair waved in tiers]. Mrs. Ledgerwood insisted on buying some things I needed for graduation, which was real sweet. She was a dominant lady but very caring, so I felt like a friend while staying there that last semester.

I enjoyed school. I was in the chorus and all the operettas, and my last year, a one-act play. I was only the maid, but I was a ham even then. I took a lot of subjects I didn't have to and worked in the library all four years. We started with 85 and I graduated as salutatorian with a class of 42.

Kinman Business School

The day after graduation I left for Kellogg to stay a few days with my family. Then I went to Spokane for the summer.

Mother had an eighty-four-year-old uncle, Ellery Guernsey, who had owned an insurance business in Duluth, Minnesota, for years, but now had his business in Spokane. He lived just two blocks from the streetcar line on north hill by Corbin Park. He had told me I could stay with them and he would send me to Kinman's business school that summer for a graduation present. Uncle Ell hadn't promised to send me through; he just said he'd send me for the summer. I took shorthand, business spelling, and got a fair amount of typing under my belt. Then I went to Kellogg to live with my parents.

1929 Crash

That fall of '29 was when everything went to hell in a handbasket. Mrs. Morgan, who had an office in the First State Bank building in Kellogg, handled insurance and also sold insurance for my uncle. He told me to introduce myself and ask if she would pass along any job opportunities so I could apply.

Several of the brass at Bunker Hill, who belonged to the Congregational Church, were kind and Christian enough to give me jobs typing business reports. I didn't have a typewriter at home. The school was nice enough to let me use theirs on Saturdays and let me sit in on typing and shorthand classes, free, to keep up my skills.

Mr. Papesh at First State Bank

In January of 1930, Mrs. Morgan called and said they wanted a bookkeeper at the First State Bank and to see Mr. Papesh, the president. So I went down and of course, I was scared spitless! He was an immigrant from one of those countries in southern Europe and spoke quite broken English, but was a very shrewd businessman who owned a lot of real estate in the Kellogg area. He said, if I wanted, I could start the morning of the fourteenth.

I got a good breaking-in because the fourteenth and twenty-eighth were Bunker Hill paydays, no matter which day of the week those dates fell on.

I'll never forget when I got up to leave, I said, "OK, I'll be here at 10:00."

He says, "Well, I don't know about you, but the rest of us are going to be here at 8:00."

That shows how much I knew about banks! But I found out shortly because the banks stayed open on paydays from 10:00 in the morning till 8:00 at night for the convenience of the public. But you worked from 8:00 in the morning until whatever time past 8:00 at night it took to balance your books. If you were lucky, you'd get out of there by 8:30. Monday through Friday, regular bank hours were 10:00 to 3:00. On Saturday, the bank was open from 10:00 in the morning till 1:00 for the public and then you came back and worked 6:00 to 8:00 for the public. But we started at 8:00 every morning and stayed until we balanced our books. For all that I got a monthly salary of $35.

But I appreciated how lucky I was because all during the Depression, I knew at least four girls who would have been glad to cut my throat to get my job.

Posting—Weight of the World

Mary Chiara, who became one of my great and good friends, was a teller who had been working at the bank since high school graduation six years before. She broke me in on the hand-posting machine. It took a lot of muscle to crank your ledger slips and statement sheets across and then crank it to return the carriage.

The ledger was made up of four books: A to F, F to L, L to R, and R to Z, with little rods you'd open up to remove the metal covers and sheets which had to be cranked through the posting machine each day.

To begin with, I posted the statements from the ledger sheets after the checks had already been cashed, sorted, scanned, and screened. Then I got broken in to work at lunchtime in the cage, waiting on the public cashing checks. But before I could do that, I had to study the accounts until I could recognize all the signatures. Sometimes, even now, if the name of an old-time customer is mentioned, if I shut my eyes, I can see their signature card.

But when I first started posting the ledger, I felt the weight of the whole world, worrying about cashing a bad check for somebody. Even if they were pretty drunk, you had to—well, I could always ask the fellow that was the assistant cashier if I were in doubt. We posted the savings ledger, which wasn't so big—let's face it, not many people were saving with the Depression on. And in between times, we had to let people into their deposit boxes.

Mary's parents had come over from Italy. Her father had been killed in an accident in the Bunker mine and a brother killed in a bicycle accident down on the Division Street bridge one Halloween. She had a sister and a younger half brother. Her mother had a rooming and boardinghouse down on Railroad Avenue.

Mary was a devoted worker. Years later, when she retired, they had a big Mary Chiara Day—and that wasn't too long before she died.

Short and Over

You had to balance your books with the front every day and again each week, mail out overdraft notices, and, at the end of the month, put out the statements. We had to post the interest in the savings ledger December 31 and June 30. Since my birthday was the last day of June, I always celebrated by posting the interest after banking hours that night. And so, I really didn't have very swinging birthdays!

There was an anomaly about balancing to the penny. If you were off five or ten cents on the ledger sheets, you had to look till you found it. One time we looked for three days to find ten cents that was off and it was on a Sunshine payroll check. But out in the cage, you had a short-and-over account to adjust mistakes. It seemed odd that out in front where you were dealing with real money, you had a short-and-over, but back where it was paper, you had to balance right to the penny.

We did it all with arithmetic and a pencil. But later, we did get electric posting equipment and that was wonderful.

Pay Cut

In the depth of the Depression, Mary got her wages cut back to $45 and I got cut to $25 a month—a bookkeeper was "low man on the totem pole." We figured if we were seen standing around out front, pretty soon one of us would be gone, so we dressed up all the old files and moved part of them down to the basement. The records that went back to when the bank started had just been stuck down there, so we sorted and filed those, too. When things started looking up, we did get our wages back up a little.

Meets Bill Lamb

When my parents had moved to Kellogg, my brothers, Dick and Art, and my sister, Helen, became friends with Mac and Margaret Lamb down at the church and young people's group. They had been getting together at their house for card games. So then I got acquainted with them, and even had a date with Mac, who was my age but still in high school. We went ice skating on a slough down at the edge of town as you headed up on a back road toward Wallace. It wasn't good skating—well, I didn't know anything about ice skating. All I knew was a little bit about roller-skating, and I didn't do all that great at that and had my scarred-up purple knees to prove it.

Mrs. Lamb, who had rented a house fairly close to us, invited us to her house one night to have lunch and play cards. And I met her son, Bill, who was still working on a stripping crew at the Bunker Hill electrolytic zinc plant.

Kissed on the Back Porch

The next time we were down there playing cards, Bill wasn't there. He came in later and he'd had a few drinks—not enough to be unsteady—but of course, I didn't know that much about liquor because to Mother, liquor was something you didn't even talk about, let alone imbibe. I weighed 100 pounds, was four foot ten and one-half inches tall and Bill was six-foot-one. He kissed me on the back porch that night as we were heading for home. He always said, later, that if it hadn't been for those few drinks and kiss on the porch, he never would have got in the trouble he did! He always said liquor was his downfall.

Bill and I had a few dates then. We hiked up the hill and he taught me to target shoot with the Colt Woodsman he'd bought when he first started working in the zinc plant. And that is one of the guns I still have because he gave it to me.

Some nights we'd just sit around and visit and play some music. Then he had this car, and so a few times we went riding around and parked awhile.

Once in awhile we'd go on a picnic and a few times we went to the show. It didn't cost much, but it still cost money, and he was trying to keep things slow because Mac and Margaret were still in school. Even though Bill's mother was doing some home nursing, as she had before and after his father died when he was eleven, he had to keep 'em afloat.

Bottles Blowing Up

Bill's sister, Margaret, and I got to be good friends. One day after work, I went by to say hello. She wasn't there, but Mrs. Lamb acted distressed and not very friendly, so I thought I hadn't picked a good day to come by and visit.

This was during Prohibition, and later I found out that Bill was capping the beer he was making. He had waited too long, and the bottles were blowing up, beer slopping all over the floor, and Mrs. Lamb hadn't had a chance to mop up yet. She was afraid I'd smell it and think they were terrible. Back then I wouldn't have known what it was!

Other Beaus

Then we had some sort of disagreement. He acquired a new girlfriend and I got another boyfriend—or two or three. When I was seventeen, I had started going with an assayer at the smelter off and on for a year and a half. Jack Sinniger was tall, had black, curly hair, and a little mustache and always called me "Little Girl." But he was twenty-seven. I went with two other assayers a few times—they were always real nice to me.

But then Bill and I ended up seeing each other again and went together for several years because he still had his family to take care of, and we just didn't have enough money to get married.

The summer of 1932, Bill and his family lived up the east fork of Pine Creek in a little settlement with a schoolhouse, store, and post office called Masonia. There was an old mine at the end of the gulch that changed names during the years and later was the Spokane-Idaho. Curtis Redding, husband of Evelyn Redding, who was the mail route lady out of Harrison for years, was the foreman of that mine at one time.

Back to Lamb Ranch in Bell Canyon

The Depression was getting worse. Bill didn't make enough money to cover rent and groceries, so they moved back to the ranch in Bell Canyon in the early fall.

At first, Bill went to the ranch on weekends. When he got cut to ten days of work a month, he spent the rest of his time working at the ranch. That way, he didn't have to pay board and room in Kellogg.

About that time, Margaret got acquainted with Jim Lyons, who worked at the Bunker Hill warehouse. So I'd ride down to the ranch with him. We played cards, rode horseback, and climbed hills. Some nights the uncles would come down and Shorty Dudley would come up, and Margaret and I would play the piano Bill had bought for her, and we'd sing and eat popcorn—real swingy!

One Fourth of July, some of Bill's mother's family came to visit. Mama (that's what I called her, too), Margaret, and I were sleeping in the bed in the only bedroom, but there were people sleeping all over the floor and in the kitchen and living room, and Mac and Bill and some of the cousins were sleeping out in the woodshed. It was wall to wall people. Next day, there was poor Mama cookin' up a storm. Somehow she always managed.

The spring on that property had little water, so pretty soon, Mac or Bill would have to haul another barrel of water down from Uncle George's place. I didn't realize until later how much of a problem it was, not having water.

Bank Holiday

[During the Great Depression more and more banks failed as people withdrew their money in fear. Newly elected President Franklin Delano Roosevelt ordered all banks closed. On March 9, 1933, Congress passed the Emergency Banking Bill, which ordered the banks to remain closed until they could be examined. By midsummer most banks had reopened.]

The First State Bank, where I worked, closed so I stayed at the Lamb ranch. But I was afraid to be gone from my parents' home very long because they might call me back. If I weren't there the day they opened, I could lose my job.

Barrel-Stave Skis

We had a late snow that March. Mac made some skis out of old barrel staves, and one clear night under a bright, full moon we were trying to ski down the hill, falling in the snow, rolling end over end, getting wet, and I was thinking, here we are, laughing and having a heck of a good time in spite of not having any money.

The bank called me back pretty soon and life went on. Bill started working more shifts.

Margaret moved back to Kellogg when she and Jim Lyons married in 1934. Mac and Mama were still at the ranch, so Bill and I came down to see them when we could.

Cockeyed Minister

Bill and I wanted to get married on Margaret's anniversary, September 21, but that wasn't going to work out. The bank had abandoned the 6:00 to 8:00 Saturday evening hours, but still was open mornings. It really didn't do to ask for any time off in 1935, but I asked for Saturday. Friday night after work, Margaret and Jim went with us to Coeur d'Alene and we were married, September 20, 1935, by a Presbyterian minister—and he was cockeyed. So Bill always swore that the minister married me to Jim because all during the service, the minister was looking at Jim and me and not at Bill and me.

Margaret and Jim went on our honeymoon with us. Prohibition had ended and there was a night club in the basement of the Davenport Hotel in Spokane, Washington, where we had nice rooms that night. Margaret and I loved to dance—Bill and Jim didn't, but they were trying to be agreeable so we dragged those reluctant fellows onto the dance floor for a bit.

The next day we drove to Coulee Dam, which they were just starting to dig with those big Le Tourneau earthmovers. The basin was filled with them and they looked humongous—but they wouldn't be anything compared with what we see now. Bill took a picture of Margaret and me standing in front of them—but we never thought to have a wedding picture taken of us!

First Home

Until then I had lived with Father and Mother. We had moved to a house with French doors and windows that is still right across the street from the Kellogg post office on South Division. Bill and I lived our first year in a miserable little four-room shack, which we rented for $12 a month. Our place was on the corner of North Division and the old highway to Wallace. The floods of '33 had left lead deposits in the sunken front yard so that even weeds were discouraged from growing there.

The zinc plant wasn't running full-time, but Bill was working all three shifts in rotation when it did—no set number of weeks on a shift—whatever seemed expedient. The long change from day shift one day to graveyard the next night was fine, but the short change from graveyard to swing shift the same day wasn't so jolly.

One-Room Shack Became Sunshine Inn

Right away we bought a lot to build a house, on West Riverside Street in Kellogg's Sunnyside Addition, from a little Frenchman who owned quite a bit of property in the area and ran a one-room place that some of the muckers and strippers used to stop at coming home from work. It developed later into the Sunshine Inn, a large, well-known restaurant and bar. We paid $200 for [the lot]. It was a corner lot and that made it more valuable. Ward and Nellie (Nederhood) Williams would be our neighbors across the street all the years we lived there.

A year later Bill went to the office at the Bunker and propositioned them to let him buy the lumber, windows, insulation, and other building materials through them. We got $500 credit and paid it back at $50 a month.

Building First House

Bill didn't know anything about building but his friend, Ed Linhart, did. So with his buddy helping him, he poured the foundation for the floor plan for a one or two bedroom, prefabricated house that Bill had seen in a book.

I wanted two bedrooms but he said, "No. It would cost $500 for that second bedroom and we can't afford it." So we went with the one bedroom.

We could have bought the house all precut and ready to build, but it did help getting "prefab" windows and doors from Portland, Oregon, at a reduced price through the Bunker.

We moved in as soon as Bill got the water in and the doors and windows so we could seal it up. That saved us rent, little bit that it was, and it helped being there where he didn't have to go several blocks each day to work on it on his time off. The studs for partitions were up, but no walls or cupboards. We had a little floor heater, a hot plate to cook on and a lumber pile in the tiny dinette for us and our guests to sit on. No room for the overstuffed chair, which was a wedding present from the bank, or the coffee table that was another wedding present or the chairs we already had stored with Jim and Margaret.

But after the house was built, Bill could see we needed the attic for storage if nothing else, so he had to figure how to make a stairway from our bedroom.

Sailboat in the Basement

Then Bill dug out the basement and put in a sawdust burner. Later, he built an 18½-foot-long sailboat down there. It was nice red oak and put together with screws. He bought the sails from Jensen Byrd in Spokane. Margaret and Jim had a floathouse on Lake Coeur d'Alene in Beauty Bay. Bill had to take the whole thing apart and reassemble it in the backyard so we could sail it that summer down there. He built a little rowboat to go with the sailboat and moored both at Beauty Bay beside the highway. Nobody collected any rent, but we paid an old fellow four dollars a month to watch over them. We'd go down there on days off and had some fun.

Mac's Horseradish Business

Going back a little, Mac had married Gina November 1, 1936. They moved to Kellogg to live at old Mr. Lafferty's. Mr. Lafferty had owned a dairy store in Harrison, but now was raising horseradish, grinding and selling it commercially for use on meats. Mac and Gina helped him and later bought him out.

Meantime, Mama stayed with them and did crochet work and sold it to Mrs. Lulu Edward, who had a dress shop there.

Daddy Reed

Then, in 1937, Mama went to California to visit Bill's Aunt Maggie [Margaret Dodd]. While she was there, she met Charles Mash Reed. She took care of his wife, who had cancer, until she died. The next year, Mama and Daddy Reed were married. He was seventy years old then and still working as head of the composing room for the Los Angeles *Times-Examiner*. He continued working there until he had a stroke at age eighty-one. Mama took care of him at home for four years until he died in 1953.

After Daddy Reed died, she remained in California and took training and became a licensed practical nurse.

No Antibiotic for Father

During the Depression, my father wasn't working full-time, but at least he was on the Bunker Hill payroll, which was all people could ask in those days. He was a big husky fellow who had never been in a hospital in his life. He caught a bad cold and infection in the glands on both sides of his neck. He saw the company doctor—we called him the "old horse doctor"—but he got worse. Mother finally nagged him down to the hospital to see the brand-new doctor, Dr. Anderson. I went to the hospital with Mother, one night after work, and his glands were swollen—just full of poison.

Dr. Anderson said, "I don't know what to do. I've done everything I can think of and nothing is touching it."

We didn't have sulfa or penicillin then. People nowadays don't realize what a miracle these new drugs are—and when we didn't have them is not that far back. He was in the hospital only a few days, and I just couldn't believe it, but he was gone. He was born August 1882 and died January 1936, so he was fifty-three, a comparatively young man. He married when he was twenty-nine and Mother was thirty. She was always so conscious of being a year older than he; it had bugged her all her life. She lived another 33 years and died in 1969.

First Baby

In 1940, Bill thought we were well enough paid off on the house that I could afford to quit work. So I did. It felt really weird being home. But soon the bank wanted me back to work while a teller or bookkeeper was on vacation, or some bank employees left for the service or war work, so I got called back to fill in till they got somebody new and was working about three days a week.

When I got pregnant I continued part-time work. I felt just fine and was going great, but I hadn't gained much weight.

When the baby was born, February 4, 1943, she wasn't premature but she only weighed two pounds ten ounces. She went right into the incubator, but she had a bowel obstruction and lived only 24 hours. I never did see her because in 1943 they weren't letting mothers get up for ten days. It was such a shock. We were so happy that first day. Bill had sent a wire to all the relatives and had passed out cigars to the fellows. Margaret's boy, Doug, was a year and a half old. It was nice that she was there to help Bill with the burial and packing away all the baby things we had ready at home.

I went back to work about a month later because I just didn't like to stay home.

Bill was working overtime and had been made a shifter for the stripping room crew and part of the time for the repair crew, too. He was in his thirties and had worked in the zinc plant since 1928. Bunker kept getting him deferred without his asking and said, "You're worth more here than you would be on the front lines." But Bill never felt quite right about being at home when a lot of fellows went into the armed services.

Angela

When I got pregnant again, I only worked to fill in for vacations. About three weeks before I was due, Margaret, Jim, and I were picking huckleberries up past Burke near the Jack Waite mine. I was getting around but was a little bit bulky and Margaret, who was pregnant but due later than I, had hysterics watching me on this steep hillside hanging onto the bushes with one arm and picking berries with the other.

Mama had flown up from California, and she and Bill were pacing up and down the hall of the old Wardner Hospital that was on McKinley Avenue, when Angela was born, August 17, 1944. When Bill heard Angela let out a scream, he said he knew this baby was hale and hearty.

It was a Cesarean birth. I had so much gas, they put a tube down my throat into my stomach, so I had nothing to eat or drink. It was a hot August. I could hear ice tinkle in the water as nurses went past my room—I could have killed for that ice water!

They wouldn't let me out of bed until the eleventh day. I walked down to the main floor to see Margaret and her baby girl, Gail, who was born ten days later than Angela.

Mother Bill

When I left the hospital for home on the twelfth day, Dr. Staley said, "You can't get out of bed till you put your girdle on, and you have to take it off after you get back in bed." Can you imagine how hard that is?

And he said I wasn't supposed to lift anything heavier than Angela, who weighed less than seven pounds. I wasn't supposed to go up and down steps. And the laundry was in the basement! She was a bottle baby because I hadn't eaten those first days after she was born.

So it ended up that Bill had to do all the "in the night" feedings and the laundry, and he always told people he was Angela's mother till she was three months old.

I got along all right but had moments of depression because I couldn't get out of the house. One night when Bill came home from work I was weeping into a pan of fried potatoes and he said, "What in God's name is the matter with you?"

And I says, "I don't know . . . I just don't knoooooow!" Boo-hoo-hoo.

I didn't work for the next two years and it was a real treat to have Bill working day shift.

Lessons for Laundry

During World War II, Mother lived with my sister, Helen, in Missoula. After the war, she came back to Kellogg, took an apartment and taught music for several years more. She hadn't much to live on—my brother, Art, sent her a little money and we did what we could. Lessons didn't bring much. If she had pupils that had talent or interest, she'd give them music lessons free or take something in trade. One lady did Mother's laundry for her daughter's lessons. Music was the passion of Mother's life!

Real Butter!

We went over to Hot Springs [Montana] in March of '46 and spent a week in a little housekeeping cabin. Butter was still hard to get, but somebody told us about a dairy at Polson where they let us have three pounds of butter. After eating margarine you colored yourself during the war, real butter was something.

It was rainy and sort of horrid. I was busy washing diapers and all this sulfur water was smelling coming out of the faucet, but Bill was enjoying the hot springs and drinking that stupid water—and trying to figure out how he could get back to living on the ranch in Bell Canyon.

Bill Buys Ranch

Uncle Joe had needed surgery during the war years and planned to sell his place, so Bill had bought it just to keep anybody else from owning it. We had no idea of doing anything with it then, but now we'd need more land. So when we got back from Hot Springs we came down to Bell Canyon to talk to Shorty Dudley about buying his ranch. He raised a few head of cattle to buy the bare necessities and from what Bill said, he bootlegged a little to supplement his income. He had been talking about selling for quite awhile and was agreeable, but wanted to stay on it. Bill said that wasn't any problem.

Bill bought a dozen head of "white faces" [Herefords] in Fairfield from a relative of a friend of ours in Kellogg. Their son got called into the navy sooner than expected. The family didn't want to keep them after the boy was gone, so Bill had to bring the cattle to the ranch sooner than he had planned. He spent that spring with Shorty in his little house across the road.

The Tent House

Bill wanted Angela and me to come down after the weather got warmer. Meantime he wanted to build a log house. I wanted to get lumber from Veazey's Mill at Pinehurst instead, but he was bound he was going to make this log house, and got Levi Lehman to help dig and pour the foundation. Then in back, he put up this little 16-by-20-foot tent house on some rock foundation for us to stay in, supposedly, just for the summer.

Margaret loaned us a big, old bed Jim had made with drawers for bedding underneath. I bought a little pasteboard clothes closet from the catalog. To help keep the mice and pack rats out, Jim built us one little screened cupboard for dishes and had a fellow down at the Bunker make two round barrels with wooden lids for flour and sugar. We had a small kitchen stove over in the corner, and a little airtight tin heater. We had three chairs and a little table Bill had built around the post in the middle of the room that held the tent roof up.

But the tent had holes in it. Every time it rained, we caught the drips in plates and pie tins set on the floor and bed. I'd listen to that splop! and plink! till I'd get mad and go to Kellogg and stay with Margaret or my brother Art until Bill got the place dried out.

Precious Spring Water

Shorty Dudley had never improved the spring in the back. Every day, he'd come over and pack two buckets of water back to his house and that did for him and his cats. The first thing Bill did was dig out the spring, cement it up inside, and put a pitcher pump on top.

Shorty kept saying, "Egad! How you people use water!"

One day when he came over to get water, he asked us to walk back with him to pick some strawberries. He had no sooner set the bucket down than one of his cats started drinking out of it.

Angela spoke up, "Mama, I want a drink of water!"

And I said, "Wait till we get over to the house!"

Shorty said, "What's the matter with you, girl? Give that kid a drink!"

Bill Quits Zinc Plant

Bill went back to work at the zinc plant for a time but had to quit because he couldn't drive back and forth while looking after the cows, building corrals, cutting hay and hauling it into Shorty's barn. The barn had a hay fork that came out of the barn loft on a track. It dropped down to pick up the loose hay and then you pulled it back up with a rope on a pulley and tripped it.

Bill replaced the tent with a single-walled board shack with a tarpaper roof. We put that pink, heavy building paper on the walls and put in a nice little heating stove. But we still called it the tent house. He had the subfloor down and one round of logs on the foundation for the log house when it snowed. I brushed it off and it snowed again. Then on Halloween it really snowed! So we could see we weren't going to do much on the log house and started doing what we could to survive in the tent house that winter. [The temperature dipped to 30 degrees below zero.]

Car Goes Kerpooey!

Our Dodge business coupe wasn't any car for being out here in the sticks with a road that wasn't maintained the way it is now, so we bought a secondhand Dodge pickup in Kellogg. It was snowing and blowing that night coming down, when the lights went out. We had just got past Ann's Place [now Cave Lake Resort], and were heading up the hill, with me holding the flashlight out the open window with the snow stinging my face so Bill could see, and then something went kerpooey! The car stopped.

Bill packed Angela, and we waded through the snow back to Ann's Place. We'd known Al and Ann Lane from stoppin' in to visit and they belonged to the Masons, too. Ann gave us something to eat and some hot coffee. Al and Bill decided there wasn't anything to be done in the wind and snow, so Al drove us home. He was afraid to drive down the canyon, so we had to walk a mile from Colby's place at the Four Corners [the intersection of Bell Canyon and Van Dusen roads].

Bill went back to get the damn thing the next day, and it turned out the hose to the radiator had come undone. The very day we'd bought it! That should have told us what that pickup was going to be like.

Groceries Via Horseback

During the winter they didn't plow out the road because the mail was delivered up on the Flats. The closest the school bus came was up at the Four Corners because nobody down here had children. Charles and Arlene Waters lived about a mile up what is now Lamb Road, on the place formerly owned by Ernie Damiano's parents.

The snow got deeper and deeper, so Bill got on Uncle George's saddle horse and rode into Harrison to Curly's store ["Curly" Ralph and Luella Cope's store] and brought groceries back in a gunnysack. After nine more days, the road district foreman hired Jim Powers to plow out the canyon with his bulldozer.

Instead of living in the tent house one winter, which we thought we might, we would live in it five more!

Back to Work

Bill had back trouble all his life. Then, they called it "lumbago." The next year, 1947, he tried to work, but some days he just couldn't get around. That fall, it was expedient that we get a little money coming in, so I went to work at the bank in Kellogg again, doing fill-in work. Angela and I stayed with my brother, Art, and his wife, Esther, that winter.

My brother kept telling me I should put in an application at the zinc plant because Bunker Hill was paying better wages for office work than any place else in the county. I knew the brass, slightly, from meeting them in the bank. I was hesitant—afraid I couldn't hack it—but I did. I worked there as a fill-in voucher clerk until the end of June, paying all the okayed bills and selling bus, milk, and boot tickets, and balancing everything up at the end of the month.

Heading Home on Halloween

I was looking forward to being home all week and not just weekends, but the bank needed me to fill in for a month or two at most for vacations. One lady that was coming from back East to be a teller didn't arrive, so I kept working "just one more week" and ended up leaving on Halloween day, and it was raining—just pouring down. Angela and I came on the train with the accumulation from working up there a year, with 22 boxes and sacks full of junk to haul home.

Bill was out hauling someplace, so we walked up the hill to wait for him at Kate Pettet's house. She was the only one I knew in Harrison.

Thomas Reed Lamb

I hadn't been home very long before I could tell I was PG [pregnant] again. I went back and forth to Kellogg on the train every few weeks that winter for my checkups. I had another Caesarean and Tom was born July 25, 1949. He was named for his two grandfathers—Thomas for Bill's father and Reed for Bill's step-father, a very wonderful old gentleman.

Tent House—Fun, Fun, Fun

All the summers we lived in the tent house, we had friends and relatives every weekend, and no water in the house. We carried water from the pump house and heated it on the kitchen range. We trotted out back to the outhouse. That winter we were still in the tent house, and that was fun—fun—fun.

Bunker Hill Zinc Plant Ups the Ante!

Bill had been hauling logs, our own and other people's. His back was really bad, his right leg going numb, so that he had to lift his leg with his hand to put his foot on the brake peddle.

So he said, "I hate to ask you, but I guess you better see if Lloyd needs you at the bank."

I called up and Lloyd said he could always use a teller. I asked what the wages were and he said they were the same as they had been when I worked there in '48.

I said, "Lloyd! This is two years later!"

I wasn't very happy about the wages but I thought, I'll have to make the best of it.

Margaret and Jim had moved to a bigger house and said we could stay there and she would baby-sit Tom that winter. Angela and Margaret's girl, Gail, had just started first grade and could easily walk to the Sunnyside School.

I was set to go when Verne Roehl, the office manager for the zinc plant, called and asked if I wanted a job. He would pay me $75 more than the bank. Whenever the union fellows got a raise, they would give the salaried people a blanket raise at the same time.

So he said, "And in another three weeks you'll get a $25 raise. Now what do you say?"

I said, "That sounds pretty wonderful."

He said, "Can you come next Monday?"

This was in the middle of the week and I thought this is pretty grim, but I said, "Yeah, I'll be there." I figured I could still be in the carpool with fellows that lived in Sunnyside.

I posted all the books with accounts numbering from 001 to 2,400, and each number in between denoted some special department or area where they wanted a separate account. There could be many accounts to be posted when a single bill was paid—no computers then—all done by hand. Verne balanced the books at the end of the month, but after I'd worked there awhile, he decided I could do it. Each one of those accounts had to balance, and all accounts balanced, down to the penny, to the grand total they had spent for the whole month and be on Verne's desk the fifth of the following month, at 8:00 in the morning, and he didn't care if I'd worked till 10:00 or 11:00 or how I got it, but it better be there by then. So I did it.

Gail Gets Rheumatic Fever

The next summer, Gail got rheumatic fever and had to have complete bed rest and quiet. Certainly it wasn't quiet with Tommy, nearly two, walking around, and impossible to keep him, Angela, and Margaret's boy, Doug, out of her room. We had been eating with Margaret and I had been paying board and room, which I know wasn't what it should have been, but it was all she would ask and all I could afford.

I found a little upstairs apartment in Sunnyside that had been used to keep spare caskets when the building housed a mortuary. I got a lady that lived out Elk Creek to baby-sit Tom, but some mornings she didn't get there in time, and I had one heck of a time getting to work. Things were hectic!

Back to Margaret's

That fall, Gail felt better and was going back to school, so Margaret and Jim fixed up their basement with a bedroom and a kitchen/living room with shelves and a little kerosene stove with burners that I cooked on. At least we could be by ourselves and not bother her. And she took care of Tommy.

That winter Bill lived there with us and worked at the zinc plant again. If Bill didn't have to work Saturday, weekends we'd bring Tommy and come down to see how Tony Dimico was doing taking care of the cattle for us and we'd check on Uncle George. Angela stayed in Kellogg with my mother, doing her music lessons.

The second year, we rented a two-room cabin on the back of Jim and Margaret's lot. Margaret went back to school for a teaching degree, so Nellie Williams kept Tom.

The next summer was a busy time. Bill quit the zinc plant and was back to working on the ranch. I had to work Saturday mornings at the zinc plant, so in the afternoon I'd head for the train to Harrison. I'd have Angela, Tom in the stroller, clean clothes and groceries in bags, get on the train and then arrive at the depot and wait for Bill to show up to take us home.

Getting back to Kellogg on Sunday was a problem. If any relatives came down, I could ride up with them. Usually we didn't have a rig that was working good enough to drive up, so if I didn't have a ride, I'd have to go back on the train Sunday morning. If I came down on the Saturday night train and went back Sunday morning, I didn't get that much done.

I felt like I was on a tightrope. Mother had kept the piano Bill bought for me before we were married until we got the walls of the log house up. I liked to sit down and play the piano, but I was afraid to start because after I played one piece I wanted to play more. A couple of times I spent a whole hour just playing and enjoying myself and I didn't have the time to spare.

Quits Zinc Plant

The end of June 1954, I'd worked at the zinc plant almost four years. We were tired of commuting. Bill thought we were squared around pretty good, so I told Verne I was going to quit. The kids and I came back to the ranch. That fall, Angela went to school in the old 1909 brick building in Harrison.

We worked on the log house. But whenever we had time, we needed more money than we could scrounge up to buy material; and when we had money to buy material, that was the busy part of the year when Bill didn't have the time.

Dishes and Dynamite

When we had moved to the ranch the first time, I had packed two big, wooden barrels with all my treasures—Haviland China my mother had given me, some hand-painted dishes and other acquisitions I had made over the years. Until the log house was built, Bill stored the barrels in a shed behind the barn. I was in a state of hysteria every time I'd look in that shed and here'd be my dish barrels sitting there with his boxes of dynamite sticks right beside them. He'd laugh and say it didn't matter as long as the caps were stored down here someplace, but I never really wanted to know where. They could be upstairs.

Whishhhhhhhhhhhoe!

Uncle George and Bill had bought the little Caterpillar about 1948 or '49 from Emery Hedlund in St. Maries. Just like in Kellogg, Bill had built the house first and dug the basement afterward. He was 'dozing out what he could and used black powder to break some of the dirt loose. He hired Hans Fabricius and his son Martin, who was a teenager, to help dig.

One day they set off this black powder and there came a flash—it just went whishhhhhhhhhhhoe!—and the lids flew off the kitchen stove, the oven door banged open, pans crashed off the stove onto the floor, some dishes fell off the table—everything in the place rattled. I was so mad I ran out in front and I can still see Hans and Martin standing there, with the black smoke swirling around them, staring at me while I was telling Bill what I thought of him in no uncertain terms.

They went home and wouldn't come back for two days. Bill said I scared away the only help he could get. The pay wasn't that much but they were willing to work for it.

Bill hired Hans and Martin Fabricius to tear down Shorty's old house. Then he spent a lot of time that winter building a canoe out of those boards. It was really nice looking when he got it done.

Spring Was a Bonus

Uncle George's spring was a good one. People hauled water from it in dry years. When Bill dug out the basement, he uncovered a still better spring, six feet below the back door. When he poured the floor for the 400 gallon storage tank, he couldn't get the water stopped with pumping, so he had to pour the floor through the water and let it set. He had to put an overflow underneath the floor and that makes the basement damp and cold, but the pump can never freeze. So that was a bonus.

Helps with Logging

I helped with the logging, off and on, weekends and vacations during the years. I skidded with the Cat when we were loading with a gin pole because Bill had to be on top of the load to set tongs. When Angela got old enough she set tongs. If Margaret's boy, Doug, was here, or anyone else, needless to say, they got pressed into service!

Office at Springston

Our finances still weren't good in the fall of 1956. There weren't many office jobs in this area, but I wrote to Russell Lumber Company.

■ Tommie helped his dad, Bill Lamb, August 1956

Charlie [Charles Russell, office manager] called up and asked me if I were interested in the job that Vivian Wilson [later Palmer] was leaving. Then he came to the house and outlined the work: payroll, correspondence, clerk in the office and post office, and sending out the prospectus on sales. The monthly salary wasn't like at the zinc plant, but I said I'd take it.

Bill drove me to Springston to work. Sometimes I'd catch a ride back to Harrison, but he still had to bring me home, so he said, "This has got to come to a screechin' halt!"

He bought an old secondhand Chevy with an automatic shift from Cy Chase. The first time Bill sent me to St. Maries alone to buy supplies for him, it stalled at the intersection by Mike's Drug—people honking at me—I about died!

I drove to work in it, taking the dike road or the back road around Anderson Lake, or into Harrison to pick up Polly Russell, who came to work at Springston shortly after I did. But whenever the Chevy got really warm, it wouldn't start.

The Springston Store had a little branch of the Harrison post office. We put mail in the few boxes, passed out General Delivery mail, made money orders, sold stamps and figured parcel delivery by air or regular mail. We didn't work Saturdays, but every few weeks, we each took a turn at keeping the post office open. There weren't many Saturday postal patrons, but Louis Bennett, the clerk who broke me in, assured me that using the postal guide, I wouldn't have a thing to worry about.

Mrs. Temple Carnegie came in with a package to mail to a missionary in Abyssinia. I looked in the postal guide, and either I was dumb or the guide wasn't definitive enough, because I couldn't decide how to mail the darn thing.

I had to tell her, "I'm sorry, but you'll just have to bring it back the first of the week." I thought I'd probably get the gate for that!

A Unique Little Place

I worked there from September of 1956 to June of 1960. There were a lot of experiences up there that would—well, we've laughed about it. It was a whole different world. I regret I never took a picture of that unique little store, mill office, warehouse, and everything. The store had a small supply, but such a diversity. Bill always said he'd call there first for hardware for repairs before he'd go to St. Maries.

When you look at the empty space now and try to picture what was there, there's not room for it: Louis and Sally Bennett's house, Harry Jensen's little shack, Rumelhart's, Ernie and Clara Smith's, the little railroad station, and Al and Glenna Ross's house. And you think about the people that lived across the bridge and above it, and there's not room. It was interesting.

Dude Ranch

For three months the next summer, 1961, Thursday Willson and I worked at the dude ranch lodge at Blue Lake for Lloyd and Rowena Jones. The worst thing was driving there. Thursday's idea of driving was like nobody else's. Oh God!

We did housecleaning, laundry, and sometimes baby-sitting for guests going to town to shop. Lloyd's Aunt Mabel was cooking, but she got mad and quit. So for two weeks, Thursday and I cooked for thirty-plus people, including the help. I'll assure you, Thursday was the main cook. Again, I was on salary, and those were long hours! We'd be there between six and seven in the morning and on Friday barbecue nights, after we cleaned up, we'd get home about eight-thirty or nine.

Writes Harrison News

I had started writing Harrison news for the *St. Maries Gazette-Record* in 1960 when Mrs. Nitkey asked me, because she was leaving after writing for many years. That summer was pretty hectic trying to keep track of what was going on. But I did manage until the next year.

4-H and World Fair

The spring of 1962, the 4-H kids and their leaders were figuring on making the trip to the World Fair in Seattle. Angela and Tom were both in 4-H and Bill and I were leaders. I had two groups in cooking, canning, and sewing. Bill had calves and sheep. Some other leaders were Red [Charles U.] and Betty Blakley, Jim and Bernice Boe, and the Jensen brothers, Verne and Art.

We were putting on a cabaret and entertainment in the gym to make money for the trip. Steve Stanley, one of the teachers, was short and tubby, but he could kick up his heels and showed Bernice Boe, Betty Blakley, Hattie Piper, Jean Fish, Sylvia Schutte, me, and some others, how to do the cancan. Boy, were we sore! We got our costumes on and the night we did it, one of the gals got drunker'n a skunk. I don't think she even knew where she was, and we had a helluva time getting through that number.

We made quite a bit of money and went to the fair on the Northern Pacific Railroad on a special excursion weekend rate for groups like ours—but of course, we had to sit up all Friday night.

Civil Service

Since I had to work somewhere, my sister had nagged me into taking the civil service exam, the first of the year of '62, to get on the rolls for working for the Forest Service.

When we got home from the fair on Thursday, the office manager at the Coeur d'Alene Forest Service called and said, "Can you be here next Monday?"

Angela was going to graduate from high school in May, and Tom would be in the eighth grade the next fall. He and Bill had decided they could bach during the week if I got work. I didn't have a place to stay in Coeur d'Alene but I said, "I'll be there."

Friend Lois Brown

I had joined the Eastern Stars in Kellogg in 1943, about a week after our little girl died, and transferred to Harrison soon after we moved. The winter before Tom was born, Lois would give me a ride to town, but she was afraid to drive down the canyon, so I'd walk up the hill to Mrs. Colby's and Lois would come over and pick me up at the Four Corners. After the meeting, I'd stay overnight with Lois, then she'd bring me back and I'd walk down the hill. And at a lodge picnic at Colby's, she had made a movie tape of Tom singing when he was three years old. So we'd gotten pretty well acquainted.

Lois had moved to Coeur d'Alene, so I stayed with her until she found me a place with Mary Johnson, where I rented a bedroom and kitchen privileges.

I stayed there during the week. That's when John and Eleanor Waters's daughter, Clara, was going to college, so Bill and Johnny fixed it between them that Johnny would come after work on Friday and bring me and Clara home. Then on Sunday night, Bill would deliver us back to Coeur d'Alene. I was busy trying to get squared around at home on weekends, get the laundry done, and living out of a suitcase—well, it was pretty hectic.

Red Tape in Budget and Finance

I worked in B and F [Budget and Finance], work I felt familiar with, paying all the bills for the office and different ranger stations. I found a lot of red tape in government that would have been dispensed with in private business. It was very frustrating. But I made some lasting, good friends, including Lois Becklund, my supervisor.

In the fall of 1963 there was an opening in St. Maries in Resources, which is timber sales. I knew nothing about timber sales, period, so it was a whole new ball game again.

Worst Challenge

The worst challenge was getting back and forth to work. Bill had bought a '62 Corvair, the first new car we'd ever had and a real lemon, I mean a *real lemon*! During that time, Bill was driving school bus, so he had to leave early, and I was on my own getting to town in the morning. I'd drive into Harrison and then ride with Charlotte Prudente. When Polly Russell started working for Cy Chase as a bookkeeper, we both rode with Charlotte.

One winter on the way into Harrison, there was a big berm on the side of the road between here and Lonnie Damiano's, just past the Dimico road. I suppose I was going a little too fast. The car spun around and made a complete circle—then it stopped, headed toward town again. Finally, I got up nerve enough to get started again.

Charlotte Prudente left our office and transferred to the ranger's office in Avery, April 1, 1964. Then I had to do all the driving because Polly Russell didn't drive at all.

Car Spins Again

The last day of March, Polly didn't ride with me. I was driving to work by myself in great, big, slushy snowflakes, going along all right till I got to that curve just this side of the Riverside, and then the car cut three figure S's. I lost control. The car whirled, slid off the road, and ended up headed back toward Harrison on that little spit of muddy ground just above the river. The whole time I was thinking: Thank God! My insurance is paid up. But then, what difference would it make to me?

And the great, big snowflakes were still coming down. Nobody was up at the Riverside, so I was startled when somebody came rapping on the door. It was Art Freeman and his son Richard. He still had his little lath mill in St. Maries and Richard was working for him.

He says, "Eleanor, are you all right? What happened?"

I said, "Well, I just went off the road—and here I am! I don't know if the car will run, and I don't know how I'm going to get back on the road."

He said, "We've got a chain in the back of the pickup." They pulled the car back on the road and Art says, "It acts all right. Do you want to drive on to town?"

I said, "Hell, no! I don't!"

So Richard drove it and I rode with Art. The car got a dreadful oil leak but wasn't hurt otherwise.

Then Polly and I bummed rides with a lot of different drivers. We rode with Polly's son Joe, who was working at the plywood mill and with Harold Drake, parts man at the Chase garage, and Betty Grant, who was working in the bank. But it finally got down to just me—I had to drive whether I wanted to or not.

Lamb's Corral

Earlier, Bill had emphysema and knew he would have to give up taking care of cows because of the dust from putting up hay in the summer and feeding in the winter. After Tom started school at North Idaho College [NIC] in Coeur d'Alene, we sold the cows.

Bill was still driving school bus, but needed something else to do to keep busy. Goldie Slane approached him to sell real estate for her, so in 1968 he got his salesman's license and later, bought Slane's Harrison Realty. Years before, he had bought the old tire-storage building [on the corner of Main and Garnet], so he put the real estate business in it. It was empty except for a desk, so he thought it would be good to bring in something for a conversation piece. We went to an auction in Deary and bought eight boxes of bottles that had just been newly dug and hadn't even been washed yet.

There were many categories of bottles: patent medicine, liquor, food, and they came in different shapes and colors that belonged to the past era. Bill studied enough about bottles to become thoroughly knowledgable and make them interesting.

He bought a few cups, saucers, plates, and vases to go with these boxes of bottles from an antique shop. Then we just worked other stuff in there gradually, and it became an antique shop, Lamb's Corral.

Breaks in New Supervisor

That spring the Forest Service moved into the new federal building in St. Maries. The section heads were mainly young college men with no training in forestry. And what really insulted you was that they would make three or four times more money than you, but you had to break them in so they could supervise [that department].

When my immediate supervisor, Jimmie (Gladys) Lowry, quit, I had to train two new girls and this new male supervisor that I disliked the moment I saw him. It wasn't that the job was so difficult. I was the only one there at that time that knew what to do.

Eye Surgery

In the meantime, my eyesight had been getting worse. I wrote to a doctor in Santa Cruz, California, that did advanced surgery on cataracts, but didn't hear from him until fall when he said to come. Here I was with this boss that didn't know anything and two new green girls, so I left pages of written instructions for making and sending the quarterly reports to Missoula, and flew to Santa Cruz. The doctor persuaded me to have him do both eyes while I was there, so I was in the hospital for over a week.

I called Bill when I got back to the hotel to tell him I had to stay for another week for a checkup before I would come home. He was telling me he was going to be a pallbearer at Buck Heuett's funeral the next day, that he'd got killed that weekend in a hunting accident. The gun got knocked off the car seat and shot him.

This was when felt tip pens first came in. They made broad lines [on the paper] that I could see with my tunnel vision. I sat in my hotel room and wrote pages of instructions to the two girls and my supervisor on what to do.

After my checkup, I flew to Seattle to visit Angela, who was now a registered nurse and working for the Veteran's Administration at the kidney center. After a week, Angela went with me to Wenatchee to visit Mac and Gina, who had a little motel there. Bill had driven to Spokane and had flown in a little plane to meet us, and that was the surprise of our lives to walk in and here he was sitting there!

Angela flew with me back to Santa Cruz for a checkup before I could get my glasses.

Back on the Job

I had left the middle of September and went back to work December 2. Got back on the job and found that miserable S.O.B. that was my boss had sent all the September reports in wrong, so I had to redo the third quarter before I could send the fourth quarter reports to Missoula. If I hadn't wanted to kill him before, now I had double reason.

Twenty-Five Below

That winter of 1968, a cold spell came, and the furnace in the new building quit working, so they sent us home. It was 25 below when Polly and I started out, but we didn't make it home. We stayed overnight at Elma Cerney's out on the point above Butler Bay. Bill came and got us the next day.

Forest Combined—Pandemonium!

In 1973, the St. Joe, Coeur d'Alene, and Kaniksu National Forests combined into the Idaho Panhandle National Forest, with headquarters in Coeur d'Alene. Part of each forest disappeared and St. Maries became the St. Maries Ranger District. Polly Russell and I transferred in mid-June to the supervisor's office in Coeur d'Alene, the same building on Twenty-third Street where I had worked before, so small they had to rent offices downtown for the engineers and some staff.

That was a terrible summer. No offices, no files! All the data for the different districts and forests just sitting there in boxes. We had to reconstruct files for all the sales from the three forests. It took weeks. It was pandemonium!

Polly and I rode to Coeur d'Alene every day that summer with Ila Matson. We also picked up Dolores De Luca Waide at Carlin Bay. Dolores was working in a restaurant and going to school part-time. Then we rode with Robert Damiano, who was working for Mrs. Chisholm at Chisholm Implements.

For that winter and spring of 1973–74, Polly stayed in Coeur d'Alene with her cousin, and I stayed with Nancy Nelson and later with Win Leaverton, and Bill or Glen Russell would bring us home weekends.

Another year went by.

I still had tunnel vision and no way in hell was I going to try driving in Coeur d'Alene, and it was getting harder to get back and forth. I would soon be sixty-two. Figuring how much ahead I'd be if I worked another three years, I thought, this is not worth it.

Last Day

The last day of work I didn't do a thing—just sat there thinking about all those years I'd worked and made a list of the things I had wanted to do. I had wanted to write poetry. If somebody was going to get transferred or retire, I wrote a little jingle about them and gave it to them when they had their party. Everybody thought that was just fine except Bill, who was always razzing me and called it doggerel. So I had bought a book about rhyming and poetry writing, but hadn't had time to read it.

Retired

I quit July 1, 1975, and they gave me a big retirement dinner at the Iron Horse Restaurant in Coeur d'Alene, with many of my family attending. It was a fun time!

The day after I got home Bill announced, "I've got plenty to do with real estate. The antique shop is your baby and you can take care of it from now on. It was your idea in the beginning." That was his story then!

Whole New Setup

All of Bill's uncles were bachelors, so I wondered if that would be carried into the next generation and we'd have another "Uncle George" in the family, because Tom was twenty-six and still not married. But he met Sharon Watland when they were working on the CETA [Civilian Employment and Training Act] crew for the city of Harrison, and they were married August 24, 1975.

Being retired and with no children left at home—that was a whole new setup. I got involved in the Harrison Hot Shots Kitchen Band, and summers I was busy at the shop.

Mexicali

Bill had heard about getting these Mexican pills for his emphysema from friends who had gone down several times to that clinic in

Mexicali. We called and made an appointment for December 4, 1979, and started down right after Thanksgiving.

Bill saw Dr. Furillo and got some pills and the list of ingredients in them. Joanne LaForce, a pharmacist at Jack's Pharmacy in St. Maries, checked and found the pills contained one drug that is used in other countries but is not recognized here. They couldn't be mailed into the United States, so all the years after, Bill had to get someone to bring them up from Mexico.

The drug helped him breathe better so that he no longer needed the oxygen tank. He didn't have one in the house until ten years later.

He tried to interest friends who had emphysema. On fellow said to Bill, "I wouldn't take that medicine when you don't really know what's in it. What if it was chicken shit?

Bill said, "I wouldn't give a damn if it was chicken shit as long as it helps me!"

School Board

I had never considered getting on the school board, but in 1982 some people who were urging me to run got my petition signed. The very first thing I learned on the school board was a blow to me. Changes suggested by other people, changes I envisioned and campaigned about, were not possible because of mandates, regulations, or because they really wouldn't have been an advantage.

I served on the board for six years through three superintendents; through the hullabaloo when Rose Lake District withdrew and went to Kellogg; through several unhappy tries to run a bond issue for a new building or revision on the present building—and heaven knows, they needed the space; and through the years when they closed the grade school in Harrison and had to use mobile classroom units. There were pros and cons about a number of issues and lots of stress when you felt like you were just spinning your wheels and getting nowhere.

I was elected the second time, and was late turning in my petition for the third, when I heard that Jean Dohrman thought she would run. I asked her if she was running because she wanted to be on the board, or because she thought nobody else was going to run.

She said, "I won't run against you, but I think it would be interesting."

I said, "That's great! I'll recall my nominating petition."

I enjoyed being on the board and made many new friends.

In-laws and Mama

I was so lucky to have in-laws that were really my family: Bill's cousins on the coast; his sister, Margaret, who was my best friend for all the years of her life, and her husband, Jim; his brother, Mac, and his wife, Gina; and a mother-in-law I could appreciate and care for. Unlike a lot of ladies of her years, she was so much fun, so young, so bright, so interested in everything, and still working when she was seventy years old. She died in 1979, just four days short of her eighty-ninth birthday.

When Angela married Howard Wilson July 28, 1979, I had a whole new family to get acquainted with.

■ MOSTLY ABOUT BILL LAMB

Easy-Going Father

ELEANOR: Bill said his father was always easy-going and pleasant. One time, Mac and Bill were out on the lake with him in their little boat. Bill dropped a wrench over the side. His father didn't get upset about it. Another time, his father came home from work and was sitting in the chair, napping. Bill and Mac ran around and knocked on the door. His Dad tried to get up and found he was tied to the chair!

His father got bald early like most of the family. One time, Bill and Mac were playing and bopped him on top of the head with a hammer, but his father was understanding and didn't get mad.

I couldn't see that happening to Bill—he was of a different temperament. I'll never forget the time on his birthday, when Angela was eight or nine. Bill was sitting at the kitchen table, reading a book and eating.

Angela came up behind him and patted him on the head and said, "Oh, you nice, old, bald-headed daddy! Today, you're just about as old as daddy's ever get to be."

He seemed to rise up and bounce off the ceiling, and she says, "Now what have I done?"

A Reader and a Mason

Bill liked fiction, but he also liked geography, history and science-fiction. He enjoyed having conversations with people on things like the Bermuda Triangle, UFO's, teleportation, and psychic powers. He read books from the library, his Scottish Rite Lodge magazine, *The Rifleman*, and *Time* until they had an article favoring gun control. He wrote them a lengthy notice to discontinue his subscription. *Time*'s editor later wrote him a personal letter saying they'd be glad to have him back on their list. "Go to hell!"—that was his answer.

■ Bill Lamb about 1941

He was fascinated with books about how civilization got started. He liked detective stories like Arthur Conan Doyle wrote. He read his set of Edgar Allan Poe many times. I guess his taste was what you'd call catholic—if it was printed matter, he'd read it.

Bill joined the Masons in Kellogg in 1939. After we moved to the ranch, he joined the Eastern Stars, too. His lodge work was one of the real interests in his life.

Never Sorry He Left

Bill always said he was never sorry he left Bunker Hill zinc plant for the ranch, although Bunker had been a lifesaver, giving him a salary when still a boy to help keep the family together. And he made a lot of friends there.

Bill had so many good memories of the summers he'd spent on the ranch, working and helping his family. And he had said it sure would be nice to be in a place where he was his own boss. He found out later that you weren't your own boss because you had three things to worry about: the weather, the lumber market, and the cattle market. And you had no control over any of them. They either made you or broke you. And your time wasn't your own. The time you could have been building and improving was the time you had to be out working to bring in some money. He later realized that we should have been making plans and saving money for five to ten years ahead instead of moving on the spur of the moment.

He did finally achieve his goal of building a log house, but without a floor plan. He knew what a broadax was, but nothing about how to use it. To cut the logs and hew them on three sides was something you didn't do in a hurry. We spent a lot of years camping in the tent house before we finally got the walls up, and then found there wasn't room for a family of four. So then he had to put in the stairway, change the roof and put the dormer on the back side to make bedroom area.

But he was glad he came back. He always felt his roots were here.

Bill Liked People

Bill was interested in people and worried about their problems. If there was anything he could say or do, anytime, he really would work at it.

He enjoyed the years he was a Hunter Safety teacher out at school and the six or seven years he drove the Bell Canyon school bus route.

All during the years, he was a gun enthusiast and liked to work on them. A lot of boys would come show him their new acquisition, or ask him about ones that needed repairs, or have him show his collection, or they'd just come to gun-talk for hours.

Bill kept a young attitude so that younger people would come to him for advice and to visit. They seemed to enjoy his companionship. And he treasured that. Sometimes boys or girls would stop in the shop downtown and tell him their troubles.

He'd come home worried and say, "Well, I hope I got 'em started on the right track."

Saw Gray—1983

I really felt sorry when he had that eye trouble. It was after he'd had cataracts removed from both eyes in Spokane. He hadn't been warned of possibilities of further trouble. One summer day he said everything looked sort of gray out of his right eye. His doctor couldn't see him until a week later. Then he performed emergency surgery, but Bill had a detached retina and a lot of damage had been done. I couldn't figure out what his eye saw after that, but it wasn't seeing enough or true enough.

He still read a lot but not as fast. I'm sure from the tools, books, and magazines on gunsmithing I still have upstairs, he had envisioned years of fiddling with the guns he'd accumulated that needed TLC. It wouldn't have been a job, but it would have been an avocation for him to work on other people's guns, because he did enjoy it very much. But he didn't have the vision in his right eye and that was a big disappointment to him.

In 1988 he had a lens implant in his left eye at Chehalis, Washington. Then he and Angela persuaded me to have both of my eyes done that same year, but later.

The Thrill of Grandchildren

Brenna [Angela's daughter] was special, being the first grandchild. Bill enjoyed watching her grow, start school, and the times she'd come to stay overnight.

Then with Tom's boys coming on [Joshua, Joseph, and Gabriel] that was a new thrill. When the boys got old enough to target shoot, he helped them. When they asked to fish in the creek down here, he'd help them figure out what they needed. He bought an old boat and little motor and took them down to the lake a few times. I don't think he fished himself; he just went to take them out. Sometimes they'd just sit and talk or go upstairs to his tiny room where he had little bits of everything collected. He got a lot of enjoyment out of being a grandfather.

Bill and Tom Shared Values

Bill and Tom enjoyed each other's company. The fact that Bill had lost his father when he was such a young boy, and had felt the aloneness and responsibility when he was really just a little kid himself, made him feel he was 'specially favored that he had a chance to have that close relationship with Tom and with Tom's boys, too.

And I thought it fortunate that Tom stayed here. I asked him why he didn't pursue making a living with his talent in music and singing, and the artwork of various kinds he seemed interested in and studied at NIC. He said that when he stayed several months in San Francisco, just after he got out of NIC, he got to thinking about people working all their lives, wanting to be in a place like he had up home. He decided to go home and find a way to earn a living so he wouldn't have to wait till he got to be an old man to come back. So he came back and worked at whatever he could find to do.

And I know Bill was hoping Tom and Angela would have a feeling for the land because he was hoping the homesteads would stay in the family. And they have. Tom owns Uncle Joe's homestead and the top of Anderson Mountain. Angela owns her grandparents' and Uncle George's homesteads.

One More Thing . . .

Well, there's one thing I didn't touch on, and I think I did it deliberately, and that was Bill's drinking problem and the effects of it. When Bill realized he had a drinking problem and quit the first time, he wouldn't go to AA [Alcoholics Anonymous]. The nine years he was sober were great, but he felt aggrieved and unhappy to think that he was different. When he quit drinking the second time, in 1973, and started attending AA, he realized he wasn't alone, that there were millions of men, women, boys, and girls out there that have the same problem. He became dedicated to the Twelve Step AA program and made himself available for advice or visits to anyone who needed him.

Many people don't like to admit being in AA, but Bill always said that a lot of people knew him when he was drinking. He realized that sometimes he hadn't been the greatest fellow in the world, so when he had given up drinking and was proud about it, he should acknowledge where his help came from.

Overcoming Ignorance

I went to an Al-Anon Assembly to learn how the spouse and family need to overcome their ignorance about alcoholism. They were saying that the people in Al-Anon, especially a wife or child, could have worse mental problems and adjustments to make than the person that drank. All the problems that had accumulated between us required a whole new way of thinking on my part. I hadn't realized that drinking wasn't something you could just turn on and off by your own will power. He wasn't lying all the times when he said, "I'll be right home." He had the best of intentions, but he didn't have the will power. It was ignorance of the problem and how to deal with it and the ignorance extended to all the family. But you have to have help from people who have training to overcome it.

I Feel at Home

I've been here long enough that I really feel at home. After Bill was gone, Angela remarked, "Mother, you know, there are a lot of places you could live where you wouldn't find people to be as friendly, caring, helpful, and compassionate."

And really, it makes you feel fortunate to be in an area where you can know and appreciate people who go out of their way to say and do things that are caring, kind, and helpful. It gives you a good feeling.

SEVENTEEN

ONNI RANTANEN

Interviewed 1985 at Spokane, Washington.

When I was a little boy in Mullan, Idaho, my parents used to tell me of the hard life they had known growing up in Finland. The country had lots of glacial stone and farms were small and rocky. There was no separation of church and state like in the United States. Part of their taxes went to support the Evangelical Lutheran Church. On top of that, the Church found ways to collect extra. People had to pay to be born and pay to be buried. And like if the oldest name person in the family died, the family had to give the Church the best cow in the barn.

The Church owned a creamery. Through the religious holidays, the creamery ran steady, and it sent out a horse and sleigh to collect milk and cream from all the little farmers. The Church controlled all the schooling, too. During the wintertime, the Evangelical Lutheran preachers came around to teach classes.

My mother said her mother was a good cook and was expected to organize the other women to serve the preachers the finest food with lots of butter. When Mother was a little girl, she'd sneak around and her mother would slip her a piece of bread with butter on it. They were so poor they could hardly ever afford butter.

My dad had the same name as mine except he had no middle name. My middle name is Mattias. Onni means "luck" and Rantanen means "lakeshore" or "seashore." Dad died June 5, 1925, and is buried in the Hunt Cemetery and has a gravestone. Later, my mother married Frank Leino.

Tales of Rich America

People felt bitter and persecuted by the Church, especially because they were so poor. When they heard tales of gold rushes in America, and how America would give you a new start and make you rich, they'd beg or borrow to get across the ocean.

My grandad on my mother's side came over first. His last name was Maki, which means "hill" in Finn. In America he changed his name to Matt Hill. My mother and her brother, Jack Hill, came over. Then my dad, Onni Rantanen, Sr., came and married my mother here.

Visit to Finland

In 1911, when I was three years old, my mother took me and my younger brothers, Arvi and Bill, to Finland on the Cunard Steamship Line.

First thing, my young cousin, Saima, and I got into mischief pulling the little carrots out of Grandmother's garden.

We had an outing in the woods that summer. The grownups stood up pitchy pine sticks all around, covered them with earth, and started them burning toward the center to bring out the tar. The sticks burned slow, and the tar ran from a hole in the center down into barrels. All night long under the polar sky, somebody played the accordion, and we sang and kept company with the man who tended the fire.

Mother had tickets to come back on the *Titanic*, which was a luxury ship and unsinkable, but another cousin, Sanna Ratio, wanted to come to America with us and had to work several months longer to earn money for her passage, so we waited for her.

That was 1912. The great *Titanic* sank. When Dad heard the news in Mullan, he was heartbroken and told his friends, "There goes my family."

As soon as Mother heard the news of the sinking in Finland, she wrote Dad, and ten days later he learned we were safe.

We came back on the *Lusitania*. I can remember walking on the deck with Sanna and looking up at those big smokestacks. We were lucky again. A German submarine sank the *Lusitania* off the coast of Ireland three years later [May 7, 1915] at the beginning of World War I.

Mullan to French Gulch

When I was seven years old, in 1915, we moved to acreage down French Gulch. I entered grade school at Kingston.

My dad had worked for the Morning Mine and the Snowstorm Mine in the Coeur d'Alene district and before that in Butte, Montana.

There were times he didn't feel so good, but he worked part of the time again in the Morning and farmed.

Dad used to get his scythe blades sharpened at Larson Siding by old man Lindroos. Larson Siding was above Mullan at the mouth of the gulch where the Snowstorm Mine was. Lindroos' granddaughter is Norma Zimmer who has been singing on the Lawrence Welk television show.

We grew hay and kept several cows and chickens and grew a big garden. There was lots to do for the seven kids in our family. I was oldest, then Arvi, William, Jack, Edwin, Violet, and Ellen. Grandad Matt Hill lived with us, too.

Grandad Fights Prize Fighter

Grandad had a friend, John Juntila. In Finn, the J is pronounced like Y. The Juntila family had run a dairy just east of Mullan for years. He'd come down to visit, and they'd sit in a two-seater swing and drink moonshine that Grandad had made for himself.

Grandad had been a good hand-driller and had worked in lots of different prospects in the Coeur d'Alenes. He had been a strong union man at Teluride in Colorado, where there had been labor trouble and state troops sent in.

There was a prize fighter there in a bar bullying people and Grandad went over and damn near killed him with his fists. Miners came to his rooming house afterwards to see the big Finn that had beat up the prize fighter.

Grandad was dying of silicosis. He and John would talk about the rock dust they had breathed in the mines. I can remember some of Dad's visitors talking to him about the rock dust, too. How they'd be working in a raise or drift, and all they had for lights was candles. The candle holder had a sharp point so you could stick it into a post, and also a hook, so you could hang on your hat. They said you could be standing six or eight feet away and you couldn't see your partner for dust.

When a miner got sick, it was always called tuberculosis so the mine owners couldn't be held liable. When miners died of what was commonly called miners's con [consumption], the doctor and coroner, Herbert Mowery, never called it silicosis. They rubber-stamped the death certificate, "extended illness."

Grandad and John said that real husky young guys from Missouri would come to work for the Hecla and other mines around Wallace, and it would sometimes be only a matter of four or five months till they died and were buried up in Nine Mile Canyon. They'd die that quick!

They said how long you'll live depends a lot on the way you breathe.

 When you are working hard, if you suck air through your mouth, you get a lot more dust in your lungs than some guy that's tight-mouthed and breathes through his nose. The nose will sift out a lot of silica.

1899 Trouble

I still remember Grandad and John Juntila settin' in that swing, talkin' in Finn, and I was a little kid, listenin', you know. They talked about the big Coeur d'Alene strike of 1899, and how the mill at the Bunker Hill got blown up. And how afterward the soldiers rounded up Grandad and Juntila, along with the other miners on the streets in Kellogg, and threw them into the bull pen. Then they said the miners tried to break out of the bull pen by digging a tunnel under the fence. The military discovered the tunnel when they almost had it finished. Tried to make them name the diggers. Tried to break them down. Made them all stand right out in the boiling hot sun. Fellows would collapse. The guards doused them with water and made them stand up again.

I don't know if Grandad was charged with anything, but he said he was one of the men held longest in the bull pen because he talked pretty broken and they wouldn't listen to him.

Grandad died in 1922 and is buried in the Hunt Cemetery. He doesn't have a gravestone, but one near him is marked "Valentine."

A Real Finn Bathhouse

We had a Finn bathhouse on our place, built by a man who really knew his business, Charles Keisala, who lived up near Bear Gulch. When I was thirteen years old, Keisala gave me a .25–.35 lever-action carbine rifle. I never forgot his kindness.

Sulo Saari used to come to our place to use that bathhouse. His last name means "island." Sulo had a rough, bulldog-looking face, but he was the most gentle man—unless he wanted to kill you. He wouldn't hurt a child.

Years later, when I was working on the Little North Fork of the Coeur d'Alene River, I heard about Sulo again. Ward Smith was checking for the Winton Lumber Company.

Ward said, "There is one pair of sawyers, a Finn named Sulo Saari and a Swede named Erickson. Most of the gangs can saw from 100 to 120 logs a day with their crosscut saw. Onni! I have checked these two several summers. Both are quick as cats and big, muscular men. They saw 200 logs a day! Every day!"

[Ward Smith appears in *North Fork of the Coeur d'Alene River*.]

First Job

By 1922, Dad was practically bedridden and dying of silicosis, too. My folks borrowed $600 by mortgaging the farm. Practically all the money we had coming in was from what eggs we could sell and the cream we took to Morbeck's store in Kingston.

I graduated at age fifteen from the eighth grade at Kingston school in the spring of 1923. I was the oldest kid in my family and they needed money so bad, I had to find a job. September 15, I said I was eighteen and got a job on the section at Enaville. That $3.04 a day really helped at home.

There were so many Greeks working on the section that I soon learned to count to 100 in their language. Listening all day long, I learned some words, too. They were all mighty nice to me.

They would say in Greek, "He's a good boy."

One of them wanted to learn to count in Finn, so I made the sound for one, "Ooksy."

He said, "Kooksy."

I said, "No, it's 'Ooksy.' "

He said, "Kooksy."

I said, "No."

He shook his head, "No good!" Then he recited, one, two, three, in Greek. He said, "Greek is lots easier," and gave up.

Plugged up Rotary

One day that winter, the train crew was sent up the branch to plow out the track. Fred Baker, who worked on the section with me, and I were sent along to clean out the switches. They were short of engineers, so they sent roundhouse foreman, Hodgson, from Tekoa, along with Jack McCarthy, the traveling engineer, to run the rotary.

The rotary plow has to be pushed by a locomotive, but it has a boiler of its own and a coal tender to run the rotary. Paturka stayed in the boiler room shoveling coal. The rest of us were in the cab ahead of the boiler and behind the whirling rotary.

Hodgson and McCarthy both got drunk on moonshine. Jack McCarthy was tryin' to wrap the whistle cord around Hodgson's neck. They were wobbling around. Jack would just about get the cord on Hodgson, and then they'd slap each other on the back and laugh.

I looked out and a lot of little chunks of coal were burning and smoking on the snow going past. Paturka must have been shoveling coal like everything, and the draft was sucking the coal from the firebox out the stack, only partly burned. Back behind us, the pusher en-

■ Onni Rantanen at the Spokane depot sheds, January 28, 1974

gine was giving us all it had with Claude Meredith as engineer and La Pierre firing.

We got to Steamboat Siding, and there was so much snow that just the switch target stuck out. That's a red disk that tops the rod above the switch so you can see which way it is turned. We headed into the siding and the rotary started kinda struggling and somebody yelled, "You're plugging 'er! Open her up!"

Hodgson pulled on that long throttle rod that runs clear to the back end. He kinda lost his balance and opened it up wide. The engine of the rotary started shaking just like when a dog picks up a rat and shakes it. The rotary was shooting snow up over the cottonwood trees, knocking limbs off. McCarthy and Hodgson was laughing and me and Fred Baker hung back in the corner, and I thought to myself, "Boy! If this isn't some railroad!"

Fred Baker was kind of potbellied, and he'd say, "They say, 'Eat an apple a day and keep the doctor away.' I'm eatin' two!"

When we backed off the siding, he and I were supposed to clean out the switches. Fred jumped overboard and went so deep that only the top of his head was sticking out of the snow. And there he was, wallowing around like an elephant in 20 feet of snow. That made McCarthy and Hodgson laugh still harder. They wiped the tears from their eyes and had another drink to Fred's health.

[Fred Baker appears in *North Fork of the Coeur d'Alene River.*]

Henry Davenport

I got acquainted with Henry Davenport, the storekeeper at Enaville, and learned to like and respect him. Years later, he special-ordered a .270 Winchester rifle for me.

He laid the papers in front of me and said, "You're a friend of mine. I don't want to make anything on it. This is just what it cost me—$62."

Henry liked the Finns. He said, "A lot of Finns went out in these thickets, cleared off the land, and made a log house. First thing you know they had a farm. Then they came down and bought stuff from me on credit. I never lost any money on the Finns."

For the lumberjacks, he had a top shelf on the upriver side of his store loaded with every kind of calked shoes: Currins, Bergman, Whites, Chippewa, Copeland Ryder.

Henry said, "There's been hundreds and hundreds of lumberjacks came here to buy calked shoes, and they'd be broke. They'd buy underwear, shirts, wool mackinaws—all their stuff, without a cent. Up the river they'd go. In the fall when the camp closed, here they'd come downriver, and this would be the first place they stopped and I'd get paid. I never lost a dime on the lumberjacks. A few bums beat me, but not the lumberjacks."

One time my family owed Davenport a lot for groceries, too. We finally got it paid off. He was a good man.

[Henry Davenport was serving on the draft board during World War II when he was shot by a young Finn. Henry Davenport appears in Neva Baker's story in *North Fork of the Coeur d'Alene River*.]

Henry Aro

At Enaville, I saw Henry Aro handle a peavey over at Benning's loading outfit. He was big and had big hands and he handled a peavey like it was a little toy. I'd stop work sometimes and watch the way he'd hook a log, twirling it, playing with it.

Henry Aro had the reputation of being a hard worker and a nice guy to work with, but he'd make a few dollars and get drunk. One fall, he was drinking over at Albert Legault's Tavern. He had worked hard all summer, like always, and had drunk up his wages on weekends. He was broke and disgusted with himself. He went home and blew his head off with a 12-gauge shotgun.

Wallace Roundhouse

The Murray train switched around Enaville, so I'd get on the engine and talk to Fred Buff, the engineer. He took a liking to me.

After I'd worked on the section two years, Fred Buff said to me, "There's a guy gonna quit at the roundhouse in Wallace. Would you like to work there?"

"Yeah!" I said. "I sure would."

He said, "By Golly! I'll arrange it for you."

I was supposed to be twenty-one, but I was only seventeen, so I lied again about my age and began work at the roundhouse, June 25, 1925, cleaning and servicing engines. I put water and oil in them, wiped grease off the rods and valves, and filled the lubricators. I was also "Call Boy." It was my job to reach trainmen on foot or by phone wherever they were sleeping in hotels, rooming houses, and cabooses and wake them in time to dress, clean up, eat, and get on the job.

One morning about 1926, we had a call to ready the little No. 704 engine used on the Murray run for a special job. Number 393 from Tekoa was setting out a car of live elk at Enaville. Fred Buff was the engineer ordered to take the car up to Hedlund's Siding at the mouth of Grizzly Creek and then across the old Hedlund logging bridge to the Grizzly Creek Flat where the elk were to be turned loose. All were in good shape except for the three that had been trampled. Those were the first elk planted in the upper Coeur d'Alenes.

Complimentary Moonshine

I was assigned to watching engines at Prichard in the summer of 1927. The crew ate at Backman's boardinghouse. There was a hall where we came in, with a whole line of wash basins, a bucket of water, and a place to throw the water after you washed. In the middle of it all set a gallon jug of moonshine and a glass, compliments of Kirt, the local bootlegger.

Claude (Buzz) Meredith was the grouchy senior engineer and he had Jack McCarthy as traveling engineer. He was a boozer just like Jack. And they hated one another. It took old Buzz a long time to wash and it took Jack a long time to wash. They came out grinning and "sure and begorra" they was happy to be eating together. I went out in the hallway and the gallon jug of moon had been lowered about three inches!

Helpful Jack McCarthy

It was Jack who got me the job firing locomotives, August 27, 1927. I was supposed to be twenty-one, but I was nineteen, so I lied again about my age. Just a year or so before this, the engines had been converted from coal to oil burners and that made firing a lot easier.

At first I fired on the freight that ran from Tekoa to Kellogg. We used to stop at "Jim, the Greek's" confectionery at Harrison for milkshakes. Then in 1929, I began firing on the Idaho Northern that ran from Enaville to Prichard. Originally, a branch line turned off up Beaver Creek and went from Delta to Ray Jefferson's hard rock galena mine at the head of Beaver Creek where it had a roundhouse. But it was no longer in use.

The Winton's [lumber company] loaded their logs at Shoshone Creek and delivered them down to Prichard to us. We'd bring as many as 35 flatcar loads of white pine down to the Winton sawmill at Rose Lake, stop there overnight, and head for Prichard with empties in the morning.

Old Slobber Stack

Our engine, a No. 729, was an old "slobber stack," a saturated engine which didn't have super-heater units and had slide valves instead of piston valves. They called it slobber stack because it always leaked steam around the cylinder saddle and valve stems and piston rods. This one leaked so bad that engine men had nicknamed it "White Wings." Wherever it traveled, it was shooting out wings of steam.

Before I got there, that decrepit old engine had soured engineer Fred Viele so much that he blamed not only the engine but the crew. He wrote a letter to Joe Ramsey, the general chairman of the engineers.

Joe Ramsey was laughing so hard he could hardly tell me what it said. "I got dead-ass Pat Langin for conductor, and Methuselah Staley for rear brakeman, and Doggie Wildflower Joe Gurlinger for head brakeman, and Three Fingered Jack Saffer as fireman. And I got that old 729 for a steam engine!"

Ore Train at Burke

In 1931, I was firing for engineer John Dickinson at Burke. In just minutes they would load ten or 15 cars of ore out of the big cement bins, and we would haul the ore down the canyon to Gem where they'd refine and concentrate it. The grade was 4.5 percent, and that's steep for a railroad.

Dickinson showed me how he held the train back. He'd set the automatic air brakes and draw ten or 12 pounds off the line. He'd hold the train down to seven or eight miles an hour. You see, you can't let the brakes remain set too long because of leakage in the brake cylinders, and the air will gradually escape. So he'd maintain the pressure by the retaining valves on each car, and meanwhile he'd be recharging the reservoirs again so he could maintain air pressure.

While he was recharging the reservoirs, he'd also use the air brakes on the big engine driver wheels—the locomotive was independently braked—to hold the train. That's tricky because you have to keep tripping a valve and releasing the locomotive brakes so your tires on the big driver wheels don't get to slipping and get hot and expand and throw a tire.

Runaway Train

Some years before this, Roy Hinkle had been engineer on an ore train that got away from him. Down the canyon she went, past Gem, going faster and faster on the five-mile grade to Wallace. The crew knew it had gone out of control and jumped off.

Just in case a train might run away, there was an old sidetrack a short distance up the canyon from Wallace, and the switch there was kept thrown into that sidetrack. Otherwise a train would come down across the Northern Pacific track and charge into downtown Wallace. The sidetrack ran up a trestle where years ago they used to haul ore to bins for a mill there.

So Roy Hinkle's engine came roaring down the canyon, shedding cars behind it as the cars jumped the track from the speed. It turned onto the sidetrack, ran up the trestle, and fell off on the ground.

Railroad men were still talking about it.

Whistles

Lots of guys just used their initials on time slips, but John Dickinson always wrote it out: John W. Dickinson. John was a good engineer, but he had an awful whistle. He could have had a ready-made cast iron whistle about a foot high and five inches in diameter that's used for passenger, freight, and switch engines. It was a nice whistle with flutes, some longer and some shorter.

Then there was the one used on the big Challenger type No. 3900 Mallets. It was 18 inches high and had a deep, vibrant steamboat tone. Beautiful!

But John W. Dickinson had badgered some machinist to make one for him, and it had the deadest sound! He used it on our ore train from Burke. We never could understand why he thought it sounded nice.

And we had to change this damned old whistle every time he went on another engine.

Lady Friend Trouble

Gossip said that back around 1923 John had some trouble because of a lady friend. He was in his engine, pulling past the Samuels Hotel, going toward the depot in Wallace, headed for Burke, when some guy came walking up the street with a rifle. Right close to the depot umbrella shed, he opened fire.

The guy took several pot shots. Dickinson was ducking and trying to stay out of sight. "Blackjack" John J. Van Tuyle, the fireman, dove right into the coal tank, and they said all you could see was his big shoes sticking out.

The rifleman missed both of them, but the engine carried bullet holes as a souvenir.

On the Bum

I couldn't find any work in the summer of 1932, so I went on the bum. I left Enaville on the No. 394 freight to Plummer and caught the Milwaukee boxcars east to Chicago. I didn't camp in the "jungles" along the way. In small towns, I'd go into a residential section and bum something to eat. In the cities, I'd hunt up the soup line.

In Chicago, I met a kid, Kermit Hayes, who wanted me to go with him to his folks' in Boston. We found a car of wheat with the door cracked open in the New York Central yards and climbed in. Going along Lake Erie, it looked like the ocean. Laying in the wheat, we went to sleep and woke up in the railroad yards of Buffalo. When we got out, you could have followed us for the first 100 yards by the wheat dropping out of our clothes along with what we cleaned out of our pockets.

We stayed with his folks in Boston until the cold told me that fall was coming on. I said to Kermit, "I've gotta get somewhere warm. I think I'll head south to Florida."

He went with me, but someplace down in Georgia, I wasn't going fast enough for him. I said, "What's the hurry? It's warm here."

Kermit said, "I'm gonna head for Jacksonville, Florida. I'll meet you there."

That's the last I saw of him.

After awhile, I bummed to Florida. I was sitting in the courtyard at Tampa watching for more coconuts to fall so I could break 'em open and drink the milk and eat the white meat. Along came a guy named

Bob Marshall. He said he and his wife had a Chevrolet car and were going to a town called Clewiston on the south side of Lake Okeechobee where he knew some people who might have work for us. He invited me to ride along.

The people had vegetable acreage. We stayed there all winter picking beans and peas and other stuff. I worked up to the job of checker. When the field hands brought a hamper full to me, I'd fasten the top and give them a slip.

Bob Marshall was building a little trailer for himself, and I was kicking in some money to help him out and also putting a few dollars aside to go home.

One day Bob said, "You're, uh, not sharing all your money like you should."

I knew the trailer was almost finished. I said, "Well, you've bought enough stuff for it."

I was sleeping on the floor in a nearby shed. In the morning around four o'clock, I very quietly got up and shouldered my pack and started down the road.

I rode the freight back to New York City and then to Chicago, where I took in the World's Fair for a week. Then I caught the Milwaukee boxcars west, 2,000 miles to Plummer, changed to old No. 393 again to Enaville, and walked home feeling a little like a world traveler.

The Kaiser and the Ox

About 1934, I worked for the Forest Service on Blister Rust at Lavin Creek and Pyrite Creek, and then at the Winton Lumber Company camp at Picnic Creek. The Nesslein brothers, Frank and George, were part of the backbone of the Winton log drive for years. They had been nicknamed the Kaiser and the Ox.

The Kaiser was hairy like a gorilla and had to shave down into his collar and then take off his shirt and shave up.

We were laying around one Sunday, and the Kaiser said to me with his mouth full of Peerless [chewing tobacco], "Where's that goddamn George? I want to sharpen my axe." George was the Ox.

I said, "I'll turn the grindstone for you."

I was cranking the grindstone and fighting off the damn mosquitoes. The Kaiser took a big spit and pulled his axe off and made a swat at them with his big hand.

"Ain't they fierce?" he says.

Then he looked around and saw his brother sitting just inside the bunkhouse door reading a "Diamond Dick" story.

"There you are, you sonofabitch. Come and turn this grindstone for me."

Then he says to me, "When he comes, just watch me lay right to 'er!"

The Ox came over and started turning the grindstone and reading Diamond Dick. The Ox was strong but the Kaiser was laying so heavy against the grindstone that finally the Ox noticed it was turning harder than usual and he says, "Why don't you go get a four-pound axe?"

"What would I want with a club like that?" says the Kaiser, and kept laying on the pressure.

[The Nesslein brothers appear in *North Fork of the Coeur d'Alene River.*]

The Kid and the Wobbly

One day in the bunkhouse, a young guy was shooting off his mouth about how he was down in Boise and how he got hit on the head.

"It damn near killed me!" he said.

An old lumberjack, Pollock Hayes, said, "What was you doin' down in Boise?"

"Oh!" the kid says, "I was in the state militia. We went there to break a strike."

Pollock was an old Wobbly. Pollock got up off the bench and cursed and damned the kid all over the place.

Charlie Mullan said to Pollock afterwards, "What would you have done if that young guy had come at you?"

Pollock had taken his shoes off and was greasing them to waterproof them for the log drive.

Pollock said, "I'd have let him have one of my calked boots right in the face!"

Married

Maxine Nearing's mother was a Hakala girl. Hakala in Finn means fir bough. She and Bill Nearing were married August 11, 1918 by Justice of the Peace George P. Walker in Wallace. So Maxine and I were married by the same J. P. on her parents' anniversary, August 11, 1937.

[Bill Nearing appears in *North Fork of the Coeur d'Alene River*.]

Runaway Log Truck

That September, I was driving an old White truck for Ed Alho. I was grinding down a steep, narrow road with a heavy load of logs. The rear springs were so weak that the load was tipping away over toward the outside away from the driver. All I had to hold the truck back was the dual transmission in the lowest gear. Alho had taken the foot brakes off.

The transmission pinged out of gear. The truck jumped ahead, running away! I had no hope I could escape out the right side. The load might tip over on me.

There was no door. I shoved my left foot on the running board and with my right hand holding the steering wheel, I looked for a chance to get away. If I jumped against the steep bank, I'd roll down into the path of the rear wheels.

As luck would have it, the bulldozer man who cleaned out the road in the spring had gouged around a big rock and left a hole next to the bank. I dove into this hole and lit on my hands and knees parallel to the wheel track. The rear tires brushed my pants as they went past.

I could hear the truck motor idling as I jumped to my feet and ran after it, maybe 100 feet, and it plunged over the bank. I stood on the edge of the road and watched the logs and chains flying as it rolled down the mountainside to the bottom of the canyon.

Up the road had been coming one of the Lehtola boys from Tamarack Ridge in a half ton pickup truck. Lucky for him, the truck had gone overboard or it would have met him head on. He saw the truck bouncing down the hillside. He stopped the pickup and went running down the hill.

When he got close to the wreck, he could see my black-and-white buffalo-checked shirt hanging in the cab. He thought it was me. He'd run a few yards, then he'd slow to a walk like he was afraid of what he was going to find. Then he'd run again.

I yelled down at him, "*Hey*! I'm up here." You shoulda seen how glad he was to see me.

Caught Lying

August 14, 1935, was when the Social Security Act went into force, and everyone had to be given a number. The railroad company sent me a letter that said, "We've got three different ages of your birth. One when you hired out on the section gang. Another when you went to work in the roundhouse, and still another when you became fireman. We must have a certified copy of your birth certificate!"

There was no getting out of it this time. I knew Mary Juntila was midwife at my birth, so I went to the courthouse for a form. I took it to

Mary. She signed it in very deep handwriting. She was old by then. I had a certificate made and took it to the office of the Union Pacific.

They said, "Well, you're old enough now, so we'll let it go."

Creeks Named

About 1937, my brother William and Fred Bentley were doing some Forest Service work on the two little creeks that come into the canyon just beyond the Rose Lake turn-off.

When they turned in their time slips, the ranger said, "You haven't put down the location."

My brother said, "We can't! The two little creeks don't have names."

The ranger said, "They do now! That first one is Rantanen and the other is Bentley Creek."

So the two had creeks named after them. But they spelled Rantanen wrong. They spelled it Rantenan.

Three Toots Service Station

Jack Welch, father of Dick and Jack Welch, owned the Three Toots Service Station at Bradley, where the railroad track branched up the east side of Silver King Gulch going to the zinc plant.

Bradley was in between two regular stations: Pine Creek and Kellogg. It was railroad regulation that if a passenger wanted to get off at Bradley, the conductor back in the train would pull the overhead cord three times. This sounded a little air whistle in the cab of the locomotive to let the engineer know he was to stop at the next way station. The engineer responded with three short toots on the locomotive whistle to let the conductor know he'd gotten the message. So that's how the service station got its name.

[Dick Welch appears in *North Fork of the Coeur d'Alene River.*]

Mining

When the woods work played out along in 1939 and 1940, I worked in the shaft of the Page Mine. The crew was my father-in-law, Bill Nearing, my brother Jack, stuttering Earl Stevens, and myself. By this time the mines were using wet drills, but still, we'd breathe a lot of dust. After Dad and Grandad died of silicosis, I had a healthy fear of rock dust.

When the sun shone in the dryhouse where miners hung their clothes, you could see the air full of dust. Walking down the drift behind guys going to work in the morning, you could see dust clouding out of their dry clothes. Then pounding rocks on the grizzly where the ore goes into the bins, every time your hammer hit the rock, it pulverized some rock dust and you breathed it. It might take years, but it would eventually affect you.

[Earl Stevens appears in *North Fork of the Coeur d'Alene River.*]

Whittlin' Engineer

I liked working with Al Olson—old A.J. I'd get plenty of practice running engine. A.J. liked to whittle things out of wood and he'd let a brakeman or anybody run his engine while he whittled.

Oliver Archer was the hardest working coal burner fireman you'd ever see. He used a great wide scoop shovel, and every time he swung that shovel, the engine threw out such a smoke that it cut off the sun. He found the toughest firing job and stayed on it for years. Nobody else wanted it.

Later, when he got to be an engineer, he said, "There's a lot of romance to running a steam engine. You can move the reverse lever forth and back, or you can shorten or lengthen the valve stroke and work the engine harder or easier, and you can adjust your throttle."

He said all this with such a serious deadpan face it made me laugh.

He said, "With a steam engine, you can do a lot of different things. But these diesels—just like running a plank through a planer."

Baldy Ross and the Cows

Andy "Baldy" Ross was engineer on the Wallace passenger for a long time. One time we were coming from Wallace toward Harrison with high water right up on both sides of the track. We had to move along and were making about 60 miles an hour. We come around the bend just above where the highway bridge crosses over the track and the Coeur d'Alene River, and here were four nice milk cows running down both sides of the track ahead of us, just outside the rails. We were close before we saw 'em.

One of the cows on my side—the fireman is on the left side—she kinda turned a little bit crossways. The pilot beam hit this other cow that was parallel with the track right in the rump and just compressed her. Her head drove right into the other cow, bent her double, and threw them both away out in the water. And there, that quick! We'd killed four cows before you could say Jack Robinson.

Another time, I was firing for Baldy on his favorite old engine No.

3202 coming from Tekoa past a little siding called Darknell. It was snowing big snowflakes so hard you could barely see. We didn't see this big, red polled bull laying between the rails till we were only 50 feet from it. The engine felt rubbery when we went over it. Then *POW*! went the air and the emergency brakes slid the wheels.

Old Baldy, first thing he done, he lit the kerosene torch. He got off with his corncob pipe stickin' out of his mouth. He walked back to the rear end of the engine where the air hose had broken in two. Then he yelled back to me, "Where's my train at?"

He held the torch up in the air to look, and there was the train, three car lengths down the track. Ten feet of steam pipe draggin' behind the engine.

We backed up, and this darn bull was right under the lead truck of the baggage car. We hooked onto the car and pulled the train up just a little. Morse Smith, the baggage guy, came out with some hooks they used for handling baggage. We took those hooks and rolled the bull out of there. Felt like a big sack about half-full of walnuts. Must have broke every bone. We rolled it down the bank.

Catching the Hoop

Out of Moscow, we had a telegraph operator, Doug Ruthstrom, a great, big Swede kid. He came out of the station with one of these solid wooden hoops for the trainmen to pick up orders. Doug planted himself alongside the track, holding out this hoop. Smitty Smith was rear brakeman on the little passenger train. Smitty was hanging onto the rear of the coach, one arm on the grab iron, and he reached out with his other to run it through the loop to collect the message which was clipped onto the hoop.

But Doug, with his big feet and 200 pounds, had a death grip on that hoop and he picked old Smith right off the rear end of the train! Of course, they stopped the train and picked up Smitty, but Smitty didn't see anything funny about it.

Buttering up the Hashers

For a long time I fired for old-timer Johnny Campbell on a passenger train. Dickinson was telling me Johnny was always buttering up the hashers in the restaurant at Starbuck.

Johnny was also always short of money, and he says to another engineer, Becky Sharp, "What do the meals cost here?"

Becky says, "Aw! They're all 40 cents."

Johnny says, "I haven't got any money. Could you lend me 40 cents?"

So Becky says, "Yeah!" and handed him 40 cents.

Johnny went and ate the meal, and was talkin' to this hasher and lit up a cigar.

The boys gave each other the wink and got out of there. Left him standing alone.

Johnny says, "What do I owe ya?"

The hasher said, "Forty-five cents. All our meals are 45 cents."

They had rigged it among them that whoever he asked, they'd give him five cents short and teach him a lesson. He was always borrowing.

Blackie Herner

They liked telling about engineer Blackie Herner, down at Farmington, back in the years when lots of people crowded the trains. Blackie had to go to the toilet, so he got out on the platform and used the one in the station.

Some character named Doobie was firing for him on this old coal-burner engine. The conductor waved "Highball!" and this Doobie started the train.

Blackie heard it and he come running out of the can, pulling his pants up. The platform was loaded with people and Blackie yelling, "*STOP! STOP! I'm the engineer of that train!*" and running for all he was worth and trying to get his pants up in front of all those people. The story was so funny, it got passed down from one generation to another.

Now, King!

At the time they were building the new Ayer Junction line into Spokane, Peter F. King was engineer on the work train. Bill Berry, the conductor, was in a real big hurry to get home early this weekend. The rails were in, but only half the ties and the whole track was still out of line. Peter King told me that the first crooked spot they hit, the engine whooped and rolled.

Bill Berry turned white where he was standing on the engine deck and he said, "Now, King!"

They hit another and he said, "*NOW, KING!*"

King could see that Berry figured this was his last ride, so he went faster and they kept hitting the crooks and swaying.

King said, "Poor old Berry hung on for dear life and 'Now, Kinged!' all the way to Hooper Junction."

Mechanic on the Fly

I fired a lot for old-timer Ed Baker out of Tekoa. We'd get an engine out of the shop and lots of times they'd leave the valve stems of the main steam valves too short or too long. Ed would listen to the engine exhaust on the first up grade and if it gave a real hard exhaust on one quarter and real light the next quarter, Ed would start muttering under his breath.

When we stopped at Plummer to unload way freight, he would get out with chisel and hammer and loosen the key and nut and adjust it. By the time we left Harrison, he'd have the engine working real good. [Al Ross, station agent three miles above Harrison at Springston, explains that "way freight" means freight that is dropped off at a point other than a station with an agent.]

Trains Broke in Two

Fred Wolff was a cocky guy and a good fireman, but by God! when he got to be engineer, he had trouble with them long freight trains. He had a Mallet locomotive, French-made and pronounced Malley. Mallets were big, powerful freight engines. We had to go through a sag and then into a tunnel, and every time he went through there, his trains broke in two [uncoupled].

Nobody could tell him anything.

"Aw!" he says, "I'm not gonna use any of you darn guy's way of doin'. I'm gonna do it the way the book says." So he'd apply the automatic brakes on the train and then finally kick 'em off, and then he'd break in two again.

Next time he said, "I'm gonna set the brakes on the engine—the driver brakes."

So he'd get clear down in the sag, and he'd ease off on his driver brakes and the rear end would be bunched as they started up the hill. The slack would *bang! bang! bang!* down the rear end, and he'd break in two again.

Kenneth M. Fink showed me the right way to do it. Without going into the fine points of it, you brake the whole train a little as you go into the sag, and then you release the brakes on the 30 cars on the head end, and leave the rear brakes set to hold the train strung out without slack. Then as you start up the hill, you pull hard with the engine and begin to release the brakes on the rear end as the cars enter the uphill.

[No long freight could ever start if there was no slack in the drawbars where cars are hooked together. No locomotive had the power to start the enormous weight of a strung out train. Assuming a train has stopped with all the drawbars strung out, the engineer gives the train a bunt backwards to put slack in the draw bars. He then bunts forward and starts the first car, which in turn bunts forward and helps start the second car, and so on till the whole train is in motion. However, when the train goes down a long hill, the cars push forward till there is no slack in the drawbars. Unless the engineer knows how to handle the brakes when the locomotive starts climbing another hill, the slack of the cars begins running backward, gathering power as it runs from one car to the next, till the violence breaks the train apart.]

Handling Slack

Kenneth Fink taught me a lot about handling trains of 100 cars or more. Like going down the long descending grade into Wallula, Washington. We had a big Mallet engine and a long train. We had to be careful because of a railroad crossing and then the yard limits ahead. Fink would get out a paper and pencil and figure the tons into the cars he had, and the cars into the tons, and how much it would push on that grade. He'd work it so the brakes would be set up on maybe the 25 head cars, and that would take all the slack out of the drawbars and bunch the whole train up against them. With the whole rear train shoving against the head, you could hold down the speed.

And if you had to stop, you could "big hole it"—set the emergency brake.

But if the train was all strung out, a sudden stop could kill somebody. The slack will buckle the cars, raise 'em right up in the air.

To give you an idea of how much slack can be in a train: I had a big train going out of Wallula of 187 cars, 12,000 tons. I had radio communication with Stanley Horner, the conductor, back in the caboose.

He said, "The brakes are all released back here, Onni."

I said, "Yeah, O.K.," and started the engine moving.

Pretty soon he repeated it, "Onni! The brakes are released back here."

"I've already moved three car lengths," I said. "You'll be moving pretty soon."

"O.K.!" he says. "We're starting to move now."

At the depot they laughed and shook their heads when we told them. We had a lot of 90-foot cars and 65-foot cars. We checked them out and our train was two miles long—the damndest train you ever heard tell of.

Lummy Derails

Poor Lummy. His name was Glen, but they nicknamed him "Lummy" because he was always complaining about his lumbago.

He was engineer on a troop train, and he had to wait on the sidetrack out at Geib, right on top of the hill out of Cheney. So the other train passed him, and he was to come off the sidetrack and go on into Spokane Christmas morning.

But Lummy forgot about the derail at the end of the sidetrack and he sailed into it and put the darn engine on the ground. Christmas morning!

The superintendent said, "I could kill you right there! Talk about trouble trying to get through the holidays with guys drinking and raising hell and then you pull a trick like this!"

What could Lummy say?

Then later, he was on one of these new No. 3900 Mallets, and he came to a curve coming into the railroad yard. This time it wasn't his fault. That whole engine went on the ground. They worked and worked, jacking up the great, heavy Mallet to build a track under it. If that wasn't the saddest thing you ever seen.

Lummy had a high voice and he cried, "Everything has to happen to me!"

Gus and Hugo Carlson

Gus Carlson was engineer and his brother, Hugo, was his fireman running the Wallace passenger. They had one of those big, high-wheeled passenger engines called Shanghai 3500s with 81-inch drivers. As they went through Chatcolet and started up the hill to Plummer, where most old-timers would pussyfoot along real quiet and easy, Gus started pushing the engine.

They were both excitable and couldn't get along.

Hugo looked over at Gus and said, "You can't run this enyine like this. What you tink, we on a freight enyine?

Gus said, "You yust keep 'er hot. I'll do the rest!"

Later when Hugo became an engineer, he was doubleheading on a troop train. Al Olson was engineer on a high-wheeled, heavy Pacific engine on the head end, and Hugo was on a little, low-wheeled, old-time slobber stack engine behind him. They were goin' down the line, and Al was letting that heavy Pacific roll. That little engine in back was a'goin' as fast as it could, and Hugo thought his little engine was going to shake to pieces.

Hugo stuck his head out the window and waved the stop sign at Al.

Al looked back and, "TOOT! TOOT!"

Then Hugo hung out further and blew his whistle.

Al looked back and, "TOOT! TOOT!" and kept right on going.

Al laughed and said Hugo was so scared, he put on the darndest performance you ever saw. Hugo tooted his whistle and waved stop all the way to the next terminal.

One day I was firing for Hugo on the Kellogg job. We had shoved some cars onto the coke track up at the smelter. Hugo was nervous that he would go too far, and was always stopping five feet or half a car short. At the last instant when he saw he didn't go quite far enough, he pulled the throttle.

As he did, the bridle rod broke off right at the boiler, and the throttle came out wide open. The engine drivers started spinning in one place with a deafening roar like bombs going off. You couldn't hear nothin'! We was boring a hole right through the rails and using up water out of the boiler. We had to do something.

Hugo was laying on the reverse lever, shoving it right down in the corner. That's the worst thing he could do. I don't know what kind of a noise it was making outside, but inside it was like everything was shaking to pieces and about to blow up.

I motioned him to hook the engine up on center.

He shook his head no!

I shoved the big Swede away, put my foot on the boiler head, and where an engine is going that way with the Stevenson link gear, it is terrible hard to lift. But when I finally started moving it, he come and helped me, and we pulled it on center and that awful roar stopped.

My ears cleared. Then I said, "Gee whiz! We'd have bored a hole right down through the ground. I don't know what woulda happened if we'd run out of water. Probably blowed up the boiler!"

So then I fixed the bridle rod and we got back down the hill.

As we got near the depot where Hugo's brother Gus was waiting to relieve him, he leaned out the side and yelled, "Gus! I'm bwoke down! I'm bwoke down!"

The Neatest Fireman

I think Scruggs was the neatest coal burner fireman the railroad ever had. I never saw him sweat. He'd keep things as neat as a pin. He seemed to know how to fire an engine easy. He'd go out on the toughest job and come back smiling, the engine and cab and his overalls spotless.

In contrast, Tillman was a tall, muscular guy and always black and sweating, but he'd keep that engine hot. John Van Tuyle was telling me that Al Tillman was in one of them rough saloons in Tekoa when Shaw, a big, husky engineer, was moving up the bar, shoving guys out of the way.

Al Tillman was standing at the bar talking, and when Shaw worked up to him, Al reached out his big hands and picked Shaw up by the shirt front and held him in the air and shook him and said, "You leave me alone!"

And Shaw let him alone!

The Fast Ride

Clyde Woodell was always in a hurry to get to town to get some more wine. He'd get pretty excited if anybody held him back. Like when his engine was second in a doubleheader, and Jack Wilburn was ahead, he let Jack know when they reached town that they hadn't come fast enough.

Jack listened. He was slow to answer and he said, "Well, I had an idear—"

And Clyde says, "Yeah! You're always full of idears goddamya! Why didn't ya get into town? We shoulda been here a long time ago."

Among the engineers, the news got around that Clyde was impatient, but Joe Searles, the bridge foreman, hadn't heard that Clyde was like that.

During a fierce snowstorm, Clyde had orders to take his high-wheeled, Mikado-type engine and clear the track of snow into Spokane.

Joe Searles said to me, "I gotta go to Spokane. Buses aren't running. Hell! I'll just get on that light engine with Clyde and ride in."

Melvin Couch was the conductor. They had orders to look out for autos.

So they started out from Tekoa. Clyde had taken on quite a few snifters.

Searles told afterward, "I was paralyzed with fear. Clyde had the throttle wide open. He'd hit a snowbank and throw snow all over. Pretty soon he'd come out in the open and snow would be flyin' by the cab. He'd hit another drift so hard that if you were standing up, it would knock you right down on the deck."

Searles said to Couch, the conductor, "Brother! I made me the biggest mistake I ever made. I shoulda never got on this engine."

And Couch said to Clyde, "Clyde! We got orders to watch out for autos!"

Clyde says, "I can't see a damn thing out there. Can't see nothin'. Might as well go!"

And he went on like a streak with the engine rolling back and forth on the deck.

Searles said, "The farther we went, the more I prayed, and the faster old Clyde went. When he hit a big drift, the engine waded in and slowed down. When he came out, he'd take off and hit the next one. It wasn't bothering old Clyde. He was in a hurry to get to Spokane to get a couple more snifters. I never took such a ride in my life!"

Now! Hit 'Er!

And Clyde had a temper. He was running engine on the Kellogg job. At a street crossing after dark, here come a guy in a car at high speed. Looked like he was going to crash them broadside. Clyde stopped the engine.

The car skidded to a stop within inches of the engine.

Clyde climbed down and walked over into the car light. Then he said, "There she is! Now, goddamit, go ahead and hit 'er!"

Test Run

One time, Claude Meredith, an old-time engineer, was giving a beautiful new passenger engine a test run over the Union Pacific track to High Bridge Park outside Spokane. The old bridge is torn down now.

The superintendent and other important railroad guys were in the engine cab, and it made Claude so nervous that when he came to a yellow block signal, he went by it and half a car length past the red signal.

That was bad. There was a spring switch there where the outside track came into another one. It worked like this: When your train came in this direction over the spring switch, the switch would throw over, and when you got past, it would flop back the other way. Well, here Claude had run over the spring switch and went by the red block, which he knew he shouldn't have done without stopping to make sure the block was clear.

So Claude backed up to correct his mistake. The switch had flopped the other way, and he put that brand new Union Pacific engine, that big, beautiful engine, with all the big shots aboard, on the ground. It was just on the entrance to the bridge. It tied up the railroad!

George Brooks—The Best

Working the extra board, all us firemen got to know who the good engineers were. For running steam engine, George Brooks was about the sharpest man I ever seen. Like going down the Snake River from Ayer Junction to Umatilla. Used to have 12 to 15 passenger coaches. George would run the engine one way and let me be engineer on the way back.

George had one eye impaired a little bit. I'd go take the physical examination and I'd memorize the damned chart they put on the wall to test eyes. Then I'd write it down for George. He'd read it once and remember it so he could quote it from memory. Then he'd go take the examination and pass it. It was just that his one eye was impaired a little bit.

But George knew steam and he knew how to get the maximum thrust out of a railroad engine and where to set the reverse lever to make the engine run faster. High temperature, super-heated steam is like an invisible gas. He'd open the throttle, then just ease it to the point where it gave the steam an expansive effect even in a dry pipe. They called it wire drawing. And handling the pressure right, that engine would really get out and go!

A lot of engineers would lose time on their runs. So the traveling engineer would say, "Well, I've got to go ride with so and so. He's doing something wrong."

A Judge of Speed

"Sunny" Jim Broyles was a real tall drink of water, slow goin' guy. But he was a sharp engineer. He'd look straight down at the ground and he could tell within a mile how fast the engine was going. You could pull out your watch and check the mile posts and that would be it exactly.

Man on the Track

We had a scary happening four miles out of Harrison at O'Gara Bay in about 1949 when I was firing for Johnny Campbell. There was snow on the ground. Old Man Causey lived further up the track near Red Cut. We never seen him, but we must have hit him in the middle of the curve at O'Gara Bay on our morning passenger run to Wallace.

When we came back, it was after dark and I was running engine. Coming around the bay, my headlight picked up something on the track ahead. It was moving like a branch would blow in the wind just outside the rail. I leaned ahead and couldn't make it out. I wasn't over 130 feet from it when it came to me that it was an arm. Old-man Causey was laying there and waving to stop us for fear he'd freeze to death that night. He'd already been there about five hours.

I threw on the emergency! Reversed the engine! Yanked the throttle wide open with the sanders on! The whole engine was shaking with the pounding.

The pilot at the front of the engine, what people call the cowcatcher, the little wheels are engine trucks that help distribute the tons of weight on the cylinder saddle and smoke box—it hit him on the shoulder or head and swung him around. I don't think we moved over a coach length past him because he was right under the baggage car when we jumped off and ran to him.

We loaded him on the train and took him to Tekoa and the doctor. I'm happy to say, he lived a long time after that.

Examination for Engineer

A man was sent out from Omaha to give a group of us an examination to become engineers: Cliff Jordan, J. J. Merriman, W. C. Walker, D. F. Egan, and me. The test was 1,000 questions on the mechanical points of a locomotive. Then there was a test of knowledge of the air brakes, and still another on rules of the railroad. We didn't have to get on a locomotive and demonstrate what we knew. After all those questions, they must have felt it wasn't necessary. I became an engineer August 22, 1947.

People used to wonder where a steam locomotive carried its sand. The first dome ahead of the cab on top held dry steam, and the second one held sand that ran down to the wheels through a flexible pipe.

If there is a heavy dew, or if it is just starting to rain and there's oxidation of the steel rail, it can become real slick. Heavy rain isn't bad because it washes the rails clean. Frost by itself isn't slick, but there is a secondary thing frost sometimes does: Where oil has dripped out of the boxes on the cars and rests along the bottom of the rail, the frost can put a little film on top of the rail and, boy! That's slick! Without sand you'll spin your drivers.

A steam locomotive can run through water up to the firebox, but a diesel can only go through about a foot of water because the traction motors are down low, and the water can get on the commutators and brushes.

In 1949, diesels began coming in a few at a time. Diesels have automatic sanders with a wheel creep relay. If one wheel starts slipping, it detects that creep and the sander will come on momentarily to stop it. Diesels are sand rigged on each side, front and back.

Train Wreck!

It happened November 8, 1973, at Milepost 202½ from Portland. It was down at what they called Port Kelly at Wallula. I was just coming off a curve with five diesel units pulling a freight train and making 40 miles an hour. Parallel to the track was a road with an empty grain truck moving alongside us. The driver in the cab was looking straight ahead. He was close enough I could have hit him with a rock. I laid on the whistle hard to remind him that we were coming to a road crossing. He couldn't help hearing me.

He was pulling past us. I laid on the whistle more. The road crossing was coming up on us.

Instead of stopping, he swung onto the crossing directly in front of us. I hit the emergency. The brakeman and fireman were saying "No! No! No! No!" And pow! We hit his trailer and ripped it off the cab and carried it across the front of the engine on down the track.

The engine was chattering and shaking. I didn't know whether to jump off and I didn't dare jump. The four diesel units behind me and the train kept pushing me. Then I felt the rails spread apart and we were on the ground, grinding ties to mush and the train still coming. As the diesels cut deeper into the ground, they slowed harder and the weight of the train came on—cars jackknifing, piling up against us, breaking.

There was a brakeman riding in the rear diesel, and he told me later, "I looked out and said, 'I'll jump!' Then here went a car over on that side. I jumped to the other side and here went a car over there. I was running back and forth and didn't know which side to get out and never did go."

When we come to a stop, the five diesels were tipped, but none of them fell over.

I climbed out and walked back alongside the train to where the truck cab was tipped against a boxcar at the road crossing. The driver had wandered off and left the diesel truck engine running wide open. Stanley Horner, the conductor, came running up from the caboose. We knew if we didn't stop that truck engine, it might burn and set fire to the boxcars. We reached into the cab and pulled all the levers in sight till we hit the right thing and the engine stopped.

Pretty soon, people came from everywhere to look. Right behind the rear diesel was a car of Walla Walla onions. The top of the car had been ripped off and the onions were spilling out. When the people left, they all took onions.

That was the worst wreck I ever saw. Afterwards, they had to jack the engines up in the air and build tracks under them. The wreck cost the railroad $400,000.

Retired

I retired January 27, 1974 after 51 years of service. I went on another visit to Finland. It had been 61 years since I was there as a little kid. The cousin, Saima, that had helped me pull up the carrots from Grandma's garden, hung onto me and cried.

PART TWO

. . . AND DOWN THE VALLEY

EIGHTEEN

IRV AND RUTH HANSON

IRV HANSON

This account is based on interviews with Irv and Ruth, letters and stories written by Irv, and information provided by Marcella Hanson.

IRVIN "IRV" STANLEY HANSON's roots go back to Norway. His maternal grandmother, Anna Theodora Dorothea Nikolena Oldsdatter Faa (1841–1899), and grandfather, Mikkel Lie Peterson (1839–1893), were born in Finnoy, Rogaland, Norway.

His paternal grandmother, Anna Christina Ribaasen, and grandfather, Hans Christian Hanson, were born in Farsund, Norway. All grandparents migrated to the United States. Irv's father, Hans Christian Hanson (1854–1921) was born in Stoughton, Wisconsin. His mother, Betsey "Ole" Peterson (1866–1961), the third of 13 children, was born in Newburg, Minnesota. The last Peterson child was born soon after the birth of Betsey's first child.

Betsey and Hans, Irv's parents, were married in 1884 in Lake Mills, Iowa, where their three children were born: Ada Camilla Hanson Dedrickson (1886–1961); Ernest "Ern" H. Hanson (1889–1977); and Irv (1896–1979).

IRV: I was living with my folks in Ontario, California, when we heard Winkleman, Arizona, was a boom camp with lots of mining jobs. Ern and his friend, Price Vail, were about twenty-three years old and experienced at bumming and finding jobs, so the three of us headed there. We caught a slow-moving S.P. [Southern Pacific Railroad] freight a few miles east of Ontario at Colton.

It was a long, heavy train, headed for Yuma, Arizona. It had to have a huge, oil-burning locomotive help it over the San Gorgonio Pass, which was about 11,500 feet in elevation. Then the helper unhooked and waited there for the next freight pulling back to Colton and on to Los Angeles.

In a few days we arrived at Winkleman, but the word had got around and the town was loaded with unemployed of all kinds. No jobs. We hung around in several big saloons and pool halls. It was warm, so we could camp out at night.

I had worked in a pool hall at Wineville racking balls and getting a lot of playing practice. In those days, pool was very much a gambling game. So I did the playing: Price and Ern—strangers to me, of course—placed bets with "live ones" on the "kid." I was careful to win only when Ern or Price had a bet on me. It worked most of the time. I had to be careful, though, when I got in a game with a traveling pool slicker!

Mascot Mine

We left Winkelman to look for work in the Mascot Mine at Dos Cabezas, a 30-mile hike. Walking or riding freight trains were our only means of travel. We waded up the Gila River, through the narrow canyon where Coolidge Dam now stands. We saw a lobo wolf and shot rabbits and quail to eat. The skin wore off our feet from wading in sharp sand, but after another few miles, we made it to San Carlos just in time for an Apache Indian celebration. The Indians sort of surrounded us but seemed to consider us harmless oddballs.

We camped out by the ruins of Fort Bowie. Just as night came on, three huge, six-foot rattlesnakes crawled out of the adobe ruins on their evening rodent hunt. Soon more snakes were all about, so we moved camp to a ridge some distance from the old fort.

Next day, 12 miles over the hills put us at the portal of the Mascot Mine. Price got a job the first day, but Ern and I had to camp out and shoot cottontail rabbits for a living. Finally we were put to work. I was a big, muscular kid and a good worker with lots of self-confidence. I was only sixteen, but put my age down as legal twenty-one to get the job, so I had to pay seven dollars road tax and five dollars poll tax.

The mine was interesting and comparatively nice to work in as the ventilation was good—so good in fact, that doors had to be closed in cool weather to control wind blast in the tunnel.

The first job I had was helping start a tunnel off the shaft where an ore stringer indicated there might be ore close by. We built a platform on timbers wedged 50 feet down in the shaft. After a couple of days, we had a tunnel started and room to work. A careless worker slipped and dumped 80 sticks of dynamite all over us as we were on the platform—60 percent powder—but no need saying, it did not explode. [Sticks of dynamite will not explode until detonated by caps.]

The fifth night, I looked at the face of the tunnel after the round was shot, and here, shining in the light of our miner's lamps, was peacock copper, 70 percent pure and very colorful. It was the richest strike the Mascot had ever found! We soon had a big stope of high-grade ore removed.

Old Hickory

One of the miners and timbermen was called "Old Hickory." He had once been an actor and comedian. At lunch break, he would arrange candles like footlights around a pile of high-grade ore and put on a comedy act to entertain us. After gaining our attention and approval, he would give a short lecture on economics and socialism, the first I had ever heard. I was too young to really get the messages, but in the years since, I have come to understand that he gave me something precious—thinking about a better social structure. Hickory was a member of the Western Federation of Miners, I think.

I got the "home for Christmas" feeling about this time and quit the mine, rode an ore car down to Willcox, and then on the main S.P. line for home.

Cold Desert

The desert can get very cold at night in December. I got in an empty boxcar with five boys from New York. They were in bad shape, but desperate to make the last miles to the "promised land" in warm, sunny Los Angeles. As we went from Gila Bend to Yuma, the night got much colder. I was wearing wool underwear, three shirts, and coveralls and was none too warm. The kids were freezing and hungry. I bought a few doughnuts and we each had two for supper. Then I showed the boys how to stuff their clothes with newspapers for insulation. We still weren't warm enough, so we lit some candles and hovered around them. Later we built a small fire in the corner of the boxcar.

Just before dawn, the train stopped at a station, and I jumped off. I noticed sparks and flame coming out through a hole in the boxcar floor. The train started and as I leaped back on, I saw that the station agent had also seen the fire. I knew he would telegraph Yuma, which was the next stop and only 15 miles ahead, and there would be a reception committee waiting for us.

As we pulled into Yuma, I could see a number of men with flash lanterns standing about where the train would stop. I had $150 in my pocket and a strong desire to get home for Christmas. I wasn't going to get caught in a jam that would be good for six months in jail.

I saw a smooth patch of sand and unloaded at about 30 miles per hour—too fast to land on my feet and run with the momentum. I had to fold up and roll. I got to my feet and started running away from the railroad tracks. One of the railroad bulls yelled, "Stop!" I ran faster. I got about 100 yards when they started shooting. I could hear bullets plop in the sand. Fortunately, we were still in gray daylight. I was so scared and running so fast, I soon rounded a protecting sand hill.

However, the excitement wasn't over by any means. At the edge of the railroad tracks, I ran into a large Yuma Indian village. I dashed between rows of hogans and woke up a huge pack of dogs. They chased me through the village and on into south Yuma, constantly barking and collecting more dogs. One of the dogs tried to bite me. By the time I got away from them, Yuma was two miles behind, and I had a ten mile hike to the next station.

Two more days of boxcars and a very dirty, sunburned kid was happily eating Christmas turkey at "Home Sweet Home," Ontario, California.

Move to Medimont

Mother wanted to get the old man away from his drinking associates in California, so we came to Medimont [Idaho] in 1917 and my folks bought a farm. Mother's sister, Marie, was married to John Snyder, who owned a small grocery store at Medimont, and that's how we happened to locate here.

My brother, Ern, and I worked around the country as loggers and came back occasionally to see the folks.

Raft Trip 1920

During the spring of 1920, Ern and I set out to trap on the St. Joe [River] and use rafts to move our camp, trapping the side streams as we went. We found a mile-long logjam close to Conrad's Crossing with plenty of cedar logs in it to make our rafts. The next morning, we loaded our gear on the rafts and started downriver.

At Broken Leg cabin, I cut a deep gash in my foot with my hatchet. I put some balsam juice on it and wrapped it with thin strips of tape.

Next day I hobbled down to the pool not far from the cabin and caught a mess of trout and made a marten set nearby baited with the fish cleanings. After dark we heard a violent rattling out there. We lit candles and here was a large, dark marten in the trap. He was worth $30, which would equal $130 of today's inflated cash. I told Ern we were due for a streak of good luck, but I was wrong.

After one day's rest, I figured I could travel on in snowshoes wearing four pairs of wool socks on my bad foot. I was surprised that it stayed warmer than the other foot wearing a rubber pack.

I jumped aboard the raft with my packsack where the rapid entered the pool and went around a sharp point of rock. We didn't know a tree had floated down during the night. The raft hit the tree and did a quick flip underwater. My feet hit bottom, and I pushed to the surface so fast that the contents of my packsack were still fairly dry.

We decided that wooden rafts were too uncontrollable in fast water, so we snowshoed out of Broken Leg taking turns breaking trail. Then we hit sign that someone had been trapping ahead of us, so we changed our plans and headed up a side stream for the top of the Bitterroot ridge.

Stranded Sheep

Close to the top of the ridge, we ran into hundreds of live sheep stranded in the snow. We heard later that a forest fire had swept through there and scattered the sheep over a large area. Not many had burned, but some 700 had walked in hot embers so they couldn't travel and had been left to die. Coyotes and foxes had been having a feast. We skinned a couple of choice sheep pelts and wrapped them around our feet to keep them warm on those cold nights. We made it into Montana, and I caught the largest white weasel I would see in 50 years of trapping.

After trapping in Oregon Gulch, we got short of grub—nothing to eat but cornmeal mush and pine squirrels—so we headed out and landed in a lunchroom at Iron Mountain, Montana. The cook had just taken several large, beautiful banana cream pies out of the oven. We each ate a whole pie.

The waitress must have told the cook. He came out of the kitchen with a big grin on his face and said, "Say! You guys sure like banana cream pie!"

When we got home at Medimont, Mother was happy to get the wool to process from our choice sheep pelts. She said it took her back to when she was an Iowa farm girl.

Kooskia Characters

It was 1923 when Ern and I lived ten miles above Kooskia. About half the population along the river were those old pioneer types, the residue of the big influx of gold miners in the early days.

This one character, John Steinman, was an old German who lived two miles up the creek above where I got my irrigation water. He panned a little gold in summer—made maybe a dollar a day. My trap line ran close to his little cabin, so I dropped in one fall, and I could see his resources were very slim. All he had was some homemade furniture, a soogan or two [thick quilts], and a few tin cans to cook in. He had a little garden, and another old guy who lived next to me on the river gave him quite a bit of produce. He had an old .45-90 rifle with black powder shells, but he was getting so old, he couldn't hunt any longer. I shot a couple deer for him. So that winter, I assumed he was getting by all right.

About once a month, he'd come walking down past our place, headed for Kooskia, and would generally pick up a ride on the road. A little after Christmas, my car was on the bum, so I decided I'd hoof it to Kooskia this morning. I got down the river about two miles below our house—I'd seen his track where it went past our house in the night. I came along and he was sitting on the bank, humped over with his head in his hands.

I walked up and said, "Hello, John!"

Then I saw he was white as a sheet and frozen solid. It was eight below zero. He could have stopped in at our house, but he was independent like a lot of those old pioneers are.

I went down and notified the authorities and helped pick him up. The coroner and sheriff asked me to investigate his cabin to find who might be his relatives, so I went up. All I found in that cabin was those tin-can cooking utensils, the homemade furniture, those two soogans, the old .45-90 and a handful of rice and three or four potatoes the size of marbles. That was all the food he had. He had no letters or correspondence of any kind. All we knew was that he left Germany when he was young to escape military service.

In those days there was no social security or relief. The only place for people like that was the county poor farm where I suppose he was headed. The sheriff told me to keep the .45-90 for my trouble.

Two old soldiers from the Mexican-American War lived about a half mile above us. I shot deer for them, too. You could look out on the hillside from my house and see 30 deer sometimes.

Honest John Kirchner

Old "Honest" John Kirchner was a fine neighbor. I let him have surface water out of my irrigation ditch for his garden. I had the water rights.

He'd sworn at some time in his life he'd never tell another lie. He wouldn't lie even a white lie. Like these guys who'd kill deer out of season between his house and mine, they'd come by and say, "Hello, John!" And he wouldn't turn his head to look, so he'd be able to say he hadn't seen them.

Then there was Hank Bimerick who lived below me and panned a little gold and scrounged around. The creek is named after him.

Kooskia Fair

Ern and I and a couple of friends, Hal and Len, had a big day at the Kooskia fair. We took an airplane ride. Len rode a bucking horse in the rodeo contest and won five dollars for the effort, plus a lot of sore bruises.

I exhibited a 32-pound watermelon at the garden booth. I won first prize—three dollars. They sold it for 10 cents a pound cut up on paper plates. It was a fine tasting melon. I only lost 20 cents on the deal.

We danced till midnight and then started the ten-mile hike upriver to our homes.

Hurry-Up Jump

Hal had a hot romance going with one of the town girls. He decided to visit her before going home. We told him we'd take a swim in the river just above the bridge and wait for him to catch up.

She was sleeping in the loft of a hay barn. It was 12 feet up but had a rope hanging on the outside wall that a good, active boy like Hal could climb up.

While climbing up, Hal noticed what looked like a nice pile of dry hay and manure in easy jumping distance from the loft. So after a brief visit, he confidently leaped out and down in the moonlight. Only the surface of the pile was semi-solid, and his 180 pounds, falling 12 feet, drove him clear to his hips in soft manure.

In his hurry to scramble out, his expensive, new cowboy boots stayed stuck in the bottom of each leg hole. He had no choice but to reach down and pull them out even though he was wearing a new silk shirt with fancy embroidery done by his girlfriend.

We heard Hal approaching our camp and knew all was not well from the sound effects. Then he leaped, clothes and all, from the bridge into the Clearwater River.

Hal told us what had happened while he cleaned his new boots and washed the silk shirt and the rest of his clothes and hung them on the bushes around our campfire.

We had speared white fish and trout and were having a fish feed. Must have been quite a sight, four naked young men cooking fish in the pale morning light like they might have come out of the past ages of evolution.

Bill Runion

Bill Runion and his brother Joe were always talking in high excitement about a new mineral discovery. They'd interest some of these old cats around Medimont and get them to furnish a grubstake to develop it.

The first time I met Bill, he hissed through the crack of my door, "Come out by the woodpile."

I said, "What the hell is it, Bill?"

"Get your packsack!" he says. "Gold! I've struck 'er at the grass roots."

I got him to come in for a cup of coffee and a doughnut. After about 15 minutes he cooled down and forgot all about the gold rush.

That was Bill. When the spring winds blew, he'd give birth to these excitements and rush off prospecting.

Bill was always spooky after dark. I stayed at his cabin near Killarney Lake one night and he never seemed to sleep. All night long he'd be getting up. Every pack rat that stirred, he would out with the old .44 pistol. I couldn't sleep at all.

The night I went up on Grassy with him, we went to hunt grouse. It was dark when we got there, so we threw our sleeping bags down in the tall grass and went to sleep.

Along about midnight, Bill jabbed me with his elbow, "H-s-s-s-t! There's a cougar!"

I whispered, "Where?"

"Right down the hill. Let's crawl down and shoot him." We started belly crawling, each with a shotgun in hand. We could see the gleam of an eye and then the eye went up higher.

Bill whispered, "H-s-s-s-t! He's goin' up a tree."

The trouble was, there was just one eye, and all of a sudden I knew. We were looking at a street light in the town of St. Maries.

Indian Encampment

Around the shorelines of Medicine Lake and Cave Lake, there was every indication that this had been a major Indian encampment site. We found arrowheads and pestles, but only one mortar. We found many trade beads and copper beads that were short tube-like sections to string on a necklace.

There was a flat stone the kids were skipping in the lake. They were all over the place. I've got 40 or 50 of them after I've given some away. There are two types—one a kind of slate and the other a kind of schist. Must have been used by trappers for scraping skins. I haven't seen them in other collections, so they must be unique to this area.

Here on our place in Medimont, unintentionally, I ran into nine burials while working my sandpit and plowing the garden. I found one femur bone longer than mine, which would indicate a person over six feet tall. That would be an unusual size for a Coeur d'Alene Indian.

RUTH: We had this sandpit and Irv and the boys had to clean off the top so as to get into the white sand down below because we were selling sand at the time. My oldest son, Lew, came up to the house and he had in his hand—I thought it was a big white rock—but it was a skull. That was the first burial found. The archaeology club from North Idaho College dug the rest and took it all to Coeur d'Alene.

After that, when Irv would run into one of these burials while plowing, he would leave the bones where they were intended to be and put the dirt back over the top. So that was the only one that was really disturbed.

One time when he was putting in a water line, he had to dig a little lower than usual to lay the pipe—and here was another burial. So he just ran the pipe underneath the bones and covered it all up again.

Our kids found—especially down by the lakeshore—these small, flat stones, very thin, and very smooth and round, maybe an inch and a half in diameter. They skipped in the lake beautifully. We didn't recognize them as artifacts for a long time. We never saw any like that in anyone else's collection except at the Maryhill Museum. We also found a lot of obsidian arrowheads and knife points. And there were two jade scrapers, which I understood came from British Columbia. These would seem to be indications of trading or travel.

Trapping Hidden Lake

IRV: The price for muskrat fur got me interested in trapping. It was over in Hidden Lake (the one near Killarney Lake) that I broke through. I was skiing along the edge, but pretty well out in it, when the ice broke. I threw my packsack and traps toward a muskrat house ten feet away. I didn't go down plunk, I sank by degrees. As I was going down, I kicked off one ski. It popped up and I laid it across the hole in the ice. I was clear down before I got out of the second ski. I worked it up with my foot and one hand and laid it across the hole, too. Using each ski in succession, I wriggled ahead to the muskrat pile and my packsack. Then I began to work myself and the packsack toward shore, putting my weight as much as possible on both skis and on the ice.

When I reached shore, my clothes were frozen stiff. I lighted a fire on the island and hung all my clothes on a limb to dry.

Since then, I always pack a ten-foot pole when I'm on ice. You're liable to break through a spot that has melted from rotting vegetation. But you can break through and still have solid ice within reach.

RUTH: Irv often came home a little wet from having stepped into a hole and going in over his hip boots. But it was rare that he would go all the way in. I was accustomed to him coming home late at night, so I wouldn't wait for him, but would always feed the kids. Of course, I worried a number of times, especially when it was cold and freezing. So this night, I was no more worried than usual, although it was much colder and he was much later.

Then he came home and told about falling in and having to dry out his clothes so he could even walk in them. And then, he still had to come down the river in the boat.

And then there was the time Irv was trapping, and going through a campground, he cut his hand on a piece of broken glass. Somebody had been shooting at bottles. The gash was bleeding pretty badly. He was closer to Kellogg than home, so he went right to the doctor. He was blood, and he was mud, and he was stinking from all that trapping stuff.

As the doctor and nurse were cleaning the wound, their noses sort of wrinkled up and the doctor said, "What, exactly, do you do?"

When Irv told the doctor he was a trapper, the doctor turned to the nurse and said, "Well! Here's the last of the mountain men!"

California Trapping

IRV: Sometimes I trap in California when I get down there in winter. Anyone in the United States can buy a trapping license in California for one dollar. They have no closed season and no bag limit on beaver and muskrat in the diked areas because the animals do so much damage. The mud is so soft that a beaver can bore a hole through in one night and flood hundreds of acres.

RUTH: When he was trapping muskrats near Sacramento, he was trying to push a stake into the dirt and fell on it. He cracked a rib. He didn't have far to walk home, but it was painful breathing.

Bears Damage Beavers

IRV: A black bear will tear open a beaver house when the young are too small to dive and he'll eat up the babies. The young are too buoyant to dive for a week or two after birth.

I chased a bear out of tearing up a beaver lodge over on Slate Creek [in the St. Joe River drainage] below the ranger station where the road comes down from Placer Creek. It was early springtime and I was out setting a few traps. This big, old bear, at the moment I saw him, was standing up with his paws holding a limb and scratching his back on the tree near the beaver house. A great, big 400-pound bear. I didn't want to hurt him, so I dropped a bullet down by his feet. He took off up an open hillside and every little ways I'd drop another .22 bullet behind him to spur him on. Pretty soon his sides were going like bellows. Winded. I'll bet he didn't come back for a few days.

Attitude on Trapping

Most of the trappers I have known have been ecology conscious. They regard themselves as benefiting the game and birds. Paddy McIntyre for example, would tell you of all the fawns he had seen eaten up by coyotes and all the birds eaten up, trying to justify his own position as a trapper. This is true enough that predators will eat whatever they can get.

As far as predation is concerned, Man is the worst. What the animals do is insignificant. Look what strip mining and logging, as done by big outfits on the Coast, does where they rip up the country. I'd include the Coeur d'Alene mining district managers as predators also. But back in the earlier days, no one thought much about pollution. It takes time to realize the danger to living things. I think this asthma I have is probably due to the lead in the dust I breathed while plowing here in the Coeur d'Alene valley.

Consider how many birds and animals have been harmed by DDT. I think most of us have some DDT in our systems.

Even the "bleeding hearts" set out rat and mouse poison and use insecticide on their shrubs and flowers and, in the process, may kill several thousand living organisms. One of the most cruel things people do is take cats and dogs and dump them.

We have to study carefully how to handle the ecology, not a study based on sentimentality, but one intelligently directed. There is some wildlife more valuable to human consumption, like ducks and some of the big game animals, and it seems only sensible to me to keep their

■ Although ill with asthma, Irv Hanson (76) still did a little trapping. Shown here at the mouth of Pheeny Creek on the Coeur d'Alene River in December 1972.

predators within bounds. On the other hand, some predators do more good than harm.

For example, I'd favor the closing of all the side streams up on the North Fork [of the Coeur d'Alene River] to beaver trapping. They do a lot of good in checking the fast runoff and erosion, while down here along the lake where they eat up the shade trees and bore holes in the railroad right of way and the dikes, they should be trapped. The fur is valuable.

The human animal has made a living from gathering and hunting for millions of years. It's part of the survival pattern. As far as I can see, there is no more reason for man to break this survival pattern than for a bear or coyote to do so.

As to a trapper feeling brutalized, I don't feel brutalized. Not, at least, to the point where I feel it's right to bomb human beings.

As far as bringing back natural habitat, there's no chance. We've disturbed that balance tremendously and will probably disturb it more. So the ecology has to be managed and these animals have to be managed by human beings. Scientific management through a lot of honest study is the key to the whole thing.

RUTH HANSON

Interviewed 1992 at Medimont, Idaho.

Dad got our place on Clark Creek from Uncle Silvenus "Veen" Buhl. He was married to one of my mother's sisters. It was three-quarters of a mile up the creek from Highway 3, and the narrow road to it winds uphill past the remains of Tom Eva's place on the left, and a little further up, the Steadman place on the right. Knoors lived north of us, the Axel Johnsons lived east of us on the south side of Clark Creek. Tom's son, Gar, and his wife, Lena, lived uphill northeast and years later bought our place from Dad. [After Gar died, Lena moved to southern California to be with her sister.]

Our place has gone through several hands, the present owners being Bill and Jan Phillips who own the Valley Mart. Nothing remains of our original log home, but the frame house we built in 1925, with its many remodelings and changes in roofline, looks good and is painted bright yellow.

Family

I was born there, December 28, 1909, three days late for Christmas. My father was Ward West and my mother was Gertrude Alice Spafford West.

There were six children in our family: Eunice, Elmer, Frank, Kenneth, me, and the youngest boy, Delbert. Eunice lives in Eugene, Oregon. She is ninety years old, still drives a car, and looks after the grandkids sometimes. All of us are living except Elmer, who was killed in an accident while working as a steelworker on a dam at Vantage on the Columbia River in 1968. Earlier, he had been working on a bridge over Kettle Falls. A boom broke. He saw this cable coming. He had to think fast and he acted fast. He rammed his leg down between two girders. When he was knocked out by the cable, he wasn't knocked into the Columbia River.

Leaded

Dad's idea was to support the family by making a living off the farm, so he bought some land adjacent to ours. He wanted to build up the production of milk and cream, so he had to work out to get cash to buy a herd of dairy cows and build a big barn.

He was working in the hay fields on the river flats. The hay grew real tall there before the lead killed it. But still there was lead dust in there and he got leaded. [As the Couer d'Alene River overflowed its banks, it deposited lead from mining operations upstream.] The doctor told him

■ Ruth Hanson, on Clark Creek (off Hwy. 3) where she was born and lived until her marriage, in front of the remodeled home built by her parents

to get out of the valley. I was about two years old when we moved away. There was no medication for it then, but he did get better, so it must have worked itself out of his system.

Then he had to decide if he should move his family back to the farm. It wasn't much of a farm then. A lot of the ground was not cleared, but he had hopes for it. Boy! I wish he could see it now!

In about two years we did move back. Then for a time he worked underground in the Last Chance Mine. His health was pretty good and he lived to be ninety years old.

Blowing Stumps

Most of the place was in timber. It took a lot of work to make a farm out of it but the soil is absolutely free of rocks and whatever you plant in it will grow.

After Dad cut the timber, he and Elmer used dynamite to blow the stumps. It was pretty exciting watching the dust explode into the air, but whew! That dynamite had an acrid smell! When we were lucky, most of the roots came out with the stump blast, but usually we had to work them out with the stump puller and it took all of us to do that.

After the stumps were loosened by the blast, they hooked a cable onto the root close to the stump, fastened the other end of the cable to a pole, and hitched the horses to the pole. Us kids would drive the horses 'round and 'round and since we were on the end of the pole, we had a lot of leverage to wind up the cable onto a drum, which broke the roots loose from the ground.

It was a big job, clearing fields. I hated that. I suppose I was about ten years old when I started—I wouldn't have had much power before that.

Smallpox Field

We called one of our fields the "smallpox field." The Johnsons divorced and their boy, Larry, who was three years younger than I, lived with us for several months during the time smallpox went through our family. Only Larry and I didn't get it. Even Mother had smallpox. She was pregnant and was worried because the baby could be born blind. All of us kids who weren't down with smallpox worked at clearing that field.

We grew hay and some grain. Archie Fortier—we pronounced it "Forchie"—brought his threshing machine over to harvest the wheat and oats. Dad had a steel-wheeled Fordson tractor to run the mill for grinding wheat coarse for animal feed. But one time, when we had a big affair and dinner at the Grange Hall down by the lake at Medimont, all local products were to be featured, so Dad ground some wheat fine, and I made the rolls from it. I suppose I was about seventeen.

Wrench in Hopper

The only accident on the farm involving machinery was when my sister Eunice's husband, Ted Cole, got hurt while filling the silo. We never knew how the wrench got into the hopper, but when it hit the choppers, it flew into a million metal fragments that cut him all around the mouth, nose, and chin.

Two Homes

Our log house was like a lean-to with a woodshed attached and we had a big log root cellar. The water supply was down under the hill, so us kids had to carry it up from the spring in buckets. We had buckets to catch the rain off the roof, too, so we didn't have to carry all the water we needed.

Years later, in 1925 when I was sixteen, we built a new house of lumber. Dad dug a ditch from the creek to the house so we had water and we had a gasoline-powered washing machine in the basement. One summer, we blanched the peas from our garden and tried shelling them by running them through the wringer, but it didn't work too good.

Lightning Cracks Wall

The next year Dad bought a radio and ran an aerial wire through the window. Lightning hit close enough that it went into that wire and cracked the window frame and then it went down and cracked the basement wall. It blew some sheetrock from the side of the room where it had come in clear across two rooms and buried the sheetrock in the opposite wall.

It happened at the time of day we would have been having our evening meal, but we knew a storm was coming, so my dad and brothers were up on the hill trying to get in some hay. I was the only one in the house. I thought the dust from the sheetrock was smoke, so I ran out and yelled to my dad that the place was on fire!

He and the boys came running down, but there was no fire. My youngest brother, Delbert, and the dog happened to be underneath the porch and both were knocked out by the lightning. I didn't think where the boy was until he came crawling out from under the porch in a state of shock. After that the dog was forever afraid of loud noises.

Model T

I ran most of the machinery on the farm and drove Dad's tractor some. My brother and I bought a little Model T Ford for $50. I had $20 that I'd saved from the $10 a month Dad gave me. Kenneth had $30.

The car had a hand throttle and three foot pedals. One of the pedals was a brake, one was reverse, and one was for the gears. Clear up was in high, halfway down was neutral. You pressed clear down and it was in low. And of course I wanted to learn to drive it. So coming home one day, I took the wheel. When we came to the barnyard gate, I pushed down on the brake and meant to push the other pedal halfway down into neutral, but I pushed too far and put it in low and we went through the gate without bothering to open it. But I learned, and that never happened again!

Pleasant Hill School

We went to the Pleasant Hill School. We followed down Clark Creek to where the road left it and walked up a trail to the schoolhouse. It set on a little rise without a flat place large enough for playing baseball! We didn't mind having to walk even during the winter snows. By the time I went to school there were four others to help me. My oldest sister is the one that had it difficult.

We all got the childhood diseases—measles, chicken pox, whatever was going through school. My youngest brother, Delbert, was about seven when he got typhoid fever. There was typhoid everywhere—Harrison was full of it. Delbert was unconscious for a long, long time. When he came to, he had no memory of anything before that—and still hasn't. Frank, who was out working around here and there, had typhoid, too, but not such a severe case and not at the same time.

I was about seventeen then. After grade school, I had stayed out a couple years to help my dad and brothers. Mother needed help in the house and with her chickens, too, but I worked more outside than in—milking cows, running the separator, washing the milking machine, and cleaning out the barn. I spent more time in the barn than in the house!

School in Kellogg

Then my brothers—even Elmer—and I went up to Kellogg to school. Elmer had been in the army, stationed in San Francisco, but he got sick. At that time, you could buy out of the army, so Dad paid a couple hundred dollars and Elmer came home. The boys bached in a little cabin right next to the print shop and found various jobs.

The West name became pretty well-known in Kellogg then, because my four brothers are all over six feet tall—one is six-foot-five—and played on the football team. They played against a bunch of big farm kids from Firth, a small school in southern Idaho I'd never even heard of, and Kellogg tied with them for the Idaho State Championship.

I stayed with the Scheuttenhelms and worked for them. I got no money—just board and room. You didn't expect anything else. Scheuttenhelm was superintendent of the Bunker Hill smelter. They had two boys and two girls. I don't remember their oldest girl's name, but the boys were John and Charles and the youngest girl's name was Mary Alice.

One time I asked the lady of the house if I could go out for basketball. She said, "Yes—if you have time." There was my answer—No!

I loved school and my grades were fine, but even though my folks came up weekends sometimes, I got homesick before I finished one year and left high school and went back to helping Dad.

Back Home

I really liked to take the dog and ride my horse up the creek on the sidehill, often up above Gar Eva's place, past the "Wood Thieves" cabin [local cabin's nickname of unknown origin], to get the cows. We were milking about 15. By that time, Dad had a gasoline milking machine. Boy! That thing made some noise! Dad put in an acetylene gas outfit for light in the barn and house and that helped a lot, but when electricity came in 1940, after I'd left home, there was no comparison!

I spent one winter in Clarkston helping Eunice. She had already taught some, but wanted to get more education at Lewiston Normal. She was pregnant and needed me to help care for her three children: Orville, Robert, and Donald. My folks hauled food down. Things were awfully tough because her husband didn't have work—there were no jobs to be had. There wasn't much meat on the table that winter! Her fourth boy was stillborn. Later, she had a fifth boy, Jerry.

When her husband died of tuberculosis, she still didn't have enough credits to teach. She could only do some substitute teaching, so she worked in one of those all-night eating joints as chief cook and bottle-washer until she remarried. Then she didn't have to work out.

Tragedy struck again. Jerry died of tubercular meningitis.

Met Irv Hanson

After that winter, I went back home to help Dad, and I met Irv Hanson. He had come back to this part of the country after he'd been gone for some time.

I often rode my horse to Medimont to the country store that was owned by John and Marie Snyder. Marie Snyder was Irv Hanson's aunt. I was standing there reading a magazine and looked up when this tall guy came in. He looked at me and I looked down at the magazine. I looked up again and he looked down. Then I looked at the ceiling. Never said a word to each other. Eventually, I got on my horse and rode back home. I was amused at the whole thing.

So we didn't actually meet until the next dance at the Grange Hall at Medimont. It began about nine o'clock—and he bought my supper.

He was 13 years older than I. He liked to get out in the hills and so did I. We rode the train from Medimont to Spokane, then another train to Coeur d'Alene, where we were married April 10, 1928, by Eugene Best, Justice of the Peace. Then we went back to Spokane and stayed about a week, till whatever money we had was gone.

We came back to this house. The house hasn't changed very much. Collected more dust. The living room is smaller now, because when we put the bathroom in, we took space from the living room.

His brother, Ern, and mother were here. I asked her what I should call her, because I didn't want to call her "Mother Hanson."

She had never cared for her name, Betsey, so she said, "Oh, call me 'Ole!'" So that's how she got that name. But it did cause a little confusion. Her brother's name was Olaf and he also was called "Ole," as were several others in the family.

Fruit Tramp

That summer, I enjoyed hiking with Irv and taking some mountain trips. In the fall, we did sort of a "fruit tramp" trip. We drove to California in a car that he and his brother, Ern, had traveled in. It was a Model T sedan. They called it a "touring" car at the time. I never saw the top on it because by the time it came here, it had lost its cloth top in the Columbia Gorge in a wind gust. They said it went sailing down over the gorge! We picked hops near Ontario, Oregon, and then we picked prunes near Red Bluff, California. We shook the prunes off the trees, picked them up from the ground, and then ran them down an inclined rack made of slats, with spaces between them, to allow the leaves and debris to fall through. Irv was paid a little extra for hauling them to the dehydrator at Red Bluff.

Slept under Wonderful Tree

For most of the trip, we slept on the ground under the stars. We discovered a wonderful tree that was deep with duff underneath it and slept there when we were going south. We worked our way down to where he used to live in Ontario, California. Then coming back north, we stayed under that tree again.

But we slept under a roof if the weather was bad. I remember sleeping in an old shed when we were picking prunes, and a few times we used our own bedding and stayed in auto courts. [An auto court, the forerunner of a motel, usually had cooking facilities, but many furnished no dishes, kettles, or bedding.]

Picking apples at Watsonville, we just spread our blankets on the ground. We couldn't have a cooked meal there, so we ate a lot of sandwiches of whole wheat bread, tomatoes, mayonnaise, and that wonderful, crisp lettuce. For breakfast we ate cold cereal with milk.

You had to be pretty strong to pick apples at that time. We had a clamp like an ice tongs that would clamp on each end of the apple box and a hook in the middle that you would hook over a limb. We took all that up in the tree to pick into. When you had a box full, you had over 40 pounds to bring down out of the tree—much of the time down a ladder.

We picked a marvelous Bellflower apple that you don't hear of anymore. Each tree was tremendous. I've never seen another quite like it.

We picked some from a ladder, but picked a lot more while climbing around. It took two of us more than a day to pick one great tree. It was strange, but we did not see any other pickers at that orchard.

I lost my wedding ring there. One morning, I was afraid of catching it in the box hook, so I took it off and wasn't careful where I put it. I lost it, and I've never had another.

Settled Down

After the harvest season, we came back here. Ole and Ern lived with us until she bought a house over in Medimont that she and Ern fixed up.

Then I started having kids. Irv trapped and we raised a big garden and had quite a strawberry patch. We sold garden produce and berries to people in the mine district—a lot to the Pik Kwik Supermarket. We had to crate the strawberries—that was two flats, 24 boxes—and take them over to the passenger train. Then customers up there collected them from the train.

When I was carrying my first child, Irv landed a job and was gone for most of the summer of 1930.

I had a lot of strawberries to pick that year. They came on when I was six months pregnant, so that made a real problem bending over. My sister came over and helped me some. I nailed the tops on the crates, addressed them, and then she hauled them over and put them on the train.

Irv was paid by the hour by the Federal Mining Company, and used his own car working with a mining engineer, Harry Gibbs, checking on existing prospect holes in the hills around Wallace. Irv liked that!

Accidents

Irv was bounding down one of those steep hills wearing work boots with high heels and six-inch tops, landed wrong and sprained his ankle real bad. He had to fashion himself a crutch to make it back to the car. And then he had to drive home because Harry Gibbs didn't drive.

There was another trip where he had to drive home hurt. He was working with Leonard Maitland up the Coeur d'Alene River. He and Leonard were sawing with a crosscut saw. Irv dropped the saw on his leg and lost quite a bit of blood. As he was driving out, headed for the doctor, he met another vehicle head on and had to take off up the sidehill. It made Leonard so mad, he wanted to get out and beat up the guys in the other car.

Cut Tendon

While he was recuperating from the sprained ankle, he had another accident. We had come home from grocery shopping. He was going to carry the milk bottle so I wouldn't have to carry so many things. As he was getting out of the car, his injured ankle gave way and he went down. It broke the bottle. The bottle cut a terrible gash in the palm of his right hand and cut the tendon.

I drove him to Kellogg, but the doctor wouldn't do anything to him that night.

Poor Ole! She came down to our place. We never locked the house at that time. She came in, and here was this blood in the wash basin and nobody around. The car was gone. We stayed overnight until the next day when the doctor would work on his hand.

By morning, the tendon had receded so much that when the doctor tried to stitch it together, it wouldn't hold. So Irv always had to pull his middle finger down by pressing his other fingers over it. Otherwise, it would just stick out. Since the nerve was cut, his finger remained insensitive, and he burned it a number of times.

His finger never got better, he just got used to pulling it down that way. His ankle got all right, but apparently the sprain weakened it so it bent a little more sideways over the years. But eventually he got back to work before his first son was born.

First Child

I thought my child was about to be born the first of September. Since Irv was using the car, he took me to Molly Ross' Maternity Home at Kellogg and then went on to work. I was to notify him when the youngster was born—but I had to wait 19 days. At that time, it was embarrassing for a pregnant woman to appear on the street, so I wouldn't take a walk till it was getting dark. Molly didn't mind my being there so long—she was getting paid for it!

After Lew was born, I had to stay down about a week as was thought to be necessary in those days. I got so weak—it was ridiculous.

Before Ed was born, Irv thought he had ulcers and wasn't feeling well, so he stayed here and his mother took care of him, and my mother took care of me over at her place. They always had a doctor in Rose Lake when the sawmill was running. I think the mill was shut down then, but the doctor was still there. The doctor had a car and came to my mother's home. Ed was born January 23, 1932. Irv was better by the time I could come back to our home.

We had a telephone installed before Dave was born October 3, 1933.

I was used to having two days of labor, so I wouldn't let them call the doctor until things were getting urgent. But this time it took too long for the doctor to get here from St. Maries. My mother and sister were here and Irv did what he could—he caught the baby. But Irv made a mistake. He made the two ties to the cord. He thought that was just to make good and sure for the baby. And so there wasn't any tie on my side at all. I did bleed some, but when the doctor came, he gave me some pills to stop it. Then he took the afterbirth and of course, that was where the blood was coming from.

Before each child was born I had a girl's name picked out, but this time, none for a boy. As the doctor was leaving, he wanted to write down the baby's name. I couldn't think fast enough, so Dave has only one. I never did pick a second name for him.

The doctor left me some anti-hemorrhage pills. I had one laying right next to my bed and little Ed came toddling along and ate it!

I stayed down a week like the doctor ordered. I wasn't supposed to do things like washing diapers, so Irv got in on washing for two babies, Ed and Dave. Lew was trained pretty early, so he was out of diapers. There were 16 months between Lew and Ed and then 20 months between Ed and Dave. Bob was born three years later, so that gave me a little rest from diapers. But they were all healthy. They had to be.

Swinging Pups

Most of the babies' wash got done at home. I didn't mind washing clothes on a washboard, but the back-breaking part was carrying water from the well and heating it on the wood range. My sister was living up the hill, not very far from where the Valley Mart store is now, and for a time we took the rest of the family wash in her car over to our mother's place to the washing machine. We'd hang out quite a wash when we got all Eunice's kids' and my kids' clothes on the line—all the time, hoping there were no pups around to swing on the sheets or pull on the long stockings!

Two Paydays a Year

After Irv stopped working for the mining engineer, he trapped. During most of the Depression that's how we made our living. We had two paydays a year: the trapping and the garden produce including strawberries. We knew how to make the money stretch and we didn't splurge.

The boys learned to help with the garden work and strawberry patch when each one was old enough to be trained to do it. And they got what they made out of it. All that Irv would withhold was just a little bit for marketing and containers. So that gave them a little incentive. Lew was always fast with his work. Ed was diligent. Dave was, too. Bob liked to look around—enjoy the world.

Played for Dances

Before we were married, Irv bought a fiddle and taught himself to play it. After we were married, he bought a saxophone and learned to play it by ear, too. Fortunately, his injured finger was on his bow hand, and somehow he managed to make that finger reach the key on the saxophone.

It must have been about 1930 when he started playing for dances with a guy named Shelton on piano, Fred Palmer on the drums, and later, Carey Connor on the piano.

Coming home one dark night after a dance, Irv saw a white horse trotting down the road ahead of him. He swung the car out to dodge around it. But just as he came up behind it, he saw there was a black horse beside it, so he had to take to the brush to get around them!

I started playing about six years later, and that was only because this Shelton couldn't make it one night, and they needed somebody to play the piano. The kids were small then, but their grandmother, Ole, stayed with them.

The first dance I played for was at Lane. The next day, both hands were swelled up like penny balloons!

My mother had taught me to read notes and play a little bit on our reed organ, the kind with a peddle you had to pump. Then I took a few lessons from a neighbor girl.

I played mostly by ear for dances. But I'd buy sheet music if I couldn't figure out the chords to go with some piece. Irv played entirely by ear. He caught on really fast after I learned it and was good at harmonizing and improvising.

We played in Medimont at the Grange Hall, Tensed, Lane, Coeur d'Alene, Kellogg, and various other places around the area. Sometimes we'd pick up Ross Ahlstrom with his drums. He is Verla Bedwell's father. And sometimes we played with Bill Noyen.

We were coming home from a dance in Kellogg, going across that flat between Rose Lake and Lane. And it was muddy. We slewed around and then slowly slid off the side of the road. It must have been about two o'clock in the morning. We were sitting there, wondering what the heck we were going to do. We didn't like to get out and get all muddy. And here came a truck along with a load of revelers from the dance.

Those guys happily got out there in the mud, picked up that car, and put it over in the road!

After another dance, we were coming home from Santa and had Kay and Norm Best with us. It was icy, with compact snow. We were coming down off the Harrison Flats, about halfway down the hill above Black Lake, when here were these horses right in the middle of the road. Irv could slow down, but he couldn't stop. When we'd go a little bit to the right, the horses would go right because that's where they could see the best. We'd go a little bit to the left, and they'd be right ahead of us all the time. Because Irv was slowing down as well as he could, we couldn't have been going over five miles an hour when we hit one of them. The horse sat right down on the radiator! It smashed it in.

We lost the coolant. The rest of the way home, we'd drive a ways and then stop to let the motor cool off. Drive a little ways more and let the motor cool again. We traded that car in!

It was quite a distance to some of those dances, like Tensed, but gasoline didn't cost so much then, and we'd get paid five dollars apiece.

Farragut

Irv went to work at the Farragut Naval Training Center in 1941, which was a hurry-up job preparing a place to train men before the United States entered World War II. Lots of carpenters found jobs there. But he was checking loads of some kind and laughing about it because here he was, probably the huskiest-looking guy there, and he was pushing a pencil. Whatever it was, it brought in some money for a change.

Of course, we went on growing produce while he was working there, and he came home some weekends to help.

Irv bought a trailer house for $25 and pulled it over that curvy, narrow old road going to Coeur d'Alene. Now it wouldn't be allowed on the highway. He lived in that and then left it up there when Farragut was finished and he came back home.

War Work

The fall of 1942 we started going to the coast to work during the school months, but always came back here to Medimont in June for the summer.

We first lived in Portland, Oregon, at Irv's sister's place. Ada had a pretty good-sized house. Irv went longshoring until he ran a spike in his foot. While he was recuperating from that, we both took a shipfitting

■ Preparing to leave for work in the Vancouver, Washington, Kaiser Shipyard during World War II. The washing machine (right) stands ready to be loaded. Ruth, Irv, Ed on Lew's shoulders, Bob, grandmother "Ole" seated behind Dave and Ern Hanson, 1942.

class at night. Shipfitting has to do with marking a seam for a cut or weld in the making of the hull of a ship. We both got jobs in the Vancouver, Washington, shipyard and Irv worked on the Ways, the first area of ship building. The shipfitters took the lines from the blueprints and measured where a piece of steel had to be cut. I worked in the assembly where they brought in the sections and parts of the hull and put them together. Mine was a pencil-pushing job—a progress checker. We used a tape to measure the footage the welders turned out an hour and each day. The last few minutes of the shift were kinda busy—a lot of arithmetic—figuring all the totals and keeping the records. I didn't see any reason for the job. It seemed to me the leadman could have done that just as well. Eventually they did eliminate that job. Because I was a woman, my pay was that of a helper—95 cents an hour. The men got $1.20 an hour, journeyman's wages.

The Garlands

Irv got acquainted with Jim Garland on the job, and he and his wife Hazel became our good friends. Jim was a folk singer. They came from Harlan County, Kentucky, where Jim was a coal miner and union organizer. He said he had almost been killed in connection with his labor work. And he wrote a book called *Take This Traveler Home*. Before coming to work in the shipyard, they had been in New York City for some time, but the family did not like it there.

McLaughlin Heights

That winter we moved from Ada's house in Portland to McLaughlin Heights in Vancouver, Washington, January 23, 1943. I remember because that's Ed's birthday. McLaughlin Heights was a government housing project just for war workers. We lived in a brand new house with new appliances: refrigerator, electric stove, table and chairs. There were no beds, so we slept on mattresses on the floor.

I didn't have to get breakfast for the boys. They fended for themselves and got themselves off to school. Lew was twelve and would usually get our supper. Each of the boys had a job. Lew did the cooking. Bob was supposed to keep the bathroom clean. He was only six. He didn't care what he did.

We had the washing machine along. I had to wash clothing about two evenings a week and then iron another two or three evenings. One day I had left clothes on the line. I hadn't expected a rain, but it did come. When I came home I didn't see any wet clothes flapping on the line. My neighbor, who did not work out, called me over and there were our clothes around her stove drying on racks.

We stayed here in Medimont for the school year beginning in 1943 and then went back to the Coast the fall of 1944. Irv didn't work in the shipyard that time. He worked in the woods near Washougal. Jim and Hazel found a house for us near them in Washougal.

Stud Gunner

My job that year in the shipyard was on the Ways as a stud gunner for $1.20 an hour, welding up the brackets for the raceway that electric wires were pulled through. We not only had to wear the hard hats but the visor to protect the eyes and face. It didn't require much special training, but you did have to have eyesight good enough to see the punch marks in the steel hull that showed where and what size stud to put there. After the stud was welded on, you took your hammer and knocked the little ceramic ferrule off. I suppose the ferrule was there so you couldn't weld the gun to the steel!

That was mostly working up overhead, so you had to be strong in the arms. There were several women on the crew, one a very husky black woman. Some members of the crew were racist and didn't want to be around blacks, but I enjoyed it. It was a great experience.

One of the bad things about the job was sometimes you had to move the machine that powered the stud gun. It was pretty heavy. We climbed ladders from one deck to the next, and one time we had to bring it up several decks.

Eleanor and Franklin Roosevelt

Eleanor Roosevelt attended the launching ceremony of one of the ships. I was well impressed when I heard her speak. I was amazed at her charming personality. She did not photograph well and when I actually *saw* her in person, she was *not* a homely person.

I was there in the shipyard when President Roosevelt died. That was an emotional event for everybody. I felt a great loss. Very much so. His pictures had shown him as growing very tired.

Long Days

Because of the traffic, it seemed like we were away from home about eleven hours every day. If you stopped at a store, there was always waiting in line, so it would be longer. Irv drove to work most of the time when we were both there. But when I lived in Washougal, I rode the bus, occasionally drove the car, or sometimes Jim Garland and I went down together because he lived in Washougal, too. The shipyard was a distance of perhaps five miles.

Our Boys

When the war was over, we came home. Irv continued to trap and we raised produce to sell. The older boys were high school age. Lew had taken clarinet lessons in Washougal and wanted to continue. Ed was interested in art mainly, but later did play the tuba in the high school band. We wanted to see that the boys could develop what talents they had. They couldn't take lessons around here, so we and Ole went together and bought a house in Coeur d'Alene at Eighth and Bancroft. We moved down there for the school term, but Irv came back here for his trapping. I stayed down there beginning the fall of 1945 and put the kids in school.

Lew and Ed graduated from the high school in Coeur d'Alene in 1948 and we moved back to Medimont. Dave and Bob went to school in Rose Lake that fall.

I had kept Lew out of school the first year and started Ed who was only five, along with him the next year. You could do that at that time. Lew made a little better grades than Ed. Being a year older made some difference. They graduated from high school at the same time, but Ed was only sixteen and that was a little young to go to college.

So Lew started college first. We sold the house on Bancroft and bought a lot from Lloyd and Opal Brooten and put up a shack for the boys to live in with an outhouse—something you couldn't do anymore.

Bob's first year of school was at McLaughlin Heights, and he didn't learn anything because the teachers were worked to a frazzle. When he came back here to the school at Cave Lake, Mrs. Merrill gave him extra help, and he went through grade school in six years. So he, too, was out of high school at sixteen. We thought that because of his age, it would be better if he didn't go to college the next year.

He got a job working with Norm Best, a highway engineer, and stayed with Norm's family in Wallace for one summer and winter pounding stakes for road surveying.

All the boys worked to help themselves through college. At that time, it didn't cost anywhere near so much and the relationship of wages to college costs were a lot more favorable. Lew and Ed had trapped some. When Dave went to Rose Lake High School, sometimes he'd walk home—which was nine miles—and trap on the way. Often he'd catch a ride part way. None of them worked out at haying. They tried to get better-paying jobs. But they did put up hay at home. They all worked some for the Forest Service summertimes.

Porcupine Under Hood

Irv started to have physical problems and difficulty breathing the summer of 1951. Bob was fourteen. Irv had breathed a lot of welding smoke working in the shipyard. There were so many particles in the air that there was sediment in the bottom of the washing machine from the clothes. And he may have frosted his lungs when trapping. He had the flu and that may have been a factor. He had asthma from then on. The doctors put him on prednisone, and he was never able to get off from it. He had to breathe.

When the smelter fumes drifted down the valley, he couldn't breathe. He thought if he could get out of that valley, he might breathe easier. So one night we went up to Eagle Peak to sleep in the back of the pickup.

We parked in a small area a little below where the lookout tower is. It was a lovely summer night. Bright moonlight.

We woke up with a start. We thought we heard something. Irv got out and looked around. We knew that porcupines had been known to eat the rubber on tires. In fact, we noticed the lookout couple had their car fenced in to keep the porkies out. Well—he didn't see any porcupine. So he got back into bed.

After awhile we heard it again. Surely there has to be something there! So he lifts up the hood and here is this porcupine, right on top of the motor, starting to chew on the hoses.

The porkie, instead of going back down the way he had come up, tried to go down the other side, but he couldn't squeeze through. Irv wanted me to give him the pliers to grab the porkie with. He was going to pull him up and throw him out. They weren't long enough. He got some quills in his hand. Then he remembered he had some long tongs in the pickup. He told me to get them for him, which I did. The tongs were heavy and it took both hands to grab the porkie. Now, he was not well dressed. He had a T-shirt on and that was all! He didn't want those tongs with the porkie to get against his bare legs, so he started whirling around and around, so centrifugal action would keep the animal away from him.

"Give me the axe! Give me the axe!"

Of course, the way he told it later, it took me a long time to get the axe. Here he was dancing with that porcupine. I did give him the axe, and it wasn't long till he conked it on the head.

Swimming in Pollution

We knew we were all swimming in a polluted lake. My childhood memories of the river flats were bare ground where nothing would grow and animals that lived there would get leaded.

Bob and my daughter-in-law, Marcella, moved to Medimont in 1978. The next year, they had the redtop grass growing on their place tested. It was contaminated enough that it wasn't advisable to feed it to cattle. Redtop is a grass that will grow under poor conditions. I think that Schlepps and those that do raise redtop raise it for seed and it will be all right planted somewhere else.

Irv's arteries stopped up. He had to have one leg amputated. Gangrene had set into one toe of the other foot. It was very, very painful. Then he had a stroke. And that was the end. 1979.

After Irv was gone, I continued growing produce for a time. But if it hadn't been for Bob and Marcella being close, I don't think I could have even tried it.

NINETEEN

FRANCES HUNT

Interviewed 1973 at Kingston, Idaho.

THE FIRST TIME I came through the Fourth of July Canyon, my third boy was a baby. We rode in a wagon behind a team of horses. The road was nothing but rocks—creek bed most of the way. We left Coeur d'Alene early—at six o'clock in the morning, bounced over the rocks all day long and made it home to Kingston by eight o'clock in the evening.

Now that baby is seventy-two years old. Awhile back, I visited him in Coeur d'Alene and timed how long it took us to get home. Only 35 minutes by car!

I was born in Lafayette, Oregon, October 10, 1880, and named Frances Martin. When I was one year old, my father, Frank B. Martin, moved my mother and me and my sister, Leona, who was four years older than I, to his homestead at Rathdrum, Idaho. That's where we were living when my mother, Mona Mae, died at age thirty-three in 1888.

Turned Loose

After that, Dad turned us loose on the public, you might say. First I stayed with a family at Rathdrum, and I had to stand on an apple box to wash the dishes. I wasn't no bigger than seven years old. Seems like I've washed dishes all my life. I stayed with two more families there, and my sister Leona stayed with me and worked, too.

We next lived with Uncle Larsh that married one of the Post girls at Post Falls. When Christmas came, he sent Leona and I upstairs while the family celebrated by eating in candlelight and exchanging presents.

When school was out and I was nine, Uncle Larsh moved his family, Leona, and me to Kellogg. He took us on the electric train from Post Falls to Coeur d'Alene, and then on a steamboat up the Coeur d'Alene Lake to Harrison, and then on up the Coeur d'Alene River to the Old Mission [at Cataldo, Idaho]. From there, we rode the narrow-gauge railroad to Kellogg. We moved into a shanty across from where Central School now is.

Uncle Larsh was a carpenter. He built the first sidewalk from the junction up to Wardner out of two-by-sixes.

At Kellogg, I worked for Mrs. Lorring. I couldn't eat at the table with them. I was hungry a lot of the time. That fall, I was ten and went to the first schoolhouse in Kellogg, right up the hill from where Safeway store now is.

Strikes, Fires, and Disappearances

During the 1892 strike at the Bunker Hill & Sullivan Mine, so many people were out of work, it was terrible. The militia came up from Coeur d'Alene. They were colored soldiers, and we were scared to death of them. Us kids went down behind where Hutton's Store is now, and peeked into the bull pen where the miners were locked up. When the soldiers said something to us, we never answered, but got out of there.

I think it was the spring of 1893 that Wardner burnt. I was living with Ermantrouts then. He had a saloon. During that terrible fire, they run out of water. Of course, his saloon burnt. The fire left a lot of people homeless.

Kingston didn't look much different than it does now—maybe a few more houses. Many years ago, we used to go across the river from Kingston and walk up the railroad track to Enaville to get the train to Wallace. Anyway, a man wanted to go across the river and this lady, Grace Waters, went down to take him across in the rowboat. They don't know what become of her. She left four little children. And the story is that when she left the house, one of the little girls said, "Mama! Don't go!" But she went anyhow, and they never saw her again.

To Canada

Mrs. Ermantrout said, "My husband has found a job in British Columbia and we are moving there."

I said, "I want to go with you."

She said, "Write your dad in Mullan. See if he cares if you go."

Dad never answered the letter, so when the time came, I went.

At that time, they were building the railroad from Nakusp over to

 Slocan Lake in British Columbia. I helped Mr. Ermantrout butcher cattle for the railroad camps. Right today I could butcher a critter just like he taught me. In between times, I waited table in two different hotels. The money I earned at the hotels was mine to do with as I pleased.

My hobby was dresses. I'll never forget the first dress I cut out. I made the sleeves straight and I could hardly get into it.

I went to school when I was in Canada, but you might say that what schooling I got, I just about stole it. I had to stay out of school whenever the people wanted me to work. If I'd have went on in school like that, I'd be in what they call eighth grade.

Winters were cold in Canada and we ice-skated a lot. We'd sit around a bonfire on the ice. Everyone was sociable. Lots of railroad workers around. In that camp, there were only six girls in their teens. I could have married half a dozen different men in Canada. You see, when you take a kid and turn 'em loose, they get old awful young.

I came back to Kingston from Canada when I was fourteen. I stayed with my uncle and aunt again, and worked waiting table in the Cataldo Hotel.

Box Socials and Dances

We used to go to box-lunch socials. Oh yes! Fix up a real nice lunch and hope a certain boy would bid and get it. But sometimes somebody would outbid him that you wouldn't want to eat with at all.

We used to go to Medimont, Dudley, and Rose Lake with boyfriends and dance till two or three or maybe four o'clock in the morning. Coming home, you'd be so tired you could hardly set on a horse. 'Course, on the railroad track, you couldn't ride fast—just let the horses walk. We had good times.

At Cataldo they built a big hall, and for years we danced the polka, schottische, and waltz there. The first music was organ, violin, and sometimes guitar. Later they got a piano. Cataldo had a saloon. There was always liquor around and all kinds of fights outside the dances. Us girls wouldn't dance with anyone who was the least bit drunk. I knew some of the boys well, but I'd refuse to dance with them because they were drinking. At the next dance they'd come to me and say, "Frances! Will you dance with me? I'm not drinking tonight."

There was one man who always wore a white shirt and one of those high, white, stiff collars. He always wore overalls that had been washed only two or three times. He was older, but he was too nice to dance with the married women—he only danced with us single girls.

The married women, of course, came with their husbands. The single girls came with their parents or sweethearts. We'd all pile into a hack and away we'd go. We always took feed for the horses, and when we got to the hall, we blanketed them so they'd be more comfortable.

Charlie David Hunt

At one dance, I met Charlie Hunt, and pretty soon he was the only one I looked at. He was thirty-two. I was fifteen.

Then, I don't know what caused it, but my finger swelled up like a boil. The doctor must have cut the cords, because since then, it's always been crooked. Anyhow, it hurt terribly so I couldn't work. I quit my job and went to stay with my sister Leona in Kellogg.

Charlie said, "We might as well get married."

I didn't want to marry quite so soon, but when Charlie's mother offered to make my wedding dress, I came back down to Kingston to be measured.

Charlie's mother's maiden name was Jeanette Buchanan. I think President Buchanan was cousin to her father.

Walked to Wedding

The Sunday of the wedding ceremony, May 24, 1896, we all walked down the railroad track to the schoolhouse in Kingston. I was wearing my dark blue cashmere wedding dress. I was only fifteen and wouldn't be sixteen until October 10.

Someone said, "Why didn't you folks come in a hack?"

We could have, but our horses worked all week, and they needed rest.

We couldn't afford a honeymoon. About two weeks later, we went to Kellogg so friends could shivaree us. We were staying at this French lady's house, and after they banged on tin cans and washtubs and jangled cowbells, we were supposed to come out and treat everybody. As a rule, they expected money to buy booze, but Charlie went out and gave them candy.

We never had a lot of money, but Charlie worked steady helping his folks farm their place, and the rest of the time he worked in sawmills or did hauling with his team and wagon.

Five Big Fat Babies

I never ate special things or got babied when I was pregnant. No! Us women done our work same as any other time. I never had a doctor with any of my four boys and one girl. Mother Hunt helped me with four of them. We had moved to Eagle when the fifth was due. I

■ Charles and Frances Martin Hunt for their 50th wedding anniversary

was going to the hospital in Kellogg, but that morning the snow reached six feet deep and the train didn't even come through, so I had my baby right there in Eagle.

I had all big, fat babies. I've heard women say, "Oh! I couldn't have a child without chloroform." But I didn't have anything.

The children were sprinkled at a church in Pinehurst when they were older, but not when they were little.

My first was named Alphonso—Mother Hunt named him. Then Tracy was my second. He died early, just four years old. Tracy Corliss—those were family names on my mother's side of the family. Tom, that lives in Coeur d'Alene, was born on Dad Hunt's birthday. When Adeline come along, and I wanted to name her June, Mother Hunt thought that was awful! She wound up being named Jeanette after Mother Hunt and Adeline after Grandmother Hunt. Frank is named after my dad, Frank Martin.

Fast Strawberry Picker

Georgia Hunt, the niece that married Pat Powers, her father is George Hunt, my brother-in-law. George was only nine years old when Charlie and I were married. He was an awful nice kid and a big help to Mother Hunt.

George married Mae Bentley. I think the Bentleys were from Oregon. They lived at Delta, out toward Murray. George met Mae when she came down to pick strawberries for Mother Hunt. Mother and Dad

Hunt raised berries and all kinds of garden truck and ran a fruit and vegetable wagon to Kellogg.

I'd get up at 6:00 in the morning, fix Charlie his breakfast, but I didn't even stop to eat. Charlie's brother, Ed, had a gold mining sluice box on the river. Well, his first wife and I raced to see who could pick the most strawberries. One day I picked 11 crates of strawberries.

Charlie's Many Talents

Many men had those great long boats they'd pole up the river with supplies to logging camps and to go on the log drives. Charlie used to cook for the drives. He was a wonderful cook on a campfire. Once after he'd been way upriver, we got word the drive camp had come down to a couple miles above Kingston. A bunch of us women got together and went up there. Charlie used what they call a reflector oven. He had 12 custard pies so pretty and brown. He had them for the men. We couldn't even talk one out of him.

If one of the horses got sick, Charlie was a regular old veterinary. He doctored everybody's horses and cows. He used to give 'em laudanum in a little bit of water. People didn't use laudanum much. It was fierce strong!

Once when Charlie came home from the woods, he told me a tree fell on top of a fella he was working with.

Charlie said, "How I ever lifted that tree, I'll never know, but I lifted it off that man. Afterwards, I couldn't even budge it."

They took the man to the hospital and he lived. Charlie was middle aged when this happened. I often think what one can do when you're excited.

Remedies

I used to doctor the kids at home. If one of them got a cold, my long suit was turpentine and lard mixed together to make a poultice. If the cold was going down into the lungs, I'd make the poultice out of cornmeal and put it on the chest. Sometimes you can make a poultice of onions—not boil 'em down, but heat them through, and put it on their lungs, and it would break up their cold in no time. Same thing for a fever.

If someone cut their hand real bad, we'd get Dad Hunt to sew it up. Then we'd bind it up real good.

I knew people that believed you could cure a wart by wiping it with a dishrag and then hiding it, and the wart was supposed to go away. That's a lot of nonsense.

Others believed if someone leaves a diaper at your house, you'll get pregnant. Fiddlesticks! Like people see a black cat cross the road and they think it brings bad luck. It's just superstition.

Some people planted by the light of the moon or the dark of the moon, but we always planted when we got ready. Never thought about the moon.

Some used to think if you drop a fork, a man is coming to visit. You can't be a Christian and believe that stuff.

Years and years ago, I had terrible headaches. I went to Spokane to a Reverend Lathe. He claimed he could heal anybody with prayer. I stayed there one winter. Never helped my headache one bit.

Then there was a minister—name was Osburn. He said, "Have you got a headache?"

I said, "I've got a headache most of the time."

He said, "Get down and let me pray for you." He put his hands on my head and prayed for me. I've never had a headache since.

Some people don't believe that, but it's God's truth and I've got the faith.

Owl Dance

Once when we lived across the river, I seen some owls have their mating dance. A beautiful moonlight night in February, we heard a half dozen of 'em talking, so we went out to see. They were on the barn roof and they were having this dance. Their wings was up and these clumsy, awkward things was hopping and dancing all around!

Before Refrigerators

We kept the milk in a cool cellar. We'd set the milk at night and the next night I'd skim the cream off. Then I'd put that cream in a churn and make butter. The milk went to the pigs, except the sweet milk we kept to drink. If we made ice cream, we had to take the team and go to Kellogg to get ice. You had to get quite a bit because it would melt so bad. Ice cream was a treat! Fourth of July was the ice-cream day. Later on, we had an ice house where we stored ice in sawdust.

I've got cookbooks, a whole bunch of 'em, but I never look at 'em. I just *do*.

When anyone was kind enough to give me anything, I always tried to return her the dish with something back. That was the early days' custom.

We had big dinners and get-togethers on holidays, and every woman tried to bring her best dish. Sometimes we'd have plays and little sketches. Had real good happy times. There was no liquor! I think if anyone had got the least tipsy, they would have been pushed out.

The Roaring '20s

When drinking became illegal, it never stopped the drinking. The men just started drinking moonshine, and that was just awful. It wasn't fit to drink in the first place. I know one man that lived off of it for a long time. He lost his mind and finally died in the asylum at Salem, Oregon.

During prohibition the women drank more or less. Always have, I guess. A woman could have a drink at a dance, but very seldom a woman would get tipsy.

I didn't wear short skirts during the '20s. Honest to goodness! Now the miniskirts, they're not as long as they used to wear shirts. I can't for the life of me see how you can dress in these little short dresses and expect to look like anything. And we didn't dance the Charleston. In our day, the smoother you danced, the better. You could put an apple on your head and dance.

Hard Times

Our hardest times around here was during strikes at the mines and during the 1930s when we had a flood along with the Depression. So many had their homes flooded and people had nothing left. But people used to give to one another, and feel responsible for one another. Different now. They look on the government to do it.

Charlie and I didn't suffer during the Depression because we was pretty well fixed. For the winters, we'd always go to town in the fall and buy two or three hundred pounds of flour, two sacks of sugar—didn't cost then like it does now. As a rule, we had our own meat. Killed our pigs, smoked 'em. Put 'em down in brine. We always had enough to eat. That was a sure thing.

But there's so many people that won't raise a garden. Even now, I think if half of these beautiful lawns was turned into nice gardens, how much better off people would be.

■ Ruth Hoerschgen and June DeGraff, 1935

■ Ruth Hoerschgen (68) at home up Latour Creek, 1984

TWENTY

RUTH HOERSCHGEN

Interviewed 1984 at home up Latour Creek, Idaho.

DAD BOUGHT THIS place from the Winton Lumber Company after it was logged off. Wintons had bought it from Latour, the homesteader for which the creek is named.

I was born here in 1916. I went through the grades right across the road at Latour Creek school. It had some 30 pupils. One of my teachers was Teresa Procopio from Harrison. The frame school building, now standing vacant because they haul the kids to bigger schools, wasn't the first school. The first was built of logs and burned about 1919.

Sawing Contest

There was a Universal Newsreel photographer in the neighborhood visiting Ladds, and he learned that women around here cut up logs for wood. This was the winter of 1935 when there had been lots of publicity about men lumberjacks, like the Higbees, competing in sawing contests. The photographer saw news value in women using axes and a crosscut saw, so he set up a contest in Rose Lake and advertised for women to come and compete for a championship. I don't remember what he offered for a prize.

The photographer had arranged for cutting down bull pine trees. It was only a little affair with the neighbors looking on—like Axel Nordstrom, Mangnus Johnson, Art Ladd, my brother Bill, my sister Mary, and Art Nordstrom.

The tree was froze hard, but June De Graff and I sawed through it in one minute and 50 seconds. Two other girl teams, Astrid Ladd with

 Lela Nordstrom, and Marion Wick with Evelyn Brigg, entered the contest. June and I won.

Lumberjanes' Trip to New York

In those days, almost every movie theater featured a newsreel ahead of the movie. The newsreel with us sawing must have showed all over the country. Here came a telegram from the New York *Daily Mirror* asking us to come to New York at $100 a week for each of us, all expenses paid, as their guests. We were both nineteen years old. June had graduated from Rose Lake High School a year ahead of me. Boy! Were we excited!

I borrowed money from my brother to get my teeth fixed, and when I came back, I repaid him out of my earnings.

We went to Spokane by train, then to Boise, and east on the Union Pacific Railroad with first-class tickets, sleeping car berths, and the privilege of eating in the dining car with money advanced by the newspaper. Some man lurked in the background, so I think we were chaperoned the whole way.

"Champ Tree Cutters Arrive Today as Guests of This Newspaper"

Monday, about noon, as we came down the steps of the Pullman car at the big train station in New York, a photographer snapped our picture. When it was printed in the newspaper, along with the headline, the cutline beneath the picture said, "Two young Amazons, June De Graff and Ruth Hoerschgen attained their championship by felling a 16-inch Oregon fir tree in one minute and 50 seconds." The newspaper had changed the bull pine into a fir tree.

The story went on: "They hail from Cataldo, Idaho, a town so small that it has not been awarded the tiniest ink spot by the mapmakers."

Jane Franklin, reporter for the New York *Daily Mirror*, took charge of us from the moment we stepped off the train. She whisked us in a cab to the Hotel Warwick and up the elevator, 30 or 40 floors, to our room.

She said, "It's my job to show you everything and see that you don't get lost. I'll give you time to freshen up and be back in two hours."

She took us down to the East River. From the concrete ramp where we waited for the big ferry, we looked up at the skyscrapers till our necks ached. Then we cruised off the point of Manhattan Island and saw the Statue of Liberty in the distance. And then going along the East River, we were crisscrossing the paths of more ferries and watching the big ocean liners moving into or out of their berths.

It was all exciting, but we were glad to get back to the hotel by early evening and into bed. It was the last time we had a leisurely rest while we were there. New Yorkers stay up most of the night, every night.

"Tall City Awes Girl Axe Aces"

Tuesday's newspaper showed a picture of us looking up at the Chrysler Building with June saying, "New York is too big, but gee! It's swell!"

And with me saying, "It's too big. I don't think I'd like to live here."

One article said we were both over six feet tall, but Jane Franklin's write-up had it right, with June, six feet and one half inch, and me, five feet nine inches.

That day they took us to the Yankee Stadium that seats 30,000 people to see the opening of the baseball season. The Red Sox were playing the Yankees.

When Lefty Gomez started pitching, June said, "We could use that boy back home!"

And I said, "I've been reading about these champs for years. I never thought I'd get a chance to really see them. Wait till the kids back home hear about it."

By the time we made it back to the hotel, it was time to eat in the fancy dining room. Then Ken Robinson interviewed us at the WINS Radio Station. It was broadcast coast-to-coast.

After that, Jane and a photographer took us to Radio City Music Hall. They took us backstage and of course, they had to take pictures of us big, strong women from the West, so they posed us standing in line with four dear little theatrical ladies—the littlest in their line-up—and June and I stood at each end with our arms stretched out and touching over their heads.

Then they suggested we form a cross-hand seat and lift the guy that played the organ, Dick Liebert. So we did that.

Wednesday's newspaper headed the pictures, "Two Fine Western Girls." "The two champion lady woodchoppers of North America, which means the lady champions of the world!" There was also a picture of us being interviewed at the "mike" by Ken Robinson.

Wednesday afternoon they took us sightseeing, this time among the skyscrapers. High up in the Empire State Building is where Walter Winchell had his offices. He came out and shook our hands and gave us his autographed picture. Then in the evening our chaperon, Jane Franklin, took us to the French Casino where we saw the Follies Bergere.

When Jane asked us what we thought of it, June said, "Of course, it's very beautiful, and I really don't think it immoral. But I'd rather chop wood the rest of my life than to have to come out like that before people without my clothes on."

"Lumberjanes Maintain Strength" and Meet Celebrities

Thursday, the newspaper started building us up as "super Amazons." We were taken to the Central Park pool and gym, and they took pictures of us climbing out of the water and shooting baskets on the gym floor.

Then back to Jack Dempsey's Restaurant for dinner. Dempsey was friendly and shook hands with both of us at once and posed with June to show that they both had the same reach—76 inches. Then they took us to Al Roon's gymnasium where this physical culture expert builds people's bodies. He taped our backs and biceps.

Al Roon said, "If the women of New York were as healthy as Ruth and June, I guess I wouldn't be running a gym to put them back in shape. They are magnificent specimens!"

We appeared for a coast-to-coast interview on Kate Smith's radio program where she asked our impressions of New York. Kate Smith is a warm, friendly person.

Then we went to Madison Square Garden, which seats 25,000 people, and saw Billy Rose's Musical Review. They took pictures of us with Jack Earl, the world's tallest man, and Major Mite, who claims to be the smallest midget alive.

"Girls View Giant Tree"

Friday they took pictures of us feeling the bark of the big elm tree we were going to cut. We were encouraged to say that the tree was dead and needed to be cut down for safety's sake, so nature lovers wouldn't make a complaint.

The New York *Daily Mirror* said, "The tree which the two Idaho Amazons will send to tree heaven, in the morning, is on the East Drive in Central Park, just north of the 65th Street Transverse. The entire process will be broadcast from coast to coast by hook-up of the National Broadcasting Company from Station WJZ, and newsreels will be on hand, too."

The newspaper also carried an editorial about the West producing strong bodies and hoping we lady woodchoppers would marry strong men and bear kids that would improve the national health and vitality.

They showed a picture of us sleeping in twin beds, side by side, on the terrace of the hotel. "No Stuffy Rooms For Our Champion Woodchoppers." They said we were retiring early to be ready for the big job tomorrow. The fact is, we were dying for sleep from the late hours.

"Girl Aces Set Record with Axe"

This is how the newspaper wrote up the tree-cutting on Saturday: "Before a crowd of almost 5,000 New Yorkers who never cut through anything more substantial than a toothpick in their lives, Ruth Hoerschgen and June De Graff made a short speech over radio station WJZ and then went to work on the giant elm. The wood was so tough they had to douse the saw several times with kerosene to prevent it sticking. The Girl Wood Fellers of the Northwest grounded the giant American White Elm in Central Park in the fast time of 11 minutes flat.

"June hails from Rose Lake that has a population of 200, while Ruth is the metropolite of the team, coming from Cataldo, which boasts more than 300 inhabitants. The girls brought their 3½ pound axes with which they made their championship record in Idaho by felling a huge tree in 1 minute and 50 seconds."

That tree was 24 inches on the stump and boy! was it hard! I chopped an undercut and we picked up the crosscut saw again and went at it. We had one of those flat whisky flasks filled with kerosene that loggers carry to squirt oil on the saw and keep it free from pitch. This elm was so hard and dry, we needed a lot of kerosene. It turned out that most of the people watching thought we were sprinkling it with holy water.

The police were trying to hold people away with a rope barrier but they kept crowding up. When the tree went down, one man was almost hit by the top. We sat down on the stump to get our breath. The crowd rushed in and surrounded us for autographs on any old piece of paper, while others were picking up slivers and sawdust grains for souvenirs.

They finally wore us out and we said to Jane Franklin, "Let's get goin'!"

Saturday night, our chaperon took us to the play, "Tobacco Road."

Jane asked us what we thought of it, and June said, "That ramshackle house of Jeeter Lester's is sure different from the kind of farms we have out home. Still, when the water flooded our house, it wasn't so nice."

New York Easter Parade

Before Easter Sunday, they had taken us to Roaman's fancy clothing store and outfitted us from head to toe so we could join the Easter Parade. June chose a suit of powder blue and I chose a brown tweed, and we had new hats and shoes to match.

When Jane Franklin asked June what she thought of the parade, June said, "Everybody sure looks swell. The women are beautiful and dress like wives of millionaires. But those silk top hats the men wear kind of get me."

Headline Monday: "It Took Two Champ Woodchoppers Of The Northwest To Show The City Girls What Real Fashions Were Yesterday"

On April 22, we made a final round of the Broadway night spots. They took final pictures of us at the Hollywood Restaurant with the chorines crowded around us, feeling our arm muscles. Then we left on the train for home.

It was a great experience!

After we came home, we were hired to give three demonstrations a day at the Spokane Sportsmen's Fair and also at the Miner's Picnic at Kellogg. We were each presented axes from a lot of different tool makers like Champion, Simonds, Atkins, and Plumb. I gave them all away except the one from Plumb with gold engraving of my name and address, and its gold is now all gone from using it for woodcutting at home.

June wasn't interested in more competing after she decided to get married.

I live on the old home place with my brother, Bill, now that my second husband has died.

TWENTY ONE

STANLEY COCHRANE

Interviewed 1973 at home in Latour Creek, Idaho.

I WAS BORN in 1911 at the Providence Hospital at Wallace. When I was a baby, Dad carried me in a packsack over Dudley Saddle eight or nine miles to my grandparents' homestead in Haley Draw. During the time I was growing up, Granddad used to tell me stories about his life back in Wisconsin.

He said they made bridges across the streams by throwing hay on the ice when the temperature was below zero. Then they'd chop holes in the ice upstream and let the water flood the hay and freeze. Then more hay and more freeze till it built up maybe three feet thick, and the sleighs could use it as a bridge to haul logs out of the marshes.

Wolves After Granddad

Granddad mostly freighted supplies to the camps. He told me he was hauling beef on a sleigh and the wolves got after him and he had to chop chunks of beef off and throw them overboard to keep the wolves from coming alongside and jumping the horses. Once when the wolf pack got too close to the back of the sleigh, he shot the leader with a .30-30. The pack stopped to eat the dead wolf, and that gave him time to get away.

My dad came out here from Eau Claire, Wisconsin, to work as secretary of the St. Joe Lumber Company at Harrison. Then he met my mother, who was a school teacher in Spokane.

Back around 1910 and 1911 when Dad owned the Dudley store, the town was busy and had at least two saloons. Tom Theriault owned one saloon.

■ Stanley Cochrane, 1973

Dudley-Latour Divide Trail

Dad donated $200 to get the trail built over the Dudley-Latour Divide. At the top of the saddle were the Papinod cabins. The trail forked right to go past the Jack Glynn cabin and then on to Grahams, Kellys, Cochranes, and swung uphill to Spencers, then down Spencer Draw to Haleys.

Where the trail forked left at Dudley Saddle, it followed a ridge down past the Gilbert homestead and to the Jeff Dean orchard in the Latour bottom. These people, and lots of others living further up Latour Creek, walked over the hill to Dudley to buy groceries and supplies.

In 1913, Dad and Mother had sold out the store to Mrs. Kelly and bought a hotel at Lakeview. There was good business for a hotel because lumberjacks stopped on the way over the hill to work in logging camps on Independence Creek.

Bluejay Eliminator

In 1917 we lived on the old Strobel place back of Killarney Lake. Old Beanbelly Thornton had a logging camp back there. Bluejays and magpies hung around his screened meathouse by the hundreds. The meathouse roof extended out over the far end of the meathouse. Old Beanbelly stuck a four-by-four through the wall. The magpies and jays would land on the blame thing just outside the meathouse. He'd wait inside till two or three lit. Then he'd come down with a big wooden maul on the inside end of the four-by-four and they'd fly up against the roof and bust their heads open.

When I came back into Latour to work in 1925, I sawed logs for Jack Glynn, who later became Kootenai county sheriff. He was hauling logs on a Model T Ford truck with those cushion tires that had holes bored through them.

Dovetail Cabin

This house I live in was built by Isaac Hill in 1900. He built it and the Finn bathhouse, dovetail. Each log is cupped to fit down over the other and moss put between for insulation. He used every kind of log: yellow pine, jack pine, tamarack, white pine, red fir, white fir, hemlock, and cedar. One thing about dovetail joints, they don't need to be nailed and can't come apart. I covered my house with board siding later.

Walt Russell Stands on Head

My son tells how when they were kids, Walt Russell [of Russell & Pugh Lumber Company] used to stop in our yard and stand on his head in the swing for them.

One time when I and John Strobel and his crew was coming home from logging, we met Walt Russell and his Model T coming through the road behind Killarney Lake. The road was too narrow to pass.

Strobel said, "I'll back up to a wide place."

"No!" Walt says, "Three or four of you jump on my running board so I won't tip over." Then he ran down off the side and back up into the road and went on about his business.

Some of Walt's crew told me that when he wanted to cross Latour Creek, he'd tie a couple of poles together ahead of each front wheel. Then he'd tie a rope to the Ford and set his boys across the creek in case he hit too deep water. Then he'd roar right across and they'd pull him up the bank.

I watched Einar Mattson build the Shoshone Motel at Cataldo. He stood on a platform using a broadaxe with an offset handle and hewed the logs as they went up. When he finished, the logs were so smooth you could almost wallpaper them.

The house of my daughter, Betty, and Jay Higbee's son, on the way to Cataldo from Latour Creek alongside the slough—that's a Mattson built house, too. Then there's another nice Mattson built house in the upper end of Smelterville.

Einar J. Mattson died at age sixty-five in 1961. His brother, Waino, lived to be sixty-one. Both are buried in the Hunt Cemetery.

TWENTY-TWO

JAY HIGBEE

Interviewed 1973 at home up Latour Creek, Idaho.

MY FATHER, Jay A. Higbee, was born in 1867. When Dad and his partner came out from Michigan and landed in Enaville, they had only a rifle and 35 cents between them. They went into a saloon and asked if anybody there would buy a deer. The saloonkeeper said, "We'll give you ten dollars for every deer you bring us."

They found their first deer down on the flat where Alford Mack lived, and Judd McKurin packed it from Latour Creek to Kingston for them. That's how they made their living that winter of 1900.

Locating Homesteaders

In the spring, they started locating people on homesteads in Latour Creek. For locating and building a cabin with a dirt floor and a shake roof, they charged $250. But if someone wanted it warmer for winter, they could give them a deluxe job, a double shake roof with dirt in between the layers for $300.

Latour Creek was named after an old Frenchman who homesteaded down where Hoerschgen lives. Some of the other homesteaders were Eli Hussa, McGuire in Larch Creek, and Cole. Cole's place was above our old home place and a quarter mile up the hill. There's a big tree grown in the middle of where the cabin used to be.

Dad wanted to locate on the homestead where Judd Van Kurin settled because it had a lot of nice white pine timber growing in the bottom. Harneys live on that place now.

Dad was sitting on the trail and along came a couple of guys, and

■ Jay Higbee, 1973

from their conversation, he took it that one of them was going to file on it. The county seat was at Rathdrum at that time. Dad started out at two o'clock in the morning and hiked through the Fourth of July Canyon on snowshoes. But when he reached the courthouse, the other guys were already there.

So Dad ended up filing on a place next to it, although later he and my mother bought and lived on the Van Kurin place and always spoke of it as their homestead.

Sewed Toe On

About 1903, Dad started logging for the Cameron Lumber Company. The logs were to be delivered to their mill at Harrison for three dollars 1,000 [board feet]. A lot of big white pine and cedar grew along Latour Creek, and they fell the trees right into the creek channel. Dad built a dam just across from the second bridge as you come up the creek so he could splash the logs down.

One day he practically cut off his big toe with an axe. He wrapped it up tight in a strip from his shirttail and came into the bunkhouse and asked his partner to sew it back on. When he unwrapped it, his partner got so sick he couldn't even pick up the needle. Dad didn't have any painkiller—he didn't drink. I never saw Dad take more than a half-dozen drinks in my lifetime. But Dad went ahead and sewed the toe back on by himself. In two days he went back to work.

The train would stop anywhere and let people off. So the next time Dr. Busby came up from Harrison, he asked Doc to look at it. Dr. Busby examined it and said, "That's as good as I could do."

Trouble with Cameron

Then trouble developed over Cameron's payment to Dad for the logs. Cameron sent a man named Brown to Dudley, and Brown hired a crew to come over the hill and drive the logs out of Latour Creek.

Dad was waiting at the log deck with a rifle. He told them, "The first man that touches one of these logs, I'll shoot."

The crew went back to Dudley and their leader told Brown, "Higbee came out and took a shot at me."

Brown said, "Higbee didn't shoot at you because if he did, you wouldn't be here."

Cameron lost the lawsuit and it broke his company. But during the bad feeling, someone blew up Dad's dam. Dad always thought it was a hired job.

Kendrick, Coeur d'Alene, Latour

About 1907, Dad moved the family to a farm near Kendrick. He didn't like farming so he moved to Coeur d'Alene, then to Rockford Bay, and then in 1916 back to Latour Creek again.

I was born in Coeur d'Alene in 1909. My sister Blanche was born in Kendrick. My brothers and other sisters were born on Latour Creek [Beatrice, Myron, Edward, Howard, and Harold]. Nine kids altogether, counting our half sisters [Hazel and Marion].

Dad died at eighty-six in 1953. Mother, Belle Higbee, died at seventy-five in 1949. They are buried in the Hunt Cemetery.

Latour Creek Railroad

L. W. Butler built a band saw lumber mill and boardinghouse on Latour Creek at the mouth of Butler Creek. I'm not sure if he homesteaded there. A pile of hand-hewn ties 14 feet high a half-mile up Butler Creek shows he meant to extend his railroad up that fork.

Many homesteaders went in with him and put their homesteads up as security. I know Kenny Norse had a whole slug of documents about it that he inherited from his dad, John Norse, who homesteaded up Latour.

To my way of thinking, Butler went at it backwards. Instead of starting at the river and building upstream so he could use his railroad to haul logs and make it pay its way, he set up his mill at the top end to build down, and this left him short of finances. Then to pay for supplies, he used a steam tractor to pull two wagons loaded with lumber, one behind the other, up the steep grade to the top of the Lane divide and down to Lane. Later, to shorten that expensive haul, he set up a small sawmill near the divide. The sawdust and slabs are still there on the Latour side of the divide on a road that turns off to the east.

He tried to hold down costs by working homesteaders, like Ole Ladd and Oscar Linder, to build [railroad] grade. They told me they only got $65 in cash for all the work they did one summer. Maybe he paid them in Latour Railroad stock also.

To save expense, he placed two-by-fours flat on his hand-hewn ties for temporary rails. He expected to build all the way to the river before replacing them with steel. He impressed people with his mechanical genius when he rigged up a Chalmers car with railroad wheels to pull little pushcars up and down on those wooden rails carrying tools and supplies. But that still didn't solve his financial problems.

After years of construction and replacing washouts, the railroad grade reached the river, but the ties and wooden rails only made it to Gilbert Draw, where the road goes over the hill to Dudley, before Butler went broke. Today, most all the bridges and pole road supports have washed away and only sections of railroad grade, shaped up on the ground, show a railroad was ever there.

On the point just below Butler's mill site, on the right-hand side going up the present road, is the grave of Butler's dog. Dad and Mother were at the burial. Butler wrapped the dog in his best hunting coat and stuck a piece of shale in the ground for a tombstone.

Butler said, "Mr. Higbee! That was a wonderful bird dog."

Mrs. Butler cried and said, "Mrs. Higbee! We loved that dog as much as you love one of your children."

Years afterward when Dad told me about it he said, "It made me mad and I thought, 'They don't know what they're talking about.'"

Tunnel Above Larch Creek

A half-mile up Latour Creek from the mouth of Larch Creek, on the left-hand side, there's a tunnel that goes in about 200 feet.

There's a shaft, and when I was a kid, we used to go in there and poke a long pole down in the dark but couldn't touch bottom. In 1970 we went back in with a light and somebody had wrote on the wall with a carbide light, "Sept. 16, 1917."

Above that tunnel is another one caved in, and that's where a man got blasted in the stomach in the winter of 1917. His two partners came past our place with a sleigh taking him to the doctor. He died soon after that.

Quartz and Tunnel

Then beyond that on the left side, the Wobbly Gulch comes out of a draw with a big rock slide, and the Wobbly cabin was up on the hill with I.W.W. signs and crayon drawings by the Hanson boys, Ern and Irv, made when they were trapping in 1917 and 1918. Just below Wobbly Gulch a trail used to take to the hillside across a little rock slide. There was some quartz laying there. Irv Hanson told me he once picked up a piece and broke it and it contained quite coarse gold. Then on up the main Latour a quarter mile from this rock slide, on the left side and below the forks just past Wobbly Gulch, there's another gulch that comes down, and in its mouth is a caved-in tunnel. I've always been curious about this tunnel because I never did hear my dad or anyone say there was a tunnel there.

About half a mile above Butler's mill site there used to be a cabin that somebody had built out of shakes and put the name Driftwood Cabin above the door.

Farther on, and three miles up Latour Creek from Butler's mill, the Shake Cabin Creek turns in from the left. Stanley Thomas built the Shake Cabin for trapping and prospecting and carried a stove in there on his back.

But continuing on up the main Latour a short ways, on the left side was where Billy Williams had a little tunnel and prospect.

I found good samples of galena in several places in that area. I'm sure that sometime ore in quantity will be found there or near the Palisades or in Pine Creek.

Ruined Creek

Back in the old days, there wasn't much water in Latour Creek, but the channel was much narrower and that's how it was possible to drive logs. When I was commissioner on the Coeur d'Alene Highway District, the Army Corps of Engineers asked permission to clean the debris out of Latour with bulldozers.

I told them, "Absolutely not! Not unless you riprap it."

But they went from the old Butler mill site up the main creek above Wobbly Gulch to the forks of Shake Cabin Creek. They took all them big cedar logs out, dozed the big rocks out of the middle of the creek where fish used to stay, and wiped out the beaver dams that made trout ponds. The flat is ruined! The timber is ruined. It makes me sick every time I go up there.

Local Cabins

Scudder was a retired engineer from the Philippines. He retired in poor health and in 1916 had Emil Johnson build him a half-dormer log house on the flat a half-mile above the second bridge. The bridge is opposite where the trail came over from Dudley down Gilbert Draw. They cleaned the creek rocks out of the bottom and made a fine garden.

The Hanson cabin stood at the mouth of Larch Creek, a rectangular, two-story log house. Just above it on the right-hand side was the John Norse cabin. Art Norse had a cabin up the right-hand side draw.

Starting up the creek you came first to the Cole cabin and then the Harry Whiteman cabin. A quarter mile to the right on the ridge was the teacher Stella Bennet's cabin. Then following the creek again, you entered the quarter mile long opening with the two Drumheller homestead cabins that Russell & Pugh used as a logging camp.

If you went straight ahead up the creek a half-mile, you came to Baldy Falls, a secluded little falls with water falling 16 feet down over shelves of rock covered with moss six inches thick, and flanked at a discreet distance by the lower and the upper Moore cabins. If you walked on up Baldy Creek, maybe four miles, you could come out at Mirror Lake beneath Twin Crags.

The falls has been ruined of its beauty by loggers and the creek gutted of timber.

Back to the field holding the Drumheller cabins: At the far end of the opening, a trail turned left to the Nelligan cabins. You could tell you were approaching Nelligans when you walked under a rustic sign eight feet overhead that spelled out "Highland Park" in letters two feet high in three-inch thick sections of trees. And a smaller penciled sign on a post alongside the trail read, "Please don't kill the park deer."

Finn Masters of Dovetail

The three Mattson boys who lived at the mouth of Latour Creek, Einar, George and Waino, did the finest cabin work. The Finns did lots of dovetail building in Michigan and then they came on West following lumbering and the mines. They'd lay a rig on the wood and mark a log, then groove the topside to make the log on top fit over the one below with packing in between. There's a nice little log cabin up the mouth of Skeel Gulch built by Mattsons.

Probably the oldest house around here is at the mouth of Latour and just toward Dudley from the schoolhouse—the old Bill Wright homestead, built before 1900. I don't believe it was built by the Mattsons.

Mother's Song

In the spring of 1919, Otto Hussa came down to our house and wanted Dad to break a big jam that he said had dammed up the creek in front of his place. So Dad sent the crew up. The men came back down and told Dad that Otto had come out and cussed them up and down because the water had washed his field. And besides, they told Dad, the logs weren't ours. So Dad sent word to Otto that he'd have to get Russell & Pugh's crew to break the jam.

Mother wrote a song about it to the tune of "Casey Jones," and when the river drivers came along, she played it on the piano and us kids sang it for them:

> Old Otto Hussa came a-stepping on the air,
> He says, "Old Man Higbee, get your logs right out of there."
> Says Higbee to this Finn man, "I do not give a damn!
> If you'd build your bridges higher,
> There wouldn't a'been a jam."

I was just a kid, but I seen that jam break. It started at where the steel bridge is now opposite the mouth of Gilbert Draw and extended up to about 200 yards below the Scudder house. When that jam all pulled at once, it shook the ground with the awfulest roar and commotion!

Dad Higbee and the Shepherd

Probably because of money Butler owed his lawyer, a number of homesteads that had been security for the railroad ended up in possession of Judge Wernette. With hundreds of sheep grazing all around me, I was bulldozing logging road on the open hillside east of where Butler's mill used to be. We were buying stumpage from Wernette and had permission to keep sheep off it. I looked down the hill and saw Dad waving his finger in the sheepherder's face. I shut off the dozer and went down.

Dad was a big man with fierce, dark whiskers and eyebrows that stuck out like cowcatchers on a locomotive. He had a deep voice that rumbled like the growl of a grizzly bear.

Dad was saying, "I want them out of here!"

The sheepherder, a lean, dark-skinned Basque, said, "No! They're hungry."

Dad said, "You'll get 'em out or I'll run you off."

The sheepherder had his two sheep dogs beside him and a .30-30 carbine in his right hand. "No! I don't run."

Dad said, "It don't make a damn bit of difference to me whether you walk or you run or I pack you off. You've got till daylight tomorrow morning." Then Dad turned and waved me back to work.

Next morning the hill was empty of sheep. That was a good thing because Dad never bluffed.

Hand-Logging

In 1925, I'll bet I pulled the longest drag of logs ever pulled in Latour. Our chute went up the Gilbert draw a mile and a half and then up the side draws too. Of course in the steep part the logs shot down.

But this was down below where we had to use a trail team. It had froze during the night and made the chute icy with a little rain on it. This was an ideal condition. I hooked the team onto the last log in the string. They kept bumping more logs ahead and when I hit the landing, I had 103 logs.

Back in 1931 we hand-logged timber clear from the top of the hill northeast of Gilbert Draw. We'd limb those big yellow pines all the way up then peel one side. Then six or seven of us would roll the tree over till the skinned side hit the skids. With frost on hard ground or a little snow, they'd really go. One tree took off, and I ran down the hill 100 feet to see it break over the first hump. I got there just in time to see it break over the last pitch three-quarters of a mile away. I've seen 'em hit a rock outcropping and split right in the middle. Some hit the bottom so hard they drove into the ground.

Depression Prices

In 1932, a guy came down from Kellogg and offered to sell me the old Billy Williams claim. There was a million [board] feet on it.

He said, "I'll take 75 cents 1,000 [board feet] stumpage for cash."

But think! At that time we was gettin' only $10 a thousand [board-feet] delivered at Morbeck's mill. And you couldn't bring a log with less than a 13-inch top. They sold some mixed timber, generally considered locally to mean red fir and tamarack, here last week for $67 [per thousand board feet] on the stump and damn poor timber, too. They required the logger to take down to a 6-inch top as well.

I was in a hunting party camped at Butler's Mill the afternoon Lois Schreckengost and Mrs. Red Watson got lost.

A guy came down from Eagle Peak and said, "There's a couple of women lost. They hunted out from Eagle Peak toward St. Joe and were supposed to come down through to the road here."

I had been hunting up toward Eagle Peak that afternoon. During the wind storm and snow, I had heard a rifle fire two shots, then a space, and two shots again—bang! bang!

I said, "I'll bet they got too far over and came down into Butler Creek and didn't find any road so they went back up the hill."

Lloyd Wilcox had an old Model A Ford. We dove up the road that leads to Rochat Peak and Baldy. Then we swung off to the right on our old logging road toward the old Higbee logging camp at the head of Butler Creek. Up high where the slide rock is, I got out and hollered. She answered. It sounded like she was straight across Butler Creek from us and high on the hillside.

I hollered two or three times and I yelled, "Stay where you are and build a fire."

I knew the brush and down stuff was awful bad below us so I said, "No use staying here because we won't bring her out this way anyhow."

That was a mistake. We should have kept the car right there with the lights on where she could see it. She must have figured we was leaving her.

Then we went down and around to the Eagle Peak road above where she might be and fired our rifles at intervals till three o'clock in the morning.

When we got back to camp I couldn't sleep. So at daylight we went back up to where we had heard her answer and fought through the brush and down timber to the bottom and up the other side. We went within a hundred yards of her body and swung down Butler Creek slope thinking she might have gone that way.

Days later we were up by Eagle Peak with the big search party. Some fellow from Spokane with hounds was afraid to let the dogs go—afraid he'd lose 'em I guess. Another guy had a bobbin' thing.

He swung it on a string and said, "She's toward Cataldo. Down the creek."

But she wasn't. That afternoon, the second time we strung out further along the slope toward upper Butler and combed downhill, we found her.

We brought her body out on the point alongside Lost Girl Creek.

Bert Russell: October 6, 1949, Lois Schreckengost, 28, who had settled in Idaho because she loved the country, and a more experienced woman companion, Mrs. Red Watson, both of Rose Lake, became separated while hunting deer in a driving snowstorm on the southeast slope of Latour Creek a half-mile southeast of Eagle Peak. Mrs. Watson hurt her ankle and built a rough lean-to of loose bark and waited patiently for help. A day later Mrs. Watson answered gunshot signals from Harold Higbee, Lloyd Wilcox, and Mel Moak and was found. They had brought food. Harold and Lloyd left their coats and Mel stayed with her all that night. Next day, they brought a doctor. In his opinion she had only a bad sprain. So with their help, she walked out. It turned out afterward that her ankle was broken.

Tragically, Lois Schreckengost, like hundreds of lost men and women before her in similar situations, ran circles on the timbered mountainside until she died of exhaustion. Her corduroy pantlegs cruelly torn, sprawled head down on the steep slope, her red hat and rifle thrown 20 feet further on, she had apparently died sometime during her first night out. Her cartridges had apparently been used up in the first hours of her wild flight before anyone learned she was missing.

Lois died about a mile up Butler Creek and west a half-mile up the hillside. Her body was brought out on the ridge between Butler Creek and what is now called Lost Girl Creek. Since Butler Creek already had a name and this creek did not, and Mrs. Watson was rescued on this drainage, it seemed fitting to place this name there. My father, W. B. Russell, and I were in the search party.

■ TWENTY-THREE

HENRY BUCHANAN

■ *Interviewed 1974 at Coeur d'Alene, Idaho.*

Kingston—1903

MY DAD'S NAME was Joseph, born 1851, and I was born 1889. The way we happened to come out from Illinois [was that] my aunt moved to Kingston and kept on till she got us out here. We came from Spokane to Coeur d'Alene on the interurban electric railroad, took the "Georgie Oakes" to Harrison, and took the train upriver to Kingston. There was just Father, Mother, and I in our family. We arrived January 9, 1903. Kingston remained my home and was the best place I ever found.

Dad got badly crippled workin' in a gravel pit for a contractor of the Frisco Mine. Somebody unhooked a car on an incline to dump. It crushed his feet up in a ball. He was on crutches a long time, and after that it was about all he could do to make a livin'. Dad was a boilermaker and machinist by trade and could do almost anything with iron. I've still got some of his boiler tubes.

Locating Homesteaders

First I worked for Red Smith, a timber cruiser at Kingston. Then I worked for Albert Hosengar locating people on homesteads. Some cruisers charged depending on how much money the homesteader had and how hard or easy he was to talk out of it.

Some saloon keepers paid others to locate homesteaders with the understanding that the saloon keeper would end up with the land and timber. The amount paid the homesteaders varied, but as a rule they got expenses and a little more.

■ Henry C. Buchanan about 1970

A homestead with a million feet of timber was worth maybe $3,000. Some homesteads had three million feet and they didn't cut the timber down small then like they do now.

Sawmills

A lot of them big cedar trees came down in high water, and I'd go along the river and cut logs out of them jams. Sound as a dollar. We got a hand winch, half-inch cable, 22½ turns to the crank. We used blocks in the line, and we could pull logs that scaled 1,000 feet right out. [A standard length log was 16 feet. To scale 1,000 board feet, it would have been 36 inches in diameter at the small end.]

Joe Avery did the buying for his dad's mill. Joe was a damn nice guy and honest. There wasn't too many of that kind. I'd put his bark mark on 'em and he'd scale 'em and pay for them right there on the Swiftwater. Then they'd go down in the log drive and they'd sort 'em out at the mouth of the Coeur d'Alene River and take 'em over to the mills at Harrison. [A bark mark was hacked into the side of a log cutting through the bark and into the wood. Generally, a double-bit axe was used. It would be something such as "hack, anchor, hack," or letters like "X" or "K" or "A."]

Most of the cedar went to Avery & Laumeister [mill] in Harrison, although they had a mill for awhile up on Eagle Creek above Prichard.

The shingle mills were always burning up. The cedar dust from the saws would just explode. I don't know how many Avery lost. But I never heard of 'em having a crooked fire [a mill burned up for the insurance money].

Buchanan Scotch Whiskey

Buchanan is a Scotch name. All through England, you see these steel signs advertising Buchanan Scotch Whiskey. I used to drink a little, but I never let it get the best of me.

The other soldiers over there with me in World War I used to say, "Hey! Buchanan! Where is all that Scotch whiskey of yours?"

I was ten months and four days in France.

Fixing Fords

Jim Hartley had the Ford garage in Wallace. Dad had a fix-it shop in Kingston and got to buyin' a few Ford parts from Jim.

So Jim says, "Joseph! How we gonna keep Henry at home when he comes back?"

"Well," my dad says, "It's been worryin' me. I don't know what to do. I'd like to see him stay."

Jim says, "Tell you what. You put in a whole stock of Ford parts. If he don't stay to use 'em, you can haul 'em back to me."

When I come home from the army in 1919, Jim said, "God! Your dad'll be glad to see you. I want you to fix my Fords."

Before I got my uniform off, I was fixin' Fords.

We didn't make a lot, but I had a good home, plenty to eat, and good credit at the store. The first owner of the Kingston store was Silas Slocum. He died, then his wife took it over.

Mary Blake

Mary Blake lived out in the woods this side of Potlatch and was a nurse in Kellogg. I had a couple of stretches in the hospital and she took care of me. I married her in 1927.

Dad Starts Lumberyard

I used to work for Al Hunt. He sold logs to Lane Lumber Company a lot. That was an awful good outfit.

Lane Lumber owed Al some money and they said, "Why don't you take it in lumber and put in a little lumberyard up there at Kingston?"

Al come down and he says to my old man, "How'd you like to have a lumberyard?"

My dad says, "What with?"

"Oh, don't worry about it," he said. "I'll fix that end of it. You look after it. If it don't come out, I'll take the short end. If I get back what I paid out, we'll split what's left."

I think Dad got ten carloads altogether. Prettiest 1-by-12's you ever saw in your life, all nicely planed. Even in those days, boards 16 inches wide and entirely clean of knots were unusual.

At Cataldo, somebody used to help theirselfs to some of our lumber during the night. Next morning the pile wouldn't be so big. We suspicioned Mac Huffin. He lived close there.

Al went to him. "Damn it, Mac! Bunch of thieves around here. I'm leavin' the lumber yard in your charge."

After that, we never lost a board!

Brother on Piano

At Kingston, there was some woman who had her husband cremated after he died and put his little urn of ashes on the piano.

Later, her brother got into an argument with a hotel clerk in San Francisco. The clerk followed him outside on the street and shot him dead. Her other brother brooded over this a good deal. He told me that he was going to San Francisco, hunt up that hotel clerk, and kill him to avenge his brother.

I gave the idea some thought and told him, "You'd better watch out or you'll be on the piano, too."

Bought Tax Land

I bought a lot of tax land beginning with the Depression years, 1932. I had 88 pieces in Kootenai County one time and 18 in Shoshone. I sold most of it. Got maybe six pieces left. I'd have had that whole Harrison Flats country if I'd had money. I saw it coming.

John Loma

Loma's place—you go up McPhee Gulch above Enaville and it's the first big draw to the left, about half a mile up there. They'd had a car burn up in a little garage, so the insurance company sent this adjuster up. This was during the time I was Justice of the Peace and Constable of Kingston. He wanted deputy protection, so they told him to get me.

The insurance adjuster said, "We ain't gonna pay for that."

This young Loma was about eighteen or twenty. He said, "I'll cut your heart out and hang it on a bush."

Loma got pretty mad at me because the insurance outfit didn't pay the claim. I used to get my tit in the wringer every once in awhile. But I didn't let it bother me.

Later on he killed a man.

[The coroner's report of September 1, 1912 said: John Lundquist, 50, Finlander. Shot by John Loma without provocation at Enaville.]

John Loma escaped. He went over across the river there at what we used to call "The Basin." It was across from the two-mile post on the railroad up from Enaville. Brush in there you couldn't see ten feet. We tracked Loma all through there, but he got out of the country into Canada. But he got caught later when he came back to the States.

That was John Loma that bit his wife's nose off. He got out of the penitentiary. He come home and this guy, Frank Ragella, was upstairs. Loma killed him with a gun. Then he grabbed his wife and bit her nose off. I don't think he was tanked up. Afterwards, she wore a rag or bandage over it.

[The coroner's report of March 26, 1921 said: John Loma, 29, Finn wife in Enaville. Gunshot wound—hands of wife—self defense].

Davenport

Andrew Maki was around seventy and young Maki was their sole support. Trouble was, the young fellow would go around the joints and fight and drink. Up there at Albert's Tavern, a bunch of 'em shoved young Maki off the porch and jumped on him with big, heavy boots. They had it in for him because he was a Finn.

The next day there was a fracas. The old man, Andrew Maki, went up there and tried to get the kid to come away, but he wouldn't. They never found out who knifed the guy at the tavern during the fracas. Didn't find the wound in his back till they got him into the undertaking parlor.

So then, young Maki went down and got into it with Davenport. There was hard feeling between them. He killed Davenport. So he went up and hid in this little shed.

Everybody wanted to shoot somebody and they did. I've been in this country for a long time and . . . of course, they riddled the shed with bullets and killed the kid.

I went to Enaville and old Andy Maki was standin' in the road—his father. I walked right up and took him by the hand.

I said, "Andrew, I'm sorry for you. Is there anything I can do?"

He said, "Henry, I was sure you was gonna come. Nobody else come."

They had shot that kid full of holes. He was up in a little chicken house or barn up in the attic.

A highway patrolman got up there and throwed his body down like a sack of bran. If it had been my kid, I'd have killed the whole goddamn outfit.

[Davenport, Maki, and Loma appear in *North Fork of the Coeur d'Alene River.*]

TWENTY-FOUR

MAGGIE NEARING KINDSVATER

Interviewed 1974 at Coeur d'Alene, Idaho.

MY DAD, Robert Beers Nearing, was an engineer for the Canadian Pacific Railroad. He used to break riding horses for other people in his spare time.

We leased ground to raise hay for our cattle. When Mother drove us out to the hayfields, she took a hoe along to kill the rattlesnakes. The poor horse would jump ten feet sideways when he heard one rattle.

Then we moved to Fernie, Alberta. I often rode in the railroad engine with my father. Fernie is near the town of Frank, where the mountain slid down and buried it with great boulders April 29, 1903. It's a coal mining town. The miners wore pit lamps, not carbide lights, but a lamp with a little wick and oil. One day there was gas in the mine and it blew up. Only one guy got out alive, and he lived only a minute or so, then he died. My father's train hauled the dead away. I don't know how many men lost their lives, but it seemed like every home in Fernie had black crepe hanging on the door.

Came to the States 1899

I was about five in 1899 when we come down to the States. Papa was a Cree Indian, born in New Medford, Connecticut, in 1856. Mother was a Canadian, Margaret Annie Goldsmith, born in Collingwood, Ontario, in 1858. She and Dad were married at Medicine Hat, Alberta. Her father, Grandad Goldsmith, was born in Abreth, Scotland, and could play the bagpipes.

Mother became an American when she married my father. Even

■ Maggie Nearing Kindsvater and siblings in 1950. Back row: Maggie, Bill Nearing, Bob Nearing, Amelia Pruitt. Front row: Florence Zimmerman, Maude Arnold, Pearl Cotton, Hazel Ahrens, May Parmentier.

though six of us kids were born in Canada, when we came across the line, I guess we became Americans. Anyway, when I got old enough, I voted.

There were nine kids in our family: Pearl, 1888; Maude, 1890; Bob, 1892; me, Margaret (Maggie), 1894; Amelia, 1896; Bill, 1898; Hazel, 1900; May, 1902; and Florence, 1904. The first babies Mama had was twin boys. If they hadn't died, there would have been 11 in our family.

Dad Fired Boiler at Harrison

Dad got a job at three dollars a day firing boilers in the Grant Sawmill that used to be right below what is now Rose's Cafe in Harrison, Idaho.

We moved into a house on the sidehill just below Sala's Cliff. Dad paid $100 for the old house. It was the buggiest house I ever seen. They crawled everywhere out of the wood and walls and ceilings. We used sulfur candles and scalding water and louse dust to kill the live ones.

Then their eggs hatched out, and we still had a house full of bedbugs. Some times it got so bad, I'd take my bed covers and go sleep on the pine needles on the hillside.

We never had no water in the house. We had to go down past Murray's to Crane's yard where a little spout came out of the mountain into a hardwood barrel and pack all our water up in buckets, even to wash clothes.

Direct below us lived the Packers. We used to throw rocks down almost to their house tryin' to get our ducks to come back up the hill from the lake. We only had three ducks and they were white. I don't know why we fed 'em. We didn't have no more than enough to eat ourselves. We had a beautiful Guernsey cow that lost her cud. If a cow loses her cud, she will die, so Mama gave her a dishrag to chew to make another one. We had a gorgeous white rooster that used to corner us kids in the old outhouse. He was so mean we were afraid to come out.

Us kids would spend hours carrying in wood for people for 10 cents. We herded cows, barefooted, out to pasture for people and got $3.50 a month. A bunch of cattle ran loose in the hills. The only thing I was scared to death of was the bulls. I found this old red-and-white milk cow running loose. I didn't know who she belonged to. I milked her on the ground to make sure she was gentle, then I drove her home. We had the loveliest milk for over a year.

Goat Sailed off the Roof

An old man raised goats at the edge of town. He gave Bob and I a little billy because the mother didn't want it. Mama gave me a ketchup bottle with milk in it and a nipple, and the goat sucked till its stomach stuck out. When bedtime came, I piled hay near my bed and made a little nest for him. In the night the little thing started, "Baaaaaa!" I got up and brought the ketchup bottle with more milk and wrapped my bathrobe around the goat and took it to bed with me.

Next morning, my mother said, "Maggie, when I went up the steps to call the rest of the bunch to get up, there you were with that homely little goat's head on the pillow right alongside yours, both of you sound asleep. So sweet! I had to laugh."

In a year that goat grew a big set of horns. We never scratched his head or teased him, he just started butting on his own. He cornered a couple of women on the porch of the Harrison Hotel and scared them silly till some men clubbed the goat away. Then he wandered up the main street and put people up trees and telephone poles.

He liked to walk over our roof, and he never fell off. One day he was bouncing up and down on the roof when my poor dad left the house and started down the trail. The goat sailed off the roof and hit Dad from behind and knocked him end over end. I won't repeat what Dad called the goat, but he took it down and pounded its nose and drove its horns right into the ground. Then Dad dragged it down the trail by the horns and sold it to some guys that worked on the railroad. I think they ate it!

Honkers on Ice

One winter night, Lake Coeur d'Alene froze clear ice, and the biggest flock of honkers thought they were comin' down to water. They all lit on that clear ice. Know somethin'! You couldn't sleep for them geese a-honkin' because they couldn't get through to the water.

We used to coast our sleds past the Presbyterian Church that stood on the hill with our neighbor's children, Ward and Katy Murray. Ward got awfully sick and died. We'd like to have died, too, because we all loved Ward.

Marked Babies

Polsons lived below us. They had butchered a deer down in the basement of their house. When Mrs. Polson went down the basement steps—she was pregnant with Stephanie at the time—she walked right into this hanging deer liver, and it hit her on the cheek. When Stephanie was born, that baby had that red birthmark right on the cheek.

In 1909, Dad ran steam engine for the Avery & Laumeister Shingle Mill in Harrison. That mill had the most terrible whistle. This young couple lived uptown pretty close to that whistle. She was pregnant at the time, and I'd see her put her hands over her ears every time that awful whistle blew.

It marked the baby. When the little girl was born, she had no ears at all—just holes. They cut her hair "Buster Brown" fashion, with bangs and combed the sides down over where the ears should have been to hide the holes.

Worked at Six

At six, I started school in Harrison. After school I'd cut wood and carry in kindling for people that had money. I didn't have anything but hand-me-down clothes—none of us did. When I was a little older, I'd do house cleaning or help with canning for two-bits a day. I worked so hard I was too tired to go anywhere or celebrate.

Anyway, Dad didn't let us go nowhere when we was young. But when I was maybe eleven in 1905, my mother told my sisters and me we could go to a masquerade and dance party. I had fixed a tiny washboard and a little tub on me, and I went as an Irish washerwoman. We was havin' a good time, but my father came after us and made us go home. Dancing was a sin to Dad.

When I was fourteen, I had a little gray pony named Buttons. Walter Boutillier had a big Clydesdale that he rode out to cruise timber on the Harrison Flats, and he asked me to go along for company.

The year after that, Grant's lumber company hauled logs off the flats down O'Gara canyon with a tractor that pulled loaded cars behind it on the road. When the Grants got the Booth place logged, they gave all the dead timber to my dad because they wanted the land cleared. I went out and stayed with him and pulled the other end of the crosscut saw. We cut cordwood for the tugboats and stove wood for people around Harrison.

Kellogg

The same year, Dad moved to Kellogg. The next year, 1910, Mama left our family Bible in Harrison with Mrs. Murray, and we chartered a boxcar to move our furniture and everything to Kellogg to be with Dad. We had two beautiful dogs named Teddy and Rufus that we left behind. Several days later they hiked up the track and found us in Kellogg. But we never got our Bible back because Mrs. Murray's house burned.

At Kellogg, Dad grew a big garden and stored winter vegetables in a pit lined with straw. I went to the Lincoln school and finished the sixth grade, but that was the end of my schooling.

That summer I worked at housekeeping for a family. I got $3.50 a week doing all the washing, dishwashing, house cleaning, and taking care of the three kids. I quit and went to work for Mrs. Browning's boardinghouse that had 150 boarders. I had over 100 lunchpails to wash. I worked from five in the morning to ten at night—or whenever I was through—for $35 a month. The boardinghouse stood where the McConnell Hotel is now. It burned down. I didn't burn it down but I felt like it many times!

I gave all the money I earned to the family. When my next to oldest sister got married, they went and took my money to buy her a wedding dress.

1910 Fire

That was the year of the big forest fire—1910. It got so dark you couldn't see the sun. People thought the world was coming to an end.

We lived right below the Bunker Mill where Papa worked for scab wages—$3.50 a day. When he got steam up and had a spare minute, he had to wheel ore into a boxcar and dump it. Ten hours a day. You didn't open your mouth about a union or you was gone.

Delayed Check

About 1915, the government sent Dad a paycheck for work he did with a packtrain at Custer's battlefield in 1876. *The Spokesman-Review* headlined it, "Government Pays After 39 Years."

Dad died about 1930. Then to be near my married sister, Amelia, Mother moved into a house on McKinley Avenue between Deadwood Gulch and the Bunker mill.

Married at Sixteen

I was sixteen and never been kissed. Along come this lumberjack, Jack Sweem, and I married him in 1910. The first home we had was on the North Fork of the Coeur d'Alene River at Graham Creek, by Carter Station. My new husband was up at logging camp, so I was alone all day long. I took one of my sisters to live with me and sent her to school.

The school was on a flat in the mouth of the creek. That old bell would ring and you could hear it for miles. Seamans and Babbits lived not far from the schoolhouse, and further up lived Tiny Mason and her husband, and way up lived Sig Pearson and his wife.

Weekends was even more lonesome because Jack, my husband, went along with the whole logging crew down to Enaville and got good and drunk and had a big time. Enaville was full of sportin' girls.

Then three years later, in 1913, Jack got a job near Harrison at the Grant Lumber Company camp, and we lived in a house in O'Gara canyon. It was the same house where Shorty Archer got shot a year later by a thief. Shot him through a suitcase.

My first husband, I'm sorry to say, he'd have let the baby and me starve to death if it hadn't been for my father bringin' us eggs and milk. Of course, I was just a kid compared to Jack Sweem. He was four years older. He worked steady, but payday, he'd walk from O'Gara, across the trestle to Chatcolet, and raise the dickens. And that ain't all. I carried water from the spring down on the road and done all his lumberjack friends' washing.

The lumberjacks give Jack money to pay me for the washings, but I never seen none of it. You know somethin'? I liked hard work and I was never a hollerer. But I wouldn't look at the likes of Jack Sweem if it was today.

Jack didn't care for nothin'. He got on the passenger train and rode to Harrison. Said he didn't have no more money. And I walked the railroad track, four miles, carryin' my baby boy. Fare was only ten cents!

Jimmy Jones Restaurant

The next year, Jack Sweem went off somewhere on a job and didn't show up again, so I divorced him. I took my two-year-old boy, Lenny, to my mother in Kellogg and got a job working as dishwasher, cook, waitress and all around workhorse at Jimmy Jones' restaurant in Harrison. I lived in our old house on the sidehill. I got up at five o'clock to go to work, cleaned up the dining room after supper, put in 12 to 14 hours a day, and got $25 a month.

I worked for Jimmy Jones, off and on, over a lot of years. They called him "Greasy Jones." You know somethin'? I saw him put a pork chop on the stove and I seen some little white maggots in it.

I said, "Jimmy! That one is no good. It's fly-blowed!"

He took it off the stove and threw it in the garbage. It wasn't his fault. They had no refrigeration back then.

Jimmy Jones would give you the last bite in his place whether you had money or not. He had a heart of gold. Only reason he didn't go broke was he was already broke when he started. I don't think he was ever married—never heard him mention a woman. I think he just grew up a loner.

And he was decent! Like me being a young woman there. I was fairly good lookin'. He never once said anything out of the way to me. And I regret I never did know when he died.

Sometimes Mama brought my little boy down and stayed with me a few days. Somebody gave me a white pony. I rode a lot and I'd take Lenny with me. Bridgemans let me use their horse, but I'd never take my little boy on that one. He was a real bugger. He'd raise right up on his hind legs intending to go over backwards with me. I'd crack him with a quirt right between the ears and set him down on his feet again.

I kept an old six-shooter at the house for protection and had a few bullets for it, but I never shot it. Dad had an old .45-70 rifle stuck away at the house and I shot it once in awhile. When it went off, there at the foot of Sala's Cliff, your ears would ring for an hour.

But one time when Amelia came for a visit, she brought a .45 Colt automatic pistol. We wanted some excitement, so I set a wooden box at the base of the cliff with a black spot drawed on it, and got off to one side a few feet. Amelia pulled up that pistol and it emptied eight shots from one pull of the trigger. The bullets struck all around me. It's a wonder I wasn't killed.

The Hoot Owls

The only time Jimmy Jones did me wrong was when he give me two big hoot owls. He kept 'em in a mesh wire fence back of his restaurant, and he'd carry water and chunks of meat up there. Jimmy called me back there and pointed at the owls that was sittin' there blinkin' their eyes at me.

He said, "Maggie! Do you want them hoot owls?"

I was so tickled to death to get 'em that I didn't stop to think.

He said, "They can't fly because they've been shut up from when they were little and never learned." He opened the door and shooed them out.

When I tried to catch them, they raked at me with their talons. So I herded them things clear up to where we lived on Murray's hill. When we reached the house, they wouldn't chase into our hen coop and wouldn't chase into the woodshed. At dark I gave up and left 'em settin' on the ground up the sidehill among the pines, blinkin' their eyes at me.

You know something? That night them owls—we had an open woodshed with wood piled up—and them owls came back that night. I had one pigeon in particular that I loved and I called her "Brownie." When I got up next morning, them two big owls was out there in the woodshed. They was sittin' up on the pile of wood, blinkin' their eyes at me, and scattered around them—mostly et—was every one of my pretty little pigeons.

The harm was done so I didn't kill the owls. Maybe they'd got tired of steak down at Jimmy's place and pigeons looked special to them. They hung around awhile, learned to fly, and left.

The Long Walk

We was servin' lunch in late October 1915 when I was amazed to see my sister, Amelia, and her husband, Fred Pruett, and my brother, Bill, walk into the restaurant. Amelia was younger than I and her husband, Fred. We girls was all married when we was fifteen or so.

I finished waitin' table and come over to 'em and said, "What are you kids doin' in Harrison?"

Bill was grinning. "You know what we're gonna do? We're gonna walk to Kellogg this afternoon."

My mother was still taking care of my little boy at Kellogg and I was so lonesome to see him I couldn't stand it.

I said, "I'm goin' with you."

So I said to Jimmy, "Let me have my pay."

I went into the kitchen and made a lot of beef sandwiches and took an extra loaf of bread. There was an extra gramophone horn in Jimmy's storeroom. It was the kind that come on those Edison phonographs with the picture of the dog in the opening of it and the words "His Master's Voice." And it was the only thing I could find to stuff the sandwiches in.

There were two passenger trains each way, every day, and we all had money, but we set out to walk it just for fun. I walked in high-heeled shoes and so did Amelia. We took along my sweet old dog, Teddy. He was brown and slick-haired. I brought along that old pistol that I hadn't never shot. Going past Anderson Lake, I tipped it up and aimed away out over the water. When the gun boomed, it fell completely apart and left me holding just the butt. And here all these years I'd kept it around for protection!

By the time we reached Medimont, you never seen so many blisters as was on my heels and toes. And Amelia, her feet was killing her. We had an old pair of rubbers like you put on over shoes, and we changed off wearing them rubbers till we couldn't hardly put anything on our feet. Railroad ties don't set an even distance apart, which makes a railroad track the hardest thing in the world to walk. You step two ties at a time and then they're uneven and you take one at a time, then skip one. We took turns walking the rails, but that's almost impossible in high heels and it's worse wearing loose rubbers.

Before we reached Lane, the down train met us. As it went past, we waved and hollered and hopped around crazy, and the engineer waved and grinned at us.

At Rose Lake, we bought some candy, peanuts, crackers, and cheese. Our roast beef sandwiches was all gone and we stuck the "Masters Voice" horn on a bush like a hat and tied some whiskers at the bottom. Us kids hadn't seen each other to play like this in a long, long time.

We hobbled past Dudley and Cataldo and Enaville, and just below Kellogg, at Sweeney, at the mouth of Silver King Gulch, it was gettin' dark and spittin' the first snow of the winter. We crawled into an old boxcar to take a rest and feeling a little bit sorry we hadn't rode the train. I used my old dog, Teddy, for a pillow.

When we crawled out, it was just breaking daylight. We had stiffened so we couldn't hardly walk. Even Teddy's legs moved like sticks. But our spirits picked up when we got to Mama's in time for pancakes. [Onni Rantanen, locomotive engineer, says that numbering from Plummer, the 31 mile post was at Harrison, where they started, and the 68 mile post was at Kellogg. They had walked 37 miles.]

Married Again and Divorced

A year or two later, I married Glen Thayer. We had two girls: Margaret, born in 1918, and Pauline later. Glen went to France in the First World War. He came home lousy with syphilis. But he didn't give it to me. I suspicioned something and asked the doctors. One of them told me. So I got a divorce.

Stayed Near My Son

My boy's name was Leonard Sweem. From around 1928, I worked in Kellogg to be with him. He grew up to be a beautiful young man with dark, curly hair like I used to have, and weighed 160 pounds. I tied myself up in him. My! I loved that boy.

He must have inherited epilepsy from his father's side because his father's sister's girl started having seizures at the same age he did. I took him to specialists and even down to Medical Lake. They couldn't seem to do much for him. I used to send to Milwaukee for the little bottle of "Lepso" and that kept down his seizures real good, but he had an awful temper. Just terrible.

We lived in a little apartment on the same side of the street as the ball park, and I helped Mrs. Cowles, who took in boarders. They used to call her one-armed husband, "Hubby Cowles." Mr. Cowles would pay Lenny a little for helping him on jobs, and that gave Lenny money to spend. I bought him nice clothes and worked for his board.

One evening in 1930, Lenny told me he was going up to the YMCA.

I said, "Promise me you won't do any boxing. It makes your heart go too fast."

He said, "O.K. I won't!"

I went upstairs to visit a neighbor woman. We were playing cards when I heard Lenny come home. I always worried that he might have another seizure. In a few minutes I come into the apartment. He had turned over on his stomach in bed and his face was so white! Then I saw those dark spots and I knew something was the matter with my boy. I got the doctor right away, but it didn't help. He was dead at only seventeen. After I lost Lenny, I thought: I'll never love another kid! But I still had my two girls to love, of course.

Albert Legault Tavern

About 1934, I worked for Albert Legault, who had a little beer parlor across the bridge from Enaville. But the best Legault is Felix and his sweet little wife. He married her when she was just a little girl, and he's always been good to her. When Felix came to visit his brother at the tavern, he'd buy candy for everybody and never drink.

But Albert was the one that punished the liquor. He was a ladies' man and got married a coupla times.

He expected me to work and work and work for low pay. Only once he paid me good. That was when I took care of him after that woman pert near killed him. Albert lived in a little trailer near the tavern. She went in, lookin' for money. She kicked the windows out and cut his arm and crippled him so he couldn't work. She pretty near beat him to death. She thought he must have money hid in his clothes, so she stole his clothes.

But he didn't have no money! Albert had cirrhosis of the liver so bad I've seen him do everything but die—and that's what finally killed him.

Husky Brothers

Along about 1935, my brothers, Bob and Bill, were among the biggest men around the river. Bill was a fighter and Bob was a log hustler. During the depression, Bob was head of a bunch of CC boys up the North Fork. I came over there with my two girls. The CC boys couldn't fish because they were out of state. So we caught trout and fried them every night for the boys. Margaret married Malcolm Pierce, one of the CC boys.

Years later, Bob was unloading logs at Enaville. He pulled the wrapper chain loose and that loosened the top log. He stooped over to pick up the fit hook and the log dropped on him.

After Bob was killed, the Forest Service named a branch of Steamboat Creek "Big Bob" after him.

My Only Good Husband

My last husband was Jake Kindsvater, the only good husband I had. He worked in the Page mine, but he was a man that got hurt every two or three months.

Sometimes I was kinda sorry that he met me. He had never been married before and was kinda innocent. We used to have fun dancin' though. I was good to him. Aw! I was good to myself. I enjoyed it.

Jake got so crippled from rheumatoid arthritis that when he walked he almost looked like he was sitting down. He had been a sailor in the First World War, so he was eligible for the Vets Hospital. They straightened him out except for his feet. But they warned him never to drink liquor again. So Jake began to drink lots of apple juice.

During the time Jake was laid up and gone to the hospital, I had to work. I lived in a little house right back of the feed store in Smelterville and for company kept my granddaughter Joanne and sent her to school. I worked as bartender for Red in the Happy Landing.

Along in the years 1924, '25, and '26, my younger brother, Bill, had done a lot of fighting in the ring. Bill would make me put on the gloves and practice with him. Some of it had stayed with me, and in 1940 I still had no problem handling drunks. When I hit 'em, they went down and didn't get up.

One morning when I put two of 'em down the road with black eyes, Red said, "I'm gonna set up a ring in the Happy Landing and put you in it to meet all comers. I'd make more money that way than off the bar."

I worked for the Happy Landing two years. It was during that time that Jake came back from the Vets Hospital—still drinking apple juice. Then his brothers threw a party down near Medimont, and Jake drank whiskey and died.

Fishing with Bill

Later years, I lived alone on the North Fork near Carrigan's place in Mrs. Schuster's little house. I loved it there. I'd walk up the river to fish. But by golly, if I seen cattle comin' down the trail, I'd climb a cliff till they went by.

My brother Bill came up. Bless him! We'd go up to Nowhere Camp, a couple of miles from Rock City, and fish and build a fire and camp out overnight. We had lots of fun. Bill stuck around a week or so and helped me cultivate and weed the garden. I canned carrots. I give everybody cabbages and berries and onions out of that garden.

But I had to leave the river and move back to Smelterville when Mrs. Schuster sold the layout. Then I broke my hip in two places and that put me in the convalescent home. Sometimes I get depressed and smoke up a whole package of cigarettes. But I'm never a person that stays depressed.

Bill's living in Spokane with his daughter and not doin' too good. If I could see him, I'd say, "Come on, you old horse and get outa that bed and git goin' because I been sick, too, you know. So Bill! Come on! We're gonna go fishin'. Yes! We are!"

[Bill Nearing appears in *North Fork of the Coeur d'Alene River.*]

TWENTY-FIVE

HENRY MORIN

Interviewed 1975 at Harrison, Idaho.

I WAS BORN April 28, 1889, at Manistee, Michigan. My parents were Albert Morin and Mary Poisman Morin. We came to Harrison in April 1901. It took us about a week, sleeping in railroad stations and making train connections after long waits. I was twelve years old. We moved into the south end of Harrison. That fall, I went to school.

Clem Peterson, who was married to Jim Early's sister, and Jim were all living there with Jim's mother in two little houses that lay between my dad's house and the Knutsen house. We'd lost some chickens and I saw Jim cleaning them.

Well, you couldn't fight 'em! So my dad, next time he saw Jim, he said, "Jim, haven't I always been a very good neighbor of yours?"

Jim said, "I couldn't ask for a nicer neighbor."

Dad said, "Things have got pretty rowdy over at your place at times, but you never heard me make a complaint."

Jim said, "No. You never have. You've been an exceptionally good neighbor."

Dad said, "Will you leave my chickens alone?"

He says, "Mr. Morin. You'll never lose another chicken."

They had a butcher here in Harrison who had a slaughterhouse up close to the Thompson place where there was a little creek [near the Harrison Boat Storage]. The butcher went out and slaughtered a nice big pig and left it hanging in the slaughterhouse.

Clem and Jim went in the butcher shop and Jim said, "I'd like to get some meat, but we don't have much money to buy meat with."

The butcher said, "You shouldn't be worrying about that. You ought to have plenty of pork at your house."

Jim said, "We've got no meat at our house!"

The butcher said, "Tell you what I'll do. I'll give you five dollars if you'll tell me who stole that pig out of the slaughterhouse."

"Well," Jim said, "I know, but I don't want to squeal on people. But gosh! I could use that five dollars."

So he took the five dollars and then whispered to the butcher, "I'm the one that stole your pig, but you can't prove it!"

Number Two Drawing

About 1908 or '09, Hedmark had the number two [lottery] drawing on the Indian Reservation and chose a homestead across the bay from Amwaco. He was a bachelor who put in just enough timber to buy his needs and a gallon of whiskey, which he drank up while laying in bed in his only celebration for the year.

He'd only sell to Russell & Pugh, and the logs had to be scaled by Walt Russell. The yellow pine was of such size that Walt Russell told about sending a boat over and bringing home 11 logs with a total scale of 10,000 board feet.

Santa Creek

I was working for the St. Joe Improvement Company when we drove logs down Santa Creek into the St. Maries River, 1908. I was with the crew running logs from McDonald's Camp, the only camp in that run from Emida to the Santa Dam. Santa Dam was in that narrow place that looks like a fish trap, those lava cliffs beside the highway just beyond the Santa turnoff toward Emida. That's the place where there were holes in the rocks and the charred wood of ancient tropical forests. [Those cliffs have since been bulldozed out.]

Lots of men. Wages three dollars a day. Four meals. It was dark when you left camp in the morning and damn dark when you got back at night.

They had a dam every place a side creek came in above our camp, so if we had a jam, we'd get it ready for the next flood from the dams above. There were no flumes—just splash dams. Below the Santa Dam, they sluiced the logs all the way to Flat Creek. Below the Flat Creek Dam, the logs were put through the loops [the S bends in the river].

The St. Joe Improvement Company had a 25-year franchise from the state to keep the St. Maries River free of snags and stuff. Then they charged everybody. Even if you towed your own logs down the river to the St. Joe Sorting Gap, at the mouth of the river, you had to pay 15 cents 1,000 board feet to the St. Joe Improvement Company. At that point, if you didn't already have a scale on that boom, you had to pay five cents per 1,000 for a state scaler [measuring each log with a scale rule to determine its footage].

Boulette and Homesteaders

My oldest sister married Louis Bond from which Bond Creek on the St. Joe River was named. He rented his meadow at the mouth of Bond Creek to Bill Theriault, who had pack strings to pack people up into the Marble Creek country.

It just so happened I was visiting my sister and Bill Theriault when Bill was puttin' up hay. That claim jumper, Ed Bouley [Boulette], was one of the crew. That's how I met him. I'll never forget it.

Ed Bouley and Gene Tyler was hired by the head of one of the biggest lumber companies to jump claims. Marble Creek was a hard place for homesteaders to stay in winter on account of being a long distance back and with deep snow. The claim jumpers would go to the Federal Land Office in Coeur d'Alene and testify the homesteader had been gone more than three months from the land, and the land office would cancel the homesteader's application. Then the claim jumper would file on it and relinquish his claim to the big lumber outfit, which would file Civil War Veteran scrip on it. The government had given scrip to Civil War Veterans, entitling them to 160 acres of land as a bonus. The big outfits had picked up the scrip for next to nothing.

The homesteaders decided to put a stop to them guys. Bouley must have been shot before the Milwaukee Railroad was built. I believe it was completed and had trains about 1909. I know there was no railroad up the St. Maries River in 1908, and the Milwaukee built this branch after the mainline was finished.

When they killed Bouley, they buried his dog with him and they left a sign there, "This is where we buried Bouley and his dog."

Rice, who homesteaded up there, knew who did the killing, but never would say.

North Fork of the Coeur d'Alene River

I scaled the first logs that came in from Big Creek [now Shoshone Creek] on the North Fork of the Coeur d'Alene River, for Stack & Gibbs.

I consider Friday the thirteenth a lucky day for me. On October 13, 1911, I was scaling a big deck of 70 to 80 thousand feet of logs stacked on steep ground near the creek. The logs were to be sent down a short chute into the creek whenever the water depth permitted. I told the men still rolling logs on the back end to be especially careful while I was scaling in front.

I was standing on the end of a log and straddling another about ten feet above the ground, and reaching out with my scale rule to scale other logs, when the men behind the log pile let a big white pine butt get away from them. The whole front of the high deck of logs started to cave out.

I felt the log between my legs drop, so I pushed myself backwards with my hands and leaped 20 feet to the ground, but I landed on my back. My head struck a piece of wood that knocked me out for a few minutes.

The other men came running around the end of the pile, afraid I'd been caught under the spillout. I lost my eyesight for two hours, but I cussed those guys out with every name I knew.

But anyway, I came out of this accident with a whole hide, so I believe Friday the thirteenth is a lucky day for me.

Tom St. Peter

There were a lot of French-Canadians from around Quebec working the drives on the North Fork. Most all of 'em were bachelors and up in years. Tom St. Peter was in his fifties and an exceptionally good lumberjack, but he could neither read nor write. He'd ask the timekeeper how big his check was and then when he went to town, he'd go to a saloon and ask the bartender if he could cash a check.

The bartender would say, "How much?"

And Tom would remember what the timekeeper had told him. But actually, Tom couldn't tell the difference between a $1 bill and a $20 bill. Of course, they cheated him if they knew him. He'd throw down a $20 bill to buy drinks, and they'd give him change for a $5 bill.

Gee! Haw!

Poor old Tom St. Peter, he'd generally end up making chute with a broadaxe. He was an expert axman, but like all the rest of the Frenchmen, he wanted to hire out as a skinner. Most all of them were good swampers, but they all seemed to want to drive a team. [A swamper cut the limbs off the logs where they lay in the woods and then cleared out brush and limbs to make a trail adequate for a team of horses to come for the logs.] All the Frenchmen were dynamite to a team. They hollered too much and hollered impossible commands.

A trail chute is a log chute with a trail alongside for horses to pull the logs because the ground is too level for logs to slide under their own weight. They'd dog a trail together and then use a spacing bar to pry the logs apart a little so when the horses started to pull, the logs would bump one another into motion.

Tom finally got his chance to drive team and was trailing on a chute.

Tom yelled, "Gee! Haw!" at the team and they pulled up the slack and stopped. [The horses were confused by the opposing commands: "Gee!" meant swing right; "Haw!" meant swing left.]

While he was doing this, I came up and sat down on the last log in the string.

The team turned around and looked at the logs. Tom yelled, "Gee! Haw! Now!" They pulled up the slack and stopped. The horses knew what they were doing, they're pretty smart. Poor old Tom didn't know nothin'.

He started spacing his logs again and he thought me sitting there kept the team from pulling them. He started after me with that spacing bar.

McGoldrick

About 1914, Stack & Gibbs had gone bankrupt, and I worked for McGoldrick Lumber Company on the North Fork of the Coeur d'Alene River. They were logging with all separate gypos [contractors].

Dave Dollar was logging for McGoldrick, logging United States timber. I know this because the government was doing all the scaling, and I was assisting Roy Lammers and check scaling, too.

The first camp was five miles above Prichard at the mouth of Lost Creek; a camp was at the mouth of Big Creek [now Shoshone Creek], and another was up one of them forks. Later, down below Prichard, Dollar had them Hopkins brothers on Cedar Creek. But this Cedar Creek loggin' was after I left McGoldrick.

The next camp was up across from Big Hank Flats on Bennett Creek, logging the old Bennett homestead. There was a gypo named Charles logging on Harvey Creek comin' into the North Fork. Then there were two Swede brothers from Coeur d'Alene logging up above on the mouth of the East Fork [now Independence Creek]. The East Fork was exactly 35 miles from Prichard by the trail. At that time, Ohio [Match Company], McGoldrick and Winton were all logging up there. I think Winton did the driving down to slack water.

Skidoo Johnny

Skidoo Johnny was skidding for Dave Dollar. Skidoo was ignorant, had no education, and couldn't keep time on the men working for him. He paid by the day and asked them to count up the days they'd worked. They worked six days a week, but they counted Sundays, too. He didn't know any better.

Dollar had this big old mare, and Skidoo was using her to skid logs down to the creek. He kept a man down on the landing to roll the logs into the creek. The mare would go down with a trail of logs, all by herself, to the landing. The landing man would knock out the logs, fasten them to her, and head her back up the hill to Skidoo Johnny. My good garsh all fishhooks! He *could* skid logs!

There was a little piece of timber on one of the branches of Big Creek that Skidoo had the chance to buy on his own. He talked Dollar into selling him this mare. He skidded himself, but he hired other fellows to skid for him, too. And I'll tell you, any men he hired earned their money. All Skidoo Johnny knew was how to skid logs, but he knew that, by jingoes! And he wouldn't have sold that mare for $10,000.

He said to me, "I have to buy a team of horses. You think Lammers would loan me money enough to buy a team of horses?"

I said, "You don't need to borrow. You go in and tell him how much money you want. Skidoo! You got over $3,000 comin'." He didn't even know it.

So we left camp, come into Wallace, and he said, "I'll buy your ticket to Spokane."

I said, "No. The company pays my fare."

He said, "Anyway, I go buy some clothes." He went and bought a pair of dress pants, dress shoes, and a white, stiff-bosomed shirt that would take a stiff collar.

The train pulled into Spokane and he says, "No more skid road for me, Henry. Where you stay?"

I said, "I stay at the Spokane Hotel so Lammers can find me when I'm in town."

He said, "You stay at the Spokane Hotel. I go there, too."

I thought: My good garsh! I'm not checkin' into no Spokane Hotel with him—not the way he's fixed up.

I said, "I'll tell you, Skidoo. You can't go no place dressed the way you are. The pants you got are too damn short for you. I'll take you to Malone and Kloss. I'll tell them to fix you up with a suit of clothes. They'll sell you a shirt with a collar already on it. Soon as you're rigged up, I'll take you over to the hotel."

He looked good in the suit. He was a well-built man. I phoned Lammers and told him about Skidoo wanting a team and that he had better than $3,000 dollars comin' and all his help was paid.

Lammers come down. "Skidoo!" he said. "Henry tells me you want to buy a team of horses."

"Yeah!" Skidoo said. "Down in the Palouse country them farmers always got good horses to sell."

Lammers says, "I'll have the barn boss go with you. You pick out the horses and I'll give him a blank check to fill out. But you got to have some other money. How much money do you want?"

"Maybe $50."

Lammers says, "We'll give you $200 or $300 so you'll have some cash on you."

And do you know! That Skidoo never went into a saloon. No, sir! And before that, he'd always go to town and get drunk. Drink it all up.

I talked him into hiring a bookkeeper to keep the books and keep time for him. "Every day, you tell your timekeeper who worked."

He said, "What else will he do?"

I said, "He probably won't do nothin' else, but he'll make money for you. You're payin' men for Sundays they don't work. The cook orders groceries and stuff he don't need. You need someone to hold him down, too."

He logged that job and made money off of it.

I kept track of Skidoo for a couple of years. The last I heard of him, he was still gypoing and makin' money on every job. And he stayed sober.

Log Rolling

My brother, Bill, and I started rolling logs about 1909. We practiced with one another, then we'd roll with some of those fellows up at the sorting works that was supposed to be champion rollers.

I told Bill, I said, "We're wettin' them fellows. They don't just drop off there on purpose."

Bill said, "I don't think they do, either. But they're supposed to be champions!"

So first time we got another chance, Bill rolled one and he dumped him. We rolled 'em in a contest and wet 'em, then we knew we were better than they were.

The summer of 1911, we spent rolling all around the country wherever there was a doings. We rolled for six days at the Astoria, Oregon, Centennial, which was in celebration of the defeat of the British attack on Astoria. We rolled in Oakes Park in Portland, and towns on the Columbia River, anywhere we had a chance to roll. If they had more than one prize, we'd try to talk 'em into one prize—winner take all. During

■ Henry Morin jumping over a stick held with both hands while brother, Bill, steadies the log, 1912

our birling in local areas, there was a lot of side money bet by loyal backers. We didn't go east. We decided to get fixed up so we could go east, but we didn't do it.

That year, we grossed $5,000. But when we got back home, we discovered we'd ended up with $40 less than we started with. Too much celebrating!

The next year, 1912, Bill and I split up to go different ways on the Fourth of July. I went to St. Maries and Bill to Priest River. We both won first money but it turned out the first money in St. Maries was only $15, doggone it!

We used to jump over a stick on a log. It was nothin' to lay down on one. We'd jump rope on a log. Pass one another. Nothin' to that. But to somerset [somersault] and come up standing on a log ain't easy. You have to give a flip.

I tried a number of times to stand on my head on a log, but I could never get my legs up. But Bill was so strong in his arms that he'd take a stick, and with a hand on each end, do a handstand on a log as small as 13 inches. He had a little notch on the log to keep the stick from slipping endo [end ways], then he'd slowly straighten his legs up. That takes a lot of strength in your arms, and I didn't have it.

Billy Delyea was good! He had awful good balance and big feet. Billy treaded a log. When you tread, you let the other fellow do the work. You roll, always facing the other fellow, watching his legs to see what he's going to do next.

My brother Bill met Delyea three times. The third time, they met in Coeur d'Alene on the Fourth of July. The purse, $125, would all go to the winner. They had a small log. They got to rolling and Delyea snubbed [stopped suddenly], and he could snub hard, too. And my brother, when he started to roll the other way, gave it a quick flip and Delyea went overboard.

Delyea could roll on a ball, but it was easier to roll that ball than to up-end a chunk [of wood]. My brother had a chunk that would just carry one man, and he'd turn it end for end. Used no pole, neither. That was better than rolling a ball.

Chet Russell was mighty good on a log, too. Darn good!

After I went to work for McGoldrick, I come out a couple of Fourth of Julys and rolled, then I quit.

Forest Service

There was very little Forest Service timber at the time of the 1910 fire. The Forest Service was two or three years old at that time and was grabbing only the stuff that hadn't been homesteaded. Most of the timber was owned by the Northern Pacific Railroad and McGoldrick.

Then, believe it or not, after the Northern Pacific had cut all they could off their ground, they turned around and traded their cut-over-burned stuff on Slate Creek for some nice stuff on Fishhook Creek. You can't tell me someone didn't get their palms greased.

The earlier Forest Rangers were practical men, most of 'em not college graduates. A ranger in the 1910 period, like Howard Drake, received $1,100 a year, but had to furnish a saddle horse and pack horse for himself.

The Forest supervisor sent me and Dodo Smith, a scaler working for the government, up the St. Joe River below Avery, to show some college men how to use a compass to find section corners and run boundary lines. Dodo was quite a drinker. He had enough liquor with him to stay drunk.

We showed 'em what a corner was like. The section lines were axe chip-marks on the trees called "blazes" and were still bright them days and easy to follow.

Dodo says, "You start 'em out, Henry."

I says, "Okay. You got your compasses. Go find a corner."

They wasn't gone five minutes before some was back. "I found a corner. I found a corner." The nearest quarter corner would be a half-mile away.

I says to Dodo, "These fellows are gonna get lost, and I'll have to

■ Ruins of 1910 forest fire up the St. Joe River

spend all my time finding 'em. You'd be no help. You're layin' around camp drunk. I quit."

Dodo says, "I'm out of liquor, so I'll quit, too."

[Howard Drake appears in *North Fork of the Coeur d'Alene River.*]

1910 Fire

That 1910 fire goin' up the bottom of Slate Creek on the St. Joe River made such a terrific draft that there wasn't a big tree left standing. Tipped 'em over, by jingoes, with roots stuck up in the air. But the trees on the hillsides stood up.

You know, if you ever got near the smokestack up at the sawmill, and if there was an opening in there, you had to hang onto your hat to keep it from getting pulled in there. Imagine a draft 35 miles long, and tree after tree with over 5,000 feet to the tree—those are big trees—and all upended.

Krause

An old German gunsmith from Wallace named Krause had homesteaded a quarter section [160 acres] on the main Slate Creek. It must have been the Northwest Quarter of Section 13, five or six miles below the forks with Dam Creek. After the main fire went through, he crawled into the creek and stayed for 12 hours. He had a coupla big soogans [thick quilts]. He'd pull himself down under water with the soogans over his head and then he'd raise up for air and this way he kept the smoke out.

I said, "Didn't the water get pretty warm?"

He said, "No. I don't think so. Of course, I was scared. Every time I'd raise up—BANG! BANG! BANG!—them big trees going down."

His eyes was all haywire from the smoke and the smoke was still so bad afterwards, he crawled on his hands and knees onto the road and up over the top of the divide, by jingoes. He couldn't see, but he knew he was on the road. By that time, there was some people coming in from Wallace looking for him. They figured he'd be dead. They found him crawling down on the other side of the ridge where the road goes down Placer Creek to Wallace.

McGoldrick on Slate Creek—St. Joe River

In 1913 I had been scaling for the Forest Service about four months, but they didn't keep me busy. McGoldrick needed somebody to run their camp on Slate Creek up the Joe River, and I happened to be in the right place at the right time and got the job. We was loggin' the Krause homestead out of Camp 1. We got a lot of timber off of it.

McGoldrick owned an awful lot of timber on the West Fork. Northern Pacific owned a lot on the main creek. Of course, there were the state sections [a 640-acre section owned by the state]. We took the cream. It was full of big white pine, cedar and spruce.

McGoldrick had logged there since 1910. They had started logging on the upper end—logged upper Slate for two years before discovering it was blue, which showed the trees were dying, but the tops weren't red yet. [When the bark beetle penetrates the inner bark, it carries a fungus on its legs which stains the wood blue and eventually kills the tree.]

He built the headquarters camp and started logging. We had a warehouse at the mouth of Slate and got busy putting a tote road right up to Headquarters. Camp 1 was at the point where the main road coming over from Wallace came close to the main Slate Creek. From this point, we built a tote road up the creek. We hauled grub to the other camps two miles above. Then we put in the dam at the forks and on up to the other camp on Dam Creek. Then we continued with this tote road—and it was an awful tote road, full of rocks and down trees. They hauled supplies in from Wallace this way.

■ Henry Morin on log drive on the St. Joe River just below the Slate Creek bridge, 1955

Headquarters Camp

I had headquarters camp and that was at least four miles from the mouth of the West Fork. We put the flume mill at headquarters camp—used a railroad civil engineer to lay it out. All the pieces were precut exactly at the mill. We started building at Headquarters camp. We flumed down the lumber, the arches and frames for the V flume. Once we got it set up, one man could build brackets as fast as two crews could build flume.

We fell all the timber downhill, which broke the tops, so we didn't have to take them. By the time we logged above there, we had a tote road and could haul the lumber on up. We had a bunch of little dams up there. We'd chute down into the little dams, and from them sluice into the flume. Every bit of it was horse logging.

The logs were big and had to be sniped. Where they dived down over humps and the log would tend to dig in the next dip, they put in partly buried saplings for the logs to ride on. The trail back up the hill was zigzag, so steep you otherwise couldn't make it. Production averaged a thousand feet to the man.

Jay Off Places

Where we couldn't use chutes, we had to skid down those steep hills with big rock outcroppings, and by jingoes, it was a job for a team of horses to get out of the way when the trail of logs started running in a trail. They had "jay off" places where it was liable to run. After horses got hit in the butt, believe me, they learned to get out of the way. All you had to do was yell, "Jay!"

Up on the West Fork, I had a little donkey [engine] and the stuff that was along the creek, we put in rollways, so we could roll the logs right into the flume. Some of those big timbers that was in the bottom itself had to be lifted up by the donkey. We'd stick up a gin pole and pick the timber up and drop it into the flume. There wasn't much water running in the flume, but they'd soon work out of our way.

Since all logs were handled by water, you had to figure on about 90 days of water in the spring. That was before the timber was all cut off. After all the timber burned off in the big fire, you couldn't depend on 10 days of water.

Down by the cedar flats, there was an awful bunch of beaver dams. They put in a camp there, just to clean up them beaver dams.

Bear

So many bear around our camp, they kept tearin' down the meat house. A couple of lumberjacks built a pen-type trap. When this fair-sized bear went in, a door fell down and locked.

Every skidding team had a chain. So the lumberjacks managed to get a loop of chain through the cracks of the log pen and around the bear's neck. Then they got another chain and put a loop on him. They worked him next to the trap door, and with about 15 lumberjacks on each chain, they let him out. If the bear started one way, the first team of lumberjacks would pull, and if he started back, the other bunch would pull. They were having a great time.

The bear did that three or four times, then he reached up with his paws and shoved these chains off his head. You should have seen lumberjacks scatter. They were not only trying to get through the bunkhouse door, but by jingoes, some of 'em were trying to climb up the outside corners of the bunkhouses where the logs stuck out.

Camp Cooks

The men went to work at seven o'clock. They were on the job ten hours—seven to five was a ten-hour day. Breakfast would be ready by six or earlier. That meant the cook had to get up at four or four-thirty to get the breakfast cooked—and they fed good.

For only 25 or 30 men, the cook would have to do it all. There wouldn't even be a bullcook. He'd have to build his own fires and carry in his own wood. Up to 50 men, all the cook had was one flunky. A 150-men camp would have a second cook and three flunkies.

If it was a big camp, both cooks might be cookin' pancakes, potatoes, ham, or bacon and eggs together. But right after breakfast, the first cook would start in on the bread, which had been settin' during the night, forming it into loaves and setting it to raise. He'd tell the second cook what he wanted sent out for lunch in five-gallon oilcans with the tops taken off. Generally the potatoes, gravy, and meat was put in a can all together so they'd stay hot. Cake, cookies, and pie went into another can. Knives, forks, and tin plates into another can. The flunkies packed 'em on their backs at noon to places where 25 or 30 men worked close together. Men working alone had to carry their own lunch.

When the flunkies took the lunch out, the first cook was generally caught up with his work, so he'd lay down for a couple of hours. If there was still stuff in the pans to be baked, the second cook would do it. The second cook had the hardest deal of the two.

You get an awful, awful good cook for 125 men for $100 a month. A lot of cooks drank. You had to watch how much lemon extract they ordered. If they ordered too much, that meant they were drinkin' it, and you just cut down on it. They didn't seem to favor vanilla extract much. I don't know why. Maybe there was more alcohol in the lemon. Them fellas could drink an awful lot of lemon extract.

If a cook got drunk, you didn't say nothin' then. You waited till you had another cook ordered out of Spokane. Soon as he came into camp, you canned the first one.

Slate Creek Lumberjacks

The lumberjacks slept in double-width bunks, laying on hay. If a man quit and a new one moved in, he was put in your bunk. If he brought bedbugs or lice along in his blankets, that was just your hard luck. If you threw out the old hay and got some new from the barn, they complained about it because hay was high priced after it was hauled up by packstring.

If a horse died, you had to make a full report to the company about how it happened. Horses cost a lot of money. But if a man got killed, nobody worried much. Just sent out word to the sheriff or coroner and wrapped his body in a blanket.

One thing you can say for the Wobblies: They cleaned up the camps and made the company furnish blankets and single bunks with mattresses. And they made the food a lot better. But they went too far.

When things got pretty strained in the camps over Wobbly activity, there were arrests of known Wobblies, but the lumberjacks hung together, and lots of times you couldn't find the names of the organizers. There was talk by the company of sabotage and violence and sending out for the sheriff or deputies.

Later, when I worked for Herrick, they called me into the office and wanted to put a star on me and give me a six-shooter.

They said, "You need the gun for protection."

I said, "I'll be a lot safer without a gun. I know them lumberjacks. Keep your star and gun."

The office didn't like it, but that's just the way I felt.

Climbing Door with Calked Boots

We had two big bunkhouses. This one had a regular-size door about three-foot wide. This Frenchman would come in, and before he'd take off his calked boots, he'd leave the door open and plant a foot on each side of the door and climb it by turning his feet so the whole sole with its calks lay flat against the wood.

I saw a little Frenchman that, where there was a ceiling, maybe seven feet high, he could take a little run and jump, place his feet flat on the ceiling, and land back on his feet on the floor.

I tell you, those Canadian-French were dynamite to fight with. They didn't fight with their hands, they fought with their feet. Some of them fellas would walk up to you and they wouldn't take their fist and hit you, they'd take a jump at you and zeet! hit you in the jaw with their feet.

I saw two of 'em in a fight—both of 'em wearin' calked boots— in a saloon down on the old-town waterfront in St. Maries. They got in a fight over a dollar bill. One of 'em tried to take it away from the other and they tore it in two. One of 'em knocked the other down and jumped up and down on top of that fella with his calked boots kickin' him in the head. He was unconscious when he got through with him. You'd think it would kill him! I had to come back in there about an hour later. There were the both of 'em up to the bar drinkin' with their arms around one another. Of course his body was pretty well protected by them heavy wool clothes—but in the head! That's the way them Frenchmen fought.

In the spring of 1913, they had cut 33 million feet of fire-killed white pine from the 1910 burn and took only big logs. They averaged four logs to the 1,000, and this was measured inside the blue and defective sap wood. A man named Dubre was boss of the drive. He brought a pile of Frenchmen with him. The pack train was busy bringing in enough booze to keep them going.

Roy Lammers came up and fired the whole gang.

Roy said, "Henry! I want you to take over temporarily while I get somebody."

I didn't know much about log drives, but there were a few good men who told me what to do. Three dams had been built on Slate Creek—one at the mouth of the West Fork, one where the road from Wallace came over the hill, and the other far up at Dam Creek near the head, perhaps 35 miles from the mouth. The dams had a head of 22 feet of water, and when opened they filled the mountain canyon with a wild flood to splash the logs down.

We had between five and six million feet on big skidways left up there when a big snowslide hit the creek and buried them 60 feet deep. We kept hitting the slide with big splashes of water and finally ate a 200-yard tunnel through it. We walked down the creek bed through the tunnel with lanterns to made sure there were no stumps to stop the logs. Then we started running the logs through. What we weren't being told by the packer, who was supposed to keep watch on his trips, was that the logs we were shooting through were jamming near the mouth of Cedar Creek.

When we got down there, the canyon was piled full of logs higher than a house and a half a mile long. A big cedar windfall stretched across the front of it. I put a Frenchman to chopping on it, but I told him not to chop it all the way through.

It was high up over the face of the jam, and he was chopping away on it, and I said, "Don't chop any more!"

He gave it another four or five wallops. The strain against it must have been terrible. He heard it start to crack. He lost his balance and fell in front of it. It snapped loose and moved only a little bit, but it moved like lightning and threw him over 60 feet up the hillside into the snow.

He just laid there and I thought: Golly! Now we've got to pack a hurt man in.

Then he got to his feet and couldn't speak. After awhile I said, "Why didn't you speak?"

He said, "I couldn't. I don't know why, but I couldn't."

One of the old river drivers told me where to set the dynamite under water in the face of the jam. Everybody connected with using the water set their watches alike and knew exactly how long it took the flood to reach any certain point. They opened both upper dams to give it all the force we had. We looked at our watches and waited for the splash to hit.

After I lighted the fuses, we climbed the hillside to watch. The water hit and man you should have seen it! The dynamite blew! It gave out a roar and an awful grinding and started moving like a big snake down the weaving canyon. Big logs that would scale 1,000 feet squirted into the air like you'd squirt cherry pits out of a cherry—between five and six million feet moving.

I had already sent word down to the West Fork dam to get everyone away because if our jam came down in one chunk, it could tear out that dam completely. Roy Lammers was coming up the creek. They told him, down there, what was happening. He saw that whole big jam come down and pour logs—water and all—right over the top of the West Fork dam and on down the creek. But it didn't hurt the dam a bit.

Roy said to me, "Golly, Henry! I don't believe you need any help up here after all. You're boss for the rest of the drive." That was a lucky one.

Once our drive hit the Joe River, we had another 20 million feet that had come from the West Fork. We had cooking spots already set up ahead of us. Those drive cooks used reflectors and turned out homemade bread, biscuits, cake, and pie. They served four meals a day. The driving went on through all the daylight hours. The drivers got three dollars a day. Big money in those days, and there was no trouble getting all the men you wanted.

We used teams of horses to drag the logs in from the wings.

Dollar had a big drive ahead of us that had come from Marble Creek. It hurt him that our logs floated down into his and his men had to move ours to finish getting their stragglers. At Scott Slough, he left around 200,000 thinking that we'd have to move them to get our own through. So I cabled a string of logs across the river just below there, piled more logs on top, and made a dam so the water would rise and pour into Scott's Slough. About the time the water rose high, my cables broke and washed the whole thing downriver. But funny thing. It wouldn't happen except by the greatest chance. The big flood downriver caused the water to come backward out of Scott's Slough and our logs floated out and left Dollar's logs where they were—stuck.

I saw Dollar in Spokane afterward and he said, "My good garsh, Henry. I don't see how you did it."

We brought that drive of between 50 and 55 million into the sorting gap at the mouth of the St. Joe River in 88 days at a driving cost of 65 cents 1,000. McGoldrick's paid me off at eight dollars a day for 100 days. I was rich.

Mrs. Flynn

Mrs. Flynn was the Queen of Marble Creek. She was a dandy camp cook. She wasn't too good lookin'; she had got to where she was big and sloppy. She liked to drink and you didn't know what minute she was going to go out on a drunk.

She was married to this Irishman, Flynn. Flynn was the first logger that I know of up on Swiftwater. He put logs out of the mouth of Big Creek, the first logs that was ever drove down the St. Joe River.

There was no railroad yet. A fellow named Hadley was straw boss under Flynn, and he beat Flynn out of his wife. Flynn drank himself to death and was buried in St. Maries.

Then they split up and she married another fellow up by Calder who, at one time, had boated lumberjacks across the river at Marble Creek. He charged 'em two-bits going into camp and a dollar coming back. They had more money coming back.

She and her man was goin' to buy a quarter section McGoldrick had up there. They moved in there but never paid nothin' and I served papers onto 'em. They was evicting her off the property and she had to go to Wallace.

She said, "Well, you wasn't afraid to come up, was you?"

I said, "There wasn't nothin' for me to be afraid about. No reason you'd do anything to me. I'm just servin' these papers. I don't even know what they say."

She said, "What's the matter with that yellow sonofabitch, your boss, Roy Lammers? He didn't have the guts to come in."

I had to go to Wallace, too, and when we came back down on the train, her nose was wet. Oh boy! It was terrible the way she was abusin' me.

I told the conductor, I said, "I never in my life—if you don't make that woman leave me alone, I'm gonna have to hit her."

So the conductor comes over and says to her, "You sit in your seat and behave yourself or we're gonna stop this train and put you off."

Bronson

Bronson was the big logger on Big Creek after Flynn. Of course, he wasn't a logger himself, he was a saloon keeper. The saloon was not too far from Tenth Street in St. Maries, close to the spot where the plywood mill is today. His gal ran the red light district. She was gettin' a rake-off from all the girls workin' down there. After the fire, when they started to put the railroad into Big Creek, she bought the first locomotive for this logger. There's a draw up there named after him, Bronson Meadows. Later Herrick bought him out.

Herrick must have taken out 250 or 300 million feet of white pine logs. The blue on the big logs would run 22 percent, and yet inside the blue, they'd scale four 16-foot logs to the 1,000. Log after log after log with 1,000 feet in each.

1918 Fire

Ed Mottern's wife's maiden name was Cavanaugh. She and Ed were married in Harrison. But before that, "Fatty" Russell, no relation of the Russells at Harrison, had located her on a homestead on Donkey Creek. He had one on the West Fork of Slate Creek. He was state scaler here for a long time. At that time, when you wanted to homestead, somebody located you on there. You came down and filed at the Federal Land Office. Each person, man and wife, could take both timber claim and a homestead, and you could get someone to build a little cabin for you, but you weren't expected to live on the timber claim. Then after so long a time you went down and proved up onto it.

Ed logged Mrs. Mottern's homestead. He had a whole bunch of logs all decked when the 1918 fire came in. All he got out with was his horses.

Marble Station

At Marble Station, Gus Saugstad had a saloon and an eating house. Mrs. Saugstad was his cook. He had some rooms with bunks up in the canyon. Ed Mottern had those cabins at Spring Creek. The McQuades came in there later and she ran a little store but never kept much stock. We used to go up there and camp in that old CCC camp layout. About 1946, when Walt Russell and I was lookin' for timber, we stayed there. Nothin' to eat. We went up to Mrs. McQuade's store. All she would sell me was a can of Spam and some crackers because she said if she sold me any more, she'd have nothing left to sell the next guy.

Lake Chutes

A lumberjack was coming down into camp alongside one of the chutes running into the Coeur d'Alene lake. He was carrying a shovel and said, "I'm not goin' to walk."

He sat down in the chute in his shovel and away he went. He didn't go very far before he was going too fast. He and the shovel jumped the chute. Boy! He got smashed up.

Another place on the Coeur d'Alene lake, the logger had built the cookhouse right alongside the chute. You'd think anybody would know better than that! Anyway, the cook was in the cookhouse cookin' and, by garsh, they got a rain and it made the chute pretty fast. Somebody turned a log loose up on the chute—which wasn't planned so long as it was wet. The log jumped the chute and went in one side and out the other of the cookhouse. Never hurt the cook, but the cook quit!

A lot of them chutes would be fast till they got down to a flat. Then you'd have to skid the logs with a team over the flat to the brow of the hill, and then they'd slide on down to the lake. Where the logs wouldn't run at all, they'd tie a gunnysack to a stick and shove it into this heated grease and, oh boy, it stunk! Then the grease monkey walked along the chute, slapping the grease on one side and then the other. They used goose neck spikes to hold the logs back in too-fast spots. A gooseneck was an inch and a half or two inches square, and they'd notch the chute where it set against it and bore a hole to drop the pointed end down.

Towline Walking

The best towline walking I ever saw was back in 1920. Frank Stratton was working on the *Reliance* tug coming downriver just above the drawbridge at Chatcolet on a weekend. He was going with the girl he later married and wanted to catch the *Flyer* to Coeur d'Alene, so he could take the electric [train] to Spokane where she worked. Frank wore his glad rags and slick-soled oxfords and, with suitcase in hand, walked down the 90 foot, two-inch manila towline from the tug to the logs without using a pikepole for balance. All the passengers on the *Flyer* crowded to the side to watch him. Then the *Flyer* dropped back to where Frank could climb on.

Frank said to Cap Laird, who was wheeling the *Flyer*, "I didn't know if you'd stop for me."

Cap Laird said, "By jingoes! I'll stop anytime to pick up a man that can do that."

Bootleggers

There were two brothers had a still up on Mica Peak that were such bad eggs, the liquor officers would never go up there lookin' for 'em. There was only a trail up to the still, but it would have been easy for the federals to have caught up onto 'em because they had to bring so much sugar in. Everybody knew they was selling moonshine. They just sold to people who came after it; they didn't deliver.

If you was a customer of theirs, why you'd go to a stump or hollow log and you'd leave two dollars. You'd go back there the next day and find a gallon of moonshine. I wasn't a drinkin' man, but guys that bought from them said they made doggone good moonshine.

The same with Virgil Guenther when he made it. He never delivered, either. I don't know where he got those little five-gallon kegs. One of these windjammers, you know what I mean, a helicopter, would come down the lake. They'd fly around a little while and pretty soon the helicopter'd come and land and grab this five-gallon keg, put it in the helicopter and away they'd hightail.

Virgil must've had a big still for the amount of liquor he was selling. It was surprising the people who bought moonshine.

Grant Hicks was a moonshiner who had the reputation of not being afraid to pull the trigger. Lute Bernhart told me that one time he was deer hunting out there close to Hicks, and lo and behold, he walked into a still.

Luther said, "I wouldn't have come up if I'd known there was a still here."

And the old man Hicks said, "If you hadn't a'been a fella that I knew, while you were still a quarter of a mile down there, you'd a'had a buttonhole in your ear."

And you know that floathouse at Silvertip, on the Joe River? All them tugboats would stop there and get moonshine.

Mike Bliss and those guys were peddling it when they had that O'Gara ferry. And that other guy there, Ernie Hamlin, was the moonshiner that hung women's clothes on the clothesline. He wore them to the dances and hid the moonshine under his dress. He'd be roosting like a setting hen on top of three or four pints and peddle them right there in the dance hall.

I don't know what Shorty Dudley, out there in Bell Canyon, had in his beer, but boy! that beer would knock you for a row. They tell me he never let it age. I don't know why he didn't let it finish working. If you put half a dozen bottles on the floor of a car and started down the road, half of them would blow up in the first mile.

Yellow Dog delivered moonshine to Spokane. One time, he carried a gunnysack full of whisky down to the Harrison depot, and one of the bottles broke. I happened to be standin' there.

I whispered to him, "My garsh, one of your bottles has broke and there's a cop right there!"

Yellow Dog said, "That don't make no difference. He ain't going to bother me." And he didn't! Yellow Dog got on the train with the gunnysack.

■ APPENDIX 1

NEWS STORIES

Morning Mine Cage Fell

The following excerpts are from the October 7 and October 8, 1936 editions of the Spokane *Spokesman-Review* newspaper.

WALLACE, IDAHO, Oct. 6.—Victims of a shaft accident in the Morning mine at Mullan early this morning, 10 bodies, some mutilated and mangled beyond recognition, lay in Wallace and Kellogg mortuaries tonight as the saddened district looked back on the worst tragedy in the history of mining in this silver-lead district.

[Those who lost their lives were: Rex Micheletta, 27; Harry McGowan, 39; Andrew Kese, 54; William R. Buchanan, 22; August Siponene, 48; Carl Donaldson, 24; Jerry Phelan, 28; Cleo Purcell, 29; Louis A. Goff, 25; and Elmer Woodworth, 46.]

Nine bodies were recovered shortly before 7 A.M. after six hours unrelenting labor. Goff's body, not located until 2:45 this afternoon, was found amid 5,600 pounds of cable that crashed in on top of the cage after it had plunged 800 feet when the cable snapped while men of the mine's night shift [swing shift] were being hoisted from the mine.

INQUEST

Oscar Wolford, the only miner called [to the inquest], testified that "I'd have gotten on the lower deck of that cage if the cager hadn't shut the door." He said that four men from 3,050 [feet] level, where he was working, reached the 3,050 station. "As I stepped out, four of 15 or 20 men on the 3050 rushed for the cage, and when the deck was loaded I gave two bells—the signal to lower the cage for loading the upper deck. I had just managed to open the upper deck door when the cage fell. It bounced—and then fell. No one had time to get into the upper deck."

The cable broke 1,200 feet above the 3,050 level . . . mine officials said at least eight or nine more would have perished had the cable's breaking been delayed another 30 seconds. Mine officials and others agreed, however, that the cage was not overloaded, although there were more in the lower deck than the mine's safety rules specify. "We find it hard to keep men from crowding into cages," said Clarence Burch, the 3,400 level's graveyard shift boss.

The men carried to death were from the 3,400, 3,200 and 3,050 levels, mine officials said, adding that at least 76 others had been hoisted from the lower workings in previous cage loads only a few minutes before.

Alex Berglund, hoistman on duty at the time, fixed the exact hour of the cage's plunge at 12:10 A.M. and said, "There had been no trouble with the cable during the night."

J. E. Berg, Wallace, general superintendent of all Federal company operations, [Federal Mining and Smelting Company which operates the Morning Mine] testified that the cable was of flat type, 3/8 of an inch thick and 4½ inches wide. "It had a breaking strength of approximately 72.3 tons, whereas the greatest weight ever hoisted or lowered in the cage that fell, including the weight of the cable, was 18,373 pounds," said Superintendent Berg. "When the cage fell, its estimated load, including 2,300 feet of cable strung out from the hoist station of the 800-level to the 3,050 station, from which it plunged, was only 11,709 pounds. This load meant there was a 12 to 1 margin of safety when the cage fell." Berg further testified that the average period for use of cable is about one year, and that this cable had been in use about 8½ months . . . the section of the cable which snapped would be turned over to cable experts for examination.

The jurors were: Paul H. Batzle, insurance man and former Shoshone county probate judge; S. H. Fairweather, insurance man and nominee for probate judge in November; M. J. Morbeck, Wallace, grocer; J. W. Osborne, Wallace, clerk; William Mullen, Wallace, county highway employee; and J. H. Foss, Mullan, retired miner.

The jury's verdict was that the accident was unavoidable.

■

Canyon Silver Crew to Get "Hawaiian Bonus"

From the *Spokesman-Review*, February 18, 1970:

The crew of the Canyon Silver Mine and their families will spend a long weekend in Honolulu as Bill Morrow, president and manager of the mine makes good "on the best bet I ever paid off."

The night shift at the property in Burke canyon broke into the ore body on the 600 level last night, and Morrow said today it "looks real good, better than on the 400 level above." Because the vein is being crosscut, the width of the vein has not yet been determined.

Morrow emphasized today, that he is picking up the tab for the Hawaiian trip, which will include 30 crew members and their families. The group will leave Spokane at 7:30 A.M. Friday and will return Tuesday.

Morrow explained the unique "bonus" by saying that about eight months ago, one of the crew asked if he would buy them a steak dinner if they hit the ore "good and wide" on the 600 level.

Morrow said he replied: "I'll buy you a steak dinner in Hawaii." He had just returned from a trip to the islands a few days previously.

Morrow said, today, he believes the crew has been paralleling the vein on the 600 vein. The crew had driven a drift 405 feet without finding the vein, then dropped back to the 300 foot mark and started a crosscut south. The ore was found 47 feet south of the drift.

While there has not been time to assay the ore, Morrow said it contains lead and silver and no zinc, and "is better than on any levels above."

"The real encouraging development," he said, "is that there is no slate in the wall. It is all quartzite." There had been slate in one wall above.

Development of the Canyon Silver, formerly the Formosa property, was begun by Morrow in 1961–62, and he said today the company "has made money all the way down."

An old 120-foot shaft was reopened and a 55-foot ore chute was opened on that level. The shaft was deepened, and on the 200 level, the ore body had lengthened to 135 feet, and on the 400 level, to 185 feet. On the 400 level, the ore averaged about 33 ounces of silver to the ton and 50 percent lead, and ranged in width from 18 inches to 9 feet.

Morrow said today, "I'm confident we have a real big ore body now."

■

Snow Slides

The *Spokesman-Review*, Feb. 28, 1936, reported three persons dead and six injured when a snowslide "swept down upon the Northern Pacific's Wallace-bound passenger train from Missoula at dusk Wednesday evening [Feb. 25, 1936]." There were several other slides including one at Burke, Feb. 27, 1936.

WALLACE, IDAHO, Feb. 27—With three persons dead and six injured, the Coeur d'Alenes tonight faced another "night of terror" as more snowslides rumbled down more gulches and continued to threaten life and property in the Burke Canyon.

The dead are: Thomas C. Byall, 68, Missoula, Northern Pacific conductor. Frank McClain, 55, Missoula, brakeman. Miss Gladys Roecker, about 28, Langer Wyoming.

They were victims of the slide that swept down upon the Northern Pacific's Wallace bound passenger train from Missoula at dusk Wednesday evening.

The injured include E. C. (Mickey) Florin, 45, Wallace, and H. E. Wheeler, 40, Burke, who were rescued after three hours imprisonment when an avalanche covered the railway passenger coach into a tomb of snow and debris. They suffered from shock and bruises but will recover unless pneumonia develops, and Florin was menaced by it, physicians said.

FIVE HOMES CRUSHED

Others in hospitals are Mr. and Mrs. Ole Erickson, Burke, and their son, Edwin, 6, and Robert Stalwick, 5, son of Mr. and Mrs. W. J. Stalwick, who were caught in a slide that crushed five homes on Church hill at Burke this morning. None was seriously injured.

Another slide this morning tore out about 1,200 feet of the Idaho Transmission company's line two miles east of the Idaho-Montana summit in the Burke-Thompson Falls district.

A slide that came down this afternoon a half mile east of last night's slide on the Northern Pacific buried the railway's tracks beneath 10 to 20 feet of snow for 1,000 feet, near the western portal of the Borax tunnel. It narrowly missed several Saltese, Mont., men walking along the track after viewing the demolished coach.

SNOW, CRASH AND DARKNESS

From hospital cots here this afternoon, both Florin and Wheeler said they had no warning of the avalanche.

"It was a hell of a sensation," said Wheeler, who was en route home to Burke, where he is a Hecla mine employee, after an extended visit in Texas. "The first thing was fine snow flying into the coach—then a crash, as the top of the coach came down upon us—and everything went dark."

"I must have been conscious most of the time, and occasionally I shouted," he went on. "Florin had been sitting across the aisle and was standing up when the slide hit. He was thrown onto the floor beside me.

"I could feel him moving for a time and tried to call to him, but got no response. Then he became quiet. I thought he was dead."

UNCONSCIOUS THROUGH RESCUE

Florin said there was no warning.

"I remember standing as I heard a noise and can remember being knocked to the floor and crawling. I guess it was under a seat," Florin said. "Then I passed out and I knew nothing until I came to in the baggage car."

He had been at Missoula visiting his wife, who was hurt near there in an automobile accident a month ago.

Both men were cared for in the baggage car last night and were brought here this afternoon, after being taken down the hill to the highway on improvised toboggans.

Dr. F. W. Rolf, Mullan, who was at the scene all night, said the woman died of injuries, probably instantly, but that "Conductor Byall and Brakeman McClain must have suffered."

He said it was indicated that the trainmen died of suffocation. Their bodies were tied in mail sacks and tobogganed down the hill to the highway for removal to Missoula.

SON SOBS IN WRECKAGE

Almost similar stories of a slide striking without warning were told by those who escaped death after a two-hour imprisonment in the debris of the Church Hill avalanche.

Mr. and Mrs. Erickson, who were found in bed, their son between them, said they were sleeping when the slide struck.

"We were wedged in tightly, but I could hear Ole calling and Edwin crying," said Mrs. Erickson.

"I also could hear the shovels and picks of the men who were digging to reach us. It seemed like hours."

CALLS TO MOTHER UNHEARD

Five-year-old Robert Stalwick gave a different version of the calamity in his childish voice.

"I thought some one was throwing a bunch of swords at me," he said. "I was mad, cause I couldn't get away and called and called to you, mudder," addressing his mother at his bedside.

The other homes crushed were those of the Hugh Cody and Mike Dunphy families and two unoccupied structures. All known danger zones in the Burke canyon had been evacuated tonight and a warning was issued to motorists to "stay out of that district."

The Burke slide came within a few hours of the 26th anniversary of the avalanche that snuffed out 16 lives at Mace at midnight, February 27, 1910. The canyon then was filled 75 feet deep and scores were injured by the slide, which was 3,000 feet long. Four more persons were killed in other disasters that winter.

Two men were killed near Kellogg in the same district in February, 1932, a mother and her son lost their lives January 5, 1933, near the scene of the 1910 slide, and the next day a man was killed at the Jack Waite mine.

TRAVEL IS DISCOURAGED

A total of .97 of an inch of rain tonight had fallen within 24 hours.

United States highway No. 10 was reopened between Wallace and Missoula, but officials discouraged travel because of the danger of additional slides.

Northern Pacific officials said they hoped to have their line open by the last of the week.

■

10-Year-Old Boy Killed in Mace Slide

March 2, 1956, *North Idaho Press* reprint of a story from Wallace, Idaho, March 2, 1936.

A snow slide that roared down off Mammoth Draw in Mace killed a ten-year-old boy early this morning and buried 18 other people.

Eight of those entombed were members of the Art Bell family and were the only ones hospitalized. They were released this morning. The others did not require hospitalization.

Killed was Timmy Spencer, son of Mr. and Mrs. John Spencer, whose home was swept off its foundation 35 feet into the creek. The parents and their 21 month-old-son, John Jr., escaped injury.

Mr. and Mrs. Spencer were in bed, with their baby between them when the slide hit. Timmy was sleeping in an adjoining room.

Sheriff's officers said it is possible that Timmy drowned. He was found in the creek beneath the debris.

Also buried in the slide were Mrs. Ray Cork and her son James, 9 months old, and Mrs. Steve Reasoner and her four daughters.

All were quickly dug out by rescuers who rushed to the scene.

Eight homes were either demolished or badly damaged. The 12 other homes in the slide area were damaged more or less with most of the damage resulting from broken windows. Several cars were buried in the slide and badly damaged.

The snow covered the valley floor to a maximum depth of about 20 feet and several homes were completely buried.

The old Mace power plant on the opposite side of the canyon from Mammoth draw, also was badly damaged.

The families in the path of the slide were asleep when the avalanche struck.

The slide wreaked damage in a path about 2,000 feet wide judging by the fact that 18 utility poles in line, spaced between 100 and 150 feet apart, were uprooted according to Wm. Featherstone, District Manager of the C.U.C.

The slide occurred at 1:13 A.M.

The slide jumped across the canyon. Snow was piled deep on top of the old Star Mine dump in the creek bed opposite the railroad crossing.

As he and other rescuers dug into the Bell home, Sheriff Gardner said they could hear a baby crying beneath the snow. The children were brought from the house into the cold air with only their night clothes on and were wrapped in blankets and brought to Wallace.

The concussion from the slide was so terrific, Gardner said, that trees 200 and 300 feet up the mountainside were knocked down. The slide seemed to hit the mine dump at the bottom of the canyon and then bounced, he said.

■

History of Slides at Burke

The worst slide occurred on George's Hill in Mace at 11 P.M. on Sunday, Feb. 27, 1910. It killed 16 persons and injured 25 others and followed an unusually heavy snowfall. A chinook and heavy rains the day after the chinook, the snow on the Anchor Mining Company dump gave way, leaving a wake of death and destruction as far as the Catholic Church in Burke. There were four major slides that winter.

In December, 1912, also on a Sunday, a slide in Millers Gulch in Upper Mace killed a young miner.

Mrs. Glenda Powell and her son Glenn were killed in a slide in Mace, Jan. 4, 1933.

Four persons were injured in a snowslide that roared down Church Hill in Burke, Feb. 27, 1936.

■

1910 Upper Glidden Dam Flood

In 1910, the Upper Glidden Dam broke flooding Burke and Mace and caused property damage, but no one was killed. In 1947, an old mine dump broke loose in Gorge Gulch, and it was reported that the flood's crest reached 45 feet. An item [probably from 1964] tells of the breaking of the Lower Glidden Dam. A portion of the road was washed out at Pig Pen, and a power pole was washed away. Upper Burke and Burke homes and basements were flooded.

■

Three Men Are Killed by Explosion Near Wallace

WALLACE, IDAHO, Dec. 6 (1907)—Shortly after 10 o'clock this morning, the boiler of engine No. 79, belonging to the Northern Pacific railroad, exploded a half mile from Wallace, on this side of Burke, on a steep grade between Mace and Burke killing Frank Rowe, a wiper, Joseph Hodge, a brakeman, and William Bulls, a fireman, while W. F. Copenhaver, engineer, was seriously hurt, and lies in the Wallace hospital, hovering between life and death.

At the time of the explosion, the engine was hauling one combination passenger and freight coach, and four boxcars. The explosion, which was heard for miles around, took place right in front of W. R. Miller's house, the last house when leaving Mace for Burke. About 15 men, women, and children were in the combination coach at the time, but beyond the fact that these heard the report, they were unaware at the time that any accident had happened as the train was traveling very slowly at the time and came gradually to a halt as the mechanism of the engine caused the emergency brakes to come into operation as soon as the accident took place.

Owing to dense clouds of smoke and steam, nobody realized at first what the nature of the accident was, and it was only after [the smoke and steam] had cleared away that the terrible nature of the occurrence became clear.

BODY IN THE COWCATCHER

The first body to be recovered was that of William Bulls, lying comparatively close at hand at the side of the track, unconscious, and with one side of the skull crushed, blood oozing from the ears, and scalded, cut and bruised all over. He was taken to one of the nearby houses, but from the first no hope could be held out for his recovery. Later he was placed on a handcar and taken to Wallace, where he was placed in the hospital, and where he died early in the afternoon without regaining consciousness.

By some extraordinary chance the unconscious body of W. F. Copenhaver was found tangled in the front part of the engine, above the cowcatcher, in what is known as the collar of the boiler. How he was thrown there is a mystery, and the only feasible explanation that can be offered is that the body in whirling through the air, was caught in the vacuum caused by the condensation of steam and drawn to that particular place by the suction. He is still alive, but the back part of his head is torn, and bruised, in a horrible manner, and he is suffering from severe scalds, cuts and burns. He was also taken to Wallace on handcar and placed in the hospital, but it is extremely unlikely that he will live. Now and again he regains consciousness for a minute or two at a time, but appears to have no recollection of anything that has happened.

SON'S BODY IN MOTHER'S YARD

The most pathetic part of the whole affair was the case of Frank Rowe, who was killed. Mrs. Rowe, the boy's mother, was engaged in her usual domestic work in a house between 150 and 200 feet from the scene of the accident, and hearing the awful explosion, went to the door to see what was the matter. Lying not 120 feet away, and in her own yard, was her son, the whole top of his head completely blown away, his skull empty, and practically every bone in his body pulverized. He had been thrown this distance by the force of the explosion, and the mother's involuntary scream gave the first clew [sic] to the searchers as to the whereabouts of his body.

Joseph Hodge, the brakeman, was blown 200 feet away up the side of the mountain, and he was, of course, instantly killed. His badly mutilated remains were the last to be discovered. Immediately after the terrible nature of the occurrence was known, Dr. C. A. Dettman of Burke was sent for, and a special train carrying Dr. Charles R. Mowrey and his assistants left Wallace, but with the exception of Copenhaver, practically nothing could be done for any of the injured men. The bodies of the dead were removed to the Worstell undertaking parlors in Wallace and the wounded to the Wallace hospital.

A coroner's inquest has been called for 10 o'clock tomorrow.

■ APPENDIX 2

JOE HILL

Joe Hillstrom, a Swedish immigrant known as Joe Hill, won the admiration and respect of union sympathizers worldwide as they struggled during the early 1900s for a living wage and humane working conditions. Hill was a member of the Industrial Workers of the World (I.W.W.), a cartoonist, and a poet, but he was best known as a writer of union songs. Set to familiar tunes and tailored to fit particular efforts, the songs were sung in the streets, in union halls, and on pickets lines. They were carried overseas by sailors and were sung in many languages.

In 1913, Utah copper mines were paying 30 cents an hour for a 12-hour shift in mines so hazardous that fatal accidents were commonplace. Joe Hill's songs and union activity contributed to a successful strike that brought some concessions from the mine owners.

Months later when a grocer and his son were killed, Joe Hill was convicted of the murder on questionable circumstantial evidence. He was sentenced to death by a court thought by many to be prejudiced.

Thousands of pleas for a pardon or federal investigation of the case were sent to Governor Spry of Utah by organizations and individuals around the world, among them Swedish Minister W. A. F. Ekengrin, Bishop Paul Jones of the Episcopal Church, and two appeals by President Woodrow Wilson. Nevertheless, Joe Hill was shot to death by firing squad on November 19, 1915.

Convinced that Joe Hill was killed for his songs of inspiration and ideals and that his death was a reprisal for union activity, 3,000 mourners sang his songs at his funeral in Utah. His body was then shipped to Chicago. Following a funeral there, 30,000 singing mourners accompanied the casket to the crematory, where they remained until the gates were closed at dusk.

Small envelopes of the ashes of this self-proclaimed and accepted "citizen of the world" were sent to sympathizers in every state except Utah, to every country in South America, to Europe, Asia, Australia, New Zealand, and South Africa. With ceremonies and singing of his songs, Joe Hill's ashes were scattered in these many places on May 1, 1916.

Joe Hill is remembered today by the song "I Dreamed I Saw Joe Hill Last Night" written by Earl Robinson and sung by many folk singers in the 1950s.

APPENDIX 3

LABOR-MINE OWNER STRIFE OF 1892 AND 1899

An account covering all the facts and interpretations of the events leading to the explosion of violence that shook the Coeur d'Alenes in the 1890s would be too lengthy and inappropriate in this oral history. However, a brief summary may explain remarks made by a few of the older story tellers included in this book.

In the early days of western hard-rock mining, the dream of "striking it rich" bridged the gap between the independent, resourceful miner and the lucky prospector who became a mine owner. They understood each other. They worked and shared the same community and relations were friendly.

As the industry developed, capital needed for higher technology to bring the ore to the surface and process it was provided by outside money, in many cases resulting in absentee owners. Hired managers lost touch with the everyday labor of mining, which created a chasm between owners and miners that ended their frontier comradeship.

As the chasm widened, managers became callous to the need of miners for a living wage and turned their attention to maximizing profits—the primary goal for which they had been hired. But mining is arduous and hazardous work, so it became imperative that the miners organize into a union to bargain for wages and safe working conditions. Union members helped each other during times of sickness and accidents, and each donated a day's pay to the bereaved family in the case of death.

For a number of years most mines were paying wages of $4 for a ten-hour day. All underground workers received the same pay scale until 1887. Then, due to a down-turn in the economy, wages dropped to $3.50. Some mines continued to pay men doing the drilling (miners) $3.50 a day but cut trammers (car men), muckers (shovelers), and all other underground workers to $3 a day. Dissatisfaction over this pay differential provoked the unions in Wardner, Wallace, Burke, and Gem to unify into a federation.

In 1891, the union built the Providence Hospital in Wallace, which was the first in the district. Prior to this, mine workers suffered inadequate health and accident care provided by a company doctor, for which the mine owners deducted a fee of one dollar a month from each paycheck. Then, at the request of the union, all the mine owners except one deposited the one dollar fee to the Providence Hospital. Bunker Hill & Sullivan owners refused to cooperate, which caused a great deal of resentment.

During the winter of 1890–1891 compressed air drills came into use. These machines could drill 12 to 20 holes per shift compared to about two holes per shift by hand drilling. This greatly reduced the cost of mining but also reduced the number of miners needed, which forced many to take work as car men and muckers. This meant a 50 cent an hour pay cut. After much negotiating, the separate mine owners signed an agreement with the union that all underground men would receive the universal pay scale of $3.50 for a ten-hour day.

But this didn't set well with the three largest companies: Bunker Hill & Sullivan, Helena and Frisco, and Gem. In October of 1891, they organized the Mine Owners Protective Association to oppose the universal pay scale and the power of the union, and they hired a Pinkerton agency detective to infiltrate the most aggressive union local at Gem.

Without warning in mid-January of 1892, all the mines closed, ostensibly to force the railroads serving the area to reduce their freight rates. Frozen in those steep mountains by heavy snows and a nation-wide depression, the miners and their families were devastated. The union set up commissaries in each town to dispense aid and food donated by farmers from the surrounding area.

The railroads finally agreed to roll back their rates to the 1890 level for hauling ore. On March 19, the companies posted notices that work could resume April 1 if men could be hired on their terms: $3.50 for drillers, $3 for all other underground workers for a ten-hour day, six days a week, and only nonunion men would be hired.

The union men refused the offer. The market was depressed, so the mine owners were in no hurry and set June 1 as the opening date.

Tempers ran hot on both sides. The union claimed the owners had been duplicitous about the freight rates, and that their real motives were to break the universal pay scale and to break the union. The mine owners claimed that due to the low prices of silver and lead, the universal pay scale agreement they had signed under duress was unreasonable.

By July 1, many mines, among them the Tiger, Poorman, Hunter and

 Morning, had worked out agreements paying the universal pay scale of $3.50, but they employed both union and nonunion labor. But the Gem, Frisco, and Bunker Hill & Sullivan mines were working on the differential pay scale and hiring only nonunion labor imported by railroad. The imported workers had to be harbored under armed guards in their mills.

The miners tried to persuade the nonunion men to leave. At the town of Gem and at the Frisco and Gem mines, there were many confrontations involving nonunion men, their armed guards, and union men. Various fist fights and gun shots left three nonunion and three union men dead and several people injured. July 11, in an effort to drive the nonunion men from the area, miners sent a load of dynamite down the penstock—a large conduit—and blew up the "old" Frisco mill which was not in use at the time according to *The Coeur d'Alene Mining Wars of 1892* by Robert Wayne Smith, page 65. The nonunion men surrendered their arms and were marched to the union hall at Gem. They were released later in the day.

Meantime, Governor Norman B. Willey declared martial law. While a company of militia was en route by railroad, union men took over the Bunker Hill concentrator at Wardner and threatened to blow it up if the nonunion men were not discharged before the militia arrived. The militia was detained at Cataldo until nonunion men were sent by rail to the Mission at Cataldo.

Although all was quiet by the time the militia arrived, they removed the sheriff and marshal from office and arrested all union men, sympathizers, and even innocent men on the street—many of whom couldn't speak English to defend themselves—and imprisoned them in hastily improvised enclosures in Wardner and Wallace called "bull pens."

Management imported more nonunion labor and opened the mines. Union men were blacklisted and forced outside the mine district to find work until martial law ended, November 18.

The needs that prompted men to band together still existed, so unionism was not destroyed. By 1899 all mines in the area, except the nonunion Bunker Hill & Sullivan, were hiring union men and paying the universal pay scale of $3.50 a day. Bunker was paying 50 cents less a day for drillers and a dollar less for car men and muckers. Bunker justified the lower scale by saying that since their mine was dry, working there did not require extra expenditure for rubber clothing. But another reason has been suggested. Bunker was a member of the "lead trust," which was a combine headed by Standard Oil that aimed for monopoly control of the markets. Membership in the trust compelled Bunker to operate on costs less than those of the independent mines in the area. As a result, the other mine owners pressured the union to either organize Bunker and force them to pay union scale, or

■ Soldiers' encampment and bull pen in Kellogg during the 1899 mining strife. *Courtesy Museum of North Idaho*

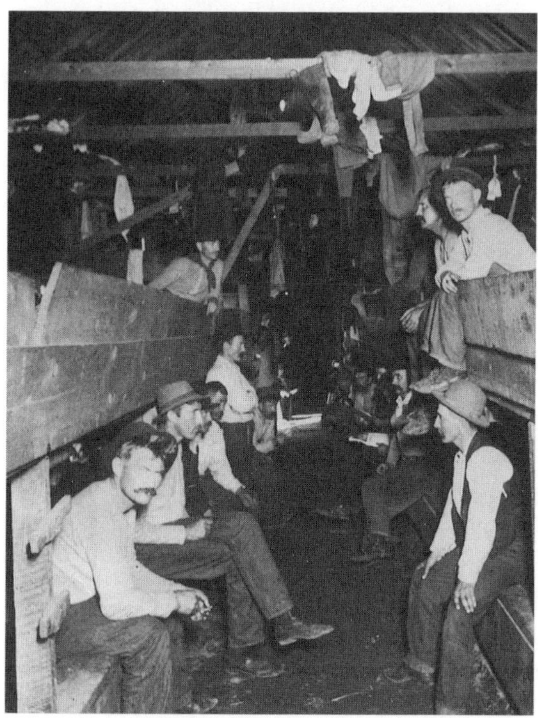

■ Bunks in the bull pen, Kellogg, Idaho, 1899. *#8-X536, Barnard-Stockbridge Collection, University of Idaho Library, Moscow, Idaho*

let them lower their scale to Bunker's. But at the same time, they were working with Bunker through the Mine Owners' Association to destroy the union.

Since Bunker fired any union man found working there, organizers recruited members in secret until April 23, 1899, when they felt strong enough to openly act as a bargaining agent and demand a universal pay scale for all underground employees, recognition of the union, and the discharge of nonunion men. Bunker refused all demands. They offered a pay differential of $3.50 and $3 and continued to fire union employees. Union men walked off the job and, on April 26, took control of the aerial tramway to prevent nonunion men from working at the concentrator.

The following is a brief account of the events that took place on April 29, 1899.

Several hundred men (many of whom believed they were on an excursion to Wardner to show the unity and strength of the union) commandeered a Northern Pacific train at Burke. The men, some of them masked and armed, loaded the train with explosives, and forced the engineer to run it to Wardner, where they blew up the Bunker Hill & Sullivan concentrator.

At that time, the Idaho National Guard was on duty in the Philippines serving in the Spanish American War, so Governor Frank Steunenberg immediately wired for federal troops to be sent into the area. When the militia arrived, the governor declared martial law. Every union man remaining in the area, and many men who were on the street by coincidence and who spoke no English, were arrested without cause and thrown in the infamous "bull pens." Some men were held for months. One bull pen was a two-story warehouse where the prisoners slept on hay on the floor without bedding until it was provided by their families. Sanitary facilities were non-existent for days. The only heat came from campfires the prisoners built outside. As the numbers increased to some 500 men (numbers vary in accounts), boxcars were brought in, bunks constructed, and the pens were enclosed in a barbed wire stockade.

Through his representative, Bartlett Sinclair, Governor Steunenberg issued a proclamation that no man could work in any mine without a state permit, which could only be obtained if the applicant swore he had not participated in any way in the strike and denied and denounced union membership. This state hiring system remained in effect until January 11, 1901, when a new governor took office and the practice ended. However, the system worked so well for the mine owners that they established and ran their own hiring agency administered by George T. Edminston, dubbed by the miners, "The King."

Despite the volumes written about the events of April 29, 1899, the truth of who was behind those events will never be known. In some accounts the union is held responsible; in others, only an inner circle of the union is blamed. It has even been suggested that spies working for the mine owners instigated and led the violence in order to destroy the union. In some accounts the concentrator had great value. In another account, old timers said the concentrator was inadequate to handle the increasing production and was slated for replacement, which makes plausible their assertion that Bunker was getting rid of the concentrator and destroying the union at the same time.

Open unionism in the Coeur d'Alenes was suppressed during this period but did rise and flourish again. In 1936, the Morning and Page mines signed a union contract; Bunker Hill & Sullivan signed one in 1942.

APPENDIX 4

MINES MENTIONED IN ROCK BURST

Anaconda Copper (Montana)
Anchor
Bedroom
Black Cloud
Black Horse
Bunker Hill & Sullivan
Caledonia
Canyon Silver
Crescent
Daddy Lode
East Colusa (Montana)
Federal
Formosa
Frisco
Galena
Golden Chest
Hecla
Helena
Hercules
Hummingbird
Interstate
Jack Waite
Last Chance
Leonard (Montana)
Lucky Friday
Mammoth #1, #2, #3
Mascot (Arizona)
Mayflower
Midnight
Monarch
Morning
Mother Lode
Page
Palisades
Pittsburgh
Polaris
Sherman
Sierra Nevada
Silver Dollar
Silver Summit
Snowstorm
Spokane-Idaho
Standard
Star
Sunshine Silver
Tamarack-Custer
Terrible Edith
Tiger-Poorman
Tramway (Montana)
Tyler
Upper Chance
White Delph

GLOSSARY

People change the meaning of words constantly as they move through different eras, locations and occupations. The definitions given here express the intent of the narrators as they tell their stories.

Bark mark—A letter or design cut with an axe through the bark and into the wood of a log to designate ownership.

Beanery—A boardinghouse where miners, loggers, or railroad workers eat.

Birling or log rolling—A contest enjoyed by two lumberjacks treading a floating log who try to dump the other into the water by swiftly rolling the log and snubbing—abruptly stopping it.

Blister rust—A fungus that attacks white pine. It affects the sapwood and inner bark and produces blisters on the exterior. It is an incurable disease, but a disease-resistant strain of white pine has been developed.

Blued—Blue discoloration of the sapwood of white pine. When the bark beetle (*Dendroctonus monticolae Hopk*) penetrates the inner bark of a white pine tree, it carries a fungus on its legs which spreads and stains the wood blue, which signifies that the tree is dying.

Boom—Logs contained in a waterway by boom sticks.

Boom chain—A short, heavy chain with a ring on one end and a toggle on the other.

Boom sticks—Floating poles with holes bored in each end to accommodate a boom chain.

Brail lines—When transporting logs by water, the logs are encircled by **boom sticks** fastened together with **boom chains** end to end or with the forward boom stick lapped over the aft one. When ropes called **brail lines** are fastened from one side of the boom to the other and force it into an oblong for towing through a narrow waterway, such as a river, it is called a **brail.** A tugboat may tow multiple brails.

Bull cook—A man who cuts wood, builds fires, and sweeps out at camps.

Bull pen—A stockade used to detain men during the employer/labor strife of 1892 and 1899 in the Coeur d'Alene mining district.

Buzzy or **stoper**—Common names for a pneumatic drill used to drill holes to be filled with dynamite for blasting. Early pneumatic drills, sometimes called **widow makers**, forced rock dust from these holes, creating a choking dust that damaged lungs and caused the deaths of many miners. Present day drills are equipped with a steady stream of water for dust control.

Cage—A metal enclosure (like an elevator only not so fancy) for hoisting men or material within a mine. **Chippy Cage** or **Chippy Hoist**—A smaller cage that runs alongside the main cage in a parallel compartment. **Skip**—Similar but usually used for carrying muck.

Cager—A man who opens and closes doors of a cage or skip to load or unload people or cargo and then signals the hoistman when ready to move the cage or skip up or down.

Calked boots—Leather boots with short spikes projecting from the leather sole which bite into the wood of a log and prevent the wearer from slipping. Pronounced "corked" boots.

Cap—Part of the bracing in a tunnel, it is a timber placed on top of a prop, stull or post.

Chute for logs—Typically, two chute sticks (poles) laid side by side, hewn to form a V shaped channel and spiked to the **cross ties** underneath.

Chute for ore—Built of heavy timbers to let ore fall by gravity down to the ore cars.

Cousin Jack—A miner from Cornwall, a county of southwest England.

Contracting—In mining, being paid by the foot in excavating and advancing the hole as opposed to being paid by the hour or day.

Dogging—In a sawmill, a log comes up the slip and onto the carriage that moves it back and forth as it is being sawed into lumber. The **setter** and **dogger** ride on the carriage. The sawyer signals the setter what size board to cut. The setter sets the saws. The dogger, standing on the end of the carriage working two levers, sets sharp hooks, the **dogs** into the end of the log to hold it steady for sawing. The sawyer may whip the carriage back and forth making it a mighty rough ride for the dogger.

Drag—Another term for a **trail** of logs which is a group of two or more logs traveling together in a chute.

Dragline—An excavating machine in which the bucket is attached by cables and drawn toward the machine.

Drift—A tunnel driven through or parallel to the course of a vein. Newly located veins are often explored by **drifting** along their length.

Drill and shoot a round—Multiple holes are drilled into the face of the stope. The holes are filled with explosives and detonated at the end of the shift. The incoming shift **mucks out** (removes the broken ore), pries down loose rock, bolts rock that may loosen, and repeats the cycle.

Dry house—A place where miners change clothes that may be wet from sweat or moisture within the mine.

Edgings—Pieces trimmed from both edges of lumber. The edgerman determines the width to make the best use of a board.

Face—The end of a stope or drift.

Fault—A fracture in the earth's crust usually accompanied by a displacement of one side of the fracture with respect to the other and in a direction parallel to the fracture.

Flume—An inclined, V-shaped channel, constructed of lumber and supported by **arches** similar to the ribs in a boat, that is flooded with water to move logs. The flume usually had a walkway on one side.

Flume mill—A small portable sawmill set up to saw lumber and dimension for constructing the flume. A flume is always built of lumber as opposed to a chute, which is constructed of poles.

Galena—A lead-bearing mineral which may also contain silver.

Gin pole—A single pole or two poles spread apart at the base and fastened together at the peak with lines running through a pulley at the top, leaning forward, and secured with guy lines so a team could be driven beneath for loading or unloading logs.

Green chain—A conveyor of freshly cut (green) lumber that is still heavy and wet before being dried in a dry kiln.

Grizzly—A grid made of steel bars used to screen boulders from the broken rock. The smaller rocks fall through into the chute. The remaining boulders are manually crushed by sledge hammer.

Hand drilling—See **single jacking.**

Headboard—Part of the bracing that forms a **timber set**, it is a board wedged between the rock wall and end of the cap.

Hot cargo—Cargo that stevedores refuse to handle.

Hoistman—One who operates the hoist that raises and lowers a **cage** or **skip** in a shaft.

Industrial Workers of the World—A union founded in 1905 for the purpose of organizing all labor, skilled and unskilled, regardless of race, creed or color, (including sailors and migratory and seasonal workers) into one big union—a concept that was the opposite of the American

Federation of Labor, which was composed of craft unions. Members of the I.W.W. were called **Wobblies.**

Jacket set—A set of timbers outside the regular timber set used for reinforcement.

Jay off—A place for a horse to escape logs traveling too rapidly while trailing. The **J hook**, a hook formed in the shape of a J used to fasten the line from the horse to the trail of logs, will readily unhook if the horse turns at a right angle.

The King—A hiring agent in the early days of the Coeur d'Alene mining district.

Lagging—Planks, two or three inches thick, used to prevent loose rock from sloughing into the tunnel.

Leaser or **leaseholder**—When a mining company has removed all the ore that can be taken profitably from their upper workings (ground closer to the surface), a vein that can be removed with little waste rock may remain. They may grant a lease to an individual, the leaser, who may hire others to mine this remainder.

Lifters—The bottom holes of a **round** drilled for blasting.

Manway—A passage to accommodate men within a tunnel, shaft, raise, or chute. Within a vertical shaft, raise, or chute, the manway is lined with a series of ladders. Each ladder bottoms out onto a platform that miners use to cross over to the opposite side of the manway to use the next ladder. This prevents the worker from falling to the level below.

Muck—Loose ore and waste left after blasting. The men who load the ore cars or chutes are known as **muckers**.

Muck stick—A shovel.

Nipper—One who brings blasting powder.

Palouser—An improvised lantern made from a tin can with a candle inserted through a hole in the side.

Pickaroon—A single-headed pick with a sharp, curved point. It has multiple uses which include moving heavy timbers and chopping ice.

Pickleboat—A narrow sled used for raising and lowering timbers and supplies in a raise.

Pickler—One who controls the separation of zinc from the solution.

Pikepole—A pole with a sharp iron point used for moving logs in water. The point has been heated and twisted about a quarter-turn (so when it is speared into a log it has some leverage) and has a curved hook a few inches from the point that is used to hook a line or boom chain.

Primer—A cap filled with compound that will ignite an explosive charge.

Raise—A vertical or inclined opening or passageway connecting one mine working level with another.

Rock burst—A miniature earthquake caused by the sudden release of pressure within the rock.

Scabbing—Working in the place of a union worker on strike.

Scaling—Measuring logs with a **scale rule** to determine their board feet. The scaler calls each number to the **tallyman** who records it in a **scale book**. Scaling may be done while the logs are loaded on a truck, decked (piled up) at a landing, or after they have been dumped into the water. Scaling while standing on logs in the water requires skill and balance.

Shaft—A vertical or inclined excavation used for finding and mining ore. It usually starts at the surface and connects the various levels of the mine. The shaft is often the mine's main entrance. Shafts are used for hoisting men, supplies, and muck, and for ventilating underground workings.

Shifter—Crew boss for a shift.

Siderite—Iron ore.

Silicosis—Massive fibrosis of the lungs caused by inhalation of silica dust. May be called **miner's consumption** or **miner's con**.

Single jacking—Early day machineless drilling where a man holds a steel bit with one hand while striking it with a sledge hammer with the other and turns the bit after each blow. **Double jacking**—one man holds and turns the steel bit while another strikes it with a sledge hammer.

Skidding—Pulling logs.

Skidway or **rollway**—Two parallel logs laid perpendicular to the chute or flume, slightly elevated and butted against the chute or flume.

Skinner—(teamster) One who drives a team of horses or mules.

Skip—Similar to a cage, a skip handles supplies or material, but more often may hoist the broken rock.

Skipway—The passage through which the skip travels.

Slimes—Ore or rock reduced to a fine powder and moistened, forming a mud.

Sniped—The end of a log beveled with an axe to make it slide easily in the chute.

Sniping—Obsolete slang from the term "to go snips" meaning "to share."

Stamp mill—An early day rock crusher in which gold/quartz ore was pulverized by heavy iron pestles that rose and fell like a pile driver. They were variously powered by mules, water wheels, steam engines, etc.

Station—An excavated room adjoining the shaft at each working level where men and material are loaded or unloaded from the cage or skip.

Stope—An excavation from which ore is removed in a series of steps. The word "stope" is an obsolete past tense of "step."

Stripper—One who removes the electrode-deposited zinc from the electrode.

Timber cruiser—One who estimates the board feet in standing timber.

Timber set—Used to prevent cave-ins, it is two posts topped by a beam or **cap**, with a **headboard** wedged between the rock wall and end of the cap.

Tram—A box-like car running on a railway or aerial tramway for conveying ore or waste rock.

Trammer—One who loads broken rock into tramcars and delivers it to the shaft.

Tunnel—A horizontal drift or cross-cut that intersects with the surface. The point at which a tunnel opens onto the surface is called the portal. Usually the opening is referred to as a tunnel if both ends reach the outside. If it has only one opening, it is usually reffered to as an "adit."

Wannigan—A raft or boat that accompanied a log drive carrying the cookhouse and camp equipment.

Wobbly—A nickname for a member of the **Industrial Workers of the World Union.**

BIBLIOGRAPHY

Blake, Oscar. *Timber Down the Hill.* N.P., N.D.

Fahey, John. *The Days of the Hercules*. Moscow, Idaho: University of Idaho Press, 1978.

Grover, David H. *Debaters and Dynamiters: The Story of the Haywood Trial.* Corvallis, Oregon: Oregon State University Press, 1964.

Hart, Patricia and Ivar Nelson. *Mining Town: The Photographic Record of T. N. Barnard and Nellie Stockbridge from the Coeur d'Alenes.* Seattle: University of Washington Press, 1984.

Jensen, Vernon H. *Heritage of Conflict: Labor Relations in the Nonferrous Metals Industry up to 1930*. Ithaca: Cornell University Press, 1950.

Magnuson, Richard G. *Coeur d'Alene Diary.* Portland: Metropolitan Press, 1968.

McCulloch, Dean Walter. *Woods Words: A Comprehensive Dictionary of Loggers Terms.* Corvallis: The Oregon Historical Society and The Champoeg Press, 1958.

Norlen, Art. *Death of a Proud Union: The 1960 Bunker Hill Strike.* Cataldo, Idaho: Tamarack Publishing, 1992.

Ojala, Gary. *The Fabulous Coeur d'Alene Mining District*. Cataldo, Idaho: N.P., 1972.

Scott, Rachel. *Muscle & Blood.* New York: E. P. Dutton & Company, 1974.

Sims, Cort. "The Log Chutes of North Idaho." USDA Northern Region, 1983. 97 pp. mimeo.

Smith, Robert Wayne. *The Coeur d'Alene Mining War of 1892.* Corvallis: Oregon State University Press, 1960.

Stavis, Barrie. *The Man Who Never Died: A Play About Joe Hill with Notes on Joe Hill and His Time*. New York: Haven Press, 1951.

Strong, Clarence C. and Clyde S. Webb. *White Pine: King of Many Waters.* Missoula: Mountain Press Publishing Co., 1970.

INDEX

The names of some working people have been included in the index just because they contributed to the development of the northwest with their hard labor.

A

B

C

D

E

F

G

H

I

J

M

N

O

P

R

S

T

U

V

W

Y

Z